HOW TO PUBLISH

YOUR NEWSLETTER

A COMPLETE GUIDE to PRINT and ELECTRONIC NEWSLETTER PUBLISHING

CAROL LUERS
EYMAN

SQUAREONE
WRITERS GUIDES

Cover Designer: Jeannie Tudor
In-House Editor: Marie Caratozzolo
Typesetter: Gary A. Rosenberg

Square One Publishers
115 Herricks Road
Garden City Park, NY 11040
(516) 535-2010 • (877) 900-BOOK
www.squareonepublishers.com

Library of Congress Cataloging-in-Publication Data

Eyman, Carol Luers.
  How to publish your newsletter: a complete guide to print and electronic
newsletter publishing / Carol Luers Eyman.
     p. cm.
  Includes index.
  ISBN 0-7570-0045-2 (pbk.)
1. Newsletters—Publishing—United States. 2. Newsletters—Design. I. Title.

Z480.N46E96   2006
070.1'75—dc22
                                                                2006000451

Printed in the United States of America

10   9   8   7   6   5   4   3   2   1

CONTENTS

$\mathcal{A}$CKNOWLEDGMENTS

My gratitude goes out to many. First, to the people who taught me what I know about writing, editing, and newsletter publishing through their own books, articles, presentations, and websites. Special thanks are due to Bonnie Heines from PennWell.

Many newsletter publishers graciously gave of their time to talk to me about their experiences, especially Robert Ellis Smith of *Privacy Journal*, Jonathan Baker of the Society for Technical Communication, Holly Watkins from the Visiting Nurses Association, and Karen Krause from the American Red Cross. Professionals who provided me technical information in their areas of expertise include Alison O'Donoghue, Rick Balboni, Dan Habib from the *Concord Monitor*, Tony Marro and Bev Martineau from American Printing, and Laurie Chadbourne and Ann Ackerman of Images and Ideas. Kay Bertrand MacMillan of the University of New Hampshire and Barbara Provencher of St. Joseph School of Practical Nursing gave me opportunities to teach adults, and my students can be sure that I learned more from them than they did from me.

At Square One Publishers, I want to thank Rudy Shur for taking a chance on me as a new author, and Marie Caratozzolo for massaging a manuscript into a book.

And most of all, thanks to my sons, Dylan and Brook, whose technological expertise surpassed mine long ago, and to my husband, Bill, for being everything to me.

A NOTE ON GENDER

To avoid long and awkward phrasing within sentences, the publisher has chosen to alternate the use of male and female pronouns according to chapter. Therefore, when referring to the third-person publisher, editor, writer, or reader of a newsletter publication, odd-numbered chapters employ female pronouns, while even-numbered chapters employ male pronouns. This gives acknowledgment to publishers, editors, writers, and readers of both genders.

PREFACE

I f you are publishing a newsletter or considering publishing one, you are not alone. According to the Newsletter & Electronic Publishers Association, although it is impossible to pinpoint the exact number of newsletters in the United States today (their registration with an organization or agency isn't required), we can still gather some clues as to the size of the industry.

Hudson's Subscription Newsletter Directory lists more than 5,000 subscription newsletters. The *Oxbridge Directory of Newsletters* includes over 12,000 US and Canadian consumer, association, and business newsletters. But these two directories list only the more formalized operations. They do not include the 1.4 million nonprofit organizations registered with the Internal Revenue Service, most of which publish newsletters; likewise for the more than 250,000 religious congregations and over 90,000 elementary and secondary schools in the United States. Thousands of businesses have also jumped on the bandwagon, embracing newsletters as a marketing tool, as well as a method for communicating with employees. The advent of the Internet has allowed even the smallest businesses to promote themselves to thousands of customers and prospects through electronic newsletters. Adding it all up, it is safe to assume that the number of people in the United States who are involved in newsletter publishing probably exceeds 1 million.

In 1995, Professor David Nelson of Northwestern University surveyed newsletter executives and estimated that the industry's revenues exceeded $1 billion. At the turn of the twenty-first century, he estimated that this number had grown to reach the $2 billion mark.

Who is behind all of these newsletters? Who is doing the legwork—the writing, editing, layout, printing, and distribution—that gets these publications to their readers? Sometimes it is the communications department of a large corporation or an ancillary group of a large publishing company. In some cases, it is a graphic arts or public relations firm, working for its clients. But it is just as likely to be a small, home-based business, whose sole employee has specialized knowledge about an arcane topic, such as international theatrical rights or object-oriented programming. It can be an individual working at home, for little or no profit, writing about a beloved hobby like quilting or rock climbing. Often it's one of a handful of paid staff members of a small nonprofit organization. And let's not forget the many volunteers, putting in time on evenings and weekends to keep their organizations' newsletters in print.

The Kiplinger Washington Letter, founded in 1923, is probably the oldest continuously published newsletter in the United States. Newsletter publishing flourished in the 1900s, particularly in the 1960s and 1970s, when typewriters and offset printing became more economical and more widely available. The introduction of personal computers and desktop publishing software in the 1980s, combined with the boom in Internet access in the 1990s, helped newsletter publishing blossom into the vast enterprise it is today.

I have been producing newsletters for nearly two decades now, and during that time I have worn many hats. I have written articles myself and edited articles for others. I have volunteered for nonprofit newsletters, hired myself out to for-profit newsletters, designed pages for print newsletters, and developed website pages for online newsletters. I have also started new publications and revived ailing ones. And whenever I conduct seminars on newsletter publishing, I am given the opportunity to pass on the lessons I've learned and the helpful techniques I've discovered over the years. But throughout my years in the business, I have never found a book on newsletter publishing that became my "Bible." Some books focus on the business side of newsletter publishing, others on design, and still others on specific newsletter types. Many lack informative, up-to-date guidelines on producing electronic newsletters. None have been able to take me from square one—starting with an idea for a newsletter—to the finished product.

When I wrap up an all-day seminar at four o'clock in the afternoon, and my bleary-eyed students are itching to go home, I have not been able to wave a book in the air and say, "Read this if you have questions after you leave here." It is for this reason I decided to pull together all of the pertinent information on newsletter production that I have amassed through my own experience, and create a practical, one-stop manual to guide you smoothly through the process from start to finish. Whether you publish a newsletter for the purpose of doing business or as a means of doing good, this book will facilitate your work. It is a comprehensive guide to producing *all* types of newsletters.

In my classes on newsletter publishing, I have had students who hoped to start a new publication and others who have taken over an existing one. In many cases, they are the ones doing the lion's share of the work with little outside help. Because many have a background in one phase of newsletter publishing—perhaps graphic design, writing, or marketing—but not in every aspect of its production, they yearn for guidance and feedback on their work.

So I have directed this book to you, newsletter publisher, who may also be called editor, managing editor, or executive editor, recognizing that in a small operation, the person with a fancy title can sometimes be found stuffing envelopes. I have tried to provide enough detail so that if you are also expected to be writer, copy editor, and layout artist, you can gain the skills to do those jobs, too. Or you can share the information with employees or volunteers who fill those roles.

For experienced newsletter publishers, I have provided plenty of ideas for doing the job more economically, quickly, and professionally. If you have been asked to give a facelift to an existing publication, this book will help identify its strengths and weaknesses, and enable you to devise a plan for improving it.

It is my greatest hope that whether you are a newsletter novice or an experienced publisher, you will find the information in *How to Publish Your Newsletter* invaluable. May it be the book you turn to time and time again to guide you in your work. If I have done my job right, you will regard it as your newsletter publishing Bible.

$\mathcal{I}$NTRODUCTION

Whether you are a novice publisher who is in the initial phase of launching a newsletter, or you are an experienced publisher who wants to rejuvenate an existing publication, the book you now hold will serve as your steadfast companion.

How to Publish Your Newsletter is a comprehensive guide, offering all of the helpful, practical information you need to plan, write, and produce a newsletter. It will help you determine if your idea for a newsletter is workable, and whether you have enough time, money, and assistance to transform your idea into a successful publication. You will learn how to write the types of articles and design the kinds of graphics that will keep readers interested and motivated to respond to your message, whether it is "Buy our product," "Renew your subscription," or "Support our organization." You will also discover the best tools and techniques for laying out, printing, mailing, and distributing both print and electronic versions of your publication. The book's extensive resource list alone will save you lots of time by helping you locate vendors, software, filler articles, legal information, clip art, and much more.

Written in an easy-to-understand, user-friendly format, *How to Publish Your Newsletter* is divided into four parts. Part One, entitled "Getting the Big Picture: Planning Your Newsletter," begins the book with chapters that help you flesh out your idea for a publication and get organized. Chapter 1, "Types of Newsletters," introduces you to the industry by discussing various newsletter categories. You will learn whether your idea fits into the category of subscription newsletters that readers buy, free marketing newsletters that entice readers to purchase a product or service, or association newsletters that have nothing to do with buying or selling.

Many publishers get bogged down in the details of newsletter production before they consider whether they are achieving their overall mission. Chapter 2, "Laying the Groundwork," encourages you to examine why you are publishing a newsletter and who will be reading it. The answers you come up with will later serve as your roadmap for choosing the most effective writing style and the best production methods for your publication.

Once you have a clear vision of your newsletter's purpose and audience, you will be ready for Chapter 3, "Setting Up Shop." Here, to devise a strategy for running your operation, you will consider a number of important questions. What distribution method (electronic or print) will work for you? How much money do you need to get started? Can you make money (or break even) on the venture? If you hire staff, how will you assign their responsibilities? How often will you publish? How will you set (and meet) deadlines?

If you are reading this book, you probably already have a general idea of the type of information you want to provide in your newsletter. Chapter 4, "Planning the Content," helps you organize that information into the types of articles that are appropriate for your purpose and audience. If you want to reproduce material from other publications, this chapter will tell you how to get permission to do so. It explains the role of advertisements in newsletters, and also gives tips on organizing your content and how to make it fit properly on a page.

Some newsletter publishers have a ready supply of readers. For instance, church newsletters are distributed to members of the congregation; school newsletters, to parents of students. Many publishers, however, must actively seek out an audience. In Chapter 5, "Finding Readers," you will learn how to use direct mail, free-sample distribution, advertising, and the Internet to find your newsletter's audience.

Part Two—"Being Clark Kent: Writing, Editing, and Illustrating Your Newsletter," contains two fact-filled chapters. Chapter 6, "Writing and Editing," shows how to gather facts for articles through research and interviewing. It also introduces the principles of writing in newsletter style. In addition to providing pointers on writing headlines and skimming aids to get the attention of your readers, this chapter includes a guide to writing different types of newsletter articles, as well as how to edit and proofread your work to make it clear, accurate, and consistent.

In Chapter 7, "Using Graphics and Photographs," you will discover how to catch your reader's eye and enrich your prose through the tasteful use of photos, drawings, charts, graphs, tables, clip art, and other graphics. This chapter also offers lots of helpful guidlines for taking interesting photographs and preparing them for clear, professional-looking reproduction.

Once you reach this point, you will focus on readying your newsletter for distribution. If you have chosen to distribute your issues on paper, you will want to move on to Part Three, "Taking It to the Streets: Producing Your Print Newsletter." Chapter 8, "Designing and Laying Out Print Newsletters," explains the principles of graphic design, helping you place articles, illustrations, and photos in a visually appealing manner on a printed page. It guides you through the process of developing a page template and laying out the contents of each issue. And it recommends the best software programs for achieving these steps.

Chapter 9, "Reproducing and Mailing Print Newsletters," will help you become informed on the topic of printing services. Here, you will be introduced to the various ways to reproduce a printed newsletter, and learn to identify the most cost-effective methods for mailing them.

If you have chosen to distribute your newsletter electronically, Part Four, "Launching It Online: Producing Your Electronic Newsletter," is your next stop. It contains three chapters, each of which focuses on a different online distribution option—web, e-mail, and PDF newsletters. You will learn how to adapt your writing to minimize the limitations of electronic formats, while capitalizing on their strengths. After learning how to design and lay out your electronic newsletter, you will discover how to test it to make sure it displays properly. In addition, you will become versed in the nuts and bolts of distributing your publication through mass e-mails.

Throughout the book, helpful checklists and sample worksheets (including blank versions that you can copy and use) will keep you focused and organized so you won't overlook the many details that comprise a professional newsletter. You will also find an extensive glossary of useful terms, as well as a broad list of resources for newsletter publishing—books, periodicals, organizations, websites, vendors, and more.

At this point, most authors would wish you luck in your newsletter publishing endeavor. But if luck were all it took, you wouldn't need this book. Instead, I leave you with the following heartfelt advice:

> *Have the patience to follow directions, the curiosity to learn,*
>   *the drive to persevere,*
> *and the humility to accept criticism and learn from the mistakes*
>   *of publishers who have come before you.*

GETTING THE BIG PICTURE
PLANNING YOUR NEWSLETTER

Before you send off your first issue to your readers, before you even start writing your first paragraph, it's important to spend some time thinking about the type of newsletter you'll be publishing, the reasoning behind it, and how you are going to get it produced. You've got to plan what your newsletter will say and, of course, find people to read it!

Part One will lead you through the steps of newsletter planning, regardless of the type of newsletter you're starting. And if you already publish a newsletter and are reading this book in the hopes of improving it, the information presented in Part One will help you tailor your publication to your purpose and audience, streamline your operations, and expand your readership.

CHAPTER 1

ᴛYPES OF NEWSLETTERS

O ver the years, I've collected sample newsletters that I have used as examples when teaching my newsletter seminars. Trying to organize my thoughts for this chapter, I hauled them out and leafed through each one, then dropped them into piles according to categories. When I was done, I found that some publications didn't belong on any of the piles. Were they newsletters at all? How could I decide?

A newsletter is a small publication that provides news for a special interest group. It's a periodical, which means it is published at regular intervals of more than one day. The term "newsletter" arose because at one time most newsletters were formatted in the style of a personal or business letter. But today their layout usually resembles that of a newspaper more than a letter.

How do newsletters differ from magazines or newspapers? First, they are published for special interest groups. That's why you'll find newsletters for people who trade carnival glass, raise roses, breed Border terriers, and manage law firms. Beyond their special audiences, newsletters differ from magazines and newspapers in three ways: production schedules, production values, and advertising policies.

The term *production schedule* refers to how often a publication is issued and how long it takes to produce. While newspapers are usually published daily, or perhaps weekly, newsletters are usually published at intervals ranging from a week to three months (although, with the rise of electronic newsletter distribution, daily newsletters have become more common). Although a newsletter's weekly, monthly, or bimonthly publication frequency may resemble that of a magazine, its content is fresher because there is a shorter interval between the writing of its articles and the distribution of the publication. How is that possible? This is where the term *production values* comes in.

Magazines are often printed in full color with photographs and graphics galore, while newsletters tend to be black and white or contain just a few colors. Magazine covers consist of artwork and headlines, while the front of a newsletter usually contains articles. Magazines run from several dozen to several hundred pages, whereas newsletters rarely run longer than twelve or sixteen pages, and often far shorter. Newsletters are most often printed on standard 11 x 17-inch paper (folded to 8.5-x-11-inches), while magazines are usually printed on glossy paper in a variety of sizes, and newspapers are tabloid size or larger. The simplicity of a newsletter's design and production values has allowed newsletter publishers to shrink the amount of time between going to press and distributing the publication to a fraction of that for the more slickly produced magazine. The complexity of printing a magazine means that its copy deadline—the date by which writers must submit their articles to the editors—is often two months before the date that the magazine appears on the newsstand. By contrast, the brevity and simple design of a newsletter and, hence, the ease of printing it, mean that its copy deadline can be just two weeks or even less before readers get their hands on the publication.

Finally, newsletters differ from newspapers and magazines in their *advertising policies*. Newspapers and magazines contain many pages of advertisements; in fact, most of their operating costs are paid by advertisers, not subscribers. Newsletters, on the other hand, usually don't accept ads or, if they do, they run very few. Most newsletter costs are paid by readers or the publisher.

Getting back to the piles of newsletters strewn around my office, I found that I was still left with a handful of publications from my original stack that didn't fit into any of my categories. One looked like a newspaper, but was addressed to a special interest group—supporters of a civil rights organization. Another resembled a magazine—it sported an artistic front cover and ran longer than sixteen pages—but had no advertisements. Where did these belong? I realized that there was no good answer to this question. Some publications have found a format that crosses the boundaries between newsletters, newspapers, and magazines, yet successfully communicates their message to a chosen audience.

And what about the newsletters that *did* fit into one pile or another? What kind of system was I using to sort them? When sorting my newsletters, I had applied the idea of genres, or types, to newsletter publishing.

Advertising is one of the many areas in which newsletters differ from magazines and newspapers. Newsletters, which rely on income from the publisher or subscribers, contain few (if any) ads. Magazines and newspapers, on the other hand, obtain most of their revenue from advertisers, so their pages are usually filled with commercials.

Once you know the type of newsletter you are publishing, you'll be ready to find out what it should look like, the type of writing it should have, and whether it can make any money. You'll be able to determine who will read it and how they will get it. In addition, knowing your newsletter's type will help you navigate through this book, reading the information that pertains to your project and skipping the information that doesn't.

To come up with my system of categorizing newsletters, I had to perform my sorting exercise three different times. First, I sorted by circulation basis. Then I gathered the newsletters up and sorted them again, this time by format. Finally I sorted them one more time, by classification.

CIRCULATION BASIS

The first time I sorted my sample newsletters, I did it by circulation basis—whether they are distributed for a price (as subscription newsletters), or free (as nonsubscription newsletters). The term "subscription" can be confusing, because some publishers ask you to subscribe to nonsubscription newsletters. By "subscribe," they simply mean put your name on a list of people who want to receive it. Just remember that you'll always pay for a subscription newsletter, and you won't pay for a nonsubscription newsletter—at least not directly. By this, I mean that you might have to join an organization to receive it.

A nonsubscription newsletter is distributed free of charge, although you may have to join a club or organization to receive it.

Subscription

We're all familiar with subscription magazines: if we like a magazine, we take the coupon that came in the mail, or we pull one of those little business reply cards out of a copy we read at the hairdresser's, fill in our name and address, enclose a check, and later (what seems like an awfully long time later) we start receiving the magazine. Signing up for subscription newsletters works the same way. Often, however, the check you write for one is a lot bigger than the one you write for a magazine. For example, yearly subscriptions to professional newsletters sold to lawyers, computer company executives, and other business readers can run into the hundreds or even thousands of dollars. But there are also subscription newsletters aimed at consumers. These carry much lower price tags, comparable to what you'd pay for a subscription to a consumer magazine.

Subscription newsletters run articles, such as insider news, trends, technical information, and how-tos, that educate their readers about a special interest. These articles are informative and relatively objective in tone. They're not trying to sell anything to their readers, convince them of a viewpoint, or persuade them to buy products or donate money. Readers are essentially hiring the publisher to provide them with information they need, but at a much lower price than it would cost them to find the information themselves.

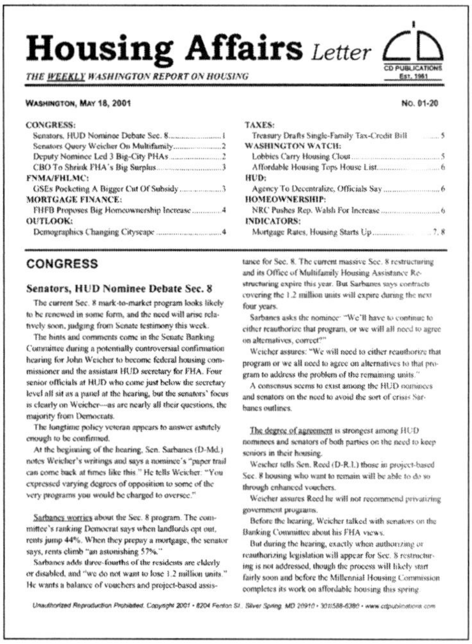

Housing Affairs *Letter*

CD PUBLICATIONS Est. 1961

THE WEEKLY WASHINGTON REPORT ON HOUSING

WASHINGTON, MAY 18, 2001 — NO. 01-20

CONGRESS:
Senators, HUD Nominee Debate Sec. 8 1
Senators Query Weicher On Multifamily 2
Deputy Nominee Led 3 Big-City PHAs 2
CBO To Shrink FHA's Big Surplus 3
FNMA/FHLMC:
GSEs Pocketing A Bigger Cut Of Subsidy 3
MORTGAGE FINANCE:
FHFB Proposes Big Homeownership Increase 4
OUTLOOK:
Demographics Changing Cityscape 4
TAXES:
Treasury Drafts Single-Family Tax-Credit Bill 5
WASHINGTON WATCH:
Lobbies Carry Housing Clout 5
Affordable Housing Tops House List 6
HUD:
Agency To Decentralize, Officials Say 6
HOMEOWNERSHIP:
NRC Pushes Rep. Walsh For Increase 6
INDICATORS:
Mortgage Rates, Housing Starts Up 7, 8

CONGRESS

Senators, HUD Nominee Debate Sec. 8

The current Sec. 8 mark-to-market program looks likely to be renewed in some form, and the need will arise relatively soon, judging from Senate testimony this week.

The hints and comments come in the Senate Banking Committee during a potentially controversial confirmation hearing for John Weicher to become federal housing commissioner and the assistant HUD secretary for FHA. Four senior officials at HUD who come just below the secretary level all sit as a panel at the hearing, but the senators' focus is clearly on Weicher—as are nearly all their questions, the majority from Democrats.

The longtime policy veteran appears to answer astutely enough to be confirmed.

At the beginning of the hearing, Sen. Sarbanes (D-Md.) notes Weicher's writings and says a nominee's "paper trail can come back at times like this." He tells Weicher: "You expressed varying degrees of opposition to some of the very programs you would be charged to oversee."

Sarbanes worries about the Sec. 8 program. The committee's ranking Democrat says when landlords opt out, rents jump 44%. When they prepay a mortgage, the senator says, rents climb "an astonishing 57%."

Sarbanes adds three-fourths of the residents are elderly or disabled, and "we do not want to lose 1.2 million units." He wants a balance of vouchers and project-based assistance for Sec. 8. The current massive Sec. 8 restructuring and its Office of Multifamily Housing Assistance Restructuring expire this year. But Sarbanes says contracts covering the 1.2 million units will expire during the next four years.

Sarbanes asks the nominee: "We'll have to continue to either reauthorize that program, or we will all need to agree on alternatives, correct?"

Weicher assures: "We will need to either reauthorize that program or we all need to agree on alternatives to that program to address the problem of the remaining units."

A consensus seems to exist among the HUD nominees and senators on the need to avoid the sort of crisis Sarbanes outlines.

The degree of agreement is strongest among HUD nominees and senators of both parties on the need to keep seniors in their housing.

Weicher tells Sen. Reed (D-R.I.) those in project-based Sec. 8 housing who want to remain will be able to do so through enhanced vouchers.

Weicher assures Reed he will not recommend privatizing government programs.

Before the hearing, Weicher talked with senators on the Banking Committee about his FHA views.

But during the hearing, exactly when authorizing or reauthorizing legislation will appear for Sec. 8 restructuring is not addressed, though the process will likely start fairly soon and before the Millennial Housing Commission completes its work on affordable housing this spring.

Unauthorized Reproduction Prohibited. Copyright 2001 • 8204 Fenton St., Silver Spring, MD 20910 • 301/588-6380 • www.cdpublications.com

Figure 1.1
Housing Affairs Letter is an example of a subscription newsletter.

Who publishes subscription newsletters? For professional subscription newsletters, often it's a sole proprietor of a business—a person with specialized knowledge about the newsletter's topic, gained through years of industry experience. Such a publisher's background can be in a business such as the stock market or the electronic-display industry, for example. It can also be in a profession, like architecture or law. Sometimes the publisher is a journalist with strengths in writing, editing, and production. Or it can be a medium or large company like Element K, which provides computer training and courseware development, and publishes newsletters like *Inside Microsoft Word* as additional products. A number of publishing companies, like CD Publications, the publisher of *Housing Affairs Letter* (see Figure 1.1 at left), specialize in subscription newsletters.

Consumer subscription newsletters are generally published by educational institutions like Harvard Medical School, which puts out a number of health-related newsletters, and by large corporations like Kiplinger's, which publishes newsletters about retirement, taxes, and investing.

Until recently, in the consumer subscription-newsletter category, you also found individuals and hobbyists who wrote about topics like raising twins or stamp collecting. Often the price of their newsletters was quite low, just a bit more than the cost of printing and mailing. Today, however, many of these publishers have replaced their print editions with online newsletters, eliminating their printing and mailing expenses, and, therefore, converting their publications to free, nonsubscription newsletters.

Nonsubscription

The bulk of the newsletters published today are not circulated by subscription. These nonsubscription newsletters are usually free, either because the readers are prospective or current customers, clients, supporters, or donors of the publishing organization, or because the readers are affiliated with the publishing organization (employees of a company, for example). Other nonsubscription newsletters are provided as a benefit to paid members of groups like trade associations and professional organizations. The gardening newsletter I receive several times a year, compliments of a local real estate broker, is an example of a nonsubscription newsletter. So are the newsletters that technical writers who join the Society for Technical Communication receive from their local chapters, and the newsletters you have probably received from charities such as the American Red Cross or the March of Dimes after making a donation (see Figure 1.2 at right).

Who produces nonsubscription newsletters? The list of publishers ranges from politicians, charities, large corporations, schools, and churches to libraries, unions, restaurants, and bookstores.

How do nonsubscription newsletters differ in content from subscription newsletters? Unlike relatively objective subscription newsletters, nonsubscription newsletters often carry a tone of persuasion. The publishers have a message to convey, and it's worth it to them to finance the production and mailing of a newsletter as a way of getting that message out. But the most successful nonsubscription newsletters balance their message with more objective articles that the publishers know will hold their readers' interest. For example, an island resort's customer newsletter would report on its new swimming pool and refurbished restaurant, subtly encouraging readers to spend another vacation there. But it might also report news that is not directly related to the resort, such as which artists appeared at a recent jazz festival on the island or the construction of a new museum there. Likewise, a cancer research foundation's newsletter would report on how to avoid exposure to cancer-causing chemicals at the same time it solicits contributions to the foundation's capital campaign. Not only do the objective, informative articles boost reader interest, they increase the credibility of the publisher.

Figure 1.2

Distributed to donors of the American Red Cross, *Update* is an example of a nonsubscription newsletter.

FORMAT

The second time I sorted through my sample newsletters, I ended up with just one huge pile. That's because I sorted them based on format—

whether they are distributed as printed documents or as electronic files. The big pile, of course, held the print newsletters. There was no other pile, because the electronic newsletters were stored on my computer. In the 1980s and 1990s, there may have been a few fax newsletters in my electronic "pile," but since the saturation of American homes and offices by personal computers and the Internet, they have been largely replaced by Internet newsletters.

Print

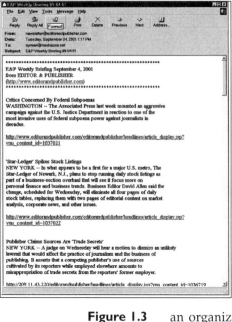

Figure 1.3
E&P Weekly Briefing is an electronic newsletter distributed via e-mail.

Print newsletters most commonly measure 8.5 inches wide and 11 inches high (the size of a typical sheet of copier paper), though occasionally they are printed on larger or smaller sheets. They usually run anywhere from two to twelve pages in length. Print newsletters are distributed through the mail; as handouts at offices, retail stores, or conferences; or as inserts to bills or newspapers. They are geared to business people and professionals as well as consumers, and they cover just about any special interest topic conceivable. It's impossible to characterize the topics or audiences of print newsletters since, until relatively recently, every newsletter was a print newsletter. Even with today's availability of electronic formats, print newsletters continue to be published on everything from computer-aided design to the history of Mississippi.

Electronic

Electronic newsletters are distributed on the Internet or on an organization's internal computer network, or *intranet*. They can be created in several forms, including web pages, text e-mails, HTML (hypertext markup language) e-mails, and PDF (portable document format) versions. Figure 1.3 at left is an example of a text-e-mail newsletter. I'll explain all of these forms in more detail in Chapter 2, "Laying the Groundwork," and in Part Four, "Launching It Online: Producing Your Electronic Newsletter."

Electronic newsletters, because of their low production costs, are often published more frequently than print newsletters. Just as newsletters are easier to produce than magazines and can, therefore, be produced more quickly, electronic newsletters are easier to produce than print newsletters and can be produced even *more* quickly. This means that they can offer *very* late-breaking news.

Note that print, web pages, and e-mail are not always exclusive types of a particular newsletter. Many print newsletters are also published in online editions. Some e-mail newsletters are not really newsletters, but rather a list of headlines that link readers to the latest issue of a web or PDF newsletter.

CLASSIFICATION

The third and final time I leafed through my newsletters, instead of looking at how they were circulated or distributed, I sorted them based on *why* they were published and to *whom* they were directed. I came up with four newsletter classifications: professional, association, consumer, and marketing.

Professional

Professional newsletters help professionals and business people keep up with developments in their fields and do their jobs better. These publications run articles about technological developments, new contracts, company earnings, new products, changes in the law, conferences, and personnel moves. In this category, I placed newsletters like *Copy Editor* (see Figure 1.4 at right), which contains language news for the publishing profession, including articles about trends in language usage, lists of words recently added to the dictionary, and reviews of related books. *Fair Housing Coach* belongs in this category as well. This newsletter trains the staffs of property management companies to avoid discrimination complaints. It explains the requirements of the Fair Housing Act and publishes quizzes to help staff understand these requirements.

In the professional category, I also include newsletters that help workers use technology, such as *Inside Microsoft Word* and *Inside Quark XPress*. Both of these publications include step-by-step instructions for completing tasks in their respective software packages. Another subset of professional newsletters includes those that help volunteer leaders run their organizations. Such newsletters are not distributed to the general membership of an organization, just to the leaders of their smaller divisions like Scout troops, chapters, or parishes. For example, the *Tieline*

Figure 1.4
Copy Editor fits into the category of professional newsletters.

newsletter runs articles directed to volunteer leaders of the Society for Technical Communication about how to recruit volunteers, run meetings, or raise money.

Most of the professional newsletters distributed in print format are circulated by subscription, but many electronically distributed professional newsletters are available free. As a rule, these publications are objective and informative in tone. Many are published by large companies like Brownstone Publishers, which produces newsletters that give plain-English legal guidance for managers in real estate, property management, and other fields. Ziff-Davis, another large company, is a publisher of technology and Internet magazines and newsletters. But some professional newsletters are published by very small companies, and are run by a person with specialized knowledge of the business or profession that is the topic of the newsletter.

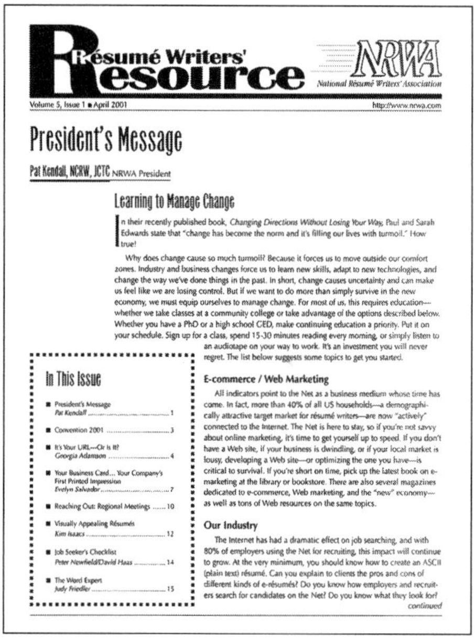

Association

If you've ever been on the board of a religious congregation, civic organization, club, or professional society, you know that one of its major tasks is to let members know when meetings are held, how much money is in the budget, who the new officers are, and so forth. Often these groups use newsletters to carry out this communication.

The primary purpose of association newsletters is to keep members of a group informed about the group's activities. Such newsletters often meet a secondary purpose of keeping members up to date about local, national, and international news, as well as issues that are related to the organization's mission but not internal to the organization. So, for example, one issue of the *Résumé Writers' Resource* (see Figure 1.5 at left) includes an article about regional meetings of its publisher, the National Résumé Writers' Association, while also containing a piece on Internet domain-name protection. One issue of the New Hampshire *Library Trustee* runs a calendar of the Library Trustees Association's events, as well as an article that discusses the rules imposed on libraries by the Children's Internet Protection Act.

Association newsletters also seek to foster a sense of community among members. That is why these publications often run photographs of members and report on milestones like marriages, births, promotions,

Figure 1.5

Résumé Writers' Resource, an association newsletter, covers both internal and external news.

and retirements. And that's also why they are written in an informal, friendly, and upbeat style.

The primary audience of association newsletters is group members. If you pay your dues and join a bowling league or sign up your child to play soccer, you will receive the league's newsletter (if one exists). Some association newsletters don't require that readers join the group; they may be distributed to the parents of students at a particular school, the employees of a company, or members of an extended family. Occasionally, association newsletters are used as a public relations tool, either to recruit new members or provide background information to a reporter who is writing about the group.

The publishers of association newsletters are frequently volunteers, especially if the organization is small. Sometimes it's the school or church secretary or another paid staff member. Employee newsletters may be produced by the company's communications department or by an outside vendor like a public relations firm or advertising agency.

Consumer

Each of us has hobbies and other interests that we pursue outside our work. Some of our interests, like health, travel, and investing, are shared by large numbers of consumers. Some well-known publishers have attracted large numbers of subscribers to newsletters that are focused on these topics. Johns Hopkins' *Health After 50* (see Figure 1.6 at right), *Consumer Reports* magazine's *Travel Letter,* and *Louis Rukeyser's Wall Street* are a few examples. Smaller publishers as well as individuals have gotten into the act as well, with publications like Gloria Pitzer's *Secret Recipes Newsletter.* These general interest newsletters carry relatively low annual subscription rates—in the $15 to $50 range. Publishers cannot charge top dollar for them because of all the competition from newspapers, television programs, magazines, and websites, which provide lots of information on health, travel, investing, cooking, and other areas of common interest.

Many of us also have more specialized interests, which range from cultivating roses to collecting die-cast toys or depression glass, and we can find consumer newsletters on topics like these as well. They are produced by publishers large and small. Among the large publishers, for

Figure 1.6
Johns Hopkins' *Health After 50* is an example of a consumer newsletter.

Consumer newsletters can focus on topics of general interest, such as cooking, travel, and investing, or on more specialized subjects, like cake decorating, sailing, and baseball card collecting.

example, is Belvoir Publications, which produces a couple dozen newsletters for aviators, boaters, horse lovers, and pet owners. Some of these specialized consumer newsletters also cost in the $15 to $50 range for subscriptions. But others, particularly if their topics appeal to more affluent audiences, can charge more, even over $100. Consumers will pay more for such newsletters if they can't get the information elsewhere. However, the prices on these newsletters are rarely as high as those sold to business or professional audiences.

Why do consumers turn to newsletters instead of the mass media for information about their hobbies and special interests? Often these interests are so specialized that the mass media does not have the expertise to cover them adequately. A newspaper might run one story about die-cast toy collectors, but it won't provide the regular coverage of new products, history, and sources of the toys that a newsletter called *The Replica* does. Newspapers simply don't have enough readers interested in the topic to cover it regularly.

In addition, the lack of advertising in most consumer newsletters adds to the credibility of the information they contain. So an amateur sailor would read *Practical Sailor* to get product reviews—of bottom paints, sailing shoes, and high-modulus ropes—that are not biased toward a newsletter advertisers' products. (The sailor also reads *Practical Sailor* because reviews of bottom paints, sailing shoes, and high-modulus ropes will never appear in mass-market publications like *Consumer Reports*!)

Marketing

Marketing newsletters are those that are published to promote a product, service, cause, or organization. In this category, for example, you'll find newsletters that are distributed to patrons of a restaurant, informing them of special offers or entertainment coming to the establishment, in the hope of attracting repeat business. You'll also find newsletters like *Intellectual Property Bulletin,* published by law firm Edwards & Angell, which carries information for businesses on patent, trademark, and copyright law (see Figure 1.7 on the next page).

Because most consumer newsletters do not contain advertisements, readers tend to feel confident in the credibility of the information they contain.

In your monthly statement from an investment firm, you may receive a newsletter that provides advice on estate planning, an explanation of municipal bonds, and other investment information. The end of each article is likely to suggest that you contact your advisor at the investment firm for more information. This is the bank's way of attracting more of your business.

Also in this category are newsletters that politicians send to their constituents to attract support, as well as those from political advocacy groups, like the National Rifle Association or the Brady Campaign to Prevent Gun Violence.

A subset of marketing newsletters consists of *syndicated* or franchised newsletters. These are published by a third party and sold to businesses or professionals who, in turn, distribute them to their customers and clients. Usually the publisher sells a syndicated newsletter to just one party in a given geographic area, so that two competing businesses or professionals don't end up sending duplicate publications to the same readers. Syndicated newsletters carry general articles related to the business or profession that are useful to its customers and clients. An example would be *Client's Monthly Alert,* a newsletter that accountants can purchase from its publisher, *Practical Accountant* magazine, for distribution to clients. The articles concern managing personal or business finances and point readers to their accountants for advice on how the information applies to their own situations. Another example is *Gardentime,* which real estate agents send to potential or existing clients. Agents can customize this newsletter by placing a photograph and personal contact information on the front and back pages. In addition to running notices asking readers to list their houses with the agent, *Gardentime* includes articles about gardening tools, gardening with children, herb gardening, and so forth, that provide a service to the reader and, in turn, foster a positive public image for the real estate agent.

Figure 1.7
Intellectual Property Bulletin is a marketing newsletter published by a law firm.

Marketing newsletters are circulated on a nonsubscription basis. You won't directly pay for them, although some are distributed only to people who are donors or customers of the newsletter's publisher. The tone is upbeat about the strengths of the company or organization and often persuasive about the benefits of buying their products, donating to the organization, or supporting the cause. But at the same time, by providing articles that directly interest or benefit their readers, they come across as more objective than the typical piece of marketing literature.

Crossing Classifications

If you are not quite sure whether to classify your newsletter as professional, association, consumer, or marketing, it may cross the boundaries of these classifications. Your newsletter may serve multiple purposes, as does *Consumer Update* from Keyspan Energy Delivery. This newsletter serves as both an information vehicle and a sales piece. It includes information that the utility must get out to its customers, like a reminder to call Dig Safe before excavating near underground utility lines. But as a way to increase the utility's sales, it may also include an article on the pleasures of using outdoor log sets fired by natural gas.

It's also possible that your newsletter serves multiple audiences. *The Kiplinger Tax Letter* is read by retirees as well as business owners and investors, so it straddles the boundaries between consumer and professional newsletters. Employee newsletters can be difficult to classify as well. Employers publish them to achieve some of the same goals as association newsletters—to publicize events sponsored by the employer and to foster a sense of community among employees—but they also can include articles that help employees perform their jobs better, in the manner of professional newsletters.

And finally, association newsletters sometimes resemble professional ones when they provide information that keep readers abreast of developments in their fields. For example, *Eye-Mail Monthly* from the American Academy of Optometry runs reports on medical research that help optometrists keep up to date on their profession, as well as articles on members who have been in the news.

CONCLUSION

Where does your newsletter fit into these classification schemes? Don't worry if after reading this chapter you're still a bit confused about where your newsletter—or your idea for a newsletter—fits. You may need more information before deciding whether your newsletter can make money on a subscription basis (or, if it's an avocation, whether it can break even); if so, Chapter 5, "Finding Readers," will give you that information. Perhaps you're feeling overwhelmed by trying to select a distribution format for your new electronic newsletter. Your fear will subside after you read Chapter 3, "Setting up Shop," which includes a helpful section on choosing a distribution method. But first things first. The next chapter starts with some important newsletter basics. It's about laying the groundwork, so your newsletter is set on a solid foundation.

CHAPTER 2

LAYING THE GROUNDWORK

The last chapter helped you determine the genre into which your newsletter fits. To develop your newsletter idea, you now need to do three things: establish the basics of why you're publishing and for whom, assess your competition, and learn how to choose and use a newsletter name. In this chapter, I'll be discussing these important factors and presenting the many considerations of each one. Taking the time to lay a solid foundation will help to ensure your newsletter's success.

ESTABLISHING THE BASICS

To make your newsletter work, it's important to clearly define its purpose, understand its audience, and decide on an appropriate style or tone. Let's take a closer look at these newsletter basics in the following discussion.

Define Your Purpose

Many organizations have developed short mission statements that describe their purpose. For a nonprofit organization, this statement drives the choice of which activities to sponsor—be they social services, historic preservation, or city park clean ups. For a business, the mission statement is a guide to deciding what to produce and what to sell. Likewise, your newsletter needs a statement of purpose to guide your choices of what to write, for whom to write, when to write, and how to present your writing.

Before you write a statement of purpose, consider some of the common reasons for publishing newsletters, which are described below. Then decide which ones apply to your publication.

To Inform

The *Boston News-Letter* was the first newsletter distributed in the United States. Primarily filled with details of English politics, this one-page publication, which eventually became a newspaper, also listed local news items such as ship arrivals, deaths, and political appointments.

One of the most common reasons to publish a newsletter is to inform readers. If you are publishing a professional or consumer newsletter, informing readers is your primary purpose. For example, *Variety Deal Memo,* a professional newsletter for the film industry, informs executives of news concerning global theatrical and post-theatrical rights and markets. Another professional newsletter, *Landlord Law Report,* informs residential landlords of changes in real estate law. *Consumer Reports Travel Letter,* a consumer newsletter, tells readers how to get the best discounts on airfares, hotels, and other travel expenses.

If you are publishing an association newsletter, your first priority is likely to inform members about group activities, such as meetings, social events, board elections, and community service projects. But you may also have secondary goals, such as informing readers of outside events like conferences, seminars, or job openings, as well as keeping them up to date in their field. For example, *Technicalities,* published by the Rocky Mountain Chapter of the Society for Technical Communication, runs several regular columns: one on chapter news, to inform members of chapter events; one on technology, to keep readers up to date on the use of technical-writing software; and a spotlight section that introduces readers to chapter volunteers.

If your newsletter is for employees of a large or dispersed company or nonprofit organization, you can use it to keep satellite offices up to date on organization-wide policies and procedures. For example, you can use a newsletter to explain a new vacation-request form to employees. Or if you adopt a new logo, you can introduce it to your employees via the newsletter, and perhaps further explain how they can incorporate it into letterheads, brochures, and other publications.

Marketing newsletters provide information, too. Usually it's information that will make readers more likely to buy the products or support the causes of their publishers. For example, if you produce a marketing newsletter for a food company, you might print recipes calling for its products as ingredients.

Marketing newsletters that are published by nonprofit organizations inform readers of news about the group itself or of outside news that has implications for the group's work. You can use such a newsletter, for instance, to inform donors about how their money is being spent, or to explain how a new tax law will affect the deductibility of their donations. Nonprofits can also use newsletters to keep readers up to date regarding the group's goals, activities, and donations. Perhaps you can publish a special issue to kick off your five-year capital campaign to fund a new science center and also announce a grant you received as the first install-ment on that project.

Informing readers is also a purpose—albeit a secondary one—of syndicated newsletters. These marketing newsletters are usually produced by a third party for a business, medical, law, investment, or accounting professional to distribute to clients. They report news in the profession-al's area of expertise in the hope that the information will motivate clients to use the professional's services.

To Motivate

Marketing and, to a lesser extent, association newsletters, list motivating readers as a primary purpose. Motivate them to do what? The answer to that question depends on the type of publication.

Corporate marketing newsletters motivate readers to buy products or services. For example, a ski area's newsletter may contain an applica-tion for a season pass as well as a calendar of special events for the upcoming season. A hockey rink's newsletter might include a coupon for free admission to a public skating session and a notice announcing that it is available for birthday party rentals.

Syndicated newsletters are subtler about motivating readers. For instance, *Cardiology Update*, produced by WPI Communications, is for cardiologists to distribute to primary care physicians; it consists of sum-maries of cardiology articles from medical journals. The top of the first page has space for the name and contact information of the cardiologist who distributes the newsletter. The information presented in the newsletter increases the credibility of the cardiologist who distributes it, and a page-one blurb suggests that the physicians who read it contact him if they have any questions about the articles. The hope of the cardi-ologist is that this increased professional interaction with primary care physicians will lead to more patient referrals.

Instead of motivating readers to buy a product or service, nonprofit marketing newsletters motivate them to donate to a cause or volunteer their time. In addition to making direct appeals for money, they may solicit donations more subtly by reporting on people who have benefited from previous donations. They might also describe the fruits of a fundraiser—say, a state-of-the-art computer system—to convince readers to donate to the technology fund. These newsletters also solicit volun-teers both directly, through help-wanted type appeals, and indirectly,

Motivating readers is the primary purpose of marketing newsletters. Those published by companies or corporations encourage readers to buy products or services, while the publications of nonprofit organizations motivate them to donate money or to volunteer their services.

Like marketing newsletters, association newsletters—published by schools, clubs, civic organizations, and other groups—motivate readers, encouraging them to join the organization or renew memberships, attend meetings, and/or participate in the group's activities.

through volunteer profiles and messages of appreciation. By illustrating the results of volunteer efforts—a new playground built by parents at the daycare center, for example—these newsletters can motivate readers to volunteer their time.

Association newsletters motivate readers as well: to join the group, to renew their memberships, to attend meetings, and/or to participate in activities. School newsletters can motivate parents to become more active in their children's education, while church newsletters can inspire readers to worship or get involved in parish outreach programs.

To Improve Your Image

If yours is a new organization, a newsletter can help you introduce it to the public by reporting news of its activities, running profiles of its staff or members, and describing its goals. If it's written in an informational rather than promotional style, your newsletter will increase your credibility and help your organization develop a positive public image.

From time to time, established organizations may need to explain to their customers the cause of business problems like delivery delays, service slowdowns, lawsuits, or product defects. For instance, you've probably received newsletters that utility companies insert into customer bills. If there's been a power outage or if water pressure has been low, the utility might use its newsletter to explain why. While it wouldn't launch a newsletter solely for this purpose, having one in place provides a convenient vehicle for getting the information out and, in this case, salvaging the company's reputation.

To Persuade

If you are publishing an association or marketing newsletter for an advocacy group, one of your major purposes is to persuade readers of the legitimacy of a political, religious, or moral viewpoint. Your newsletter can achieve that purpose through editorials, news articles, and features that support these views. As you'll also want to persuade readers to act on those views, your newsletter might provide material to encourage such action. It may offer, for instance, suggested language to use in writing letters to congressional representatives, sample ballots to help readers select favorable candidates, or directions to protest marches.

To Thank

Even a small amount of recognition goes a long way toward motivating people to donate their time or money. For a business, a newsletter is a place where you can show customer appreciation by running a spotlight on how they use your products or by conducting an interview with one of their employees. For nonprofits, a newsletter is a good place to thank donors and volunteers. Many nonprofit newsletters include a page listing individual and corporate donors along with a suggestion that readers patronize those businesses that have made donations. You can also publicly acknowledge services that have been donated to you by businesses, or recognize volunteers by publishing their profiles, or perhaps listing those who have reached one, two, or five years of service.

To Build Community

An association newsletter is a great vehicle for helping members get to know one another. Professionals join associations so they can network with others in their field. If the association's newsletter notes new jobs, promotions, research, and business pursuits of members, it helps members achieve that goal. Members of social or hobby organizations like to read about fellow members' leisure pursuits or milestones like marriages, births, or relocations. Employee newsletters can increase morale by reporting on both work and leisure-related activities of its staff. Another way in which they build community among readers is to run interviews, profiles, and photographs of group members, teachers, clergy, or office staff.

Recognizing your customers, employees, donors, or volunteers in your publication is an excellent way to show your appreciation and to encourage their continued efforts.

To Solicit Media Coverage

Distributing a newsletter to members or subscribers gives you some publicity, but you can leverage that exposure by regularly sending your newsletter to newspapers, magazines, radio stations, television stations, and/or Internet news portals. They may pick up a story and give it wider distribution. And reporters who receive your newsletter will be more likely to think of you when they are looking for experts to quote, examples to cite, or topics for feature stories. If, however, you want the media to cover a specific event, not just your day-to-day activities, send them a press release instead.

To Reduce Mailings

A hiking club finds itself exceeding its postage budget. Poorly planned last-minute mailings of meeting announcements and dues renewal notices are eating up the money. The group could save on postage—and copying costs—by combining these notices into a regularly published newsletter.

Even if you aren't paying for postage, you can still benefit from combining notices into a newsletter. For example, if parents of students at your elementary school complain that notices stuffed into their children's backpacks never seem to make it into their homes, you can combine these notices into a weekly newsletter that parents will become accustomed to looking for every Friday.

Now that you've had a chance to think about some of the purposes of newsletters, it's time to write a statement of purpose for yours. First, make a photocopy of the Newsletter Planning Worksheet found on page 316. In addition to the following guidelines, a completed sample of this worksheet is provided, beginning on page 26, to help further guide you in filling it out. Now, take a look at the first two items on this form.

I. WHAT ARE THE PURPOSES OF YOUR NEWSLETTER?

For this item, simply check off those purposes that apply to your publication. In our completed example on pages 26 and 27, the purposes of the newsletter *Wildlife Watch*—published by the Hampshire Wildlife Society—are to *inform* readers about wildlife preservation in Hampshire County; to *motivate* them to volunteer, donate, and participate in the group's activities; and to *thank* donors and volunteers.

2. WRITE A PURPOSE STATEMENT FOR YOUR NEWSLETTER.

In twenty-five to forty words, explain why you are publishing this newsletter and for whom. Mention your newsletter's benefits to both the reader and your organization. Look at the purpose statement of *Wildlife Watch*. Notice how it describes both its purposes and its audience. It includes benefits to the reader (becoming informed about chapter news and wildlife preservation) and benefits to the organization (motivating readers to volunteer, donate, and participate). What follows are more examples of purpose statements.

Professional: *Store Strategist* informs owners of retail stores about revenue-enhancing management tips and techniques.

Consumer: *Quilter's Corner* helps amateur quilters master their hobby by

Your newsletter's purpose statement should include how the publication will benefit the group or organization that publishes it, as well as the readers themselves.

informing them about new techniques and products, exhibits, and people who pursue the craft.

Association: *Library Link* is published by the South Central Association of Libraries to inform area librarians of general developments in library science and of the association's chapter events. It also encourages and helps them to network with other local librarians.

Marketing: *Telecom Sentinel* is published by Irvington Telecom to inform customers of developments in fiberoptic telecommunications technology, to motivate them to purchase Irvington Telecom products, and to thank them for their business.

You can use your purpose statement whenever you need to quickly describe your newsletter to advertisers, vendors, and candidates for staff positions. Notice that I didn't include readers in this list. That's the purpose of a *tagline,* which you'll learn how to compose later in this chapter. In addition to describing your newsletter to readers, a tagline will appear on its front page.

Understand Your Audience

When you publish a newsletter, you must pay close attention to your intended audience. Knowing to whom you are talking affects what you write, how you write it, and how you present it on the printed page or the computer screen.

Don't overlook the fact that your newsletter may have a primary and a secondary audience. A newsletter for elderly clients of a home health-care service may also be read by adult children of those clients. A youth soccer league publication may be read by both the parents to whom it's addressed and the players themselves. Depending on your purpose, you may want to include material of interest to both audiences.

Here, we will take a look at some characteristics you should know (or discover) about your audience. We will consider their demographics, level of education, interest in what you have to say, and familiarity with your organization.

Demographics

Demographics are the characteristics of a particular segment of the population. They include the statistics gathered by a census, such as age, sex,

Knowing the demographic profile, educational background, and interest level of your audience will affect what you write, how you write it, and the way in which you present it on the page.

As you can see, this completed worksheet clearly defines the purpose, audience, tone, and editorial posture of the newsletter *Wildlife Watch*.

Newsletter Planning Worksheet
for
Wildlife Watch

1. What are the purposes of your newsletter?

✓ Inform about _____ wildlife preservation in Hampshire County _____

✓ Motivate to:

    ✓ volunteer   ✓ donate   ___ join or renew membership

    ___ attend meetings   ✓ participate in activities

___ Improve organization's image

___ Build community interaction and involvement

___ Persuade of a political, religious, or moral view

✓ Thank donors, volunteers, and customers

___ Solicit media coverage

___ Coordinate procedures among offices

___ Reduce number of mailings

___ Other: _____

2. Write a purpose statement for your newsletter (25 to 40 words).

Wildlife Watch informs members of the Hampshire Wildlife Society about chapter news and about wildlife preservation in Hampshire County; motivates them to volunteer, donate, and participate in society activities; and acknowledges the contributions of donors and volunteers.

3. Who is your primary audience?

Demographics:

Age _____ adults 25–55 _____

Sex ✓ M   ✓ F

Race _____ mixed _____

Ethnic group _____ mixed _____

Religion _____ mixed _____

Geographic location _____ Hampshire County _____

Income level _____ mixed _____

Disability status _____

Educational level:

___ Some high school   ✓ High school graduate   ✓ Some college

✓ Bachelor's degree   ___ Master's degree   ___ Doctoral degree

Familiarity with topic:

___ High   ✓ Medium   ___ Low

Interest, motivation to read your newsletter:

___ High   ✓ Medium   ___ Low

Familiarity with organization:

___ High   ✓ Medium   ___ Low

4. Can you identify any secondary audiences for your newsletter?

Friends and/or colleagues to whom Society members pass along the newsletter.
Similar demographics.

5. What is the appropriate tone(s) for your newsletter?

___ Conservative   ___ Stylish   ✓ Cost conscious
___ Upscale   ✓ Casual   ___ Formal

6. What is the appropriate editorial posture for your newsletter?

✓ Advocating   ___ Objective   ___ Predicting   ___ Personal

A blank copy of this Newsletter Planning Worksheet is found on pages 316 and 317.

race, ethnic background, and religion. Other demographic information includes geographic location, income level, and disability status.

Knowing the demographics of your audience will help you choose a writing style, usage conventions, and a design that will appeal to your audience. For example, if you know that a large portion of your audience is over age fifty-five, you might choose to use a more formal writing style than you would for younger people. You should keep the age of your audience in mind when deciding the type of slang to allow as well—if your review of the middle school play describes it as "da bomb," you will flatter the young actors, but their parents will think you're calling it a flop.

Age also tells you what knowledge you can assume your audience has. People born before the early 1960s will know that Richard Nixon is the president who was "not a crook," but this reference will go over the heads of most younger people.

Age, sex, and disability status influence newsletter design. Older audiences tend to appreciate larger type, as do people with visual impairments. Bright neon colors and bold graphics typically appeal to a younger audience. Color choice also might be a consideration if your newsletter is directed toward males rather than females, and vice versa.

The geographic location of your audience can determine the topics you write about and the type of language you use. For example, people in the northeastern United States aren't interested in detailed information about the construction schedule for a new highway in Los Angeles—unless your newsletter is for a travel club that's planning a trip there. Writing an article that reminisces about sipping *frappes* at an ice cream stand will make a Bostonian's mouth water but leave a Midwesterner scratching his head, since "frappe" is a term for "milkshake" and unique to the Boston area. Likewise, you can use baseball analogies in your writing, perhaps saying that your capital campaign "hit a home run," but if your audience includes recent immigrants, they may not understand what you mean.

Factor in your audience's age, sex, geographic location, educational background, and other characteristics when determining the writing style, language usage, and even the typeface to use in your newsletter.

Education Level

How much schooling do your readers have? In what subject areas? Understanding your readers' educational level means knowing not only whether they have PhDs, bachelor's degrees, or high school diplomas, but also their familiarity with the topics in your newsletter. A medical newsletter aimed at consumers, like Tufts University's *Health & Nutrition Letter,* may have well-educated readers, but they may not have degrees in health-related fields. Knowing that, you would have to translate medical terminology into plain English. You'd also need to provide certain back-ground information when necessary. If, for instance, you are writing about cirrhosis, it would be important to first review the function of the liver before going into the physiology of the disease.

An audience of physics PhDs who are reading a newsletter that sum-marizes recent research will expect a formal, technical writing style. Flashy graphics, bright colors, and informal, slang-filled language will cause them to question the credibility of the publication.

Knowing your audience's educational level, along with their age and income level, can also help you decide whether to publish a print or elec-tronic newsletter. Older readers and those with lower incomes and less education may not have access to the Internet, although that is rapidly changing as computers make their way into more and more households each year.

When deciding whether to publish a print newsletter or an online version, consider the age, schooling, and income status of your audience. Some people, especially those with lower incomes and education levels, as well as those who are older, may not have access to, knowledge of, or interest in the Internet.

Interest and Motivation

Some newsletters are invited guests in readers' homes or offices; others are like door-to-door sales reps who need to convince customers to let them in. Professional, consumer, and association newsletters tend to fall into the first category, while marketing newsletters are likely to fall into the second.

If you have readers who do not subscribe to or request your newslet-ter, you have to convince them to read it—via enticing graphics, attrac-tive photos, attention-grabbing opening paragraphs, and brief articles. But if your newsletter contains information that is important to your audience, you won't need to work as hard to get them to read it.

If one of the purposes of your newsletter is to persuade your audi-ence of a viewpoint, you'll also need to consider the degree to which they already hold that view. If your readers are undecided, you'll need to devote substantial newsletter space for material that supports your view-point. If, on the other hand, they already support your view, you can use more space to motivate them to act on those views—vote for a favorable candidate, attend an organizational meeting, and the like. Don't expect your audience to include your opponents: they are already convinced of the opposite point of view, and it's not a good use of your time to try to win them over to your side.

Familiarity with the Organization

Volunteers for a regional running club spent dozens of hours each month producing a twelve-page newsletter. Filled with tips on stretching, race strategy, and diet, it also included photos of its members crossing the finish line (often as winners) at road races. A typical photo caption read, "Anne and Sarah are up to their usual antics at Falmouth." Members who had been at Falmouth read the caption and understood it, but those who weren't—the less active members as well as the new members—read the caption and asked, "Anne who? Sarah who? What are their usual antics, and when have they been up to them before? And where the heck is Falmouth?" This caption and others like it said to the less-active members, "Our club is a group of insiders. We all know each other, and we know what each other's usual antics are."

The running club may want to attract and retain members with its newsletter, but the publication's insider tone may have the opposite effect. While the content of this particular newsletter showed that the editors understood the demographics, level of education, and interests of its audience, they ignored an important audience characteristic: familiarity with the organization.

If yours is an association newsletter, remember that the subset of your readers who are either new to your group or not active in it is your primary audience. Your active members—executive officers, committee chairs, those who attend meetings—already know eighty percent of what you report in the newsletter, because they hear it announced at meetings or they talk informally with other members who are "in the know." If written sensitively, your newsletter can turn your inactive members into active ones.

Researching Your Audience

How do you gather information about your audience? If you need cut-and-dry data like demographics, visit your public library. Ask a reference librarian to point you to almanacs, statistical abstracts, census reports, and other reference books or databases that provide demographic information, such as the number of orthopedic surgeons in the United States who are under thirty-five years old, or the percentage of college-bound high school seniors who smoke.

The Sourcebook of ZIP Code Demographics is one example of a business reference book. It provides, by state and zip code, data on the likelihood of consumer spending for financial services, home products, entertainment, and personal items. *The Lifestyle Market Analyst* contains information on the interests, hobbies, and activities that are popular in various geographic and demographic markets in the country. In addition, the

When assessing your audience, be sure to check the reference section of your local library. Most include helpful resources for gathering information ranging from statistical data of consumers in various areas of the country to their general interests and spending habits.

Encyclopedia of Business Information Sources can steer you to databases, directories, and other sources of statistics relating to dozens of fields, ranging from aviation, advertising, and masonry to the mushroom and pasta industries. The Resources section, beginning on page 323, provides more details on these and other research sources.

If other periodicals that are related to your newsletter's topic are available, try checking out their advertiser's kits. Often found on a periodical's website, these kits usually contain demographic data on the audience.

If you have an existing newsletter, you can find out more about your readers by inserting a survey into an issue or two. In addition to collecting demographic information, you can ask readers how much background knowledge they have in your subject area or how familiar they are with your organization. Another method of getting this information is to conduct a focus-group discussion with a sample of your readers.

You may also have experts right in your organization who can help you. Your company's salespeople and marketing staff know their customers. Your school principal knows what percentage of families is new to the school each year, or how many children qualify for the federal free-lunch program. Your fundraising staff knows the demographics of your donors.

Finally, you can consult trade publications in your field. They often carry data, such as demographics of people who hold various occupations, buy certain products, or use social services.

Use what you've learned in this section to complete items 3 and 4 of your Newsletter Planning Worksheet:

3. WHO IS YOUR NEWSLETTER'S PRIMARY AUDIENCE?

Fill in the characteristics of your primary audience. As you can see from the completed sample worksheet beginning on page 26, the primary audience for the *Wildlife Watch* newsletter includes the members of the Hampshire Wildlife Society, which is made up of men and women from twenty-five to fifty-five years of age who live in Hampshire County. They are of mixed backgrounds, races, religions, and income levels; and they are typically high school and college graduates. They are also familiar with the *Wildlife Watch* newsletter and are interested in its issues and focus on preserving the county's wildlife.

4. CAN YOU IDENTIFY ANY SECONDARY AUDIENCE(S) FOR YOUR NEWSLETTER?

In addition to your target audience, does your newsletter have one or more secondary audiences? The sample *Wildlife Watch* has identified friends and colleagues of Hampshire Wildlife Society members, who may be given copies of the newsletter by the members. Demographically, this secondary audience is similar to the primary audience.

Choose the Right Style

Now that you have determined what you will be saying in your newsletter and who will be reading it, you have to choose a style in which to present it. When it comes to style, it's important to set the right tone and use the most effective editorial posture.

Set the Right Tone

It's your anniversary. You and your spouse go out to dinner at the finest restaurant in town. The menu includes dishes like Timbale of Osetra Caviar, Basque-Style Lamb Stew, and Sautéed Radicchio. The lights are low, the music is classical, and the artwork is original. The furniture is richly upholstered and the waiters wear tuxedoes.

The next day you stop at a deli on the way to your daughter's state soccer tournament. A top-forty radio station blares in the background. The cashier yells, "Two tuna on rye" to the guy making sandwiches, and you hand over a ten-dollar bill. You and your daughter sit at a Formica table to eat, and in a total of twenty minutes, you're out of there.

These two restaurants serve separate purposes and very different clientele (for newsletters, think "audiences"), so they deliberately set a tone and mood. The first establishment, visited for special occasions, is formal and stylish. The second, catering to people in a hurry who don't want to spend a lot of money, is casual and "no frills."

Although a newsletter plays no music and serves no food, its writing style, layout, color, and paper (if print format) still convey a mood and tone. Choose a tone that will appeal to your audience and achieve your purpose. If your purpose is to motivate or persuade, your writing will advocate opinions and actions. If you seek to inform readers, your writing will be more objective. If you are soliciting donations from an audience with little money to spare, you might choose a frugal design, but if

The writing style and general appearance of your newsletter should convey a tone that appeals to your audience and achieves the purpose of your publication.

you're appealing to large-income donors, you may choose a design that's more expensive.

Using black ink and white paper, because they are less costly than colored, signals to your readers that you are watching your budget. Color (particularly four-color) text and photos hint that your publication has more money to spend. A design with lots of white space looks expensive because it says that you can afford to buy lots of paper. Bleeds—the use of ink that extends to the edge of the paper—add to the expensive look. Mailing a newsletter in envelopes instead of placing address labels on the back page also gives a pricier impression.

There are times, however, when other considerations trump cost, and you might choose to use an expensive production technique even though you want your organization to project a frugal image. For example, if your newsletter contains confidential information, you would use envelopes regardless of cost. Or if you wanted to draw attention to your writing and better communicate your message, you might select a newsletter design that uses extra white space. The overall tone of your newsletter is not set by just one design element.

Your topic can help you decide whether your newsletter should convey a formal or informal tone. Association newsletters, particularly when they relate to a leisure activity or when the publisher and readers know each other personally, are designed and written in a more casual style than professional newsletters.

Also consider the image you want to nurture for your organization when developing your newsletter's tone. Fashionable colors and splashy typefaces give you a stylish, up-to-date look. Pastel colors and graphics that are placed at an angle convey informality. Muted colors, traditional typefaces, and justified columns of consistent widths convey a more serious, conservative image. In Chapter 8 you'll learn more about creating a mood and tone through newsletter design.

Writing and usage styles also convey the level of formality of your newsletter. If you write in the second person (using "you" and "your," as I do in this book) and allow abbreviations, slang, or contractions, your newsletter will sound less formal than if you write in the third person (using "he," "she," "one," and "they") and avoid abbreviations, slang, and contractions. Chapter 6 goes into greater detail about developing writing and usage styles.

The samples in Figure 2.1 on page 34 illustrate newsletters with formal, informal, cost-conscious, and upscale tones.

Design elements of your newsletter—colors, typefaces, column width and alignment, amount of white space, placement of graphics—all convey a certain mood and tone to readers.

Figure 2.1

Setting the tone for your newsletter's look.

- Justified columns, muted colors, and traditional typefaces contribute to the formal tone of *Heart Murmurs.*

Source: Patricia O'Brien and Julie-Anne Evangelista, Cardiovascular Program, Children's Hospital, Boston, MA.

- Bubble-like geometrics and a light-hearted photograph contribute to the informal tone of *The May Report.*

- The use of black ink and plain white paper shows readers of the Monadnock Humane Society's *Advocate* that the organization is trying to keep its newsletter production costs down so it can spend more on the animals it aims to protect.

- *Westlaw Edge* conveys an upscale tone with a bleed around the word "edge" in the banner, a full-page table of contents, and, inside, elaborate graphics.

Heart Murmurs

The May Report

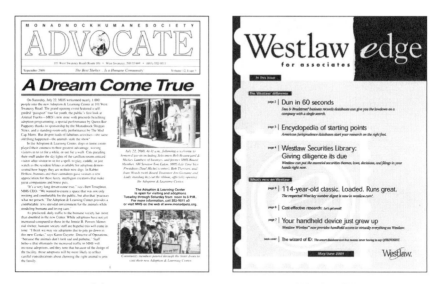

Advocate

Westlaw Edge

Use the Right Editorial Posture

Editorial posture is the position or slant that a newsletter's writing takes on the topics it covers. The editorial posture you adopt depends on the purpose of your newsletter. It can be advocating, objective, personal, or predicting.

If your purpose is to persuade readers, you'll adopt an editorial posture of advocacy. For example, *Tony Perkins' Washington Update*, published by the Family Research Council, an organization formed to promote conservative family values, contains writing that attempts to inspire readers to fight for policies that reflect those viewpoints. The writing in this type of newsletter is often contentious and argumentative.

If your purpose is to inform readers, your writing will be more objective. You might write how-to articles in which you might offer step-by-step procedures to help your readers accomplish certain tasks. A research-based health newsletter might objectively summarize the results of studies that draw conflicting conclusions about the causes of breast cancer. But that same newsletter could also take on a posture of advocacy by including an editorial calling on Congress to increase funding for breast cancer research or an article encouraging readers to get regular mammograms.

Some newsletters are written in a personalized manner. For example, financial wizard *Louis Rukeyser's Wall Street* is written in the first person (using "I" and "me"). A picture of Rukeyser appears on page one, and his signature appears on the last page. This conveys to readers the idea that they are receiving his personal investment advice. Another common editorial posture for investment and business newsletters is one of prediction, forecasting business or financial-market trends.

You're ready to finish up the Newsletter Planning Worksheet now. The remaining two items will help you choose the most effective style for your newsletter.

> Depending on the purpose of your publication, its editorial posture can be advocating, objective, personal, or predicting.

5. WHAT IS THE APPROPRIATE TONE FOR YOUR NEWSLETTER?

After carefully considering your newsletter's purpose and audience, it's time to decide on the most appropriate tone. Check one or more of the options presented in this section to help in your decision. As seen in the sample worksheet beginning on page 26, *Wildlife Watch's* tone is casual and cost conscious.

6. WHAT IS THE APPROPRIATE EDITORIAL POSTURE FOR YOUR NEWSLETTER?

In this final section of your worksheet, choose which editorial posture—advocating, objective, predicting, or personal—is best suited for your newsletter. As *Wildlife Watch* is the newsletter of a society that supports and promotes wildlife preservation, its editorial posture is "advocating."

Keep this worksheet handy. As you continue reading the book, you'll want to refer back to it to guide you in making decisions about planning, writing, and designing your newsletter.

ASSESSING THE COMPETITION

If you are considering launching a subscription newsletter, you'll want to research the competition. If you aim to turn a profit on your newsletter, you need to know whether other newsletters cover the same topic for the same audience. Don't necessarily be discouraged if you *do* find such newsletters. There may still be room in the market for yours if it offers something the competition lacks, such as deeper knowledge of the field, more contacts with insiders who can provide valuable information, better writing, or more timeliness.

When preparing to launch a newsletter, don't be discouraged if you discover existing newsletters that cover the same topic as yours. As long as your publication offers something desirable that the others don't—better writing, more timely information, greater knowledge of the field— there will be a spot in the marketplace for it.

If the goal of your subscription newsletter is to cover an avocation without necessarily turning a profit, you should still find out if similar newsletters exist. You may be surprised to find another publication that does a good job of covering your topic, and then decide not to reinvent the wheel by starting your own publication.

The best way to research the competition is to consult newsletter directories. Some of the best-known directories include *Newsletters in Print, Oxbridge Directory of Newsletters,* and *Hudson's Subscription Newsletter Directory.* Newsletter directories usually list publications by subject area, but they also include indexes that list them by title, publisher, and/or geographical region. For each newsletter, they provide information such as the publisher's name, address, phone and fax numbers, and e-mail and website addresses. They also include the editor's name, a description of the newsletter's audience and purpose, its frequency, price, year established, circulation, available formats, and advertising policies.

More-specialized newsletter directories are also available. For example, *Legal Newsletters in Print* lists legal, legislative, and regulatory related newsletters, bulletins, and reporting services published in the United States. *MarketWatch* lists investment newsletters classified by type of investment such as mutual funds, stocks, bonds, and currencies.

In addition to being available as printed books, some newsletter directories are also distributed in easy-to-search electronic formats, such as CD-ROMs or databases that are accessible on the Internet.

Advocacy and the Tax-Exempt Nonprofit Organization

If you are a tax-exempt nonprofit organization, you need to consider your IRS status when choosing an editorial posture for your newsletter. Examples of the classes of IRS tax-exempt organizations and the sections of the Internal Revenue Code governing them include charitable organizations, § 501(c)(3); social welfare organizations, § 501(c)(4); labor and agricultural organizations, § 501(c)(5); and many more.

IRS regulations dictate the amount of legislative lobbying and political campaigning that each of these types of organizations can engage in and still maintain their tax-exempt status. Running articles and editorials in your newsletter that promote legislation or candidates could jeopardize your nonprofit status. For more information, contact your attorney or visit the IRS web page on tax-exempt organizations at *www.irs.gov/charities*.

Once you have identified competing publications listed in these newsletter directories, you'd be wise to familiarize yourself with them. At a minimum, you should write or e-mail the publisher to request a sample copy. Better yet, develop a broader understanding of how they cover their subject by subscribing for a while or by reading several issues at the library. If you can't find the newsletter you're looking for at your local branch, try visiting a large city's public library or a university, law, or business library. The average public library doesn't carry many newsletters because of the specialized nature of their audiences and topics.

In *Publishing Newsletters,* Howard Penn Hudson discusses how the success of a subscription newsletter depends on whether its intended audience can find other ways to access information on the same subject. Paul J. Bringe, a newsletter publisher and direct marketing consultant, notes several market conditions that indicate the need for a newsletter:

■ *If periodicals are published for the audience and topic, but are not timely.* For example, a monthly magazine on your topic may exist; but, as I mentioned in Chapter 1, there is a long lead-time between the writing of magazine articles and their delivery to readers. Your readers may need news within a week or two of its occurrence. A newsletter can offer that timeliness.

■ *If magazines are unable to address the market, because the market is too small to attract enough advertisers to support them.* Since most subscription newsletters don't run advertisements and their production costs are lower than those of magazines, you can fill the information gap with your newsletter.

■ *If a professional audience is unable to get information on your topic elsewhere.* In other words, no newsletters, newspapers, or magazines exist in that particular field.

To determine whether these conditions exist for your newsletter's market, you can refer to a periodicals directory, such as *Ulrich's Periodicals Directory, Standard Periodical Directory, Publist.com,* and *International Media Guides.* Several websites offer a directory of electronic newsletters and discussion lists, but they are not comprehensive. These directories are akin to newsletter directories except that they list magazines, newsletters, newspapers, journals, electronic journals, and monographs. The type of information they provide for each periodical is similar to that provided by the newsletter directories: publisher contact information, frequency, circulation, and so forth. Just as you used newsletter directories to obtain copies of competing newsletters, you should use periodicals directories to help obtain copies of competing magazines, journals, or newspapers before launching your publication.

More information about newsletter and periodical directories is in the Directories section of the Resources section, beginning on page 323.

ALL ABOUT THE NAME

Choosing the right name for your newsletter is key. People should be able to recognize your publication from across the room based largely on its nameplate.

Another area to consider when developing the idea of your newsletter is its name. To identify your newsletter, you need to give it a title and decide how to display it in your nameplate, along with your logo and tagline. (Nameplates, logos, and taglines will be discussed in a moment.) You may also want to make sure your name is protected by registering it as a trademark or an Internet domain. Some newsletters will also need to have an International Standard Serial Number. This section will help you complete all these tasks.

Nameplates, Names, Logos, and Taglines

Your newsletter's *nameplate,* also called a *banner,* is the first place a reader's eyes fall. It is typically set at the top of the first page and commonly includes the newsletter's title, logo, date, and tagline. Nameplates are usually set off graphically in some way—often they appear within a box or above a horizontal line called a rule, which sets it apart from the rest of the newsletter. People should be able to recognize your newsletter from across the room, based largely on its nameplate. This means if your newsletter's name is too long, you'll have to set it in type that's too small to make instant recognition possible. Yet you want your readers to know up front who publishes the newsletter and why. How do you do it?

Hypothetically, let's say that you have been put in charge of creating the newsletter for the Hampshire Wildlife Society. Your first idea for its title is simply *The Hampshire Wildlife Society Newsletter.* Right off the bat, it's obvious that this title is too long. What can you do? First, you can save space in the nameplate by avoiding the use of the word "newsletter" in the title. Readers will know it's a newsletter by its size, the type of paper it's printed on, the formatting, and the content of the articles. Including the word "newsletter" in its name is redundant. After all, you don't go to a newsstand in Grand Central Station and ask for *The New York Times Newspaper,* you request *The New York Times* or just *The Times.*

If you get rid of the word "newsletter" in this example, you'll be left with *The Hampshire Wildlife Society*—the name of the publishing organization. Consider whether you need to include this name in the nameplate. For professional, consumer, and subscription newsletters in which you are selling information, your organization or company's name may not need to be so prominent. For marketing and association newsletters in which you are selling your organization or company as well, you do want it prominently displayed.

Most companies and organizations use a *logo*—often a symbol or trademark—to identify and communicate their name. If you have a logo, you can display it within the nameplate at a size that is large enough to be visible but not so large that it dominates the nameplate. If your logo does not include the name of your organization (or abbreviates it), you can also include *logotype,* which spells out the name. Alternatively, you can display your logo and/or logotype elsewhere on page one—perhaps in the lower right- or left-hand corner.

Back to our newsletter example. If you use the Hampshire Wildlife Society's logo in the nameplate instead of using the society's name in the title, there will be nothing left—it will have no name at all! So what you'll have to do next is come up with a word or two that expresses both the purpose and the topic of the newsletter. Readers are more likely to remember names that have a double meaning, perhaps one meaning that pertains to the subject matter and another that pertains to writing or communication. For example, Beaver Brook Association, a nature preserve, calls its newsletter *The Log;* the Sacramento, California, Chapter of the Society for Technical Communication publishes *The Capital Letter* (Sacramento is the capital of California); and the Cardiovascular Program at Children's Hospital Boston publishes *Heart Murmurs.* If the two

Your newsletter's name should be short enough to fit properly in the nameplate. It should also reflect the topic or purpose of the publication. Here are some examples:

Healthy Outlook
South Nassau Communities Hospital

Independent
PMA—the Independent Book Publishers Association

The Log
Beaver Brook Association

Heart Murmurs
Cardiovascular Program at Children's Hospital Boston

Youth Sports Journal
National Alliance For Youth Sports

words in your title are alliterative (they start with the same initial sound)
the name will also grab people's attention. For our example, the name
Wildlife Watch works for the Hampshire Wildlife Society. It's a catchy
alliterative title that is descriptive of the society's goals. It also has other
important qualities—it is short enough to fit across the nameplate even
when set in large type. It is also easy to pronounce and spell.

Don't give your newsletter a name like *News Notes, Newslines,* or
News and Views. These titles, while clever, have been used so often that
they have become trite. If you have trouble thinking of a name, check out
Quick & Easy Newsletters by Elaine Floyd. This book lists over 700 words
from A ("About") to Z ("Zoom") that you can use in a newsletter name.

Finally, compose a *tagline*—a short phrase that communicates the
newsletter's purpose, audience, and/or benefit to readers. Figure 2.2 on
page 41 presents the taglines of three newsletters. *Deal Memo* uses "The
global newsletter of theatrical and post-theatrical rights and markets."
Andrew Harper's *Hideaway Report* uses the tagline "A connoisseur's
worldwide guide to peaceful and unspoiled places." *Property Manager's
Protector* uses "How to safeguard people, property & profits." If you
incorporate the name of your organization into the tagline, you don't
need to repeat it in logotype in the nameplate.

Wildlife Watch communicates its audience, purpose, and publisher by
using the tagline "News for friends of the Hampshire Wildlife Society."
Figure 2.3 on page 42 displays the before and after nameplates of our
hypothetical newsletter. Notice how the newsletter's revised nameplate,
including its publisher, purpose, audience, and logo, takes up the same
amount of space as the original one.

Registering a Trademark

You can register a trademark—a brand name—with the federal government for your newsletter's title. Registering a trademark means that no
one else in the United States can use your newsletter's name on a product that would cause confusion, mistaken identity, or deception. For
example, if you registered *Wildlife Watch,* your newsletter's name, no one
else could use this name on their newsletter. But someone else could
name a board game or a wristwatch *Wildlife Watch,* because it's unlikely
that people would confuse these products with a newsletter.

If you ever get into a legal fight over use of your name, you will have
certain procedural advantages if you have registered your trademark. If
you haven't, you could be forced to stop using your name. If you don't

Information Media Group.

Harper Associates, Inc.

Copyright, Brownstone Publishers, Inc., 149 Fifth Ave., New York, NY 10010-6810. Reprinted with permission. For a free sample issue or to subscribe, call (800) 643-8095.

Figure 2.2
Three nameplates (banners) with taglines that clearly communicate each newsletter's name and purpose.

register your trademark, you still have a common-law right to use the name (assuming no one else has established use of the same name), but that right applies only in the geographic area where you are using it.

You may have noticed that some newsletter names have the ™ (trademark) symbol in their banners. The symbol indicates that the publisher is claiming the trademark on the name. Once the publisher completes registration of the name, he can replace the ™ symbol with ®, which means it has been registered.

Whether you plan to register your trademark or not, it's a good idea

Figure 2.3

As seen in the top example, the type in the original nameplate for this newsletter is too small to be read from across a room. Below it, the revised nameplate packs the name, audience, and purpose of the newsletter, as well as a logo, into the same space as the original.

Original Nameplate

Revised Version

to do a trademark search before choosing a newsletter name, so you don't use one that is already established. You can do this by searching the records of the US Patent and Trademark Offices (USPTO) at *www.uspto.gov*. And although you aren't required to use an attorney to register a trademark, the process of both searching and registering may go faster and more reliably if you do. You can obtain applications and further information on how to apply at the USPTO website.

Registering Internet Domain Names

If you've ever surfed the Internet, you've used a domain name. A domain name is the string of letters that uniquely identifies a website. *Whitehouse.gov* and *amazon.com* are two examples. Domain names were developed so that web surfers would not have to remember the sites' underlying addresses, which are long series of numbers and periods (such as "207.151.159.3").

Does your newsletter need an Internet domain name? It depends. If your newsletter will be one of several items available on your website, it probably doesn't need its own domain name. You can simply link to your newsletter from the home page of your company or organization. But if you suspect that potential readers might try to find your newsletter online by entering its name in their browser's address box (rather than using a search engine like Google or Yahoo! to find you), then you might want to register your newsletter name as a domain name. That way, potential readers won't end up at unrelated or (worse!) competing sites when looking for you.

You can obtain a domain name through any company that has been accredited by the Internet Corporation for Assigned Names and Numbers (ICANN) to act as a registrar. These companies set their own prices, ranging from about $10 to $35 per year, for registering domain names. Many of them offer a search facility on their website that lets you find out whether your chosen domain name has already been taken. You can find a list of accredited registrars at *www.internic.net/regist.html*.

About International Standard Serial Numbers (ISSNs)

An ISSN is an International Standard Serial Number that the National Serials Data Program (NSDP), a part of the Library of Congress, assigns to periodicals, including newsletters. The ISSN uniquely identifies a periodical, regardless of what country or what language it is published in. You've probably seen the corresponding number—an ISBN—on the back of books. You may even have used an ISBN when calling a bookstore to order a book. If you know the ISBN, you don't have to tell the bookstore clerk the author, title, or publisher of the book. Similarly, the eight-digit ISSN identifies a newsletter or other serial publication.

An ISSN is a number that uniquely identifies magazines, newsletters, and other serial publications. Depending on your needs, you may or may not have to apply for one.

Libraries use ISSNs to identify, order, and check in publications. They also use them to file interlibrary loan requests. Large newsletter publishing companies find ISSNs useful when processing orders via computer. Newsletter directories include ISSNs as one of the pieces of information distinguishing each publication. The US Postal Service uses them to regulate controlled-circulation publications. Finally, the Copyright Clearance Center, which collects fees for reproduction of copyrighted material, uses ISSNs to monitor payments.

Is it necessary to have an ISSN for your newsletter? Generally, you will *need* an ISSN if:

■ You will be mailing your newsletter via Periodicals mail, a category reserved by the US Postal Service for certain qualifying periodicals (for more information, see Chapter 9).

■ You expect libraries to circulate your newsletter. Not just public libraries, but also corporate, nonprofit, university, or legal libraries.

■ You anticipate (a) that others might request permission to reproduce copyrighted material from your newsletter, (b) that you would require payment for the granting of such permission, and (c) that you would have the Copyright Clearance Center handle those payments.

You will probably *want* an ISSN if:

■ You are publishing a subscription newsletter.

■ You want your publication listed in newsletter or periodical directories.

You can obtain an ISSN through the NSDP of the Library of Congress. There is no charge for requesting or using an ISSN. Applications are available at *www.loc.gov/issn*. When filing the application, you will have to provide a sample issue or a copy of the title page or the masthead, which is a listing (often boxed) of the newsletter's staff and other information about its operation, such as address, website, circulation, and reprint policy. The masthead appears in the same spot in each issue. (Chapter 8 provides more information on mastheads.) For electronic newsletters, you can provide the website address or e-mail an actual issue with your application. The NSDP suggests allowing about a month to receive your ISSN.

If you publish your newsletter in both print and electronic formats, you will need a separate ISSN for each one. And if you change the title of your newsletter, you will have to apply for a new ISSN.

Display your ISSN in every issue of your newsletter. Most publishers place it in the masthead. You should also include your ISSN in any catalogs or advertisements that sell or display your newsletter (both direct mail and space ads), and in any other place where details of your publication normally appear.

CONCLUSION

By now, your newsletter idea should be taking a clear shape in your mind (and on your Newsletter Planning Worksheet). You may even have a name for it. At this point, you're done with the theoretical steps of newsletter planning; it's time to get organized and get the project rolling.

CHAPTER 3

SETTING UP SHOP

I f your project were a movie, you would be ready now to raise several million dollars, cast roles, build sets, hire a crew, and get the project on the road. But it's not a film, it's a newsletter. So instead you're going to choose a distribution method, create a budget, hire a staff, assign responsibilities, and implement effective schedules and tracking charts to help maintain a smooth production—in other words, set up shop.

CHOOSING A DISTRIBUTION METHOD

The newsletter of a handheld-computer users group had been published sporadically over the years. After its first editor moved to Chicago, the group appointed a second editor, who produced one issue and then relocated to Florida. After a year with no newsletter at all, the group finally found a third editor. Six issues later, with printing and postage bills exceeding $500 per issue, the elapsed time from copy deadline to mailing reaching six weeks, and the pending resignation of the layout artist, the group decided to take its newsletter online.

Should you follow suit? It's important to decide now which type of newsletter you will be publishing, because your choice will drive your budget, staffing, and scheduling decisions, which are discussed in this chapter. Your choice will also determine whether you proceed through the chapters in Part Three (Taking It to the Streets: Producing Your Print Newsletter) or Part Four (Launching It Online: Producing Your Electronic Newsletter) of this book.

Your newsletter's audience and purpose should determine the best format. An electronic format made sense for the handheld-computer users

Distributing your newsletter online has some obvious advantages over distributing print versions. Without having to make stops at the print shop and post office, you can get your publication out in a more timely fashion—and it will save you money. And from an environmental point of view, eliminating the use of paper is an obvious plus.

group since its members were (by definition) computer literate. Can you say the same about your members? This is where the audience research described in Chapter 2 comes in handy. Having some idea of the type of computer hardware, software, and Internet access your audience has can help you make sound decisions about delivering your newsletter electronically. In addition, regardless of their *ability* to access your newsletter online, ask yourself: Are your readers *motivated* enough to seek out your newsletter on their computers? The reduced costs of electronic distribution are enticing, but what price will you pay in readership, response rates, or the goodwill of your audience?

In many ways, you can win your readers' hearts by distributing your newsletter electronically. By reducing the delays that are inherent in using print shops and the post office, you can deliver your news in a more timely fashion. By eliminating paper, you are showing concern for the environment. Readers who like what they read can easily forward your newsletter to their friends and colleagues. And, like the handheld-computer users group, you can benefit by saving money on printing charges and postage.

On the other hand, you may find that your online newsletter gets fewer readers than your print version. Many people simply prefer reading on paper rather than a computer screen. Others may prefer reading newsletters while straphanging on the subway, or in bed before nodding off at night. Still others simply won't be willing to make the effort (or won't know how) to open a web page or portable document formatted (PDF) newsletter.

Print Newsletters

Most print newsletters are distributed through the US mail, but other avenues are available as well. You may arrange to distribute a free general-interest newsletter at any number of community drop-off points, such as libraries, universities, restaurants, supermarkets, or other public venues. Insurance agencies, banks, physicians' offices, and other businesses that regularly meet customers or patients in their offices can hand out their newsletters there. Retail stores can offer their newsletters to customers at the checkout counter. You can also distribute your newsletter at conferences, meetings, and trade shows that members of your audience attend. You might find it cost-effective to distribute your newsletter as an insert to a newspaper or a mailing that a third party regularly sends to your target audience.

Electronic Newsletters

There are four formats for distributing your newsletter electronically. They are web newsletters, text e-mail newsletters, HTML (hypertext markup language) e-mail newsletters, and PDF (portable document format) newsletters. In the following discussion, I describe these formats and help you evaluate whether they will work for your publication. My evaluation criteria include ease of layout, distribution costs, design capabilities and legibility, linking capabilities, and ease of obtaining and reading. Later, in Part Four, I'll give you more details on how to produce a newsletter in each format.

Web Newsletters

A *web newsletter,* which is created in HTML format, appears as a set of pages on your website. With this type of newsletter, you get the benefit of inexpensive, quick distribution plus the ability to let readers easily link to other locations and e-mail addresses on the

Figure 3.1
Web Newsletter
Inexpensive to distribute and reasonably simple to lay out, web newsletters can incorporate graphics and color easily and at a nominal cost.

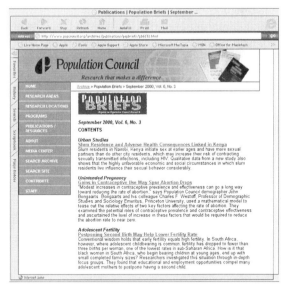

site. For example, you can allow users to click on an article listed in the newsletter's table of contents, enabling them to jump right to that article, or jump from the midpoint of an article back to the top.

Although you don't have complete control over the layout your readers see on the computer screen, you can still format a web newsletter attractively, as seen in Figure 3.1 at right. You can include photos, graphics, and text in color without the added cost that is incurred with print newsletters. Once you become comfortable with web-page development software, you'll be able to lay out your newsletter more quickly than with print or PDF formats.

Accessing a web newsletter is fairly simple for readers, especially if you send them an e-mail announcement of each issue that lets them click on a link to the newsletter's web page. And if you have readers who object to reading on the computer screen, you can accommodate them by providing an easy way to print out the newsletter.

Text E-Mail Newsletters

Of the various types of electronic newsletter formats, *text e-mail newsletters,* which are sometimes called *e-zines,* are the easiest to design and lay out. Figure 3.2 at left is an example. Readers need only know how to check their e-mail to receive this type of newsletter. Distribution costs are minimal. These newsletters can include links to visit websites or to send e-mails. Best of all, they download in no time!

On the other hand, text e-mail newsletters lack the ability to create the pleasing layouts that readers have become accustomed to since the advent of desktop publishing. They are delivered as plain text, meaning they don't include any formatting like bold or italicized text, varying typefaces, or special characters, nor do they contain graphics or photos. You cannot set up columns or tables in a text e-mail newsletter.

In spite of these drawbacks, if you follow the steps for producing text e-mail newsletters, which are explained in Chapter 11, you can still make them highly readable, and you can be confident that the way the newsletter looks when it arrives will be reasonably close to the way it looked when you distributed it.

HTML E-Mail Newsletters

HTML e-mail newsletters are similar to text e-mail newsletters in that you distribute them as e-mail messages to your subscribers. But unlike text e-mails, the HTML format allows the use of different fonts, type sizes, and colors, as well as pictures and photographs. Figure 3.3 on page 49 is an example. HTML e-mail can also contain links to websites, e-mail addresses, and locations within the newsletter itself. But, as with a web newsletter, you won't have complete control over its appearance on your reader's screen.

Your audience needs minimal computer expertise to read HTML e-mail newsletters. For most readers, accessing them is as simple as checking their inboxes. However, you'll need to take care when composing these newsletters to avoid creating large, lengthy messages that will be slow to download if your readers don't have high-speed Internet connections. Another drawback to this type of newsletter is that some of your readers may be using e-mail software that is not sophisticated enough to display it correctly. Formatting an HTML e-mail newsletter is more complicated than laying out a text e-mail newsletter, but simpler than laying out a print or PDF version.

PDF Newsletters

Have you ever received an electronic document that you weren't able to open on your computer? Maybe a graphic designer you hired sent you a

Figure 3.2
Text E-Mail Newsletter
Although easy to design and lay out, text e-mail newsletters, like *Inspired2Write*, are delivered as plain text. They lack the visual appeal offered by graphics, photos, and various typefaces.

file for a brochure she created in Quark XPress; but since you didn't own Quark XPress, you couldn't open the document. And you weren't about to go out and spend hundreds of dollars on the software just to proofread one brochure! Or maybe your sister sent you her family holiday letter as a Microsoft Word file. Things were looking good this time—you did own Microsoft Word, so you were able to open the document. But the layout was a mess. Why? Because she had used her favorite font, Lucida Calligraphy, which you didn't have on your computer. So the letter was displayed in the bulky, type-written-looking Courier font instead.

Adobe Systems created the portable document format (PDF) to take care of such problems. This format allows people to read documents such as brochures, manuals, and newsletters, even if they don't own the software or the fonts that were used to create them. A PDF document looks just like its original version.

Adobe also developed software known as Acrobat, which lets you convert files from their original format— Microsoft Word, Quark XPress, Adobe PageMaker, or any other format—to PDF. Acrobat sells for about $300 (a scaled-down version is included in some other Adobe products, like PageMaker and FrameMaker). Adobe also developed a free software program called Adobe Reader, which enables people to read PDF files. To download this program, simply go to *www.adobe.com*. As so many websites use PDF files, a great many Internet users have already installed Adobe Reader onto their computers.

Figure 3.3
HTML E-Mail Newsletter
In addition to including different fonts, type sizes, and colors, an HTML e-mail newsletter can also contain links to websites, e-mail addresses, and locations within the newsletter itself.

PDF files retain all the attractive formatting and graphics that you can include in print newsletters. You can use color—in photos, graphics, or text—at no extra cost. As with web and e-mail newsletters, PDF newsletters can contain clickable links to websites and e-mail addresses, as well as links to other parts of the newsletter. For your readers, viewing a PDF file onscreen is similar to viewing a scanned newsletter. And those who find PDF newsletters difficult to read online have the option of printing them out first.

Most publishers who use PDF newsletters post them on their websites. When readers go to the sites, as long as they have Adobe Reader installed, the newsletter is displayed on their web browser, as seen in Figure 3.4 on page 50.

Laying out a PDF newsletter takes the same amount of time as laying out a print version. But if you are publishing for a mixed audience—

some who prefer an online newsletter and some who prefer print—you might want to create both versions. Once you lay out a print newsletter, converting it to PDF involves just a few easy steps. As with all online formats, the cost of distributing PDF newsletters electronically is minimal.

For your readers, PDF newsletters require a bit more computer knowledge than web page and e-mail newsletters. Some computer novices may not be comfortable downloading Adobe Reader. If you deliver the PDF file as an e-mail attachment, they will also have to know how to open it. But these are not difficult tasks, and with a small amount of training, or perhaps an explanatory page on your website, most readers will be able to handle them.

Assessing Criteria for Distribution

Now that you are familiar with the various formats for print and electronic newsletters, you can assess which method is best for your publication. To help insure you make the right choice, Table 3.1 on page 51 assesses and compares each format based on the following criteria:

Figure 3.4
PDF Newsletter
PDF newsletters can retain all of the attractive formatting options and graphics that are available in print newsletters.

■ **Ease of layout.** How long will it take to lay out the newsletter?

■ **Distribution cost.** What is the cost of distributing the newsletter to readers, whether by mail, e-mail, or website posting?

■ **Design capabilities and legibility.** How sophisticated a page design does the format allow you to create? Is the page design easy to read?

■ **Linking capabilities.** Does the format allow readers to link to websites, e-mail addresses, or to other parts of the newsletter?

■ **Ease of obtaining.** Can readers with minimal computer skills easily obtain your newsletter in the format?

Managing Change in Distribution Format

If you are considering changing your print newsletter's distribution format to an electronic one, try to poll your readers first to determine if they will accept the change. Also try to find out if they would prefer receiving text e-mails, HTML e-mails, web pages, or PDF versions. Depending on their response, you might consider publishing in more than one format

TABLE 3.1. ASSESSING AND COMPARING NEWSLETTER FORMATS

The table below assesses the criteria—the advantages and disadvantages—of each newsletter format. Ratings are based on the following key:

Poor = ■   Good = ★   Best = ★★

Criteria	Print Version	Newsletter Formats			
		Web Pages	Text E-Mail	HTML E-Mail	PDF Version
Ease of layout	■	★	★★	★	■
Distribution cost	■	★★	★★	★★	★★
Design capabilities; legibility	★★	★	■	★	★★
Linking capabilities	■	★★	★	★★	★★
Ease of obtaining	★★	★	★	★	■

to accommodate the needs of different groups. For example, if a large group of your readers needs the improved timeliness of an electronic newsletter, but another group still wants a printed publication, you can mail out a print version and also post one in an electronic format on your website. This way, readers can access the online newsletter without having to wait for its arrival by mail. They also have the option of reading the material onscreen or printing it out first. Some publishers continue to publish print versions for their main newsletter issues, but use e-mail to publish short updates between issues.

Multiple formats are also a good solution when you aren't sure of your audience's technical abilities, the hardware and software they use, or the speed of their Internet connections. Let's say, for instance, you would like to publish in HTML e-mail format instead of text e-mail to take advantage of its formatting capabilities. Some of your readers, however, may use programs that don't display HTML e-mail properly. You can accommodate those readers by also publishing a web page or text e-mail version of your newsletter.

If you decide to change your newsletter's distribution format from print to electronic, give your readers reasonable notice by announcing it in several issues of your print newsletter. And be sure to include a request that asks readers to go to your website and submit their e-mail addresses. Repeat this request in your membership renewal forms and any other print publications you distribute. You may find it easier to gain

If you are going to change the distribution method of your newsletter from print to electronic, be sure give readers ample notice. Announce the change in several issues of the print version before making the switch.

Case Study: STC Boston Takes Its Newsletter to the Internet

Five years is a long time to plan a change in newsletter format, but the results were worth it for the Boston Chapter of the Society for Technical Communication (STC). Preliminary discussions went on for several years, but once the decision was made, it took the planning committee just six months to design and publish the first online issue of the *Boston Broadside*, according to former chapter president Jonathan Baker.

Chapter leaders pressed for the change when they realized that the $30,000 annual bill for laying out, printing, and mailing a twenty-four-page, two-color newsletter to more than a thousand technical communicators every other month left the chapter little money to spend on anything else.

They took a studied approach to the change in format. First they enlisted volunteers Barbara Veneri and Ann Savitisky to survey other STC chapters to find out which formats they were using to distribute their newsletter, and to gain some insight from their experiences with similar audiences. They also surveyed their own members to get a feel for which formats would be well received. The results of their research led them to publish an HTML-format newsletter that was available on the chapter's website.

reader acceptance of the change if you phase it in, distributing in both print and electronic formats for a few interim issues.

CREATING A BUDGET

How you budget for your newsletter depends on the type of publication you are producing. If it's an association or marketing newsletter from which you do not expect to make a direct profit, budgeting will involve simply estimating your costs. You might also hope to offset your expenses with a bit of advertising income.

If you are publishing a subscription newsletter from which you *do* hope to make a profit or at least break even, budgeting will be a bit more complex. In addition to estimating costs, you'll have to set a price for subscriptions and possibly advertisements, estimate your income, and determine whether you can make a profit. In either case, the Budget Worksheet on pages 318 and 319 will help you get started. Make a photocopy of this form and fill it out as suggested in the following section. Use the completed sample on pages 56 and 57 as a guide. To help with your calculations, you might also consider setting up a computer spreadsheet that corresponds to the Budget Worksheet.

They developed a template, tested it, and posted samples on the website before rolling out for publication a few months later. When they discovered that a newer version of Adobe Acrobat allowed them to easily convert the HTML newsletter to PDF, they decided to provide the newsletter in both formats. The HTML version satisfied their onscreen readers, and the PDF version was easily printed by those who preferred hard copy. When each new issue became available, the staff sent out an e-mail announcement to members that included the newsletter's cover page and links to each article. After going online with the newsletter, the chapter eased the transition by continuing to print and mail out a four-page version for the first few issues.

The chapter is pleased with the decreased cost and improved timeliness of its newsletter. A temporary loss of $5,000 to $7,000 per year in advertising revenues (ads were suspended during the transition to simplify production) were recouped when a mechanism for including ads in the online newsletter was worked out. At that point, the net gain of going online approached $30,000 per year. In addition, where in the past, printing added a minimum of three weeks to the newsletter's production schedule, the online version is available to readers immediately after layout.

Has the transition been successful? The editors know that the newsletter is being read, since it records an average of 900 hits per month. To keep in touch with reader needs, they include a feedback form in the newsletter and solicit additional comments in periodic member surveys.

This worksheet uses a simple method for calculating income and expenses, and for determining whether you can break even or make a profit. If you would like to use a more sophisticated method to project profit and loss for a subscription newsletter business under a number of different business scenarios, I recommend consulting *Starting & Running a Successful Newsletter or Magazine* by Cheryl Woodard.

Income

The primary source of income for newsletters is revenue from subscriptions. Some newsletters, usually association or marketing types, also receive income from advertisements. Traditionally, subscription newsletters have shied away from advertising. If you plan to generate income from your newsletter, the following information on subscription pricing and advertising rates will help you determine its projected revenue and assist you in setting up a realistic budget.

Pricing Subscription Newsletters

How do you put a price on a subscription for your newsletter? You might expect to simply add your costs to your desired profit, and then divide

Subscription cost should be based primarily on three factors—the availability of information on the newsletter's subject matter, the benefits readers will derive from the publication, and the audience's means of paying for it.

that sum by the number of subscriptions you expect to sell. That's certainly part of it, but you must also consider what price the market will bear for your publication. This depends on three factors: your subject matter, the audience you are targeting, and the benefit the audience receives from your newsletter. Let's take a closer look at these factors.

■ **Subject matter.** A major determinant of the price the market will bear for your newsletter is the availability of information on your subject matter. Little information is available in the mass media on esoteric topics, such as the African telecommunications market. Yet, a certain group of people in the telecommunications industry needs that information, and realizes it would cost a lot of money to gather it. That's why they are willing to pay a publisher like Information Gatekeepers over $1,000 for a one-year subscription to *Africa Telecom*. On the other hand, information on popular consumer topics like home decorating or gardening is widely available. Readers can find it with little effort, so they won't be as willing to pay a premium for a newsletter on these topics.

■ **Audience.** Different audiences have differing means to pay for a newsletter. Newsletters aimed at businesses can charge the most. Newsletters for executives of nonprofit organizations must charge less, and those for consumers, who must pay for the publications out of their own pockets, must charge the least.

■ **Benefit.** What is the benefit readers will enjoy by reading your newsletter? An investment newsletter aimed at consumers can charge more than a gardening newsletter, because readers expect to realize a monetary return on their subscription dollars. Business readers will pay top dollar, presumably because they expect the information they get from a newsletter will help their companies reap financial rewards or save on expenses. Nonprofit executives can also foresee benefits from paying a few hundred dollars to subscribe to a newsletter that relates to their work. For example, disabled-services professionals can read *Disability Funding News,* which promises to increase their success in raising funds and receiving grants.

Once you've assessed the availability of your subject matter, the means of your audience, and the benefit you are providing, check out the competition. Compare the frequency and length of their newsletters to yours. Generally, greater frequency and more pages translate into more value to the reader. However, also keep in mind that busy professionals and business people have little time to spare and want to get the information they need in a concise format. Padding a newsletter with articles that are distantly related to your subject matter does not add to its perceived value.

Next you'll want to calculate how much total subscription income you need to cover your estimated expenses, which will be covered in a moment. Once you have that figure, calculate how many subscribers you would need at various reasonable subscription prices to cover these costs. Try to learn the circulation of similar publications to get a reasonable estimate of how many subscribers you can attract.

Many newsletter publishers test the market by distributing offers with different subscription prices, and then waiting to see which produces the best response relative to price. Other pricing strategies include offering introductory subscriptions at a low price or free, offering discounted charter subscriptions for people who subscribe during your first year of publication, and giving discounts on long-term subscriptions.

In recent years, many subscription consumer newsletters have been converted from print publications with low subscription prices to free online publications. Many publishers of these newsletters produce them more for love than money. To meet their printing and mailing expenses, they had to charge for subscriptions. But when use of the Internet became more popular, it made more sense to publish online newsletters and offer them free, forgoing subscription revenues, but still breaking even.

Many of those publishers also came to recognize one of the facts of Internet life: readers are rarely willing to pay for online content, including newsletters. Some Internet publishers have been successful producing brief, free newsletters in which they promote their fee-based newsletters that contain more extensive content. The successful online newsletters that charge for subscriptions tend to be those that are print based with online viewing as an option.

Once you have estimated your Annual Subscription Income, enter this figure in the Budget Worksheet.

Setting Advertising Rates

How do you know what to charge for a newsletter ad? This depends on two factors: the value of the target audience to the advertiser, and your production costs. To demonstrate the value of your audience to advertisers, it's important to offer them hard data about circulation and reader

Here's a fact of Internet life—most readers are resistant to paying for any online content, including newsletters. Successful online newsletters that charge for subscriptions are usually print based with online viewing as an option.

If you plan to publish a newsletter that makes a profit or breaks even, an annual budget is necessary. In the completed worksheet below, the sample newsletter is a monthly publication. It does not contain ads, and the publisher plans to spread the startup costs over a three-year period. A blank worksheet, which you can copy and fill in with the specific details of your publication, is found on pages 318 and 319.

PROJECTED INCOME
A newsletter's primary income is the revenue generated by subscriptions. Some newsletters also count on income from advertising.

Multiply per-issue ad income times number of annual issues. (This newsletter has no advertisements.)

PROJECTED EXPENSES
Newsletter expenses are divided into three categories: startup costs, per-issue costs, and fixed costs.

Startup Costs
These one-time expenses are required for the initial setup of your newsletter. They involve equipment and supplies, and the services of either staff members or outside vendors.

As the total startup cost in this example is to be spread over three years, it is divided by three to determine the annual startup amount.

BUDGET WORKSHEET		
	Itemized Amount	Total Annual Amount
PROJECTED INCOME		
Subscription revenue	$100,000	$100,000
Advertising (per issue)	0	
Advertising total for year		0
TOTAL ANNUAL INCOME		$100,000
PROJECTED EXPENSES		
STARTUP COSTS		
Equipment:		
Computer	$2,500	
Printer	200	
Scanner	200	
Fax machine	0	
Modem	100	
Office furniture	0	
Camera/photographic equipment	0	
Software	1,500	
Manuals	100	
Clip art	100	
Installation of utilities, Internet services	100	
Services:		
Planning/Design	600	
Training	200	
Marketing and promotion	30,000	
Legal and accounting	4,000	
Other		
Total Startup Cost	39,600	
Total Annual Startup Cost (39,600 ÷ 3)		$13,200

	Itemized Amount	Total Annual Amount
PER-ISSUE COSTS		
Management	0	
Writing	0	
Editing	100	
Photography	0	
Artwork	0	
Layout	400	
Printing	500	
Mail services	300	
Postage	130	
Mailing list services	0	
Other		
Total Per-Issue Cost	1,430	
Total Annual Per-Issue Cost (1,430 × 12)		$17,260
FIXED COSTS		
Rent	0	
Utilities, including Internet access	0	
Owner's salary	50,000	
Fulfillment services	2,000	
Website hosting and Internet access	1,500	
Marketing and promotion	5,000	
Insurance	200	
Legal and accounting	700	
Other		
Total Fixed Costs	59,400	
Total Annual Fixed Costs		59,400
TOTAL ANNUAL EXPENSES (includes startup, per-issue, and fixed costs)		$89,760
PROJECTED PROFIT		
Total Annual Income		$100,000
minus Total Annual Expenses		− 89,760
equals Total Annual Profit		= 10,240

Per-Issue Costs
These costs are incurred with each publication. They include editorial expenses, such as those for writing, editing, and layout, as well as publishing costs, such as printing, postage, and mailing.

Multiply per-issue cost times number of annual issues (this example has twelve) for total annual per-issue cost.

Fixed Costs
Incurred over a specific period (usually one year), fixed costs, such as rent, utilities, and insurance, do not vary with the number of issues published.

PROJECTED PROFIT
Simply subtract the Total Annual Expenses from the Total Annual Income for a quick look at your potential Annual Profit.

demographics. (Chapter 2 offers suggestions for doing audience research.) Also, do a little homework to see what similar publications charge. When considering ad rates, it's important to factor in your production and distribution costs for the ads. For example, if advertisements add four pages to an issue of your newsletter, how much will your printing and postage costs increase?

Advertisers will have a slew of questions about your production requirements, schedules, and prices. To simplify answering these queries, create a rate card like the one illustrated in Figure 3.5 on page 59. This card should answer the following questions:

■ What are the dimensions and prices of full-, half-, quarter-page, and any other size ads you accept?

■ Do you provide discounts for multiple insertions?

■ Can you guarantee an ad will be placed in a certain position in the newsletter?

■ Do you accept black-and-white, two-color, and/or four-color ads?

■ What are your deadlines for reserving space in each issue, for sending payment, and for submitting copy (the ad itself)?

■ How much commission, if any, do you pay to advertising agencies?

■ What is your circulation? What are the demographics of your readers?

■ Do you provide layout services for advertisers?

Tax Considerations for a Small Newsletter Business

Section 455 of the Internal Revenue Code allows small newsletter businesses to defer subscription income into the future years during which the subscription is fulfilled. In other words, if you collect $200 this year for a two-year subscription, you can spread that income (and consequently the amount of taxes you pay on that income) over the two years during which you are bound to send the newsletters to the subscriber. This allows you to retain some cash to pay for the newsletter's writing, printing, and mailing costs over the two-year period. Subscription-fulfillment software can help you keep track of this deferred income. Contact your accountant for more information.

ADVERTISEMENT RATE CARD FOR *WRITERS' ROUNDUP* NEWSLETTER

Ad Sizes and Cost

Ad Size	Dimensions (width x height)	1 insertion	4 insertions
Full page	$7^1/_2$ x 10 inches	$300	$900
Half page	$7^1/_2$ x 5 inches	$200	$600
Quarter page	$3^3/_4$ x 5 inches	$100	$300

Deadlines

Issue	Space Deadline	Copy Deadline	Payment Deadline
Winter	January 3	January 10	January 3
Spring	April 3	April 10	April 3
Summer	July 3	July 10	July 3
Fall	October 3	October 10	October 3

Other Information

- *Writers' Roundup* is read by 1,100 writers who typically hold bachelor's degrees or higher, are between ages 25 and 54, and live in the Lakeland region.
- All ads are black and white.
- To inquire about availability of layout services and special ad placement, call (800) 555-1114.
- No commissions paid.

Before you can tell advertisers the acceptable dimensions of the ads, you'll need to know your newsletter's design. For print newsletters, this information is provided in Chapter 8. Design guidelines for online newsletters are presented in the chapters in Part Four.

The next step in filling out your Budget Worksheet is estimating the yearly income you expect to receive from advertising. For this, simply multiply your projected ad income per issue by the number of issues you will be publishing per year. Let's use *Writers' Roundup* as our example. By expecting to sell one full-page and one half-page ad per issue at the single-insertion rates of $300 and $200, the publisher anticipates $500 in revenue per issue. Multiplying that $500 by the number of issues per year (four), means an estimated $2,000 in annual advertising revenue is expected. This figure would be entered in the Annual Advertising Income box of the Budget Worksheet.

Figure 3.5

Advertisement rate card answers the most common queries of advertisers.

Costs

Updated annually, *Writer's Market*—a guide to publications that accept freelance submissions—includes a section called "How Much Should I Charge?" As a newsletter publisher, you will find this section valuable as it provides estimations of the time required for newsletter writing, editing, and layout, as well as the hourly rates commonly charged for these tasks.

Newsletter expenses can be divided into three categories: startup costs for new equipment, supplies, and services; per-issue costs, which come with each publication; and fixed costs, which are incurred over time. Estimating these costs on an annual basis will help you establish a yearly budget.

For prices of equipment and supplies, such as computers, software programs, and office materials, you can search online or look through print catalogs of retailers or manufacturers. For costs of services, such as newsletter writing, editing, and layout, contact vendors in your area for estimates. You can also find hourly rates and estimates of the amount of time required for these services in the book *Writer's Market*, which is revised yearly. Some websites of writer's organizations also contain this information. You can also quickly find rates for electronic mailing list services through online searches of these companies.

At this point, you may be unsure of the items to consider in your budget. For example, do you need to buy a page-layout software program or can you produce your newsletter using the word processing program you already own? In later chapters, I'll provide more specific information that will answer this question and others like it. At this point, I'll briefly mention some of the more commonly needed items you might consider.

Startup Costs

Chances are, you may already own some of the equipment and supplies you'll need to publish your newsletter. But you'll want to budget for the items you don't own, as well as services you'll need. Consider the following equipment and services, which you may (or may not) want to include in your startup budget.

■ **Equipment.** If you are going to use professional page-layout software, you'll need a relatively powerful computer. You'll also want a printer for checking proofs. If you can deliver newsletter files to your print shop electronically, you won't need an expensive printer; but if you must deliver camera-ready copy, a good-quality printer is important.

Startup costs for launching a newsletter fall under two main categories—equipment and services.

You may also need a scanner to convert hard-copy photographs into digital form, and a fax machine if you plan to send proofs to offsite reviewers who don't have Internet access. Since electronic newsletter files can be quite large, a high-speed modem and a high-speed Internet connection are useful for transmitting your newsletter to the print shop.

You may also need to purchase office furniture and basic office supplies, a camera and other photographic equipment, and perhaps a telephone system.

For print and PDF newsletters, you'll need either word processing or (preferably) page-layout software. For PDF newsletters, you will also need software that lets you convert a word processing or page-layout file to PDF format.

For HTML e-mail and web page newsletters, web-authoring software is a must. For text e-mail newsletters, you can use a simple text editor program, which comes with most computers or can be downloaded inexpensively from the Internet. Regardless of your distribution format, you will need an e-mail program and a web browser. These, too, usually come bundled with a new computer.

Depending on the complexity of the graphics you intend to use, you may need to purchase an illustration program or a graphics editor. You

A Warning to Nonprofit Organizations About Unrelated Business Income Tax

The IRS allows tax-exempt nonprofit organizations to earn income on activities that are related to their missions, without being liable for taxes on that income. For example, a nonprofit theater company is not required to pay taxes on the money it earns selling tickets to its plays. But the IRS does require nonprofits to pay taxes on income earned from trades or businesses that are *unrelated* to their missions if the income, minus certain deductions, exceeds $1,000 per year. So if the theater company earned money by operating a restaurant year-round in its building, the IRS would see that income as unrelated and taxable.

The IRS considers income that is earned from publishing advertisements in the newsletter of a nonprofit—even if the newsletter's content pertains to the mission of the nonprofit—as unrelated,

taxable income. So if your organization's total unrelated income, including revenue from advertising, exceeds $1,000 per year, it is subject to the Unrelated Business Income Tax (UBIT).

The IRS does not treat the publishing of certain advertisements—those that are considered to be "acknowledgements"—as an unrelated business and does not include those revenues in the organization's unrelated-business income. When deciding which ads qualify as acknowledgements, the IRS looks at the amount of commercial benefit the sponsor could reasonably assume to derive from placing such ads. For more information on the UBIT, contact your attorney or accountant, or refer to IRS Publication 598, *Tax on Unrelated Business Income of Exempt Organizations*, available at *www.irs.gov/pub/irs-pdf/p598.pdf*.

Many computers come bundled with various software programs. Make sure you know which programs your computer has before purchasing them separately.

may also need to buy scanning software, although a program is often included with the purchase of a scanner.

To maintain a mailing list of subscribers, a database software program may prove to be helpful. If you are running a newsletter business, you might consider purchasing a subscription-fulfillment software program that will also maintain your mailing list. An accounting software package is another useful startup investment.

For all types of software, you might want to budget for buying manuals, which are not always bundled with software. Other supplies that you may need to purchase include clip art and stock photographs. And don't forget about estimating the cost of installing utilities, Internet connections, and other wiring in your office.

■ **Services.** Service costs include the startup work done either by your own staff or by outside vendors. For work done by your own staff, estimate the number of hours they will spend on a task, and multiply that number by their hourly pay rates (including the cost of benefits). For vendors, enter the fee they quote you for the service. Startup services typically include the following:

- *Planning.* Includes time spent developing the newsletter's purpose, tone, and editorial posture, as well as researching its audience; budgeting; scheduling: deciding how frequently to publish, planning the content for the first year, and creating a schedule for staff to follow in producing each issue; and recruiting staff: screening candidates for in-house positions created for newsletter publication and interviewing vendors.

- *Designing.* Involves creating a desktop publishing template into which the layout artist will place text and graphics for each issue.

- *Training.* Cost for sending staff to classes on newsletter planning, writing, editing, design, layout, and software use.

- *Marketing and promotion.* The money spent soliciting subscribers through direct mail or space advertising. This will be a fixed cost as well as a startup cost, and will entail a significant initial investment.

- *Legal and accounting expenses.* Fees for obtaining trademarks, incorporating a newsletter business, and setting up financial books.

Allow a substantial portion of your startup budget for marketing and promoting your publication to gain subscribers. Money spent in this area is considered a fixed cost as well.

If yours is a nonprofit newsletter, you can reduce your costs by recruiting volunteers and soliciting donations. Keep in mind that it is often easier to get donations or volunteers to defray your startup costs than it is to get them to reduce your per-issue and fixed costs. In other words, you are more likely to find a volunteer who is willing to spend a day training your staff or setting up your computers than it may be to find one who will commit to laying out your newsletter every month. Likewise, a photo shop might be more willing to donate some camera equipment than it would be to edit the digital photos that are used in each issue.

Once you have totaled your startup costs, you'll also need to calculate what you will be spending on them each year. Keep in mind that although these costs don't recur every year, their useful lifetime is limited—computer hardware and software become obsolete and need to be replaced or upgraded, staff needs periodic retraining, and you may eventually want to redesign your newsletter. So during each year that you publish your newsletter, you should account for a portion of these startup expenses. First, decide over how many years to spread them. Then, as shown in the Budget Worksheet, divide your startup expenses by the number of years. This will give you your Startup-Costs-Per-Year figure.

Although startup costs do not recur every year, the equipment purchased during the initial stage will require periodic repairing, replacing, or upgrading. New programs may require staff retraining. Be sure to allow a certain portion of your yearly budget for these expenses.

Per-Issue Costs

Per-issue costs are those incurred with each issue you publish. They include the cost of services (again, either the number of hours your own staff spends on a task, multiplied by their hourly pay rates, or fees you pay outside vendors to do your work) and any supplies needed for each issue. When you get estimates from outside vendors, be sure to ask whether all supplies are included in the quote.

Editorial costs like writing, editing, and layout will remain constant regardless of the number of subscribers you have. Publishing costs—printing, postage, and mailing-list services—will vary with the number of subscribers. Calculate them using your estimate of the average number of subscribers. Consider costs of the following common per-issue necessities to come up with an estimate for your budget:

■ **Management.** Estimate the time of a managing editor for scheduling, initiating, and overseeing each issue. Depending on the length of the newsletter, the number of staff being supervised, and the number of meetings required, this estimate can be anywhere from three to sixteen hours per issue.

■ **Writing.** Freelance writers are usually paid by the word, and rates vary widely, depending on whether the topic is general or specialized. For current rates, check the latest edition of *Writer's Market*, available at

The quality of your writers will determine the amount of editing your newsletter needs. Amateur writers may cost less than professionals, but your editors will have to spend more time going over and polishing their work.

libraries and bookstores. Once you have decided on your newsletter's length and design, you'll be able to calculate the approximate number of words it will take to fill it (detailed in Chapter 4). After researching the per-word rate for writing in your subject area, multiply that rate by the total number of words it will take to fill up the space.

■ **Editing.** This includes the three types of editing: content editing, copyediting, and proofreading (discussed in detail in Chapter 6). Rates are based on the level of skill required, with content editing costing the most, copyediting somewhat less, and proofreading the least. Again, *Writer's Market* is helpful in determining how much to pay. The amount of editing your newsletter needs will directly correlate with the quality of your writers. If you rely on amateur writers, your editor will have to spend more time polishing their work. Expect a copyeditor to spend one or two hours on a four-page newsletter; a proofreader, under an hour.

■ **Photography.** This includes expenses for film and developing, which you can avoid by using a digital camera. If you use a professional photographer, you will pay for the shoot. If you plan to re-use the photos in future newsletter editions, obtaining this permission may cost an additional fee.

■ **Artwork.** Often, you can save money on artwork by using clip art or free graphics like boxes, rules, and display type. If, however, you need custom diagrams or other artwork, you will have to get estimates from graphic artists.

■ **Layout.** Layout artists often charge by the hour. Expect them to spend about an hour per page, depending on the number of times you ask for changes. Instead of an hourly rate, see if you can get a price quote for a set rate, based on the number of pages in an issue. This will help you more accurately predict your per-issue costs. Generally, you'll pay more to brick-and-mortar firms for this service than to freelancers who work out of their homes. *Writer's Market* lists both hourly and per-page rates for newsletter layout.

■ **Printing.** If you photocopy your newsletter in-house, include paper and toner under printing supplies, and staff time under services. If you will be using a print shop, be sure to get at least three quotes, as rates can vary greatly for the same job.

■ **Mail services.** If you prepare your newsletter for mailing yourself, include supplies like mailing labels, wafer seals, and envelopes, as well as staff time for preparing the mailing. For print newsletters, you can hire a mailing house, which will prepare your mailing in accordance with Standard Mail (bulk) regulations.

■ **Postage.** Check out current postal rates for your newsletter's size and weight with your local post office. Look into reducing postage costs by using Standard Mail or nonprofit rates, if applicable. (Chapter 9 offers more information on special mailing rates.)

■ **Mailing list service.** You can enlist this type of service to distribute your e-mail newsletter, or to send an e-mail notification of a new issue of your web newsletter. It can also take care of subscribing and unsubscribing readers.

Enter these figures in the Per-Issue Costs section of the Budget Worksheet, and total them. Multiply this total by the number of issues you publish per year to obtain the Annual Per-Issue Costs figure.

Fixed Costs

Fixed costs are those incurred over a specified calendar period—usually one year—and they do not vary with the number of issues you publish. Examples of fixed costs include rent, utilities, and insurance.

If you are publishing an employee newsletter for your company or one that markets its products, and the company does not charge these costs to your department, don't enter them in the budget worksheet. This might also be true for a nonprofit agency or a corporation whose newsletter is just one of the activities of its communications department. However, if these costs *are* charged to your department, enter them in the Fixed Costs section of the Budget Worksheet.

If you don't have an office, or if you are budgeting for a volunteer newsletter, you won't need to enter estimates for rent and utilities. But do enter annual figures for any of the following fixed costs that you expect to incur:

■ Salary of the owner of a newsletter business.

■ Subscription fulfillment services.

■ Website hosting and Internet access fees.

■ Insurance.

■ Professional fees, such as those paid to an accountant for preparing tax returns.

Expenses that do not vary with the number of issues you publish fall under the category of fixed costs. Rent, insurance, and utilities are typical examples.

Once you have totaled your fixed costs, enter the figure in both the Total Fixed Cost box and the Annual Fixed Cost box on the worksheet (they are one and the same).

Profit and Loss

Now you can calculate your total annual expenses by totaling up the Annual Startup Costs, the Annual Per-Issue Costs, and the Annual Fixed Costs on your worksheet. If you are publishing a subscription newsletter for profit, you can then get a quick look at your potential profitability. At the bottom of the Budget Worksheet, subtract your Total Annual Expenses from your Total Income to arrive at a figure for your projected pretax profit or loss.

ASSIGNING RESPONSIBILITIES

Although one member of your staff might be capable of handling a variety of publishing tasks—writing, editing, creating graphics—it is not recommended. This practice is likely to result in errors, omissions, and a one-dimensional publication.

How many employees or volunteers do you need to pull together a newsletter? Typically, you'll need one or more writers, editors, graphic artists, and managers. Although you can often have one staff member handle several of these publishing tasks, don't ask one person to do it all. Why? Because it will undoubtedly result in errors, omissions, and a newsletter that is one-dimensional. Even professional writers should have another person edit and proofread their work. And multiple staff members, in addition to providing more sets of eyes to correct errors, provide diverse perspectives on editorial content.

Producing a newsletter (unless it's a weekly or daily) is not a full-time job, but it does require enough work so that a paid staff will need to free up time from other responsibilities to complete it.

Newsletter Roles

Depending on the size of your newsletter, the number of people responsible for its production will vary. However, there are a number of key jobs that are common to most publications.

Heading up your newsletter staff is the *managing editor*. This person has first and final responsibility for every step of the publishing process. She sets schedules, develops budgets, and recruits staff. She also gets the wheels rolling when it comes time to begin work on each issue and oversees each stage of production to make sure the work is getting done.

Many organizations also create an *editorial board* to oversee the publication. Generally, this board includes the managing editor and perhaps two or three others who have a broad understanding of the newsletter's purpose and audience. It is responsible for planning the articles and themes for the upcoming year's issues. Brainstorming for creative ideas is always more productive when more than one person participates. The editorial board also reviews the newsletter before it is distributed. Keep the board small—four people including the managing editor is plenty.

Additional newsletter roles include a writer(s), content editor, copyeditor, and proofreader. The *content editor* should be someone who is familiar with the purpose and audience of the newsletter as well as its topic. The *copyeditor* needs to be versed in the rules of the English language as well as the newsletter's usage style (more on this in Chapter 6). The *proofreader*, in addition to having a sharp eye for typographical errors, must have stellar spelling, punctuation, and grammatical skills. Often, one person can fill all of these roles.

On the visual side of production, you'll need a graphic artist, a layout artist, and possibly a photographer. A *graphic artist* (also called a *graphic designer*) is responsible for setting up your newsletter's design template; this person must have the ability to create a visually pleasing page. A *layout artist* takes the text of the articles for each issue and places it into the template that has been created by the graphic artist. While the layout artist and graphic artist are often the same person, a graphic artist needs a higher skill level than a layout artist. Once the design is created, the layout artist simply follows the graphic artist's specifications, although she will have to make decisions, adjustments, and changes depending on the requirements of each issue. She must be skilled in operating page-layout software.

If you accept advertising in your newsletter, an *ad coordinator* or *sales representative* has the job of soliciting ads, answering advertising inquiries, and receiving ad copy and payment.

Whether you assign these newsletter roles to in-house staff members or you use outside vendors, be sure to clearly spell out—preferably in writing—who is responsible for doing what and when. If you write out the job descriptions for each role, be sure to include the following information:

■ **Who gives assignments?** Who is responsible for giving article assignments to the writer for each issue? Who will send each staff member the newsletter copy—either to edit, lay out, print, or distribute electronically?

It doesn't matter if your staff is large or small, or whether the work is done in-house or by outside vendors—job descriptions and assignments should always be clear and specific. Be sure to spell out (preferably in writing) who is responsible for what and when.

20 Ways to Stretch Your Newsletter Budget

Want to get extra mileage from your newsletter's budgetary dollars? Some of the following suggestions apply to print newsletters, some are for electronic publications, and many can be used for both.

Content

1. Look for aspiring writers (journalism students, at-home parents trying to launch a freelance career) who are willing to work for free to add published clips with their bylines to their portfolios.

2. Ask published authors for free articles. In return, list their bios with information on how to buy their books, as well as their website addresses or other contact information. If your newsletter is electronic, you can provide links to their websites.

3. For association newsletters, try to reach an agreement with the editor of the newsletter of another chapter or of a related organization to occasionally reprint each other's articles.

Design

4. Use one of the newsletter templates that comes with page-layout software instead of paying a graphic artist to design one.

5. Avoid designs that include bleeds (ink that is printed all the way to the edge of the paper). They require the printer to use oversized paper and then trim it to size, which adds to your costs.

6. Use a preprinted shell for your front and back pages to get low-cost two-color printing.

Layout

7. For nonprofits, find a volunteer who uses desktop publishing or web-authoring software at work, and is willing to donate a few hours of training in its use.

8. Trade a sponsorship notice in your newsletter for free layout services.

9. Check for typos, errors, and omissions *before* sending files to layout. Layout artists charge more for excessive proof corrections.

Paper

10. Instead of using expensive color ink, add visual appeal to your newsletter by printing it on colored paper.

11. Check with the postal service to see whether printing on a lighter-weight paper would reduce your postage costs.

12. Use standard paper sizes. Odd sizes require printers to trim edges, waste paper, and, in turn, charge you extra.

Printing

13. Negotiate lower prices with a print shop in exchange for a long-term contract.

14. Plan ahead for the number of copies you'll need. If you use offset printing, you'll incur big overhead charges for additional print runs.

Mailing and Distribution

15. If you're mailing over 200 pieces, look into using the reduced Standard Mail postal rate.

16. Apply mailing labels to envelopes *before* adding postage, so you don't add postage to more pieces than you need to mail. Such costly mistakes add up.

17. Use the US Postal Service's address correction and return services to update your mailing list. This will help prevent future mailings to incorrect or nonexistent addresses.

18. Use a free online mailing-list service for web or e-mail newsletters. (For more information, see Chapter 11.)

19. If you publish a marketing newsletter that you distribute for free, periodically (every year or so) insert a form in one of the issues for readers to fill out and return to you if they want to continue receiving it. This way, you won't waste money mailing the newsletter to people who don't read it.

Miscellaneous

20. If you are registered as a nonprofit, you are not required to pay sales tax on your purchases. Be sure to obtain a card for this from the state, and then present it to retailers when making purchases.

■ **What approvals are needed?** Who must review or edit articles before they are passed on to the layout artist? Who needs to approve the layout before it is submitted to the printer, posted on the website, or distributed via e-mail?

■ **Where and how is completed work sent?** To whom should the copy editor deliver edited articles? To whom should the layout artist send the completed page-layout file? Where should the printer deliver the printed newsletters? What medium should be used to deliver these items— e-mail, postal service, CD, or flash drive? And in what file format—text file, PDF file, word processor file, or something else?

■ **What reminders are needed?** Does the layout artist need to call the print shop to give an estimated delivery date for the current issue? Does the mail house need to be informed of any production delays? Should the managing editor phone volunteers to invite them to an envelope-stuffing party?

■ **Who communicates with outside vendors?** Consider assigning one person to be the liaison to your freelancers, print shop, mail house, and so forth. This will prevent the vendor from receiving conflicting instructions from multiple staff members.

As you define responsibilities, don't forget to spell out who has final say on spending. Unanticipated expenses can always arise, even if you've developed a yearly budget. The need to report on an unexpected situation—a natural disaster, for instance—might require you to print a larger newsletter than originally budgeted for. The postal service might

Be sure to make your staff aware of who has the final say on schedule changes, and whose approval is required for any additional expenses.

raise its rates in the middle of the year. If so, you'll need to know who can approve exceeding your budget to cover the increase.

You'll also need to identify the person who has final say on schedule changes. Regardless of the amount of planning you do, a time will come when someone wants to stop the presses to include a late-breaking story, or your layout artist schedules a last-minute vacation and wants to delay publication for a week. Who decides whether your deadlines can slip?

Reviewers

When your newsletter is completed, it should be given a final review before publication. To preserve printing and distribution deadlines, limit the number of reviewers. Two sets of eyes—one for focusing on content accuracy, and another for catching typos and grammatical problems—should be enough. And let the reviewers know in advance when to expect the job, and when they must have it completed.

You'll find that everyone wants a finger in the pie when it comes to reviewing the newsletter before publication. It's essential to have *some* reviewers, but not too many.

Often the managing editor doesn't have the expertise to review all of the publication's content for appropriateness and accuracy. So it's prudent to have the editorial board read articles and review photos and artwork. Include the leader—be it a marketing executive, the principal, or the pastor—who understands the legal and political ramifications of printing each story. For example, an editor of a school newsletter might want to write an article reporting why a teacher has been dismissed. If the principal is on the editorial board, he will decide which portion of the information about the dismissal can be published and which portion constitutes private personnel matters that cannot be released to the public.

Usually there is a window of just a few days (sometimes just a few hours!) on the production schedule during which reviewers are supposed to do their job. But for many reviewers, especially those in high positions, reading newsletter copy is at the bottom of their to-do list. How can you prevent delinquent reviewers from causing you to miss deadlines? There are a number of ways.

First, warn them well ahead of time of when you expect to need their help. (The next section on creating a production schedule will help you do so.) Second, when they agree to be reviewers, make them aware that although this job shouldn't take a lot of their time, you will need it done promptly. Third, if there are multiple content reviewers, get them to agree to simultaneous reviews. In other words, Janet should not insist that Charlie read the copy before she takes a look at it—you will never meet your deadlines that way. Finally, limit the number of reviewers. You can probably get away with two people: someone to review content for accuracy and appropriateness, and a copyeditor/proofreader for catching typos and grammatical mistakes.

Recruiting Staff

So how do you go about finding writers, editors, layout artists, and photographers to be a part of your newsletter staff? Perhaps one of the easiest (and often overlooked) ways to find qualified individuals for *any* newsletter position is to simply ask around. Print shops do business with writers, editors, graphic artists, and photographers all the time. They can steer you to skilled, reliable people. Desktop publishing services and advertising agencies can offer you their own services or point you to qualified individuals. Graphic artists know editors and editors know writers. To find photographers, look at the credits on photos you like in local newspapers and magazines, and then contact the photographers to find out if they do freelance work. When you identify a person you think may be qualified, ask to see examples of their work, both to get an idea of its caliber and to determine if they have experience in the type of newsletter you are producing.

You can also look to your own employees or colleagues for help. Have any shown interest or skill in writing or layout? Is there a serious amateur photographer among them? You can bill their new assignments as a way to expand their portfolios. Some of these people may have latent skills you can develop. For example, your office manager, whose typing and English skills are flawless, could become a crackerjack editor after attending a proofreading and copyediting workshop. Or that sales rep with a studio art degree may have the artistic sense needed to do your layout once she is trained to use page-layout software.

Keep in mind that writers and editors sometimes consult periodical and newsletter directories to find places to sell their work. Getting your newsletter listed in a directory is usually free and may generate job inquiries from qualified people. Most directories list publications by topic. This helps writers and editors align themselves with publications that cover subject matter for which they are best qualified. The Resources section, beginning on page 323, lists these newsletter and periodical directories, for both print and online publications.

Serious writers, editors, and layout artists usually belong to at least one professional organization to keep apprised of developments in their fields, to network with colleagues, and to find work. Most groups, like the Editorial Freelancers Association (*www.the-efa.org*), maintain websites

When searching for qualified writers, editors, layout artists, or photographers in your area, try contacting professional organizations, such as the American Society of Journalists and Authors and the National Press Photographers Association, for possible leads.

Volunteers are precious commodities. They offer their time, often while balancing paid jobs and personal obligations. Be sure to acknowledge their efforts in your publication.

that include job banks. You can post both permanent jobs and freelance assignments on these sites for members to search. A number of these organizations post member resumes you can search through, but if poring through resumes is too time consuming, you might consider using a writer referral service like that offered by the American Society of Journalists and Authors (*www.asja.org*). For a fee, they will take your job posting, screen candidates, and refer qualified members to you.

Because they can send and receive work via the Internet, writers, editors, and layout artists don't necessarily have to be located in your area. But if they are to cover local events and people, photographers do need to be nearby. Professional organizations can point you to photographers in your area. Try the National Press Photographers Association at *www.nppa.org* or the American Society of Media Photographers at *www.asmp.org*.

Journalism schools are another avenue for connecting you to writers and editors. If you're operating on a limited budget, consider hiring students or recent graduates. Writers Write at *www.writerswrite.com/journalism/jschool.htm* contains links to dozens of schools of journalism, both in the United States and abroad.

If you are a nonprofit organization, you will probably try to recruit volunteers to fill at least some staff roles. Keep in mind that it can be difficult to enforce strict deadlines with volunteers who are balancing your newsletter with paid work and family obligations. You have to consider the amount of quality and promptness you can sacrifice in exchange for their free services. It may also require an extra helping of tact to explain to a volunteer writer why you had to cut her 1,400-word article down to 500 words.

Also, ask your volunteers if they can commit to meeting your deadlines month after month. You might have more luck asking volunteers to share duties—for example, two layout artists could alternate working on issues. And be sure to give credit for the work of volunteers and for donated items in your masthead or bylines.

CREATING SCHEDULES

When you hear the word "scheduling" in the context of newsletter publishing, you may think first of planning dates for writing, editing, printing, and distribution. But long before anyone writes a word, you'll need to schedule what to report on and when to report on it. With the help of your editorial board, you will have to schedule your newsletter's frequency (how often to publish); decide on its length (how many pages to publish in each issue); create an editorial calendar (plan the type and topic of articles to run in the coming year); and develop a production schedule (set deadlines for writing, editing, layout, printing, and distribution for each issue).

Scheduling When and How Often to Publish

How do you decide whether to publish your newsletter quarterly, bimonthly, monthly, or weekly? The amount of available staff, as well as your budget for writing, layout, printing, and distribution, play a large part in answering that question. But what you have to say and why you are saying it are just as important.

The newsletter, by virtue of its name, contains news. Because readers expect the information to be timely, newsletters are usually published at least four times a year. If the interval between issues is any longer than three months, the "news," which may be as old as six months, becomes stale. Newsletters with contents like stock prices, interest rates, or sports scores need to be published most frequently.

Do some research up front to find out when the information you want to provide in your issues becomes available. Let's say your parent's group wants to run a calendar that includes community events for children. Find out from the library, children's theater, and local bookstore how far in advance they plan their events. If you publish quarterly, will they be able to give you details on what's happening two or three months from your publication date? You may discover that in a quarterly newsletter, you can include only events for the first two of the three months between issues. Some newsletters that are published infrequently solve this problem by also publishing shorter interim issues. For example, *News & Views*, the newsletter of the Philadelphia Metro Chapter of the Society for Technical Communication, publishes up to twenty pages, six times a year. But it also publishes *News & Views Light*, a four-page update that is distributed between regular issues. The *Light* edition contains reports of recent chapter meetings, details of upcoming meetings, and response forms for attending them.

A trend for e-mail newsletters is to allow subscribers to choose how frequently they want to receive issues. For example, a reader might be able to select whether to receive daily issues or weekly digests.

In addition to how often to publish, you'll need to decide when to publish. If your publication is for a professional audience, keep its

Many frequently published e-mail newsletters let subscribers choose how often they want to receive issues. A subscriber may, for instance, have the option of receiving a daily newsletter only once a week.

yearly business cycles in mind. Consider whether your readers are more likely to read an issue that arrives during their busy season, or during their downtime. If you publish a political newsletter, take the schedule of Congress or state legislatures into consideration. For consumer newsletters that cover seasonal topics, like skiing or gardening, publish frequently as that time of year approaches and less often as the season winds down.

If you publish bimonthly, avoid mailing in August and December. In August, readers won't always receive mail promptly because of vacations. In December, not only do readers have hectic schedules revolving around holiday activities, increased mail volume may cause delivery of your newsletter to be delayed.

Setting Your Newsletter's Length

Although there are no specific rules regarding newsletter length, generally, the more often you publish, the shorter the issues.

Now that you've figured out when and how often to publish, you have to decide how many pages to publish for print newsletters, or words (or screens) for electronic issues.

There are no hard and fast rules saying that every issue of a newsletter should be the same length, but budgeting your time and expenses is easier if you have an idea of how long the issue will be. Generally, the more frequently you publish, the shorter the issues.

Robert Abbot, author of *A Manager's Guide to Newsletters*, believes the frequency and length of your newsletter should also depend on the "ability and willingness" of readers to respond to your messages. He uses a marketing newsletter published by an automobile dealer as an example. When the newsletter's message is "come in for an oil change," readers are quite able and willing to respond, because they know their cars need regular oil changes and because the work is inexpensive. But when the newsletter's message is "come in to buy a new car," readers are less able and willing to respond, because their old cars may be running just fine and they can't afford new cars very often.

Abbot advises publishing short, infrequent newsletters for communicating messages to which readers are very able and willing to respond. It won't take a lot of words to persuade the readers (those in need of an oil change, in this example) to act. But to communicate messages like "buy a new car," to which readers are not readily able and willing to respond, he advises publishing longer, more frequent newsletters, as these readers need lots of convincing.

How does Abbot's advice translate to the nonprofit world? If you're

Independent Contractors

It is common for newsletters to hire outside people to do writing, editing, and layout. But how do you know if these workers should be treated as employees or as independent contractors? The answer to this question is significant, because if they are employees, you must pay payroll taxes and premiums for federal unemployment, state unemployment, and workers' compensation insurance. If you are audited and are found to have wrongly classified a worker, you could be required to pay all back taxes owed, as well as interest and penalties.

The IRS uses a "common law test" to determine whether a worker is an employee or an independent contractor. The agency looks at the facts of each case in three main categories: behavioral control, financial control, and the type of relationship itself. No single test, but rather the overall picture, determines the IRS's ruling on each case.

When assessing *behavioral control,* the IRS looks at whether you have the right to direct and control the worker concerning how, when, or where to do the work; what tools to use; and where to purchase supplies. Having such control indicates that the worker is an employee. If you train the worker about required procedures, the worker may be considered an employee as well.

To determine *financial control,* the IRS looks at whether the worker has a significant investment in her business—has she, for instance, purchased her own computer hardware and software? If so, she is likely to be considered an independent contractor. The IRS also considers if you reimburse her for business expenses, such as those incurred for travel and phone calls. And it considers whether the worker has an opportunity to realize a profit or incur a loss.

The third part of the IRS test is concerned with the *relationship* between you and the worker. If you pay her benefits, she is probably an employee. (But if you don't pay benefits, the worker could be either an employee or an independent contractor.) As part of the "relationship" test, the IRS looks at whether you and the worker have a written contract that spells out your relationship. You should consider having an independent contractor enter such an agreement with you from the start of your relationship. Ask the contractor how her business is legally structured, whether it has any employees, whether it does work for multiple clients, how its services are marketed, and so forth. This will help you determine whether the worker would qualify as an independent contractor.

Not only the IRS but also the Department of Labor and your state's unemployment compensation board, workers' compensation insurance agency, and tax department have their own definitions and rules regarding independent contractors. Each of these agencies can audit you to determine if you are wrongly treating employees as independent contractors.

As an employer, it is important to familiarize yourself with the requirements of all these agencies by contacting the IRS (*www.irs.gov*), and the US Department of Labor (*www.dol.gov*) as well as your state's unemployment compensation board, department of labor, tax department, and workers' compensation insurance agency. Your local office of the Small Business Administration (*www.sba.gov*) may be able to help you as well.

Most readers don't like having to scroll down a computer screen to finish reading an article. It is one of the major reasons (along with the less-than-optimal resolution of computer displays) that web and e-mail newsletters are typically shorter than print versions.

asking readers for small donations or one-shot volunteer help, keep your appeals brief. If you're asking for large contributions for a building fund, you'll need to work harder to convince readers of your organization's credibility, financial stability, and ability to complete the project.

Abbot's suggestions make a lot of sense for marketing newsletters, published by for-profit or nonprofit organizations, whose purpose is to *motivate* readers to buy, donate, or volunteer. However, to *inform* readers, a major purpose of consumer and professional newsletters, longer articles and more pages may be needed.

Length also depends on distribution format. Printed newsletters usually run anywhere from two to sixteen pages. Publications longer than sixteen pages start crossing the line between newsletters and magazines (or newspapers). PDF newsletters can also run from two to sixteen pages, because most readers print them out rather than read them on the computer screen. But e-mail and web newsletters, because they are usually read on-screen, should run shorter. The more your readers must scroll down the screen to finish an article, the less likely they will be to read it. Poor resolution of computer displays also reduces the willingness of readers to read lengthy e-mail and web newsletters.

Another consideration in planning length is whether or not your readers are paying for your newsletter. If your subscription newsletter was marketed as an eight-page monthly publication, readers may become disgruntled if you slack off and produce just four pages.

Creating an Editorial Calendar

Have you ever picked up a December issue of a home decorating magazine and found elegant photos of, say, a colonial home outside Boston, bedecked with evergreen garland and wreaths, set off against a carpet of new-fallen snow? Considering that the magazine hit the newsstand around Thanksgiving, and the publisher needed several weeks lead time to get the photos developed and the magazine printed, did you ever stop to wonder how they found that snow-covered yard? The timing would put the photo shoot in October, long before it snows—even in Boston.

The trick? No, not snowmaking equipment, just good long-term editorial planning. The pictures were taken a year earlier, when the editors already knew—because of their efficient planning—that the piece would be running in December.

The editor of any periodical, including newsletters, needs to plan its content well ahead of the publication date. Such planning allows time to recruit writers, illustrators, and photographers; get permission to reproduce copyrighted material; and do any necessary research.

In addition, editorial planning helps you remember recurring events that are easy to overlook amid the chaos of meeting the deadline for a current issue. Let's say your newsletter is published every other month: the January/February issue is mailed January 3, the March/April issue is mailed March 3, and so forth. Your group holds executive board elections in May, and your bylaws state that members must receive written notice of the nominees in April. Will you remember in January or February (which is when you'll be planning and writing the March/April issue) that you have to publish the list of nominees for a May election? If you map out an editorial calendar for the year, you will!

Here's a handy technique for doing yearly planning with your editorial board: Tape large sheets of paper to the wall, labeling one for each issue of the year. Brainstorm articles, columns, calendar items, and notices that you want to publish over the course of the year, jotting each one down on yellow post-it notes. Include meetings, conventions, trade shows, and fundraisers, as well as reminders to readers of deadlines and other dates in your budget or business cycle. Also list any holiday or seasonal items that you'll need to publish.

Place the yellow notes on the large sheet of paper corresponding to the appropriate issue. This technique makes it easy to see the year's calendar at a glance and to move the yellow notes around based on the group's consensus. Record the results of your planning in an editorial calendar. Set up the calendar as a grid, like the one illustrated in Figure 3.6 on page 78. Include a column for each of the year's issues and a row for each type of article. Alternatively, you can record the calendar on a large whiteboard prominently displayed in your offices for staff to refer to later.

Once you create your production schedule, which is explained in the next section, you may have to move some of the yellow notes to a different issue because of lag times for printing and distribution. For example, if yours is a monthly publication and the issues are mailed out during the second week of the month, will your readers get adequate notice of the Memorial Day picnic if it is announced in the May issue? You may have to publish that notice in the April issue as well.

Developing a Production Schedule

The publishing industry is notorious for its deadlines. Why? Probably the most important reason is that publications lose their value if they

Planning the content of your newsletter for the coming year will give you ample time to recruit any of the contributors—writers, illustrators, photographers—you need for each issue.

	Winter Issue	Spring Issue	Summer Issue	Fall Issue
EDITORIAL CALENDAR FOR *WRITERS' ROUNDUP* NEWSLETTER				
Feature Article	-Membership drive	-Announce conference	-Partnership with Eastern Region	-Conference report
Website Reviews	-Dictionary sites	-Style and usage sites	-Editing sites	-Training course sites
Book Reviews	-New dictionaries	-New edition of *American Style Guide*	*-Editing for the Novice*	*-Getting the Most Out of Training Courses*
Member News	-Announce new senior members	-Profile of new president	-Profile of new vice president	-Report on membership stats for year
Software Tip	-Creating pictures in Word	-Converting FrameMaker files to PDF	-Organizing favorites in web browsers	-Defragmenting a hard drive
Miscellaneous	-Announce new board members	-Solicit scholarship applications	-Announce scholarship winners -Solicit new board members	-Announce slate of nominees for board
Calendar	-Monthly meetings -Dues deadline	-Monthly meetings -Scholarship deadlines -Conference registration	-Monthly meetings	-Monthly meetings -Christmas party -Deadline for mailing board-election ballots
Photos	-Christmas party	-New president	-Scholarship winners -New vice president	-Local session at national conference

Figure 3.6

An editorial calendar helps map out the content of your newsletter for the upcoming year.

aren't distributed on time. Think about it. If your September newsletter goes out two weeks late, all the events you have announced in that issue that were to occur during the first two weeks of the month will be over before your readers hear about them. Your readers won't get the news they subscribe for, and you won't get the participation of those you publish for. Likewise, the readers of a business newsletter will expect you to provide *timely* information that they can use to get a step up on the competition.

Another reason deadlines are so important is that readers expect your newsletter to arrive after a fixed interval of time, and they'll start to worry and complain if it doesn't. Finally, if you accept ads, your advertisers will expect you to deliver a dependable publication; if you don't, they may take their business elsewhere.

Setting Deadlines

It's a fact of life: most people need deadlines to get tasks done. As newsletter editor, you will need to set deadlines for writing, editing, layout, printing, and distribution. How do you do it? By drawing a red circle around random dates on a calendar? Not exactly.

Begin by talking to the people who are responsible for each production task. Not only should you find out how many hours or days they estimate it will take to do their job, but also how much *elapsed* time is involved. For example, your printer may know she'll need three hours to prepare and then run the press for your newsletter, but this doesn't necessarily mean she'll have your job ready three hours after you deliver it. The press may be set up for another job when you deliver yours, or there may be a number of jobs already scheduled at the printer's ahead of yours. This means your newsletter will have to wait its turn. For this reason, you should allow a few days in the production schedule for such scenarios. (You might also consider calling the printer in advance to schedule an appointment for your publication.)

Similarly, let's say you find a freelance layout artist for your newsletter, but she is already committed to producing a project for another client on the tenth of each month, which is when your newsletter layout deadline falls. You'll have to add a few days to the schedule to accommodate her previous commitment.

Be aware that most people overestimate the speed with which they can accomplish their work. So consider adding a day or two to whatever estimates you receive. And when staff and vendors say they can finish a job in "X" number of days, find out if they mean elapsed days or business days.

Once you have these estimates from staff and vendors, sit down with a yearlong calendar. Circle your desired distribution date, then count backwards to set deadlines for printing, layout, editing, writing, and planning—in that order. Avoid setting deadlines that fall on weekends or holidays. When you have gotten the dates laid out on your calendar, create a production schedule like the one in Figure 3.7 on page 80. After customizing the schedule to include your newsletter's projected issues for the year, fill in the specific assignments and deadlines. You might want to substitute the names of the staff members and vendors to make it even clearer as to who does what and when. For example, instead of having "Editor assigns articles to writers" in the first column, write "Anne assigns articles to Marvin and Alex."

When scheduling deadlines for your publication's contributors—writers, artists, printers, etc.—be aware that people tend to underestimate the time it will take them to accomplish their job. For this reason, it is a good idea to add a day or two to the estimates you receive.

PRODUCTION SCHEDULE FOR *WRITERS' ROUNDUP* NEWSLETTER				
Assignments	Winter Issue	Spring Issue	Summer Issue	Fall Issue
Editor assigns articles to authors:	January 2	April 2	July 2	October 2
Authors deliver copy to editor:	January 9	April 9	July 9	October 9
Editor delivers edited copy to layout:	January 12	April 12	July 12	October 12
Layout delivers layout file to editor:	January 17	April 17	July 17	October 17
Editor delivers layout to proofreader:	January 19	April 19	July 19	October 19
Proofreader returns corrected layout to editor:	January 22	April 23	July 22	October 23
Editor delivers final layout to printer:	January 29	April 30	July 30	October 29
Printer delivers newsletters to mail house:	February 5	May 4	August 6	November 5
Mail house mails out newsletters:	February 12	May 11	August 13	November 12

Figure 3.7

Sample one-year production schedule for a quarterly newsletter.

Getting Staff to Meet Deadlines

Staff and vendors will have an easier time meeting your deadlines if you give them a copy of the production schedule well in advance. Ideally, you should give them a schedule for a full year. This will allow them (and you) to make necessary arrangements for getting the work done when business travel, special projects, vacations, and other commitments conflict with a deadline.

You cannot expect vendors to meet their deadlines if you have not met them yourself. If you and the proofreader originally agreed on a three-day turnover, for instance, don't expect her to finish the job in two days if you deliver the copy to her a day late. In fact, if you miss a deadline by more than a day or so, your vendor may have already promised that later time to another customer, which means your work will be delayed even more.

If possible, try to keep the scheduling consistent from issue to issue. For example, if you publish monthly, for each issue you could schedule the writers' deadline on the fifth of the month, delivery of the copy to the printer on the sixteenth, and distribution of the publication on the twenty-eighth, with minor adjustments for weekends. Likewise, for a weekly newsletter, your deadlines might be Mondays, Wednesdays, and Fridays. Your staff will have an easier time remembering deadlines if they are always the same.

A common complaint of newsletter editors is that they have a hard time getting high-level staff to meet their deadlines for writing articles. This often happens with the ubiquitous "President's Message." Although the president and the newsletter's editorial board may agree that it's important to include such a message in the publication, presidents and other high-level executives often have difficulty finding the time to write it. Rather than exclude the executive viewpoint, some editors have resorted to writing the column themselves and then presenting a draft to the president, who can usually find a few minutes to edit the piece to her liking. Some editors are able to schedule a meeting with the president, find out what she wants to say in her "message," and then write it for her. Others have found presenting an outline to the executive is enough to help get her started.

To keep my newsletters on track, I like to schedule reminder dates— I call them "nag" dates—on my own calendar. On nag days, I e-mail or call the staff members who have deadlines coming up as a gentle reminder. This also gives me an idea of how far they have gotten with the assignment and if they'll be able to meet the upcoming deadline. If I were using the production schedule illustrated in Figure 3.7, when working on the winter issue I would remind my authors on January 7 or 8 that their articles are due on January 9.

Scheduling reminder dates (I call them "nag" days) helps prevent any scheduled deadlines from getting blown. On those days, contact anyone with an upcoming deadline as a gentle reminder. This will also give you an idea of how he or she is coming along with the assignment.

Keeping Track of Articles

To keep track of where each newsletter article stands in the production cycle, it is helpful to use a log like the completed sample in Figure 3.8 on page 82. Make a copy of the blank Article Tracking Log found on page 320, or use it as a guide for making your own. Feel free to add and/or remove columns from this form as needed for your particular newsletter. You'll find this type of log to be a handy and helpful quick-reference guide to the articles you're running in the issue, who's writing them, and any work that is pending.

With all of the factors involved in newsletter production, if you do not keep track of the articles, it is very easy for one or two to be overlooked. Imagine having a beautifully laid out publication, only to discover at the last minute that the information for one of the columns is missing. Maintaining a good tracking system will help prevent this type of crisis from occurring.

ARTICLE TRACKING LOG - WINTER ISSUE FOR *WRITERS' ROUNDUP* NEWSLETTER						
Article	Writer & Contact Info	Word count	Assigned? Date	Received? Date	Edited? Date	Placed in layout?
Conference	Maria Blackwell 310-555-3040 mb565@gln.net	700	☑ January 2	☑ January 4	☑ January 7	❏
Website reviews: Dictionary sites	Francine Budreau 310-555-6970 fran@wbn.com	600	☑ January 2	☑ January 6	❏	❏
Book review: New dictionary	Francine Budreau 310-555-6970 fran@wbn.com	500	☑ January 2	❏	❏	❏
Member news: Announcement of new senior members	Michael Jefferoff 310-555-6060 jeffer77@nnt.com	100	☑ January 2	☑ January 7	☑ January 8	❏
Software tip: Creating pictures in Word	Michael Jefferoff 310-555-6060 jeffer77@nnt.com	600	☑ January 2	☑ January 7	❏	❏
Announcement of new board members	Maria Blackwell 310-555-3040 mb565@gln.net	400	☑ January 2	☑ January 3	❏	❏

Figure 3.8
A tracking log helps you maintain the status of each article in the production cycle.

CONCLUSION

This chapter mapped out a lot of important material to help get your newsletter off to a successful start. You've nailed down the concept of your publication, as well as some necessary details for getting it off the ground. You are aware of the various newsletter formats and distribution methods, know the basics for creating a budget, and understand the roles of various staff members. You also know how to keep your production running smoothly through the implementation of effective schedules and tracking charts. So what's next? It's time to focus on what your newsletter is going to say.

CHAPTER 4

PLANNING THE CONTENT

By now, you have developed your newsletter idea and planned the logistics of your operation. You may be itching to put words on paper, but hold back just a bit longer. You're not quite ready to *write* your newsletter yet; but you *can* start planning the type of material to publish. The information in this chapter will help you decide the types of columns and articles to run, how to organize them, and how to make it all fit in the available space. If you were in Hollywood perched in a film director's chair, you'd call this process *storyboarding*—putting together a set of sketches showing the important action and scene changes in your movie. But you're not in Hollywood and you're not planning a movie. You're probably sitting at a desk (in a comfy swivel chair if you're lucky) while considering the appropriate subject matter for your newsletter. Instead of storyboarding, we'll call this step "planning your content"—a little more mundane, but to the point.

DEFINING YOUR CONTENT

Newsletters contain two types of content—editorial and advertising. Editorial content includes the stories and articles written by your editorial staff. Advertising content is the material used to promote sales of a product or service. Although advertisements are more commonly found in newspapers and magazines than in newsletter publications, they do appear in some association and marketing newsletters.

Editorial Content

How do you decide the type of editorial content to include in your newsletter? For the answer, first consider your purpose. What do you want to achieve through your publication? Many inexperienced editors make the mistake of printing too wide a range of material, selecting articles without thinking about whether or not they achieve the newsletter's purpose. For example, consider a newsletter for mothers of young children that includes articles about gardening. As the purpose of this newsletter is to inform its audience about childrearing, gardening articles don't achieve that purpose—unless, of course, they pertain to helping children plant gardens.

If the primary purpose of your newsletter is to, perhaps, persuade people of your point of view, you would run different types of articles than you would if your purpose is to keep readers informed about the work of your company or organization. Table 4.1 on page 88 is designed to help you zero in on the most appropriate kinds of articles for your particular publication. But first, it's important to know that editorial content falls under two main categories—*internal* news and features, and *external* news and features. You should also know where to find this information, how to fine-tune it, and when you must obtain permission to print it.

Internal News and Features

A newsletter's editorial content falls under two main categories—*internal* news and feature articles, and *external* news and feature articles. Internal material highlights the work of the company or organization that sponsors the newsletter; external material covers happenings in the outside world that are relevant to the newsletter's purpose.

Articles or columns that reflect internal news highlight the work of your company or organization. What follows are some specific articles types that commonly fall under this category. As you can see, some of them overlap.

■ **New products, programs, and services.** Give lots of attention to the accomplishments of your company or organization, whether it is launching a new product, establishing a drug prevention program, or setting up a blood-pressure screening clinic.

■ **Frequently asked questions.** Use your newsletter to answer the questions, suggestions, or complaints of clients and/or customers. In addition to keeping your readers informed, this type of column can help reduce the amount of time you and your staff spend handling such questions by phone or e-mail.

■ **Meeting reports.** Keep readers informed by reporting on actions taken at board of directors' or membership meetings. Summarize presentations given by guest speakers at special programs or seminars you sponsor. Getting a taste of what goes on at your meetings can help motivate your readers to attend in the future.

■ **Chapter, regional, division, or committee reports.** By including reports from other chapters, regions, divisions, and committees, you'll keep readers in all locations abreast of company or organization news.

■ **Contributor acknowledgments.** Running thank-you notices and contributor lists let your donors and volunteers know you appreciate them.

■ **Profiles.** Publishing biographies of employees, members, volunteers, or donors helps readers get to know one another and increase their sense of belonging to a group. Acknowledging these people for their contributions to the organization is also likely to motivate others to do the same.

■ **Announcements.** Inform readers of such matters as procedural changes, upcoming board elections and annual meetings, and proposed changes to bylaws. You can also announce new hires, resignations, transfers, and retirements. In a more informal newsletter, you can also run wedding or birth announcements (with permission).

■ **Accomplishments.** In an employee or professional association newsletter, note achievements of staff or members, including promotions, publications, and awards. Not only does such a column keep readers informed of their colleagues' accomplishments, but it also helps them get to know one another.

■ **Benefits of membership.** Your newsletter may get passed on to people who aren't members of your organization, so be sure to seize the opportunity to highlight the benefits of joining. Such an article also reminds current members of why they should renew their memberships.

■ **Calendar.** List events sponsored by your organization, like your symphony's concert dates, or the date of your store's summer clearance sale. Don't forget to include deadlines (for paying dues, completing forms, submitting newsletter articles, and so on). If space permits and the information fits your newsletter's purpose, include outside events as well.

In an employee or professional association newsletter, you can help create a sense of community among readers by running articles that mention notable achievements of colleagues or members. Publishing biographical profiles of employees, members, volunteers, or donors further fosters this connection.

The editorial content of your newsletter doesn't have to include all of these types of internal news articles. Consider only those that are pertinent to your publication and help achieve its purpose.

External News and Features

If you have the time and money, and it suits your newsletter's purpose, consider running stories about relevant happenings in the outside world. The following list offers some possible ideas:

Along with running internal articles about your company or organization, consider including stories or happenings from the outside world that may be relevant to the organization and its areas of interest.

■ **Reports on government legislation and regulations.** Monitor publications of legislatures or agencies that have jurisdiction over your readers' areas of interest or expertise. Write articles that summarize their findings or other newsworthy information. For example, an association of educators of gifted children might follow the progress of gifted-education legislation through Congress, while an investment industry newsletter could cull news from the Securities and Exchange Commission.

■ **Local, national, or international news.** Report on external news that affects your readers. For example, if your health clinic runs an exercise club for seniors, your newsletter can summarize the latest findings on the benefits of exercise for the elderly. In the same article, you can quote members of the exercise club, describing how participation has affected their own health. In an advocacy newsletter, use news reports to back up your arguments. For example, to get readers to write their senators in support of low-income housing, summarize a current news report about increasing homelessness.

■ **Educational articles.** Do your readers want to know how to use a new technology, teaching technique, or piece of equipment? Educational and how-to articles are well suited to all types of newsletters. Book, software, and website reviews are other types of educational articles that are ideal for newsletters.

■ **Research reports.** Monitor professional journals so you can summarize the latest research that would be of interest to your audience. Discuss how your readers can apply the findings to their work.

■ **Conference reports.** Conferences are often *the* place to learn about research, new products, and trends. Since many interested readers can't attend conferences because of the time, travel, and expense involved, fill them in on the proceedings with summaries of research presentations, seminars, and keynote speeches. Give your readers a feel for what happened behind the scenes—the general mood in the industry or profession, the networking, and the inside take on the official pronouncements.

■ **Editorials.** If your newsletter's purpose is to persuade its readers, most of your content will incorporate your organization's point of view. But if your newsletter is primarily informative, confine proselytizing to editorials or letters to the editor.

Now that you are familiar with the most common internal and external types of articles, it's time to take a look at Table 4.1 on page 88. This table will further help you determine which columns or articles offer the most suitable content for your particular newsletter.

Selecting Content for Your Audience

Once you've settled on the types of articles to run, you have to fine-tune the topics of those articles so they appeal to your audience. Earlier in the chapter, I gave an example of a mothers' group newsletter that inappropriately ran articles on gardening. Its editors had simply assumed that because many women like to garden, and mothers are women, their readers would appreciate the information. If they had surveyed their audience first, they would have discovered that the readers weren't as interested in gardening as they were in developing parenting skills, which was the main purpose of the newsletter.

Likewise, you need to know why your audience reads your newsletter. If they are new teachers, they'll want basic information on classroom management. But if they are veterans who have taught for twenty-plus years, they'll be looking for more advanced material. If yours is a regional publication for pharmacists, is it necessary to report news from the US Food and Drug Administration? Or do your readers get this information elsewhere and look to you for updates on local regulations instead?

If you are publishing a marketing newsletter, try to find a balance between content that promotes your products and services, and content that is useful to the reader. For example, rather than starting an article with a plug for your health club's aerobics classes, cite research demonstrating the health benefits of aerobic exercise, and then conclude by explaining how your program provides those same benefits.

Sources of Information

So how do you find information for your articles? There are several ways. You can subscribe to a clipping service, which will send you news articles from print publications, TV and radio shows, and the Internet that are related to your subject on the day they are published. Some Internet-based clipping services are free (in exchange for personal information), while others will charge you based on the level of service or the number of clips delivered. Most clipping services send either printed copies of the articles by fax or mail, or electronic versions via e-mail or web page. The Resources, beginning on page 323, list some of these services.

Press releases are another excellent source of information and leads

Information for your publication can come from a variety of sources. Clipping services search out news that is related to your subject from various media outlets—newspapers, magazines, television, radio, and the Internet. Press releases from relevant companies or organizations are also good sources for article leads. And through their feedback, your readers themselves can be possible contributors.

TABLE 4.1. DETERMINING NEWSLETTER CONTENT

Based on the purposes of your particular newsletter, the table below will help you determine the type (or types) of articles that are most suitable for it. Simply find the column(s) that describes your newsletter's purpose, then scan down to the checked boxes, which indicate the types of articles that can help you achieve that purpose.

Article Types	Newsletter Purposes						
	Inform	Motivate	Improve image	Persuade	Thank	Solicit media coverage	Reduce mailings
Internal news and features:							
New products, programs, and services	✔	✔	✔		✔	✔	
Frequently asked questions	✔	✔	✔	✔			✔
Meeting reports	✔	✔			✔		✔
Chapter, regional, division, or committee reports	✔				✔		✔
Contributor acknowledgments					✔		
Profiles	✔	✔	✔		✔	✔	
Announcements	✔	✔			✔		✔
Accomplishments	✔	✔	✔			✔	
Membership benefits		✔					
Calendar of events	✔	✔				✔	✔
External news and features:							
Reports on government legislation and regulations	✔	✔		✔			
Local, national, and international news	✔	✔		✔			
Educational articles	✔						
Research reports	✔						
Conference reports	✔						
Editorials				✔			

for articles. Companies and other organizations are more than happy to make their press releases available to editors. Contact those that are important to your industry or field and ask to be placed on their distribution lists. You can also subscribe to a press-release distribution service, which sends releases on specified topics as they become available. See the Resources section for more information.

If you decide to let a third party prepare all of your newsletter's content, you can distribute a syndicated newsletter. As described in Chapter 1, syndicated newsletters are produced for business, medical, law, investment, or accounting professionals to distribute to their clients.

Finally, your readers themselves can be a fruitful source of editorial material. Solicit their feedback in the form of letters to the editor, responses to previously published articles, descriptions of personal experiences, and tips that will be of value to other readers of the newsletter. Just be sure to use your editorial discretion in deciding which reader feedback to publish. If necessary, do some fact checking on the information they have provided.

Understanding Copyrights and Agreements

As a newsletter publisher, you must understand two sides of the copyright-law coin: (1) how the law affects your ability to reprint material in your newsletter that has been published elsewhere, and (2) how to protect your newsletter from being reproduced by someone else without your permission. In addition, you must know how to reach agreements with your contributors, who allow you to use the material they produce for you.

Using Copyrighted Material in Your Newsletter

Sometimes while planning your editorial content, you may come across an article, a passage from an article, or a graphic that is exactly what you need in your newsletter. While you may be tempted to reproduce that material, think twice before doing so.

Under current copyright law, no material can be quoted without permission of the publisher unless the material falls under the *fair use* provisions, which allow for limited copying of published works without permission. While at one time these provisions were fairly liberal, at this point, fair use generally allows people to quote from copyrighted material only for news reports, reviews, classroom instruction, and discussions. Nevertheless, in practice, many publishers often follow the older,

Under current copyright law, the fair use provision allows for the limited reprinting of a previously published work—generally for the purpose of news reports, reviews, and classroom instruction. However, permission from the copyright owner is required to reprint even small excerpts from poems and song lyrics.

more generous fair use laws, and permit the reprint of copyrighted material that is less than a paragraph in length. Note, though, that the situation is different when the quoted material takes the form of song lyrics or poetry. In these cases, reprint permission from the copyright holder is generally required even when the excerpt is very small.

Where does that leave you, the newsletter editor? Keep in mind it is always a wise practice to get reprint permission from the publisher of the quoted work. Because people interpret fair use laws in different ways, and because of the time involved in getting reprint permission, many editors avoid quoting from other people's work. But if, after considering these facts, you *still* feel that the quoted material would add to the value of your newsletter, by all means contact the copyright holder for permission. To find out who holds the copyright, look in the masthead of the periodical, or on the page following the title page of a book. If the publisher holds the copyright, contact them directly. If it is the author, send him a letter in care of the publisher. If you are from a nonprofit organization or your newsletter is distributed free, mention it, as that may induce the copyright holder to reduce or waive fees if they normally charge them. Note that it can take several months to receive a response. Once you do, keep the permission letter on file to refer to in the event of a future dispute. A sample letter requesting reprint permission is found on the page at right.

Protecting Your Newsletter from Copyright Infringement

As a publisher, you want to be assured that no one can reproduce material from your newsletter without your consent. For this reason, it is important to have some basic knowledge about the United States Copyright Law.

A copyright is a federal law that protects original "works of authorship," which can include anything from a poem to a drawing to a computer program to a newsletter article. Your ideas and concepts are not protected, but your finished work is. Under copyright law, no one can reproduce, adapt, distribute, perform, or display your work unless you formally grant that person the right to do so. Moreover, a copyright is yours as soon as you put your work down on a piece of paper. It is yours whether or not you have registered your work with the United States Copyright Office.

You can help protect your work by simply placing a copyright notation on the work itself. This is referred to as a *common copyright*. It's

You are considered the owner of your finished work—a poem, an article, a play, a drawing, a computer program, a newsletter—even if you have not formally registered it with the US Copyright Office.

This standard permission form requests the right to reprint previously published material. Be sure to send out this form on letterhead with your address, telephone number, and other contact information.

(Current Date)

Jane Smith, Publisher
The New York Telegraph
555 Main Street
New York, NY 11111

Dear Ms. Smith:

I am the editor of *Writers' Roundup,* the newsletter of the Lakeland Writers' Association. I am writing for permission to reprint "The Art of the Obituary" from page 23 of the November 13, 2005 issue of *The New York Telegraph.* (See attached copy of the page.) I would like this article to appear in our upcoming spring issue.

Please provide me with the desired credit line and specify where you would like it to appear:

_____

_____

I would greatly appreciate your consent to this request. For your convenience, a release form is provided below, and a copy of this letter is enclosed for your files. Should you not control these rights in their entirety, kindly let me know whom I should contact for reprint permission.

Thank you for your attention to this matter. I look forward to hearing from you.

Sincerely,

Carol Luers Eyman
Carol Luers Eyman

I (We) grant permission for use of the material requested above.

Signature _____

Name _____ Date _____

important to understand that this notation isn't necessary to establish copyright. As explained earlier, copyright was established as soon as you wrote the article. However, this notation does serve as a visual reminder that you have the rights to that piece of work. Any of the following copyright notations, placed in the masthead, will serve the intended purpose of reminding the reader that you own the rights to the material in your newsletter:

Although a copyright notation, such as the ones seen at right, isn't necessary to establish ownership of your newsletter, placing one in the masthead will serve as a visual reminder to readers.

Copyright 2006 by Lakeland Writers' Association

© 2006 by Lakeland Writers' Association

Copyright © 2006 by Lakeland Writers' Association

If the option of common copyright does not provide you with an adequate feeling of security, or if you have a special reason to fear infringement of your work, you can register your work with the US Copyright Office. Formal registration gives you certain legal benefits. If anyone *does* violate your copyright by publishing part or all of your work, the formal copyright registration will speed up any legal battle and avoid complications. And if the work is registered with the copyright office within three months of its appearance in print or before any violation of your rights occurred, you will be awarded the money to pay for any legal expenses, as well as compensation for the wrongs committed against you. A willful copyright infringement, where it's clear that the user stole your work on purpose, carries with it damage awards up to $100,000 per infringement.

Registering your newsletter is easy, and you can do so at any time, even years after the material was written. It is more economical to register several issues of your newsletter at a time, rather than each one individually. The registration process begins by filling out an application form, which can be downloaded from the Internet or obtained through the mail. (See the Resources beginning on page 323 for contact information.) Return the completed application form and the required number of copies of your newsletter to the Copyright Office along with a check covering the copyright fee. The office will mail you a certificate of registration once your application has been reviewed and accepted. Be aware that neither the fee nor the sample newsletters will be returned to you.

It should be noted that despite the extra protection afforded by any copyright protection, many newsletter publishers do not choose this option because of the fees and time involved. Also keep in mind that only your *words* are copyrighted, not your ideas or your newsletter's title. In some cases, newsletter publishers are happy to receive the free publicity gained by having their material reproduced elsewhere. Many newsletter publishers establish common copyright through a notice in their masthead, as described earlier, and then state that their material may be reproduced as long as the source is credited and/or the editor is informed in advance.

Agreements

As a newsletter editor, you must also be sure that you have proper permission from your contributors—authors, photographers, and artists—to use their work in your publication. How you obtain permission depends on whether or not the contributor is your employee. You do not need permission to print material that your employees produce as part of their job, which is considered *work for hire.*

When freelancers and people other than employees contribute to your newsletter, it is best to have them sign a contract or a letter of agreement, as seen in the sample on page 94. This agreement should state the conditions of your purchase of the material they create. It should stipulate the following:

■ **Article description.** The topic of the article, its length in words, and any additional materials (such as sidebars or graphics) that the writer is to provide. For artists and photographers, this would include photographs, illustrations, and/or other graphic material.

■ **Submission details.** The submission deadline for the material and the format in which it is to be submitted (text file via e-mail, for example).

■ **Revisions.** The number of revisions you can request for the material, and whether or not you must pay a fee for them.

■ **Kill fees.** Whether you must pay the freelancer if you decide not to use the material after it has been submitted. Also, stipulate if you must return the unused material to the freelancer along with all rights to publish it.

■ **Payment details.** How much you will pay for the work and when you must issue payment.

■ **Rights.** When you accept material for publication in your newsletter, you purchase some of the contributor's rights to reproduce, adapt, distribute, perform, or display his work. Usually, periodical publishers purchase "first serial rights," also known as "first North American Serial

Unless an agreement has been signed to the contrary, employers are considered the owners of any work that their employees prepare or produce within the scope of their jobs.

If you have written a relatively short article—a personal essay, for instance—you may receive a contract that is shorter than the standard agreement. Most contracts, though, roughly offer the same basic terms. So although your contract may vary from the following in setup or format, the items it covers will probably be similar to those included below.

Contributor Rights Agreement

Date: 11/15/20 _ _

Contract between: Mindy Wilson (writer) and Stay at Home Mom (publisher).

Article Details:

The writer agrees to prepare an article on the subject of Home Office Security (the "Work") with a word length of 800 words. The writer will provide the following additional materials for said Work: sidebar of resources, photo of interview subject Carol Parsons, with compensation included in total fee. The Work will be delivered to the Publisher in e-mail text file format by the following date: January 31, 20−−. The writer agrees to provide one revision of the Work.

A kill fee of 20% ($120) will be paid in the event that the final Work is unacceptable to the publisher. A kill fee will be paid under the following circumstances only: 1) The Work does not meet the requirements the publisher had in mind 2) The writer refuses to provide a rewrite of the Work 3) The publisher changes editorial direction and no longer needs the Work.

The publisher agrees to reimburse the writer for the following expenses with documentation: telephone calls.

Should a major rewrite be requested, the writer will receive, in addition to regular fee, the following compensation: $50.

Finally, the writer will be provided 3 (three) copies of the publication in which his/her Work appears.

Payment Details:

The publisher agrees to pay the writer $600 within 30 days of receipt of said Work, given that all agreed-upon requirements have been met. This fee purchases First North American Serial rights only. All other rights reserved by the writer. The publisher also agrees to reimburse the agreed-upon expenses within 30 days of submission of receipts. Kill fees will be paid within 30 days of notification, should this be necessary.

Other Legalities:

The publisher agrees to provide the writer the final, edited version for consideration while there is still reasonable time to make changes. The writer reserves the right to withdraw her name from the Work without affecting payment should a disagreement about the final draft occur.

The writer guarantees that the Work is accurate to the best of her knowledge and does not contain any material that could be construed as libelous or defamatory. In return, the publisher agrees to provide and fund counsel to the writer should any litigation result from above mentioned article.

Mindy Wilson	_December 1, 20−−_
Writer	Date
Linda Stern	_November 15, 20−−_
Publisher	Date

Rights"—the right to publish the material before any other publication does. This allows you to publish the material only that one time; however, you can purchase other rights, such as second serial (reprint) rights, electronic rights, and performance rights.

Of course, there is room to negotiate with freelancers on many of these contract terms. For more information on periodical-publishing contracts and agreements, see *How to Publish Your Articles* by Shirley Kawa-Jump.

Advertisements

To generate extra income, some newsletters run advertisements. When planning the content of your newsletter, consider the pros and cons of accepting ads before deciding to include them.

First, think about whether the presence of advertisements in your newsletter will cause your readers to question your objectivity. You may be familiar with the magazine *Consumer Reports,* which tests and rates products. Published by the nonprofit Consumers Union, the magazine runs no advertising. This is to assure that its writers and testers are not influenced to report favorably on products from companies that advertise in the publication. Similarly, to avoid the appearance of influence on its editorial content, most professional newsletters don't publish ads. However, it is becoming common to find advertisements in professional newsletters that are distributed free on the Internet or via e-mail.

Advertisers can be quick to complain about how their company, products, or services are portrayed in the editorial content of your publication. This can make it difficult to avoid promoting their products (either intentionally or unintentionally). For instance, if you include software reviews in your newsletter, you have to be wary of favoring your advertisers' products or of limiting the products you review to those of your advertisers.

If you can avoid caving in to advertiser pressure and are vigilant about the objectivity of your editorial content, running advertisements won't necessarily tarnish your newsletter's image. But be sure to clearly distinguish the ads from editorial copy. Usually it's easy to tell the difference between graphical ads and editorial content. Problems tend to arise with ads that contain mostly text, like those you often see on the op-ed pages of newspapers. Ask the advertiser to submit this kind of ad in a typeface that differs from the ones used in your editorial headlines and

If you run advertisements (or plan to run them) in your newsletter, they should be easily distinguishable from your editorial content. This is especially important for ads containing all text and no graphics. Have the advertiser submit the ad in a typeface that is noticeably different from the type used in your editorial text and headlines. And set the ad apart from the rest of the text by placing it in a box and inserting the words "Paid Advertisement" below it.

To preserve the editorial integrity of your newsletter, don't overload it with advertisements. Make a decision regarding the amount of space to devote to articles (a percentage of the issue, a minimum number of pages, or the amount of screen space in online versions). Once this has been established, you can decide on ad placement in the remaining space.

text, then box the ad to separate it from the rest of the page. Also, insert a footer below it that reads, "Paid advertisement."

To maintain the editorial value of your newsletter, establish standards on how much space to devote to advertising in each issue. You can follow the example of some publications and use a proportion, such as 40-percent advertising and 60-percent editorial. You might also want to establish a minimum amount of editorial content (say, four full pages) and then allow a certain number of advertising pages above and beyond that. For web newsletters, you'll want to establish guidelines describing how much screen space can be devoted to advertising, and whether pop-up ads will be allowed. Instead of devoting a number of areas of the screen to ads, you can assign them to a designated spot and rotate them every few seconds. For text e-mail newsletters, Chris Pirillo, author of *Poor Richard's E-Mail Publishing*, suggests limiting advertising to a maximum of two or three ads of three to six lines per issue.

To find advertisers, contact companies that sell goods or services aimed at your target audience. If yours is a general-interest regional publication, local consumer-oriented businesses and professionals are potential advertisers. Having your newsletter listed in a directory of newsletters or periodicals can also yield inquiries from advertisers.

ORGANIZING YOUR CONTENT

As a preteen, my son had a set morning routine: shower, dress, make breakfast, and grab section two of the local newspaper—home of his beloved *Garfield* comic strip. He knew just where to find it, right after the sports news and before the advice columns, because the newspaper's editors organized the content in the same way every day. Likewise, you can help readers of your newsletter quickly find the information they need if you organize the content consistently from issue to issue.

The content of most newsletters falls into the categories of news, features, regular columns, sidebars, and advertising (if applicable). In a well-organized newsletter, each category appears in the same general location in each issue. The following discussion defines these categories.

News

News is commonly defined as "information on recent events, particularly those that are significant or uncommon." Traditionally, the most important news stories run on page one of a newsletter, just as they do in a newspaper. If you run several short news stories, you might consider grouping them into a news briefs column. For example, as shown in Figure 4.1 at right, the newsletter *Professional Apartment Management* groups short news items about court cases involving landlords and tenants into a column entitled "Owners in Court."

Your newsletter's subject matter may lend itself to a number of topical categories. For instance, a university's alumni newsletter could run news under "Academic Highlights," "Athletic Highlights," "Research Highlights," and "Alumni Highlights." An international business newsletter might organize its noteworthy news by region—"The Americas," "Europe," "Asia," and so forth. Such categories create a framework for the articles, helping your readers put them in context before they even start to read them.

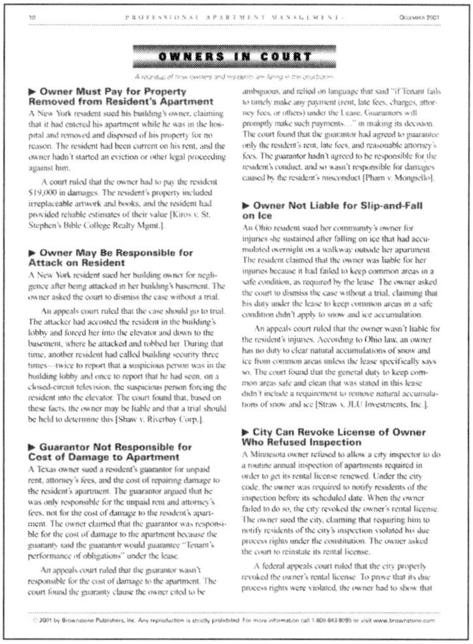

10 PROFESSIONAL APARTMENT MANAGEMENT December 2001

OWNERS IN COURT

▶ Owner Must Pay for Property Removed from Resident's Apartment

A New York resident sued his building's owner, claiming that it had entered his apartment while he was in the hospital and removed and disposed of his property for no reason. The resident had been current on his rent, and the owner hadn't started an eviction or other legal proceeding against him.

A court ruled that the owner had to pay the resident $19,000 in damages. The resident's property included irreplaceable artwork and books, and the resident had provided reliable estimates of their value [Kiros v. St. Stephen's Bible College Realty Mgmt.].

▶ Owner May Be Responsible for Attack on Resident

A New York resident sued her building owner for negligence after being attacked in her building's basement. The owner asked the court to dismiss the case without a trial.

An appeals court ruled that the case should go to trial. The attacker had accosted the resident in the building's lobby and forced her into the elevator and down to the basement, where he attacked and robbed her. During that time, another resident had called building security three times—twice to report that a suspicious person was in the building lobby and once to report that he had seen, on a closed-circuit television, the suspicious person forcing the resident into the elevator. The court found that, based on these facts, the owner may be liable and that a trial should be held to determine this [Shaw v. Riverbay Corp.].

▶ Guarantor Not Responsible for Cost of Damage to Apartment

A Texas owner sued a resident's guarantor for unpaid rent, attorney's fees, and the cost of repairing damage to the resident's apartment. The guarantor argued that he was only responsible for the unpaid rent and attorney's fees, not for the cost of damage to the resident's apartment. The owner claimed that the guarantor was responsible for the cost of damage to the apartment because the guaranty said the guarantor would guarantee "Tenant's performance of obligations" under the lease.

An appeals court ruled that the guarantor wasn't responsible for the cost of damage to the apartment. The court found the guaranty clause the owner cited to be ambiguous, and relied on language that said "if Tenant fails to timely make any payment (rent, late fees, charges, attorney fees, or others) under the Lease, Guarantors will promptly make such payments..." in making its decision. The court found that the guarantor had agreed to guarantee only the resident's rent, late fees, and reasonable attorney's fees. The guarantor hadn't agreed to be responsible for the resident's conduct, and so wasn't responsible for damages caused by the resident's misconduct [Pham v. Mongiello].

▶ Owner Not Liable for Slip-and-Fall on Ice

An Ohio resident sued her community's owner for injuries she sustained after falling on ice that had accumulated overnight on a walkway outside her apartment. The resident claimed that the owner was liable for her injuries because it had failed to keep common areas in a safe condition, as required by the lease. The owner asked the court to dismiss the case without a trial, claiming that his duty under the lease to keep common areas in a safe condition didn't apply to snow and ice accumulation.

An appeals court ruled that the owner wasn't liable for the resident's injuries. According to Ohio law, an owner has no duty to clear natural accumulations of snow and ice from common areas unless the lease specifically says so. The court found that the general duty to keep common areas safe and clean that was stated in this lease didn't include a requirement to remove natural accumulations of snow and ice [Straw v. JLU Investments, Inc.].

▶ City Can Revoke License of Owner Who Refused Inspection

A Minnesota owner refused to allow a city inspector to do a routine annual inspection of apartments required in order to get its rental license renewed. Under the city code, the owner was required to notify residents of the inspection before its scheduled date. When the owner failed to do so, the city revoked the owner's rental license. The owner sued the city, claiming that requiring him to notify residents of the city's inspection violated his due process rights under the constitution. The owner asked the court to reinstate its rental license.

A federal appeals court ruled that the city properly revoked the owner's rental license. To prove that its due process rights were violated, the owner had to show that

© 2001 by Brownstone Publishers, Inc. Any reproduction is strictly prohibited. For more information call 1-800-643-8095 or visit www.brownstone.com

Figure 4.1
In a column called "Owners in Court," *Professional Apartment Management* newsletter places news briefs about court cases involving landlords and tenants.

Features

Features are special articles that are prominently run in your newsletter. Like news, feature articles can cover recent events, but often from a special angle or point of view. They also cover events in a manner that is less time sensitive than standard news articles. For instance, a university newsletter might run a late-breaking *news* story about the endowment of a faculty chair by a graduate. In the next issue, the newsletter could run a *feature* profiling the donor of that endowment, detailing his previous and current donations to the school. The information in the feature is timely because of the recent endowment, but it is not as late breaking as the news story.

Newsletter articles that qualify as features include profiles of executives, customers, employees, volunteers, and donors; educational or how-to articles; and historical material.

Regular Columns

Columns that regularly appear in each issue are the mainstay of newsletters. Typically, they include such topics as the president's report; an editor's message; questions and answers; book, software, or product reviews; tips; calendars; and editorials. When you come up with an idea for an article, think about whether its subject matter and length make it appropriate for placement in one of these columns. For example, Figure

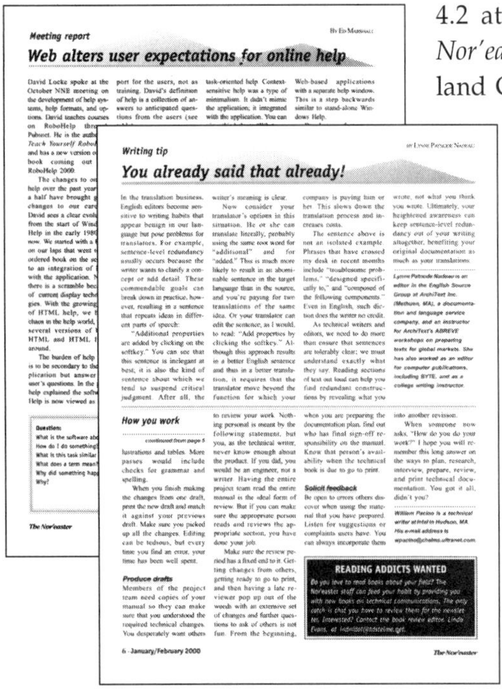
Meeting report

Web alters user expectations for online help

Writing tip

You already said that already!

How you work

READING ADDICTS WANTED

6 · January/February 2000

The Nor'easter

Figure 4.2
"Writing tip" and "Meeting report" are two regular columns that run in *The Nor'easter.*

4.2 at left shows two columns that appear regularly in *The Nor'easter*—a newsletter for members of the Northern New England Chapter of the Society for Technical Communication. One of these columns called "Writing tip" presents an article on how to avoid redundancy in one's writing. "Meeting report"—another of *The Nor'easter's* regular columns—includes an article on creating online help files.

Sidebars

Sidebars are boxed items that accompany news or feature articles. They often contain supplemental material or information that refers to or relates to the articles. For example, alongside a news article describing your organization's latest fundraiser and all of the effort involved in its success, you can include a sidebar in which you list the names of the volunteers and the jobs they did for the event. Or perhaps in the fall issue of your local parenting newsletter you run an article called "Making the Most of Autumn," which encourages family outings and activities. In a sidebar, you can list addresses of area petting zoos, pumpkin patches, and apple orchards that welcome the general public.

Sidebars are also useful for providing explanatory material, such as driving directions, a list of definitions, or other information that would interrupt the flow of the main article. They are also good for citing information that readers may want to find quickly or refer back to later, such as a list of names, phone numbers, or websites. As shown in Figure 4.3 on page 99, *Professional Apartment Management* newsletter uses a sidebar to list all of the legal citations mentioned in that particular issue. This makes it easy for readers to locate the citations quickly.

Advertising

In print newsletters, small text-only advertisements can be arranged in a column of classified ads. Larger ads, called *display ads,* are usually interspersed throughout the editorial content for greater visibility. If possible, they should be placed near related editorial material. In e-mail newsletters, ads are usually grouped in left- or right-hand columns. Avoid interrupting articles with ads, as many readers won't bother to scroll past the ad to finish the article.

Grouping and placing news, features, regular columns, sidebars, and ads are just part of organizing a newsletter. In Parts Three and Four of this book you will also learn how to use layout and typography to visually communicate the organization of your newsletter to its readers.

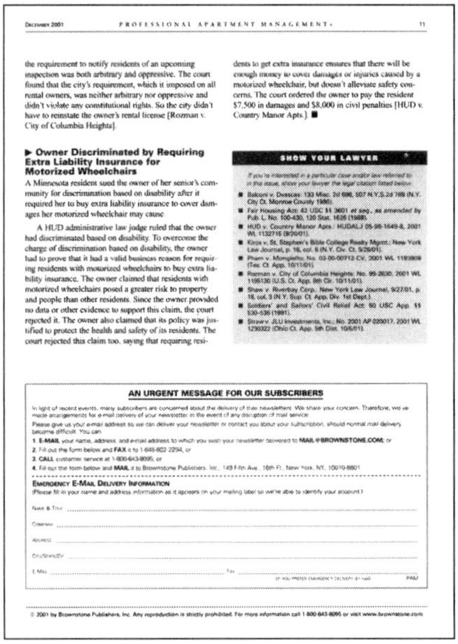
December 2001 PROFESSIONAL APARTMENT MANAGEMENT 11

the requirement to notify residents of an upcoming inspection was both arbitrary and oppressive. The court found that the city's requirement, which it imposed on all rental owners, was neither arbitrary nor oppressive and didn't violate any constitutional rights. So the city didn't have to reinstate the owner's rental license [Rozman v. City of Columbia Heights].

▶ Owner Discriminated by Requiring Extra Liability Insurance for Motorized Wheelchairs

A Minnesota resident sued the owner of her senior's community for discrimination based on disability after it required her to buy extra liability insurance to cover damages her motorized wheelchair may cause.

A HUD administrative law judge ruled that the owner had discriminated based on disability. To overcome the charge of discrimination based on disability, the owner had to prove that it had a valid business reason for requiring residents with motorized wheelchairs to buy extra liability insurance. The owner claimed that residents with motorized wheelchairs posed a greater risk to property and people than other residents. Since the owner provided no data or other evidence to support this claim, the court rejected it. The owner also claimed that its policy was justified to protect the health and safety of its residents. The court rejected this claim too, saying that requiring residents to get extra insurance ensures that there will be enough money to cover damages or injuries caused by a motorized wheelchair, but doesn't alleviate safety concerns. The court ordered the owner to pay the resident $7,500 in damages and $8,000 in civil penalties [HUD v. Country Manor Apts.]. ■

SHOW YOUR LAWYER

If you're interested in a particular case and/or law referred to in this issue, show your lawyer the legal citation listed below.

- Fair Housing Act: 42 USC §§ 3601 *et seq.*, as amended by Pub. L. No. 100-430, 120 Stat. 1626 (1988).
- HUD v. Country Manor Apts.: HUDALJ 05-98-1649-8, 2001 WL 1132716 (8/20/01).
- Rozman v. City of Columbia Heights: No. 99-2630, 2001 WL 1195130 (U.S. Ct. App. 8th Cir. 10/11/01).
- Shaw v. Riverbay Corp., New York Law Journal, 9/27/01, p. 18, col. 3 (N.Y. Sup. Ct. App. Div. 1st Dept.).
- Soldiers' and Sailors' Civil Relief Act: 50 USC App. §§ 530-536 (1991).

AN URGENT MESSAGE FOR OUR SUBSCRIBERS

In light of recent events, many subscribers are concerned about the delivery of their newsletters. We share your concern. Therefore, we've made arrangements for e-mail delivery of your newsletter in the event of any disruption of mail service.

Please give us your e-mail address so we can deliver your newsletter or contact you about your subscription, should normal mail delivery become difficult. You can:

1. **E-MAIL** your name, address, and e-mail address to which you wish your newsletter delivered to **MAIL@BROWNSTONE.COM**; or
2. Fill out the form below and **FAX** it to 1-646-602-2294; or
3. **CALL** customer service at 1-800-643-8095; or
4. Fill out the form below and **MAIL** it to Brownstone Publishers, Inc., 149 Fifth Ave., 16th Fl., New York, NY, 10010-6801

EMERGENCY E-MAIL DELIVERY INFORMATION

(Please fill in your name and address information as it appears on your mailing label so we're able to identify your account.)

Name & Title ______

Company ______

Address ______

City/State/Zip ______

E-Mail ______ Fax ______

PAM

© 2001 by Brownstone Publishers, Inc. Any reproduction is strictly prohibited. For more information call 1-800-643-8095 or visit www.brownstone.com

Figure 4.3
On this page of *Professional Apartment Management*, a sidebar entitled "Show Your Lawyer" lists legal citations for the cases and laws referred to in that issue.

MAKING YOUR CONTENT FIT

Before you design the pages of your newsletter, consider the amount of space you plan to allocate to the different types of material you are including. Will you be devoting a lot of space for member news or just a quarter page? Will your book reviews be of sufficient interest to warrant a full page? You may want to vary the allotted space from issue to issue, but set up general guidelines for length, based on the importance of the articles to your newsletter's purpose.

As you produce each issue, particularly if it's a print newsletter, sometimes the material you receive may be too long or too short to fill the available space. When this happens, you'll have to either find additional material or cut your content to fit. How do you do it? Read on.

Assign Article Length

It will be a lot easier to fit your copy into each issue if you plan ahead and specify an article length—in the number of words—to your writers. You can come up with this number once you've created a design for your newsletter (discussed in Chapter 8 for print newsletters, and Chapters 10 through 13 for electronic versions). Decide on which page you expect to run the article. Say you plan to run a principal's message in the second and third columns of page two. Although you know how much space you have for the message (two columns) you still need to figure out how many words will fit into that space. There are some common ways to determine this.

One technique is to create a few files on your word processor that contain varying numbers of words. Begin by copying an existing file that contains only text (no graphics) or by creating one on your own. The file should be several pages in length. Run a word count on it, then start deleting text from the file until it contains only 500 words. Save this file and name it something like "word count 500." Now copy this file to a second file, cut it down to 300 words, and save it as "word count 300." Repeat these steps to create 200- and 100-word files, as well.

Next, decide which of these word-count files comes closest to filling the allotted space (in our example, the space is in the second and third columns on page two). Copy the text from that file and place it in your newsletter template. Format this text in the same typeface and point size you plan to use in the final layout. If it doesn't fill the space, make a copy of one of the other word-count files, and paste it at the end of the text from the first file. Once the allotted space has been filled, do a word count. Then subtract words to account for the space that will be occupied by headlines and/or graphics. Your final word count will be approximate but still useful to the writer, who will have a good idea of how long the piece should be.

Do the same for the other pages of your newsletter to get a general idea of how many words it will take to fill a full page, a half page, and a quarter page. When you pass these numbers on to your writers, the content will come much closer to fitting the allotted space than it will if the authors have no guidelines.

Another technique for estimating article length is to use a text file called "copyfit.txt." If you own PageMaker (a software package for laying out newsletters), you may already have this file on your computer's hard drive. You can also search the Internet for "copyfit.txt" to find a site that allows you to download this program. The file contains 1,000 words, each five letters long (the average word length in the English language). A number following every twenty-fifth word notes how many words are in the file up to that point. Place "copyfit.txt" in your newsletter template, formatting the text in your selected typeface and point size. The number that appears at the end of the space you are measuring is the approximate word count for that space.

Creating Filler

It is a good idea to maintain a collection of backup articles of different lengths. Whenever the editorial content of your newsletter runs short, you can draw from this on-hand collection.

In spite of your best planning efforts, there will be times when you will need to stretch your newsletter content. Even if you measure your pages and assign articles to fit, you may find yourself with empty space. To avoid a last-minute scramble for additional copy, keep a collection of backup articles on file. Whenever your writers produce more articles than you can fit into a single issue, hold onto the ones you don't use. If they aren't time-sensitive, you can use them in future issues.

Alternatively, use canned or filler articles, which are provided by writing services and can be downloaded from the Internet. If they are free, the providers will probably require you to include some sort of commercial attribution—an advertisement or a link to the producer's website. Check to see if the licensing agreement allows you to modify the article because you will want to be able to edit the material to fit the tone and writing style of your newsletter. The Resources, beginning on page 323, lists sources of filler articles.

Cutting Copy

There will be times that you simply won't be able to fit all the articles that have been contributed to a single issue of your newsletter. Your budget may allow printing only four pages, even when you have enough copy for eight. Or maybe you can afford eight pages, but you've received enough copy to fill nine. Since printing nine pages would mean leaving the tenth page blank (making for a very awkward layout), you'll have to make some cuts.

This may require, as journalists say, "killing" entire articles. If you take this route, obviously begin by dropping the least important and least timely articles. (Hopefully, you can save them for a future issue.) If you find that an article is too long to fit into its assigned space, instead of killing it, you may be able to shorten it. In Chapter 6, the "Editing" section, beginning on page 152, helps you decide how to cut a paragraph or more from an article while maintaining its readability and accuracy. In Chapter 8, the section on "Fitting Copy," beginning on page 228, presents tips on how to make less-extensive cuts.

CONCLUSION

The information in this chapter has helped you identify the various types of editorial and advertising content that meet your newsletter's purposes and appeal to your audience. It also presented the basic steps for organizing that content and making it fit into the available space. Finally, this chapter has made you aware of the steps you must take before reprinting any previously published material—as well as how to protect the editorial content in your newsletter from being reprinted without your permission. Now, it's time to focus on your audience.

When you find yourself with more copy than you can fit into the allotted space of an issue, you will have to do some cutting. This could mean paring down an article or killing it entirely. If the dropped article is not time sensitive, save it for use in a future issue.

CHAPTER 5

FINDING READERS

Some newsletter publishers have audiences handed to them—publishers of employee newsletters distribute their publication to staff; publishers of alumni newsletters, to graduates; and publishers of church newsletters, to its members. Publishers of subscription newsletters, however, must actively seek out readers if they are to survive. For these publishers, the task of finding readers never ends. Even if they meet their first-year circulation goals, they must continue working hard to keep their readers interested enough to want to renew their subscriptions; and they must continue looking for new readers to replace those who don't. For publishers of marketing newsletters, finding customers for their products or donors to their cause is an ongoing task.

Remember that the first goal of any marketing plan should be to focus on the target audience. Take a cue from the Hollywood studios, who advertise new films through previews. They show these coming attractions at movie theaters before the featured films, because they know that people who are at the movies today are the ones most likely to come back tomorrow. They also preview new film releases on television programs that attract the same people who are likely to find those films appealing. Likewise, you can direct your marketing focus on your target audience by appealing to them through the publications they read, the Internet sites they visit, the mailing lists they are on, and the associations they've joined.

The number of subscriptions a marketing tactic brings is not your only concern. Selling your newsletter cost effectively is another very important goal of your plan. You must calculate what it's costing you to bring in each of those subscriptions. An ad in a national magazine might bring in a slew

If you promote your newsletter through different marketing methods—direct mail, advertising, telemarketing, Internet marketing—be sure to set up a system for evaluating which method generates the best response.

of new subscriptions, but the price of the ad may be so high that you'll lose a great deal of money on the deal.

Some publishers don't expect to make a profit from their newsletters, particularly if they are free publications that are used to promote other products and services, or to attract donations to their nonprofit organizations. If you fall into this category, you must be particularly wary of the costs of finding readers. If your marketing budget is very low or nonexistent, the marketing methods presented later in this chapter offer inexpensive suggestions for gaining publicity.

For any marketing method, you'll want to set up a system for gathering data on its effectiveness. For instance, if you advertise in magazines, you can print a code on the reply coupon to determine which ad in which publication drew the most responses. If you promote your newsletter online, you might consider using a different e-mail address for responses on each ad or website, so you can determine which ones are working best. If you keep track of the code for each subscriber in your database, down the line you can also determine which marketing techniques generated the most loyal subscribers, based upon their renewal rates.

In this chapter, you'll discover some commonly used newsletter marketing strategies—direct mail, advertising, telemarketing, and Internet marketing, as well as approaches like soliciting media coverage and distributing sample copies. No one method is right for every newsletter; you may have to test several techniques until you hit on the ones that work for you.

DIRECT MAIL

Traditionally, subscription newsletter publishers have achieved the best marketing results through *direct mail*. With this method, subscription solicitations are sent directly to individuals at their homes or offices. Although the effectiveness of direct mail has suffered in recent years as readers have become increasingly swamped with solicitations, it is still the method of choice for many publishers.

Using direct mail marketing to enroll subscribers to your newsletter involves the following steps: obtaining mailing lists of people who have an interest in the subject matter, preparing a sales offer, mailing it out, and evaluating the results. Although direct mail can be very effective, if you are not experienced with it, be careful. Even minor oversights can lead to serious, expensive mistakes. So unless you know what you're doing, you would be well advised to get some help with the process. Hire a consultant, attend a seminar, or at least read a few books before conducting a campaign. The US Postal Service provides information about direct mail on its website (*www.usps.gov/directmail/welcome.htm*) as does the Direct Marketing Association (*www.the-dma.org*).

The number-one key to a successful direct mail campaign is using the right mailing list. It is more important than the cost of the subscriptions or the design and content of the sales literature in your mailer. Direct marketers claim that the right list can draw up to ten times as many customers as the wrong one.

In the following section, I'll cover the basics of direct mail. This involves finding a market, using house and/or rented mailing lists, constructing an offer, and designing and writing your direct mail piece.

Finding a Market

Whether or not you can realize a profit on your subscription newsletter depends on the *payback* in subscription revenue you can achieve from your promotions. The potential payback, in turn, depends on the size of your newsletter's market, the cost of promoting your publication to that market, and the subscription price the market will accept.

According to Patricia Wysocki, executive director of the Newsletter and Electronic Publishers Association, a business-to-business newsletter needs a potential market of at least 20,000, of which it can expect to reach 10 to 15 percent. A general-interest consumer newsletter has a much larger market than a narrowly focused professional newsletter; but, as you will see, the larger market for the consumer newsletter does not guarantee greater profits.

How do you determine the size of your market? By researching the size of mailing lists available for it (more on finding mailing lists later in this chapter). If you can't find or compile lists of the people in your market, your market does not exist.

The cost of promoting your newsletter and the subscription price the market will accept for it will determine your potential payback. Subscription price depends on whether you are targeting a professional or a consumer audience. Professional subscribers, whose employers usually foot the bill, are willing to pay more for a newsletter than consumers, who pay out of their own pockets. In addition, professional subscription newsletters typically offer information that is not available elsewhere. This gives them greater value to subscribers than consumer newsletters,

When preparing to launch a direct mail campaign, you can determine the size of your market by researching available mailing lists. If you cannot find or compile lists of the people in your market, take it as a sure sign that your market doesn't exist.

Response rates for direct mail campaigns vary, ranging from a fraction of a percentage point to 5 percent or more. The mailing list used, the cost of the subscription, and the type of offer proposed are all response-rate factors.

which compete with numerous other mass market publications on the same topic. As Howard Penn Hudson points out in *Publishing Newsletters*, it's difficult for consumer newsletters to make a profit. Even though its market for potential subscribers is huge, a consumer newsletter must be priced low. Furthermore, the cost of promoting this type of publication is very high. Let's look at an example.

When you do a direct mailing, the return on your investment depends on the percentage of the people you solicit who actually buy subscriptions. This is known as your *response rate*. Response rates vary from a fraction of a percentage point to 5 percent or more, depending on the list used, the price of the subscription, and the type of offer (a three-month free trial subscription versus a discounted one-year subscription, for example).

Let's compare the differences in direct mailing costs between a professional and a consumer newsletter. Cost factors for each publication include renting or compiling mailing lists, as well as writing, designing, printing, and mailing the direct mail package. Except for writing and designing, all of these costs will increase as the number of packages you mail increases.

We'll say that the professional newsletter can charge $200 per year for a subscription, and the consumer newsletter can charge $40. For both publications, your plan is to send out a mailing to 50,000 prospective subscribers. We'll assume that your mailing list will draw a 2-percent response rate, which translates into 1,000 subscriptions (.02 response rate x 50,000 mailings = 1,000 subscriptions).

Your income from the direct mailing of the professional newsletter would work out to $200,000 ($200 per subscription x 1,000 subscriptions = $200,000). For the consumer newsletter, it would be only $40,000 ($40 per subscription x 1,000 subscriptions = $40,000). Yet you spent the same amount on the direct mailing for both.

You might respond by saying, "Well, since there are more potential subscribers out there for my consumer newsletter, I'll simply invest in a larger mailing." But to match the $200,000 income of the professional newsletter, you would need to sell five times as many subscriptions. (The consumer newsletter costs one-fifth of the professional one—$40 instead of $200—so you would have to send direct mail to five times as many people.) Not only would you spend much more money than you would to solicit the professional audience, if you achieved five times the number of subscribers, your costs to print and mail each issue of your newsletter would be far greater as well. The same $200,000 in income for the professional and consumer newsletters translates into far lower (if any) profits for the consumer newsletter after these higher promotional and production expenses are paid. So, even though the size of the market is smaller, the potential for profit is higher for professional newsletters.

The goal of direct mail is twofold. As you have seen, selling subscriptions is one goal. Gathering names of prospects for future mailings is the other. Many newsletter publishers are satisfied to break even or make a small return on their mailings. They know that later on they can reap bigger profits when these customers renew their subscriptions. Selling renewals is far less expensive than selling subscriptions. Instead of single-digit response rates, publishers often realize rates of more than 50 percent on renewal mailings.

Once you know your market, the next step is finding out if mailing lists of people in your target audience exist. You can either rent them or compile house lists.

Using House Lists

House lists are mailing lists you create yourself. They include your current customers as well as anyone who has requested information about your newsletter or other products you sell. House lists also contain people whose subscriptions to your newsletter have expired, and those who have responded to previous mailings you have done using rented lists. (When you rent an outside mailing list, you are allowed to add the names of any responders to your house list.) People who have registered on your website should be added to your house lists as well. (Be sure to clearly indicate how you will use the personal information that people provide when they register.) Acquaintances from trade associations you belong to and conferences and seminars you've attended are other additions to your house list.

Elaine Floyd, in *Marketing With Newsletters,* suggests that if you're publishing a marketing newsletter to promote your company's products or your nonprofit's services, your house list should also include your suppliers and vendors, such as accountants, lawyers, bankers, subcontractors, print shops, and mailing houses. She also recommends including your employees, so they know what your customers are reading. You may be able to expand your house list by swapping names with companies that target a similar audience but sell noncompeting products. For example, if you publish a newsletter for elementary school teachers, you might trade mailing lists with a textbook publisher.

House mailing lists include current and former subscribers, people who have requested information from you, and anyone who has responded to your mailings from a rented list. Visitors who have registered on your website and industry acquaintances are other possible house list additions, as are your suppliers and vendors.

Before adding names to your list, always check for restrictions on their use. Don't assume that you can use a list just because you can get your hands on the names and addresses. Many associations and clubs do not permit the use of their members' names and contact information for purposes that are not related to the business of their organization. Members can become irate if their names are misused.

If you use house lists, you'll avoid paying fees for list rental, but you'll need to devote staff time to creating and maintaining your list. You'll also have to purchase database software and pay for an address correction service to maintain current mailing addresses (more on this in Chapter 9). If you don't have the time for these tasks, you can hire an outside vendor to maintain your house list.

Using Rented Lists

Response lists contain names of people who have previously responded to a direct mail offer. They are more expensive to rent than compiled lists, which include names gathered from sources such as telephone books, industry directories, and conference attendees.

If you are just starting out in newsletter publishing, you may not have a house list, or it may be too small to generate enough subscribers. In such cases, you can use a list created by someone else. I call these *rented lists*, because most list owners don't allow you to purchase them, but you can rent them for each mailing.

There are two types of rented lists: compiled and response. *Compiled lists* are gathered from telephone directories, lists of association members, lists of conference or seminar attendees, industry directories, public records, and the like. *Response lists* contain the names of people who have already responded to direct mail marketing, such as mail order buyers, magazine subscribers, and people who have requested free literature in response to a mailing. Response lists almost always draw more customers than compiled lists, so they cost more to rent.

Finding Lists to Rent

Mailing list *owners, managers,* and *brokers* are the main sources for finding lists to rent. Owners are the originators of the lists. For example, the owner of a list of people who attended a pharmaceutical seminar is the pharmaceutical company that sponsored the seminar. The owner of a list of members of a petroleum industry trade association would be the association itself. Some owners handle the rental of their lists themselves, while others hire list managers to manage and market them. Still others use list brokers, just as a homeowner uses a real estate broker to rent or sell his house. List owners and managers have a financial interest in the renting of their own lists, while brokers are paid a commission (by the owners) for the lists they rent. Brokers work with you, helping to identi-fy appropriate lists. They also know where to get them and how they have performed for other direct marketers. Brokers will also take care of the administrative details of renting the list, from verifying information about a list to gaining approval of your mail piece from the list owner. You can find list brokers online, in the Yellow Pages, and through direct marketing periodicals such as *DM News, Direct*, and *Target Marketing*.

One obvious advantage of using house lists is that you don't have to pay for rented ones. You will, however, have to devote time to maintaining the entries. This means updating addresses, adding new names, and deleting others.

Direct Marketing List Source, published by SRDS Media Solutions, is a detailed source of information for list brokers, managers, and own-ers. Browsing through this book, which may be available at your public library, can also give you an idea of the types of lists that are avail-able for rent. And check the websites of the American List Counsel (*www.amlist.com*) and Edith Roman Associates (*www.edithroman. com*) for information on available lists.

Understanding List Data

Before deciding to rent a list, it's important to evaluate it properly. The owner, manager, or broker should provide you with detailed informa-tion about the list, which usually comes on a *data card*. Figure 5.1 on page 110 is a mailing list data card from the American List Counsel for its data-base of accountants. Although the information on data cards may vary from list to list, this sample card is fairly typical, and includes the fol-lowing:

1. Size/total number of people on the list. If you are going to be run-ning a test mailing of say, 10,000 names, and that mailing is successful, you'll want to be sure the number of names on the total list is large enough to continue your direct mail campaign.

As you can see from Figure 5.1, the total file contains 505,800 names and addresses of accountants. Within this list, a more specific listing of 3,200 accountants at "Big 8" firms" is also available, as well 362,800 names of CPAs only.

2. Price of the list. Typically, mailing lists are rented on a per-thousand name basis. In our example, the price is $60 per thousand names.

3. Audience profile. This includes an overview of the types of people found on the list, including the various selectable, more specific listings. In this sample list, 134,900 of the addresses provided are at a place of business, and the rest are home addresses. This section also indicates that you can select subsets of the list like CPAs, small firms, and female practitioners.

Figure 5.1
Sample Mailing List Data Card
This data card from the American List Counsel provides detailed information on its mailing list of accountants.

- Size of list.
- Cost per thousand names.
- Audience profile.
- Additional list information.
- Type of labels or computer media on which the list is available.
- Available criteria for tailoring lists.
- Payment, cancellation fees, and other terms.

ACCOUNTANTS DATABASE

ALC's Accountants Database puts you in touch with over 500,000 accounting professionals.

① KEY SEGMENTS ②

505,800	Total File	$60/M
3,200	Accountants at "Big 8" Firms	$60/M
362,800	CPA Only	$60/M

③ AUDIENCE PROFILE

We've expanded our accountants list to include non-accountants in the tax preparation field. CPAs are now distinguishable from the rest of the file. IRS electronic filers and tax preparers are also separately selectable. Over 243,000 records have phone numbers and the file includes more that 185,000 women.

134,900	Business Address	83,500	Small Firms (2-10 Employees)
370,900	Home (3-Line) Address	164,200	Female Practitioners

MARKETING INSIGHT

Accountants perform a broad range of accounting, auditing, tax and consulting activities for their clients who may be corporations, governments, nonprofit organizations or individuals. Almost all states require CPAs and Public Accountants to take continuing professional education courses for renewal of their licenses, so these accountants are great prospects for continuing education mailings. They are also responsive to offers for financial publications, accounting software, and other products or services that will help them stay abreast of technology relating to their field, and changes in tax law.

TERMS AND CONDITIONS

Allow 1-3 working days to process order. Payment due 30 days from mail date. Any order received at ALC is subject to a flat cancellation fee. Net name arrangement negotiable. File run against NCOA. 20% commission to authorized brokers on base rate. Unlimited usage, 2x base/minimum plus selection plus output material charges. **⑦**

USAGE

- Kiplinger Washington
- MBNA America
- Practitioners Publishing
- Prentice-Hall
- Quotemaster USA
- Real World Training

Toll-Free 1-800-ALC-LIST

Gender:	70% Male
	30% Female
Minimum:	5,000
Source:	Directories
Updates:	Semi-Annually **④**

Addressable Material:
- PS Labels
- Cheshire Labels **⑤**
- 9TR 1600 BPI Tape
- Diskette
- E-Mail

SELECTION CHARGES ⑥

State/SCF/Zip	$6/M
Specialty	$6/M
Gender	$6/M
Key Code	$2/M
PS Labels	$7.50/M
Mag Tape	$25/F
3x5 Cards	$25/M
Sheet List	$15/M
Phone Numbers	$15/M
Diskette	$25/F
Unlimited Use	$120/M

ALC Contact:
Maria Scarpulla, x2980
maria.scarpulla@alc.com
(609) 580-2980
Lisa Edelstein, x2909
lisa.edelstein@alc.com
Fax Orders To:
(609) 580-2866

ALC
American List Counsel
data management for the digital age

www.amlist.com Fax 609-580-2866
4300 US Highway 1 CN-5219, Princeton, NJ 08543

4. Additional list information. This provides additional information on the list, such as the percentage of males and females listed, the minimum number of names per order, and the source of the names. Our sample data card shows that the mailing list contains 70 percent males and 30 percent females; the source of the names is from directories; and the database is updated twice a year. It also states that 5,000 names is the minimum rental amount.

5. Addressable material. This section notes on which type of mailing labels or computer media (diskette, e-mail) the list is available.

6. Selection charges. This area provides further criteria for tailoring your list. For example, you can choose names of accountants from certain states or names of female accountants only; you can also have your list key coded or addressed on pressure-sensitive (PS) labels. (More information on these and other criteria is detailed under the following section, "Estimating List Rental Costs.") Each of these selections comes with an additional charge. For example, according to this sample card, if you want your list to include females only, it would cost an additional $6 for every thousand names.

7. Terms and conditions. This includes information such as expected order processing time, payment terms, and cancellation policies.

By closely examining this data, you can make an educated guess as to whether the list might address your market.

Estimating List Rental Costs

List owners quote the price of renting their lists at a cost per thousand names. If the data card says the price is $175/M, it means you'll pay $175 for every thousand names you rent (most owners set a minimum of 3,000 to 5,000 names per order). In addition, you will be charged for any selection criteria, such as a listing of names by state, specialty, or gender.

You will also be charged for key coding. A key-coded list includes a special number that appears within the name and address of each person on the list. That number, which serves as a code, will appear on the reply cards you receive, indicating which mailing the card came from. This will help you track which mailings were the most successful.

Let's say you want to rent 5,000 names from the "Accountants Database" illustrated in Figure 5.1, and you want only accountants from certain states. You also want the list to be key coded and on pressure-sensitive labels. You would be charged as follows:

5,000 names @ $60/M	$ 60.00 × 5 = $300.00
State selection @ $6/M	$ 6.00 × 5 = 60.00
Key coding @ $2/M	$ 2.00 × 5 = 10.00
Pressure sensitive labels @ $7.50/M	$ 7.50 × 5 = 37.50
Total rental	$407.50

Budget your money wisely. When launching a direct mail campaign with a mailing list you have never used before, run a small test mailing first. If the response rate is acceptable, you can roll out a subsequent mailing to a larger portion of the list.

Of course, when budgeting for the entire direct mail campaign, you'll have to include the costs of designing and printing the direct mail pieces themselves, as well as the price of postage.

Testing and Rolling Out

Before investing tens of thousands of dollars in a mailing to a large list you've never used before, conduct a *test mailing:* mail to a small portion of a list you have selected, and then evaluate your response rate. This will help you determine if the list is worth investing in further. Typically, test mailings are sent to at least 5,000 names to assure some statistical validity. (Also, 5,000 is often the minimum number of names a list owner will allow you to rent.) An experienced list broker can help you decide how many names to include in your test.

If you achieve an acceptable response rate in the test mailing, you can then rent a much larger portion of the list and *roll out* a mailing to those names as well. Many direct marketers recommend reusing a successful list again and again with increasing frequency until the response rate declines to a point at which the mailings are no longer profitable. Also remember, when you rent a list, you are allowed to use the names for only one mailing (unless you rent it again). However, when people respond to your mailing, you are allowed to put their names on your house list, which you can use as often as you like.

Constructing the Direct Mail Offer

Before you decide whether to mail out a letter, brochure, business reply card, sample issue, or some combination of these items to your prospective subscribers, you have to decide what you are selling. The answer may seem obvious—you are selling your newsletter. Yes and no: you are not just selling the newsletter, you are selling a subscription to it. And a subscription can come in many flavors and varieties. It can last for one year or three years. It may carry a money-back guarantee or come with a free industry report. The price may be reduced for a limited time only.

It can be difficult to predict which type of offer will draw the most responses. For this reason, you might consider sending out half of a mailing with one offer and the other half with another. To determine which offer is more successful, key code the reply cards to reflect the offer they contain. Typical subscription offers include one or more of the following to attract potential subscribers:

■ **Trial subscriptions.** A free or paid short-term subscription, usually for one to three months. This allows potential subscribers to evaluate the quality of your newsletter by reading several issues. Follow these trial issues with a series of letters encouraging the subscriber to renew. A variant on the trial subscription is the *forced free trial*, in which you send out a series of free, unsolicited trial issues.

■ **Discounts.** Lower-than-normal priced subscription (perhaps within a certain time limit) that returns to the normal price upon renewal. Some publishers offer discounted charter subscriptions to those who subscribe at the newsletter's inception.

■ **Optional terms.** The longer the subscription term a responder chooses, the deeper the discount he receives. So, if the newsletter costs $100 for one year, you might offer two years for $190 and three years for $270.

■ **Gifts and premiums.** Responders receive a gift if they subscribe or request more information. To assure that the responders have potential to become buyers (and aren't just responding because they want a free mouse pad), choose a gift, such as a special report, that is related to your newsletter's subject matter.

Along with any special subscription deal you offer, be sure to include the payment terms. For instance, you must specify if payment must be enclosed with the response or if you will bill the subscriber later. Do you accept credit card payment? If so, which cards do you accept? If the subscriber is paying by check or money order, to whom should payment be made?

Whichever deal you offer will depend on your budget and the sensitivity of your audience to price. Again, trial and error—testing one type of offer on half of your mailing list and another on the other half—may give you the best indication.

Writing and Designing the Direct Mail Piece

Once you've decided on the type of offer you want to sell through direct mail, you can begin thinking about how to design the sales literature itself. The direct mail piece on page 114 serves as an example. It includes all of the basic components, including the sales letter, reply card, and reply envelope.

If you're new to direct mail, it is helpful to work with a direct mail writer or consultant. You'll find a listing of marketing consultants and

Along with using the right mailing list, designing an effective direct mail piece is a key factor for a successful campaign. Working with a direct mail writer or consultant is recommended if you are new to this type of marketing method.

The components of a good direct mail piece must meet certain criteria, as seen in this sample.

1 A good sales letter attracts attention, arouses interest, and creates desire.

■ First page has an eye-catching headline that also highlights a special offer.

■ Informs readers why the newsletter is important specifically for them.

2 Reply envelope is sized to easily fit the reply card and contains:

■ Preprinted mailing address.

■ Lined area for subscriber's return address.

■ Message of urgency to processing department to create sense of importance.

■ Website address on back flap.

3 Reply card includes all pertinent information.

■ Name of newsletter.

■ Subscriber's name and address (preprinted in this example).

■ Price.

■ Special offers.

■ Subscription length.

■ Payment method options.

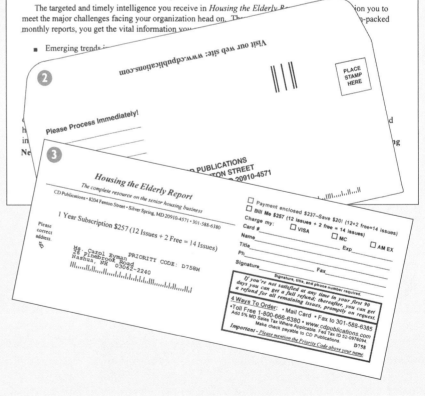

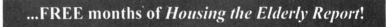

Discover the _most_ complete resource for the business of housing the elderly.

And get...

...FREE months of _Housing the Elderly Report_!

Dear Senior Housing Professional:

Here's your best opportunity to gain the same powerful information advantage that hundreds of your colleagues in the senior housing and elderly care profession already enjoy--_Housing the Elderly Report_!

The targeted and timely intelligence you receive in _Housing the Elderly R_____ion you to meet the major challenges facing your organization head on. _____-packed monthly reports, you get the vital information y_____

■ Emerging trends

Visit our web site: www.cdpublications.com

PLACE STAMP HERE

Please Process Immediately!

CD PUBLICATIONS
TON STREET
20910-4571

Housing the Elderly Report
The complete resource on the senior housing business
CD Publications • 8204 Fenton Street • Silver Spring, MD 20910-4571 • 301-588-6380

1 Year Subscription $257 (12 Issues + 2 Free = 14 Issues)

Please correct address.

Ms. Carol Eyman   PRIORITY CODE: D758M
26 Pinebrook Road
Nashua, NH 03062-2240

☐ Payment enclosed $237–Save $20! (12+2 free=14 issues)
☐ Bill Me $257 (12 issues + 2 free = 14 issues)
Charge my:
Card #
☐ VISA   ☐ MC   ☐ AM EX
Name
Title   Exp
Ph.
Signature   Fax
Signature, title, and phone number required.

If you're not satisfied at any time in your first 90 days you can get a full refund; thereafter, you can get a refund for all remaining issues, promptly on request.

4 Ways To Order: • Mail Card • Fax to 301-588-6385
•Toll Free 1-800-666-6380 • www.cdpublications.com
Add 5% MD Sales Tax Where Applicable. Fed Tax ID 52-0976094.
Make check payable to CD Publications.

Important - Please mention the Priority Code above your name

D758

copywriters who have newsletter experience on the website of the Newsletter and Electronic Publishers Association (*www.newsletters.org/ page.cfm?name=recsuplist*). You can also get some help with designing direct mail pieces from the US Postal Service. Its website (*www.usps.gov/ directmail/templates*) offers Microsoft Word and Quark XPress templates you can download.

When writing and designing direct mail pieces, marketers follow four basic steps to generate positive responses. They remember these steps with the acronym AIDA: (1) attract **A**ttention, (2) arouse **I**nterest, (3) create **D**esire, and (4) call to **A**ction. The direct mail package can achieve this purpose if it includes the right materials that are prepared properly. What follows next are the items commonly found in a direct mail package for newsletter offers.

Sales Letter

Along with an eye-catching outer envelope, a well-written sales letter with a catchy headline is a key element for *attracting the attention* of potential subscribers (step 1 of AIDA). Newsletter sales letters often reach four to eight pages—longer than the typical direct mail letter. The theory behind this length is that people who are not interested in the newsletter will promptly throw the entire mailing away, while those who *are* interested will want as much information as possible before signing a check.

The sales letter also *arouses the interest* of the readers, fulfilling step 2 of AIDA, by emphasizing how they will benefit from reading your newsletter. Don't spend time writing about how you came up with the idea for the newsletter or what you go through to produce each issue—most readers aren't interested. What they do want to know is what's in it for them. Tell the reader how subscribing will increase sales, satisfy customers, or improve employee productivity.

The sales letter also fulfills step 3 of AIDA by *creating desire* in the reader. How? By describing your offer—a trial subscription, free gift, special discount, or whatever else you may be offering—in an enticing way. It should be an offer the reader won't want to pass up!

Reply Card

The reply card fulfills step 4 of AIDA by *calling readers to action*. It also makes it easy for potential subscribers to order your newsletter. The reply card should contain all of the information subscribers will need if they throw out the other pieces of the mailing. It should include the

Memorize the following rhyme to help stay focused on the customer as you write a sales letter:

Tell me quick and
tell me true
Or else, my friend,
to heck with you
Not how this product
came to be
But what the darn thing
does for me.

price, length, special discounts, and any other terms of the subscription, along with simple instructions for placing an order. The reply card must also have a place for subscribers to provide their names and addresses, indicate the desired offer, and fill out payment information such as credit card number and expiration date. When sending out the offer, you can choose to apply the mailing label to the reply card and insert it so the label shows through a window envelope. This way, subscribers don't have to bother filling in their names and addresses when preparing the reply card.

Subscribers may want to fax you their orders. For this reason, be sure to print your reply card on light-colored stock in a size that will fit in their fax machines.

Reply Envelope

As a courtesy to potential subscribers, reply envelopes for consumer newsletter offers are generally postage paid.

Usually, the reply card is designed to fit inside a reply envelope, so subscribers can enclose a check. Even if they choose to pay by credit card, they'll need the envelope to hide their account information. For consumer newsletter offers, reply envelopes are usually postage paid, to spare the subscriber the inconvenience of finding and paying for a stamp. For professional newsletter offers, the envelope may or may not be postage paid. Some publishers feel that it isn't necessary to prepay the postage on envelopes, particularly for subscribers whose employers are paying for the subscription and not likely to be concerned with this cost. Furthermore, the envelope may get lost or misplaced when the employee sends the reply card to the accounting or purchasing department for payment.

Outer Envelope

The purpose of the outer envelope is to attract attention and stand out among a stack of mail. It should entice the recipient to open it. To help achieve this goal, on the front or back of the envelope print teaser copy— a phrase or sentence that entices the recipient to open the envelope and see what's inside. For professional newsletters, keep in mind that administrative assistants are often the first ones to see the mail. You'll want your envelope to look important enough for them to pass on to their bosses.

Direct marketers are always coming up with different techniques— from applying first class postage to using oversized envelopes to excluding their return addresses—to get their envelopes opened and, therefore, improve their response rates. Only testing, and perhaps the advice of a direct mail consultant, can determine whether these techniques will work for you.

Optional Items

In addition to the standard items included in a direct mail package for newsletter sales, a few other items are sometimes part of the package as well. For instance, some packages include a brochure, which might contain testimonials from satisfied subscribers, biographies of the writers and editors of the newsletter, or pictures and descriptions of gifts or premiums that are part of the offer. Another option is a lift letter, so called because it tends to "lift" response. The outside of a lift letter usually says something like "Read this only if you are still undecided." Inside, the letter offers additional reasons for subscribing, and it is usually signed by the publisher of the newsletter.

You might think inserting a sample issue in the direct mail package is a good idea, but it is not recommended. For starters, it can be expensive. Furthermore, the issue may not show potential subscribers the variety of editorial content that they would receive over the course of a full subscription. A better option would be to include a one-year index of the newsletter, giving readers a more comprehensive idea of the material contained in the publication.

Adding a brochure, lift letter, or premium offer to your direct mail package may be a good way to increase the response rate. Including a sample issue of your newsletter, however, is not recommended. It can substantially increase your mailing cost and, more important, it will not fairly reflect the variety of topics covered by your newsletter over the course of a year.

After reading through this section on direct mail, you can see how launching such a campaign can be an effective marketing tool for gaining newsletter readership. As you have also seen, it requires thorough consideration and serious attention in many areas—zeroing in on the right market, finding and using the most effective mailing lists, making an enticing offer to potential subscribers, and designing an irresistible mailer. Done properly, a direct mail campaign can garner successful results.

ADVERTISING

Another way to find subscribers for your publication is through advertisements. If you are considering this route, keep in mind that it is less important to advertise in publications with large circulations than it is to advertise in smaller publications that reach people who might be interested in your newsletter's subject matter. If you run ads in mass market publications like large newspapers and consumer magazines, it's a good bet that you'll be disappointed by your response rate—particularly in light of the high prices you'll be paying for such ads. Even advertising in a small local newspaper, which charges lower advertising rates, can be fruitless (unless your newsletter has general, local appeal). Instead, identify the media outlets—be they print publications, Internet sites, or other media—that are most likely to reach your target audience.

Print Ads

Newspapers and magazines that are read by members of your target audience may be good sources of subscribers for your newsletter, and, therefore, good places to run your ads. To find such publications, visit a business library or a large public library and ask the reference librarian to direct you to publications directories. These references list publications by subject matter or industry. Examples of publications directories include *SRDS Business Publication Advertising Source, Consumer Magazine Advertising Source,* and *Ulrich's Periodicals Directory.*

When you have decided on the periodicals you feel are likely avenues for reaching your audience, consider hiring a professional copywriter to create an attention-getting print advertisement. Be sure the ad includes a response mechanism, whether it's your toll-free telephone number or a coupon for the reader to clip and mail back to you. Also consider offering either a free trial subscription or another free or low-priced product, such as a sample issue or an industry report that is related to your newsletter's subject matter. This strategy will provide you with qualified leads—names, addresses, and telephone numbers of people who are interested enough in your topic to respond to your offer. Once you have this information, you can then follow up with a subscription solicitation via direct mail or telephone.

House Ads

Because people other than subscribers may read your newsletter, insert a subscription reply card in every issue. Be sure it contains all of your contact information, including your e-mail address.

I am always amazed that I can pull a half dozen subscription reply cards out of the various magazines I receive in the mail. They are usually inserted adjacent to what is called a *house ad*—an advertisement for the publication itself. Considering their widespread use, house ads and reply cards must work.

Not every reader of your newsletter will be a subscriber, so be sure that each issue contains a reply card. On it, include your mailing address, as well as a phone number, fax number, and/or e-mail address for readers who want to respond quickly.

Subscribers to professional newsletters often share printed versions with (or forward electronic versions to) colleagues or friends. You can encourage readers to pass along your print publication by including a "route to" box on the back. Readers can fill in the names of their coworkers and route the newsletter to them via interoffice mail. You can also encourage readers to pass along your electronic newsletter simply by asking them to forward it to others who might be interested. You might also include a stipulation that they must forward the publication in its entirety. This way, the "forwardees" will have all the contact information they need if they are interested in subscribing.

Internet Ads

Banner ads (graphical ads that usually appear along the top, bottom, or sides of the computer screen), *pop-up ads* (small boxed ads that "pop up" on top of other windows), and simple *text ads* are common forms of Internet advertising. Many Internet users find pop-up ads as annoying as e-mail spam. As a result, many people disable them from appearing on their computers. For these reasons, I don't recommend using pop-ups to advertise your newsletter.

When advertising online, avoid using pop-ups. Many people find these ads annoying and, therefore, disable them from appearing on their screens. Banner and text ads are much more effective.

On the other hand, banners ads can be worthwhile if they are used properly. In a marketing seminar held by ContentBiz, an e-mail newsletter that covers new-media industry news, eight Internet publishers discussed successful techniques for marketing subscriptions to e-mail newsletters and websites. These experts believed that banner ads are productive. However, they all agreed that simply placing them on general-interest websites is not effective. Instead, they suggest linking this type of ad to keywords on search engines. This means, for example, if your newsletter covers sailing, it would be a good idea to buy an ad that appears only on the search engine page if a person entered "sailing" as a keyword. Placing banner ads on other subject-related websites can also be effective.

The experts also agreed that placing ads in e-mail newsletters that are related to your subject matter, particularly those distributed through paid rather than free subscriptions, yield a good number of responses for the cost of the ad.

Other Advertising

Advertising on radio and television stations that serve general audiences is not recommended for your newsletter, which is aimed at a specific group of people. You might, however, consider advertising on cable or satellite stations that run specialized programming (finances, golf, parenting, real estate, etc.) that may be more tightly targeted to your audience. Prices for advertising spots on these stations are also lower than those for general interest channels.

TELEMARKETING

Unlike a direct mail campaign, which can take months to prepare, launch, and assess, a telemarketing campaign can be completed quickly.

Telemarketing was severely restricted in 2003 with the implementation of the Do Not Call Registry. This registry prohibits most for-profit organizations from calling consumers who have placed their phone numbers on the list. However, business-to-business telemarketing is not subject to these restrictions, although calls by a business to home-based businesses and consultants may be restricted. In addition, telemarketing can be a "turn off" to prospects, who may not appreciate your phone calls interrupting their work or dinner.

Most subscription newsletter publishers use telemarketing in some way, says Patricia Wysocki of the Newsletter and Electronic Publishers Association. Many use it to solicit renewals. But if you decide on telemarketing as a means of selling your newsletter, first consider the following. You will need a well-targeted list of prospects. You will also have to charge high subscription prices to offset the expense of paying hourly fees or commissions to a professional telemarketing firm. If you have a large number of prospects, you may find it more cost effective to telemarket in-house.

One advantage of telemarketing is that you can complete a campaign quickly. Direct mail, on the other hand, can require up to three months for developing the package, printing and mailing it, renting a mailing list, and receiving responses. Another advantage is that speaking to prospects and subscribers on the phone allows you to get valuable feedback on whether or not your newsletter serves their needs.

You can find a list of recommended telemarketing consultants, as well as detailed information about the rules concerning the Do Not Call Registry, on the websites of the Newsletter and Electronics Publishers Association (*www.newsletters.org*) and the Direct Marketing Association (*www.the-dma.org*).

INTERNET MARKETING

Whether your newsletter is print or electronic, you can use the Internet to find readers. You can solicit subscriptions through e-mail and/or by promoting your publication on your company's or organization's website.

Soliciting on Your Website

If you publish your newsletter on the website of your company or organization, many of your prospects will be people who happen upon the site after finding it through a search engine. Make sure that it's easy for these surfers to subscribe to the newsletter by placing an online subscription form (or a link to one) on every page of your website. Remember, people who get to your site via a search engine will not necessarily arrive at the home page or even the main page of your newsletter. A few potential subscribers might be willing to navigate through two or three links to find the subscription form, but don't count on it. Better to place it right in front of their noses. And your subscription form doesn't have to be long. If your newsletter is free, the form can be a simple box in which subscribers can enter their e-mail address.

> When publishing a newsletter on the website of your company or organization, be sure to place an online subscription form on each page of the site. Many people who arrive at the site will get there through a search engine and may not necessarily end up on the home page or the first page of the newsletter.

Of course, before people can fill out your subscription form, you'll have to get them to visit your website in the first place. How do you increase traffic? One of the cheapest ways is by mentioning your web address as often as you can—on all printed matter like letterheads, business cards, invoices, and brochures; in the footers on each page of your printed newsletter; when you're interviewed by the media; and on the packaging for other products you sell.

In addition, you'll want to make sure that Internet search engines list your site whenever people search for content that is related to your newsletter. There are two ways to list your website, because there are two ways that search engines find sites. Some use the first method; some use the second; and many use both.

The first way of listing your website is to actively inform the search engines that it is out there—a process appropriately called submitting your site to the search engine. Through this process, your site is entered into the search engine's directory system. You've probably visited online search engines and noticed that they display a directory of categories (arts and entertainment, business, computers, travel, and so forth) under which you can search for the information you need. Sites are placed into these categories by human beings—either the person who submits the site or people who work for the search engine company.

To submit your site, visit the main page of various search engines, such as Google (*www.google.com*) or Yahoo! (*www.yahoo.com*). Look for a

Online Newsletters
To Charge or Not to Charge?

As the Internet has evolved, the number of people who use it has grown exponentially—and generally, they expect to use it without charge.

Publishers of print material are much more successful in charging for their publications than online publishers are. Generally, online newsletter publishers do not (and should not) view their publications as major sources of revenue, but rather as a means of promoting other products or services. This offers them the potential to generate a small revenue stream through advertising and a low number of paid subscriptions.

So, the question is: *Can* you get readers to pay for your online newsletter? The answer is: Sometimes. The next question is: How?

A number of online newsletter publishers have been successful finding paying subscribers by implementing a few techniques. For instance, some offer free newsletters consisting of brief summaries or teaser articles that let readers know more information is available to paid subscribers. Others use a similar technique in which they offer a few complete articles free of charge, while advertising the availability of additional articles for paid subscribers. Many publishers allow free access to their website's search facilities, enabling readers to search through a listing of the newsletter's articles and other material. The ability to read the articles, however, is available only to paid subscribers.

As another alternative, some publishers of print newsletters have begun to ease into online distribution without sacrificing revenues by offering their subscribers a discount when they order the online edition instead of the printed form. Some give subscribers the option of paying a bit more to subscribe to both the print and online editions. Another method of getting readers to pay for online newsletters (although a less successful one) is to publish the newsletter free for several months or even a year, and then convert it to a paid publication.

Readers may also perceive more value in an online newsletter that comes in portable document format (PDF). This type of formatting retains all of the attractive fonts and graphics that appear in a print publication. When readers print out this type of online newsletter, it looks very much like the version they would receive in the mail.

Although Internet users have been spoiled by the wide availability of free content online, one or more of the techniques just described may prove successful in attracting a continual stream of paying readers to your publication.

link that says something along the lines of "Submit a site" or "Add your site." Click on it, then follow the directions. Each search engine will ask you to submit a category (they provide extensive listings) for your site. Be very specific. For example, if you publish a newsletter on the commercial marine industry, dig down through several category levels before listing your site. So, instead of listing it under one basic category, such as: "business-and-economy/business-to-business/transportation," you'll do better by listing it more specifically in the "business-and-economy/business-to-business/transportation/maritime/newsletters" category. If you aren't sure where to list your site, put it where several of your competitors are listed.

The second method by which search engines list websites is through a software program called a "crawler" or "spider," which searches for sites and lists them in an index. When a web surfer enters keywords into the search engine, the engine looks at this index and ranks the pages based on their relevance to the keywords. Then it displays a list of the pages, usually ten at a time, to the surfer. Your goal is to get ranked in the first ten hits (or at least in the first twenty) found by the search engine.

If you hire a web developer to create your web newsletter, ask her to help improve its chances of achieving a high ranking in search engine hits. Work with her to incorporate keywords and phrases into your web page that pertain to your newsletter. In our example, keywords such as "commercial marine industry," "tugboats," "fishing vessels," and "shipyards" might be appropriate.

If you develop the web pages yourself, you can increase the number of hits returned by search engines in several ways. First, place important keywords and phrases in both the headlines and the first twenty-five words on the page. Be aware that these search engines will not find keywords that are placed in image maps and other graphics—they must be part of the HTML. This means you should use ALT tags to add keywords to graphics. Another way of increasing hits is to include a TITLE tag in your HTML that expresses your subject matter in four or five keywords.

Most search engines offer both paid and free mechanisms for submitting your site. If you choose a free submission, it can take several weeks or even several months for your site to be listed. And many search engines don't accept free submissions from commercial sites. If you pay for a submission, your site will usually be listed in a matter of days. So you may want to consider allocating part of your marketing budget to search engine submission fees. For more information on increasing traffic to your website through search engine optimization, visit the site *www.searchenginewatch.com.*

Whether or not you create your own website, you can still hire a consultant to help you optimize your site for search engines. You can also pay a consultant to submit your sites to search engines, a process that can be tedious and time-consuming. More information on such services is listed in the Resources section beginning on page 323.

Placing significant keywords and phrases in both the headlines and the first twenty-five words of your online newsletter will result in an increased number of hits through search engines.

Soliciting Through E-Mail

Although soliciting your newsletter through e-mail might seem like an easy, inexpensive marketing method, it is likely to be viewed as spam. By doing so, you run the risk of losing both sales and your reputation.

You might view e-mail marketing as a low-cost alternative to direct mail. All you have to do is buy a list of e-mail addresses to solicit your newsletter subscriptions. Internet etiquette, however, frowns upon sending out unsolicited marketing e-mail, more commonly known as *spam*.

It's true that some e-mail lists contain addresses of people who have supposedly agreed to receive such mailings. Once upon a time, when they ordered a product on the Internet, signed up for an e-mail newsletter, or filled out some other type of website form, they checked a box indicating their interest in receiving other offers. Often, these boxes are already checked, and those who are filling out the form must actively remove the check mark (as instructed in the fine print) if they don't want the offers. Many users don't even notice the box, so they unwittingly add their e-mail addresses to mailing lists. Even those who check these boxes intentionally often forget they have done so, or they may fail to associate your offer with a long-forgotten form they once completed.

The point is this: when you send your solicitation to the addresses on an e-mail list, the word will soon get out to your audience—from colleague to colleague or through discussion groups or bulletin boards—that you are a spammer. Your sales and, more important, your reputation will suffer.

OTHER MARKETING METHODS

A number of effective marketing methods for newsletters, both print and online versions, are more subtle and sometimes overlooked. Some of these strategies include gaining public recognition of your expertise, distributing free samples, and networking with other businesses and publications in your field. Unlike most of the marketing methods discussed so far, many of these techniques can be implemented without spending a lot of money.

Solicit Media Coverage

For many publishers, one of the most effective forms of marketing is getting their newsletters mentioned in newspapers and magazines, or on radio and television. To make this happen, you have to contact the editors and/or producers who determine what their publications or programs cover. Using a press release, let them know about the launching of your newsletter, the results of an industry survey or forecast you've produced, or an important article you've published.

Just as you target direct mail campaigns to people who are interested in your subject matter, focus your media campaign on journalists who cover your subject matter. If you are successful, you may net yourself an appearance as a guest on a TV or radio show, or a profile in a print article. On the Internet, you can find a number of press-release distribution services, which will send your release to journalists who have indicated an interest in your subject matter. Most of these services charge several hundred dollars; however, the newswire service PRWeb (*www.prweb.com*) offers this service for free.

One key to gaining media coverage for your newsletter is to pitch it at a time when editors are looking for material on its topic. So be ready to write a press release whenever a news story breaks that relates to your newsletter's topic, or at any other time the information is salient, such as during a big trade show. You can also give free subscriptions to influential reporters and editors in your industry. If they read your newsletter regularly, they'll be more likely to write about what you report or turn to you when they need quotes from an expert in your field.

Build Your Credibility

You can build a reputation for your newsletter by making yourself and your writers and editors known as authorities on your subject matter. Contact the people who organize conferences and trade shows in your field and volunteer to give a presentation at the event. Be sure to include the name of your newsletter in the biographical information you provide to the organizer.

If you don't have public speaking experience, consider starting out by teaching adult education classes. Continuing education departments of colleges and universities are always looking for part-time teachers. Often you can suggest a topic and design a course or one-day seminar yourself. Your newsletter will benefit in several ways. After taking your course, your students will be impressed by your expertise and become likely subscribers; your name and biographical information will appear in the school's catalog, which will be read by your students as well as others who don't attend your class; and teaching will help keep you in touch with the needs and experiences of members of your newsletter's target audience—your students.

Writing articles for related publications will further enhance your

By sharing your knowledge and expertise on the subject matter of your newsletter, you can build your reputation as an authority. Write articles for related publications; volunteer to speak at conferences and trade shows in your field; design a course or seminar for an adult education class; and participate in online discussion groups.

reputation. If the publication cannot pay for your work, consider creative ways to barter it. Request that the article include your biography, information about ordering your newsletter, and a link to your newsletter's website. Perhaps you can place an ad in the publication in lieu of payment, or their staff can write an article that you can run in your newsletter.

You can also build your credibility by participating in online discussion groups and posting well-informed answers to the questions of participants. Some marketers suggest including a description of your newsletter and its website address as part of your signature in the e-mail messages you post. Just be cautious about doing so. As Chris Pirillo, author of *Poor Richard's E-Mail Publishing*, points out, members are often opposed to the use of discussion groups to promote commercial ventures. He recommends that you follow the guidelines of each group. If they don't prohibit it, you can add your website address to your signature once you have participated in the group for a while and established some credibility.

Distribute Sample Copies

Whenever you give out sample copies of your newsletter, be sure they include some means by which people can subscribe—a reply card, a coupon, a toll-free number, an e-mail address.

When you attend or speak at conferences, trade shows, or seminars, ask the organizer if you can rent a booth from which you can distribute free issues of your newsletter along with order forms. You are likely to see a higher response rate from this distribution method than you would with direct mail. This is because the people who pick up the samples, in addition to being members of your target audience, have shown interest by approaching your booth.

Even if you can't attend an event, the organizer may provide opportunities for you to promote your newsletter. For instance, if a packet of freebies is distributed to attendees, you may be able to include a sample copy of your newsletter in the packets. Although you'll have to pay a fee to the organizer for this opportunity, you'll avoid direct mail expenses like list rental and postage.

If you publish a nonsubscription marketing newsletter for customers of your retail business or clients of your professional practice, you can give out samples at the checkout counter of your store or in your waiting room or reception area. You can also distribute them along with other marketing literature you give to prospective clients and customers. Whenever you give out sample copies, make sure they contain a coupon, reply card, toll-free number, or some other means by which people can let you know they want to subscribe.

Marketing Advice from a Veteran

If longevity is a barometer of success, then Robert Ellis Smith has made it. Since 1974, he has been publishing *Privacy Journal,* a monthly newsletter based in Providence, Rhode Island, that reports on new technology and its impact on personal privacy.

Although longevity has brought visibility to his publication, Smith is still proactive about marketing. "My most successful marketing strategy has been making my own mailing lists," he says. "There simply are no lists for rent out there that define my market." He creates his lists from the attendee rosters he receives at conferences on privacy issues. By paying admission fees, Smith reasons, conference participants have already shown that they are willing to spend money for information about privacy, so there is a good chance they'll buy a subscription to *Privacy Journal.* His reasoning is sound, as evidenced by the impressive 6-percent response rates he typically achieves when mailing to his house list. His strategy is also cost-effective—attendee lists are usually provided to him free as a conference participant. And Smith never has to pay for these conferences; he attends either as a member of the press or as a speaker.

Bartering has played an important role in Smith's marketing plan. Often he exchanges his services as a conference speaker for a booth at the conference, where he can sell his newsletter and the numerous books he's published on privacy. When he can't attend a conference, he'll sometimes distribute a brochure for the event in one of his newsletter mailings. He does this in exchange for an unstaffed booth, where visitors can pick up sample copies of his newsletter and other marketing materials. These conference booths have been his second most effective source of sales.

What marketing advice does Smith have for the newsletter publisher who's just starting out? First, network with your peers. He finds that newsletter publishers are very open about sharing successes and failures with one another. During his early days of publishing, while still in law school in Washington, DC, Smith's most valuable source of advice was a small network of newsletter publishers called the Newsletter Association of America (which has since evolved into the Newsletter and Electronic Publishers Association).

Second, Smith advises taking a hands-on approach to marketing. When asked if he had ever tried a marketing tactic that went completely wrong, he recalled hiring some not-so-seasoned consultants to coordinate a direct mailing. Instead of relieving him of the marketing workload, they required an enormous amount of his time. Before they could write an effective sales letter, he had to explain his market, his field, and his publication. Then they rented mailing lists and sent out a mailing that cost him a lot of money and produced disappointing results. As a result of this experience, Smith cautions that newsletter publishers should never completely delegate copywriting for direct mailings. Publishers and their editorial staff know their niche market best.

Over the years, Smith has become widely known in the field (he wrote the definition of "privacy" for the *World Book Encyclopedia,* and he has testified before Congress on the subject), but he still actively seeks notice from the press. He provides free copies of his newsletter to a few reporters who he knows will quote him in their articles. He writes letters to the editors of large-circulation newspapers. He distributes press releases, like the one in which he ranked the fifty states into five tiers, based on the strength of their personal privacy laws. Associated Press picked up that story, netting *Privacy Journal* considerable publicity.

Swap Ads, Links, and Other Publicity

Networking with other businesses that share your audience, but don't directly compete with you, can be a fruitful way to gain publicity and market your newsletter. For example, if your publication is for administrators of hospital medical records, find a company that produces medical-records software and is willing to place your ad on its website in exchange for placing its ad on yours. Or you could simply swap links to each other's sites. (There's an added benefit to swapping links—having numerous sites that link to yours can improve its position on the results pages of search engines.)

Another option is to trade "co-registrations." At the bottom of your subscription order form, you can include a check box in which subscribers can indicate if they'd like to receive information about the other company's products. Likewise, the other company can include a check box on its order form for people who are interested in hearing more about your newsletter. Be specific about the type of information they will receive and from whom, so the subscriber doesn't think the information is junk mail or spam when it arrives.

When your newsletter mentions prominent companies, publications, trade organizations, and individuals in your industry, be sure to let them know. Often they will mention the coverage in their own publications or link to your article from their website, giving you greater exposure in turn.

Solicit Renewals

Offering high-quality editorial coverage of your newsletter's topic and providing first-rate customer service to subscribers are effective ways to ensure subscription renewals.

The Newsletter and Electronic Publishers Association surveyed its members on their renewal rates. Business-to-business newsletters reported an average *conversion rate* (renewal after the first year of subscribing) of 61 percent and an average renewal rate of 75 percent. Consumer newsletters reported rates of 35 percent for conversions and 64 percent for renewals. As you can see, long-term subscribers are the most loyal. Because subscribers are less likely to renew after the first year than after succeeding years, your overall renewal rate should increase after your first few years in business. Since it's far cheaper to renew existing subscribers than to recruit new ones (you don't have to rent lists, renewal sales literature is not as extensive, and the response rate is far higher), you'll want to make every effort to retain your readers. The two most effective ways to do this are by providing high-quality editorial coverage of your topic and giving first-rate customer service.

Publishers usually solicit renewals through a series of letters, sometimes starting "at birth" (with the first billing letter) and continuing until after the subscription expires. The number of letters in the series varies with each publisher. As for responses, some subscribers will renew as soon as they receive the first notice; others will wait until it gets closer to the expiration date. As a general rule of thumb, continue sending out renewal notices until they become more expensive than soliciting new subscriptions.

Each successive renewal notice should be worded and formatted differently from the previous one (novelty increases the likelihood that the subscriber will pay attention to them). In addition, make it easy for subscribers to renew through such practices as accepting credit cards and allowing them to be billed later. If you offer a gift or a discount for renewal, do it in one of the early notices. By making such offers late in the renewal series, you will train your subscribers to wait till the last minute to renew. And never format a renewal notice like an invoice—US postal regulations forbid sending out bills for something the recipient hasn't ordered. If your subscriber has not previously agreed to renew, you can't bill her for a renewal.

Finally, even after they expire, your former subscribers are some of your best prospects. Patricia Wysocki of the Newsletter and Electronic Publishers Association says that many newsletter publishers send direct mail to their "expire lists" four times a year or more, and they receive better response rates with them than with any of their other mailing lists.

CONCLUSION

Once you've considered all of the strategies for finding readers, you should be able to outline a marketing plan for your newsletter. As you choose your marketing techniques, consider where and how you can best reach your audience, as well as how much money you can spend. And remember that the best marketing plan may be to follow your instincts about what will work. Test it, gather data on the results, and decide whether to repeat it—or try something new.

PART TWO

*B*EING CLARK KENT
WRITING, EDITING, AND ILLUSTRATING YOUR NEWSLETTER

In the *Superman* TV episodes that filled many of my childhood afternoons, reporters Clark Kent and Lois Lane seemed to spend more time in the custody of gangsters than they did at their typewriters putting out a newspaper. Certainly their exploits made for better TV than discussions of how to write a news story. But even in the 1950s, when the two finally did sit down at their typewriters, they followed many of the same news-writing techniques still used today. Chapter 6 takes a look at these techniques, showing you how to gather information, develop an editorial style, and edit your work for clarity and accuracy.

If Clark Kent's colleague, photographer Jimmy Olsen, were still around today, he'd be pleasantly surprised by the increased importance of photos and graphics in twenty-first century journalism. But with this emphasis on visuals comes a need for editors with a basic understanding of graphic arts. If you have a background in design or amateur photography, you've got a head start. If, however, you're relatively new to using illustrations, photos, and other graphics in your newsletter, fear not. Chapter 7 offers plenty of easy-to-follow tips and advice for making the most of visuals.

CHAPTER 6

WRITING AND EDITING

'I've met so many people, from college freshmen to corporate executives, who are afraid to write, who apologize for what they write. If you feel the way they do, following a step-by-step process that includes brainstorming for ideas, gathering and organizing information, writing a first draft, and then revising and editing the material will help. You'll be happy to hear that you already completed the first step back in Chapter 4, when you brainstormed for article topics. In this chapter, you'll be going on to the next steps—gathering and organizing information, and then drafting and revising that material into articles that are appropriate for your newsletter's purpose. You'll also learn how to write headlines and use skimming aids to enhance your articles.

The second part of this chapter is devoted to editing your articles for readability, accuracy, and consistency. I'll show you how to cut an article to make it fit in the allotted space, and then we'll talk about getting it right, down to the last detail, by proofreading. You'll also see why it's a good idea to wait a few days or at least a few hours before editing your own work.

GETTING THE FACTS

The first step in writing a newsletter is gathering information. You will have to do some research, conduct interviews, and then organize the information before you start to write.

It's easy to find information on almost any topic through Internet searches. What's hard is making sure the information is reliable. Begin with a search engine like Google (*www.google.com*), and then be on the lookout for websites sponsored by reputable organizations, such as government agencies, nonprofit organizations, and educational institutions. Newsletter Strategy Session (*www.newsletterwriter.biz/nss/reference.shtml*) offers a list of links to online research and reference sites that are especially useful to journalists.

Another good site is the Internet Public Library (*www.ipl.org*), which contains a general reference center and can also link you to available online periodicals and newspapers. Most of the public-, corporate-, and academic-library sites offer links to reliable websites. Libraries also provide access to online subscription databases that contain quality information on topics ranging from investments to genealogy to politics. These sources, which typically come with hefty subscription fees, are usually free to library patrons.

You can search periodicals from your public library's website by using online services, such as EBSCO, which offers an A-to-Z database of periodical titles that can be located by keywords or through searching by author, titles, or subjects. Also try newspaper archives, which you can search on their individual websites. You can also sign up for daily news briefs from the newspapers or magazines that focus on your particular field. Books are another great starting point for finding basic information on a topic, although some may be too general or out of date to provide the specialized, current information that newsletters offer. Reference books like the *Encyclopedia of Business Information Sources* will lead you to directories, manuals, trade associations, and databases that are important to your field.

If you are writing an article about an industry or an issue, turn to the association or organization that represents it, like the Dairy Farmers of America or the American Booksellers Association. They can provide the most current studies and reports. A number of professional organizations and universities publish press releases, research findings, and statistics at Newswise (*www.newswise.com*) and Profnet (*www.profnet.com*). The federal government also issues reports and statistics at Fedstats (*www.fedstats.gov*), where you can contact federal organizations, such as the Department of Labor, Justice, Education, or whatever department is appropriate for your research.

Most people love to talk about themselves or their area of expertise. When conducting interviews, try to ask questions that encourage their responses. It is always better to have too much information than not enough.

For many of your newsletter articles, you'll want to conduct interviews. Interviews can provide the quotes and anecdotes that give credibility and color to your articles, lead you down paths you might have missed in your research, and help you verify information you've found elsewhere. To find interview subjects, contact the people mentioned in press releases you've gathered, or use the research websites mentioned above to find experts. You can also contact associations, universities, or businesses mentioned in the preliminary data you gathered for your article.

A good interview starts with thorough preparation. That means coming up with a broad outline for the article, deciding which area of expertise the source will address, and composing a list of questions for that particular interview subject. Have more questions ready than you think you'll need, and try to avoid asking questions that result in a "yes" or "no" answer. Instead, keep your questions open-ended. Use one of the reporter "basics"—Who, What, When, Where, Why, or How—to open each one.

If at all possible, try to conduct your interviews in person. When you are talking to someone face to face, it is easier to clarify points, understand the subject's perspective, and gather all the necessary information.

The manner in which you conduct interviews is every bit as important as adequate preparation. By approaching your subject in an appropriate way, taking good notes, recording the meeting, and double-checking facts *during* the interview itself, you'll make both the interviewing and the writing processes much more pleasant, effective, and accurate.

Once you have done your research and conducted your interviews, you will want to organize the information you have gathered into an outline. Experiment with several different ways of organizing the topics until you hit upon the one that makes the most sense for your article. If you are working on a news story, organize the topics in order of importance. You can also organize your stories chronologically, topic by topic, person by person, or from most common to least common occurrence.

> Whenever possible, try to conduct interviews in person. Speaking to someone face to face makes it easier to clarify points and understand the subject's perspective.

UNDERSTANDING THE PRINCIPLES OF NEWSLETTER WRITING

Research tells us that nowadays people get most of their information from printed matter by skimming headlines, subheads, illustrations, and tables of contents. They are less likely to read the full text of articles. This is particularly evident among newsletter audiences, who often read the publications standing up as they open the mail. They browse the front and back, scan the large and bold text, and look at the pictures. When they *do* read an article, most people are reluctant to jump to another page to finish it. Good newsletter publishers are aware of these habits of typical readers, so they favor brief articles that quickly come to the point. And they pack information into their headlines, subheads, and other skimming aids.

The rules for newsletter writing are likely to differ from those you learned in English class. Newsletter writing is concise, informal, and conversational. It uses short, simple words in short, simple sentences.

To help you understand good newsletter writing style, study newsletters from established publishers like Lawrence Ragan Communications (*www.ragan.com*) or Brownstone Publishers (*www.brownstone.com*). Read first-rate newspapers like *The New York Times, The Washington Post,* or *The Wall Street Journal.* And take a look at some of the writing books mentioned in the Resources section beginning on page 323. If you think you need further study, consider enrolling in a college journalism or business writing course.

In this section, I'll show you how to set the tone and mood of your publication through writing. I'll also show you how to select vocabulary and details that don't confuse (or insult) your audience. I'll cover how to write concisely, clearly, and accurately. And finally, I'll offer pointers on how to get readers to respond to your writing.

Selecting a Tone

Your writing style, the types of stories and illustrations you run, and the page design you choose all contribute to your newsletter's tone. Most newsletters, even conservative ones, tend to use an informal writing style. Informal writing includes some contractions, such as "can't" (cannot) and "won't" (will not); it also uses occasional first and second person pronouns, like "I," "we," and "you." An informal style puts some—but not a lot of—distance between the reader and the writer.

Newsletters that are very informal adopt a casual writing style. Often, these are association newsletters in which the writers and readers know one another. Or they might be newsletters for a young, hip audience, such as fans of a rap group or video-game enthusiasts. Casual writing includes many first and second person pronouns as well as slang and colloquial expressions. With this type of casual writing, there is no distance between writer and reader.

If your newsletter is informal or casual in tone, go ahead and bend some of the strict grammatical rules you learned in school. Incomplete sentences (fragments) are okay if you use them sparingly—and knowingly. It's fine to end an occasional sentence with a preposition or split an infinitive if the sentence sounds right when doing so.

Your writing will also suggest a mood, whether it's factual and objective or opinionated and argumentative. Within one newsletter, you might print objective news articles beside opinion pieces and humorous essays. Just remember to choose a mood that is appropriate for the subject at hand: humor doesn't belong in a news story about the firing of your company's president, nor sarcasm in a profile of your hospital's most dedicated volunteer.

Selecting Vocabulary and Detail

When writing for your newsletter, give your readers the amount of information they need to understand the story. For instance, you wouldn't tell your spouse how old your child is; you wouldn't tell Iowa state legislators which political party their governor belongs to. You *would* tell an audience of Texans whether the governor of Iowa was a Democrat, Republican, or Independent. Likewise, real estate brokers would be insulted if your article explained what the MLS (Multiple Listing Service) is; however, it would be appropriate to spell it out and explain it to first-time homebuyers.

It's important to take the same care in choosing vocabulary. In general, writing in newsletter style means replacing uncommon words with short, concrete synonyms. However, if you know that your audience shares a common, specialized language—a jargon—go ahead and use it. Hockey fans will understand references to hat tricks and cross checks, just as computer specialists will know about motherboards and packets.

Writing Concisely and Clearly

Regardless of who your newsletter audience is, you'll want to write concisely for three reasons: concise writing is easy to understand, busy readers have short attention spans, and newsletters have limited space.

Select specific, concrete words that convey lots of meaning. Use specific verbs, like "stammer" for "speak jerkily," and specific nouns, like "avenue" for "wide street." Another way to be concise is to avoid carelessly repeating words or ideas. In the following sentence, the italicized words can be deleted with no loss in meaning:

> In September, she started *her first day on* her new assignment.

Another way to be concise in your writing is by using lists when you mention three or more related items. When each item in a list is set off as

Concise writing is perfectly suited to newsletters, which themselves are often short with limited space. Brief and to the point, this type of writing is also easy to understand and lends itself to busy readers with short attention spans.

For writing that is clear and concise, cut out unnecessary words (such as those in italics at left), while preserving the meaning of the sentence.

a bullet or numbered point, readers find the information easy to scan, to find later, to organize, and to remember.

Using the active instead of the passive voice further improves clarity. Often, rewording a sentence in the active voice will save you words. The active voice also makes clear who the actor is. For example, *Mistakes were made by all parties* and *The discrepancies were not explained by the accountant* are in the passive voice; while *All parties made mistakes* and *The accountant did not explain the discrepancies* are in the active voice.

Writing Accurately

You want your writing to be as accurate as possible, both to maintain your newsletter's credibility and to avoid legal problems. The following section offers guidelines on how to do this by explaining the laws on libel and how to avoid libel suits. Helpful information on choosing reliable sources, as well as maintaining a speaker's meaning when transcribing quotes, is also presented.

Avoiding Libel

As a publisher, if you have printed false material that defames a person's character or exposes him to public ridicule, and you have not done what a "reasonable reporter" would have done to verify that information, you can be charged with libel.

Libel is the publication of false information that defames a person's character or reputation, or exposes a person to public ridicule, hatred, or contempt. Material in headlines, captions, and photographs, as well as in the body of an article, can be libelous. Publishing false statements made by a person you interview can subject you to a libel suit. You can be sued for libel by individuals, businesses, associations, religious organizations, and unions.

Accusing someone of participating in criminal activity or improper sexual conduct, or claiming that someone has a "vile disease" or is a racial or religious bigot, are a few examples of the topics that can bring libel charges. Even if the article doesn't mention names, if it gives enough details to identify the person, you can still be sued. As a publisher, you are at fault for libel if you publish material that is false *and* you have failed to do what a "reasonable reporter" would do to verify that information. The courts find different levels of fault based on whether the person is a public figure or a private individual.

Public figures include government officials, celebrities, and people who have voluntarily taken a major role in a public controversy. When you report on them, or on matters of public interest, the plaintiff must show that you printed the material with "malice"—you either knew what you printed was false, or you showed "reckless disregard" for the truth (by not reading relevant documents, by not talking to sources on both sides of the story, by relying on anonymous sources, and the like).

On the other hand, a different standard of fault applies when reporting on private individuals. The rationale is that public figures have more access to the media and can more easily refute information that damages their reputation. Private individuals, however, with their lesser ability to set the record straight, do not need to prove that you acted with malice, only that you were negligent in printing the false information by failing to exercise reasonable care in verifying the information.

How can you avoid publishing libelous material? First, take all reasonable care to assure that your information is true. Double-check the facts of the story. Do your research—speak to sources on both sides of the story. If these sources do not respond to your calls, mention your attempts to reach them in the article. If one of your sources quotes information to you from a memo or other document, read the document yourself. Keep backup material for your research—notes, tapes, transcripts, and documents. Be wary of using sources who insist on remaining anonymous when they make potentially libelous statements. Also ask yourself if the source may have questionable motives for making defamatory statements about others. Be sure to back up such claims with other documentation.

Second, have questionable material reviewed by at least two people with authority in your organization—an editor, publisher, or executive. If you have any doubts, also have the material reviewed by your attorney before publication. Don't print it unless you are certain it's not libelous.

Consider purchasing libel insurance to protect yourself against lawsuits. Even the most diligent publishers can be sued—rightly or wrongly—and forced to pay legal fees in their defense.

Evaluating Your Sources

Just a small effort on your part to check the reliability of your sources can contribute greatly to your newsletter's accuracy. When working with sources, always question the validity of the material. What qualifications (jobs, academic degrees, certifications) does the author hold? How is the material presented? If the source material is poorly written or full of typographical errors, you can rightly question whether it was checked for accuracy. If two of your sources contradict one another, do more research to find out which one is right.

You'll also want to evaluate the motives of the person or organization providing the information. Commercial organizations are out to

Be sure to verify the source of any information you obtain for your articles. And before publishing any questionable material that is potentially libelous, have it reviewed by an attorney.

make a profit. While their information is not necessarily inaccurate, it may be presented in a way that best serves their profit motive. Look for indications that the material is current. Check the copyright date. Is it this year, or five years ago? If you have obtained the information from a web page, when was the site last updated? Do the links still work? Even if your source is not a commercial one, recognize that some nonprofits are advocacy groups whose purpose is to get legislation passed favoring their cause, so their views are not without bias. I don't suggest that you ignore information provided by people with these motivations, just be sure to verify what they tell you. Finally, be careful about using information from anyone with questionable motives. For example, a person who gives you controversial information about a company from which he was recently fired may be holding a grudge against that company, so the information is likely to be suspect.

When reporting the results of a research study or poll, find out who conducted the research and who funded it. Studies funded by government agencies or universities are less subject to bias than those funded by corporations or political parties. Consider the size and scope of the sample. Smaller, localized studies carry less weight than large, national ones. Also ask how the participants were recruited. A poll taken on a website includes only people who bothered to visit that site—hardly a random sample.

Transcribing Quotations

Quotations add interest and realism to newsletter writing. They show that you had direct contact with the subject, which supports the accuracy of your reporting. So quote people whose statements are well phrased, or controversial, or lend credence to the gist of the article. However, don't quote a monotonous recitation of events or statistics if you can concisely and accurately paraphrase the information.

Quotations can add interest and lend support to the gist of an article, but don't overuse them. And stick to those that are short and meaningful.

You cannot always transcribe everything your interview subjects say into your article. Some may use street language and words that are not fit to print. Others may ramble. Editors disagree on how to treat such quotes. Some allow writers to correct small grammatical errors in quotations. Many remove stammering—the "ums" and "errrs" and "you knows" that everyone uses from time to time. Most writers do not quote nonstandard English unless it contributes to the purpose of the story, such as an article depicting a typical day in a juvenile detention center.

If the person you interviewed spoke clearly and well, you can use those quotes in their entirety. If using the full quotes will confuse readers or cause other problems, here are some accepted techniques for handling the material:

■ Paraphrase the words of the person interviewed.

■ Paraphrase most of the statement, quoting just the words that add flavor. *Anson says they applied for the grant unsuccessfully four times before "hitting the jackpot" in 2006.*

■ Use the quotation, leaving out insignificant, troublesome material such as stammering, slips of the tongue, poor syntax, or irrelevant ramblings. This method is acceptable if you substitute an ellipsis, which is symbolized by three periods in a row (. . .) for the words you are omitting. Just be sure the omissions do not change the meaning of the person's words.

■ If you need to add a word or words to a quote for better clarity, place the additional material in brackets. *"The only true expert in the field is [Albert] Smith."*

Using quoted material appropriately, whether in its entirety or in combination with paraphrasing, can lend credibility, flavor, and added interest for your readers.

Encouraging Reader Response

To achieve your newsletter's purposes, you'll want your readers to respond to your articles. If yours is a marketing newsletter, you'll hope to generate sales or donations. If it's an advocacy newsletter, you'll want readers to perhaps write to their senators or sign a petition. In a professional or consumer newsletter, you'll want readers to use the information you give them to do their jobs better, save money, make more money, or improve their health. So don't forget to tell them directly how to act on what they've read. This means that you must always provide them with a response mechanism, such as an order form, a website address, or a phone number.

ORGANIZING ARTICLES

Chapter 4 introduced the types of stories you can run in your newsletter. This section offers suggestions on how to organize them. The two primary article formats are news stories and features.

> Instead of using a direct quote that is a meandering or monotonous recitation of an event or occurrence, paraphrase the material.

News Stories

For news stories, the inverted pyramid writing style is the journalistic choice. Articles written in this style present the most important information at the beginning, and follow with information in decreasing order of importance. When necessary, editors are able to shorten these articles by cutting copy from the bottom without fear of deleting important material.

Picture an Egyptian pyramid. It has a broad, square base with triangular sides that come to a point at the top. Now invert the pyramid—the widest part is at the top and the point is at the bottom. Journalists organize their news stories in the image of an inverted pyramid. The wide part of the pyramid represents the most important part of the story and belongs at the top of the story. The narrow part represents the least important information and belongs at the end. Journalists use this *inverted pyramid* style for two reasons. First, if the story needs cutting, an editor can easily cut from the bottom up, knowing he won't be cutting the important part. Second, readers who don't finish the articles—and many don't—will understand the main idea because it was presented in the beginning.

You can report the most important information in a news story by answering six questions: who, what, when, where, why, and how. Start your story with one or two sentences that summarize its crucial points. This is known as the *lead*, and it should answer the first four questions— who, what, when, and where. Notice how the first two sentences in the sample news story at right give those facts.

If you have trouble writing a strong lead, write the rest of the story first. Once you've immersed yourself in the entire story, the lead may pop out at you.

After the lead, use the next part of the story to put its facts in context—to answer the questions why and how. Explain why the story is important to your readers and how it will affect them. Let them know how the news relates to what has happened in the past and how it may influence what happens in the future. Don't leave your reader asking, "So what?" at the end of the article. In our sample news story, for instance, the news is put into context beginning with the fifth paragraph, explaining the point of view of people bound by the new law, its link to larger legislation, and the political context of its support.

You can add depth and fairness to your story by documenting the facts with information from one or several sources—people, documents, organizations—that you've consulted. If you can't reach people who represent both sides of the story, document your efforts to do so: "The company did not return telephone calls requesting a response."

As you write your news story, include information in the order of decreasing importance. News stories don't include a formal conclusion, since there's a possibility that the last paragraph will be cut during editing.

In a news story, the most important information—the main idea—leads off the article, followed by information in order of decreasing importance.

Anti-Terrorism Law Imposes New Rules on Charity Telemarketers

By Debra E. Blum

Under a law signed by the President last week, charities and the professional fundraisers they hire must abide by a new set of disclosure rules when making telephone appeals. The new law expands the Federal Trade Commission's rules that govern telephone sales of goods and services to include telemarketing of charitable gifts.

When the commission issued its sales-call rules in 1995, it exempted calls made by or for nonprofit groups. Now, charity appeals are subject to those rules, plus a new set of disclosure requirements laid out in the new law. According to the statute, solicitors must "promptly and clearly" state that the purpose of the call is to ask for donations, and they must state the name and mailing address of the charity on whose behalf they are calling. The law also says that callers must make "other disclosures as the Commission considers appropriate."

The FTC has not yet spelled out what, if any, additional disclosures it may require.

Critics in the telemarketing industry say the new disclosure rules are burdensome and will be costly to charities because calls will be longer and less likely to engage potential donors. Most worrisome to telemarketing officials is the FTC's new power to add additional disclosure rules as the agency sees fit.

"That's a wide-open door that essentially says, 'If you are making calls on behalf of charities, the federal government is taking over, and it can ask for whatever it wants,' " said Lee Cassidy, executive director of the Direct Marketing Association Nonprofit Federation.

PART OF USA PATRIOT ACT

The charitable-solicitations provision was originally contained in a bill introduced by Sen. Mitch McConnell, Republican of Kentucky, early last month. No action on the bill followed until key elements of it were put into a wide-ranging piece of anti-terrorist legislation not long before it was passed by both houses. The law, known as the USA Patriot Act, broadens the government's ability to gather information in the hunt for terrorists.

The charitable-solicitations bill was intended to deal with problems of fraudulent fund-raising that were expected to be "dramatically worse" following the attacks on September 11, according to a written statement from Mr. McConnell's office.

But nonprofit leaders and telemarketers are skeptical that the new law offers any more ammunition in the fight against fundraising fraud or terrorism. Instead, they contend, it simply piles another layer of regulation onto charities that already are subject to myriad state and local fundraising laws.

Features

In a feature story, which is not as time sensitive as a news story, the goal of the lead paragraph is to catch the reader's attention and draw him into the article. The main idea is summarized next in a nut paragraph, which is followed by supportive information, and then a formal conclusion.

Feature stories cover people, places, and events, and are written from a special point of view or angle. They are not as time-sensitive as news stories, so the writer and editor have more time to come up with interesting angles, which often develop as they go along. For example, while doing research, the writer may come across some information that generates an idea. Having extra time also allows the author to write more creatively. However, don't mistake a license for creativity for a license to bend the truth. Accuracy in a feature article is as essential as it is in a news piece. Because of the increased flexibility of features, you will need to take extra care that you don't introduce bias in your writing style, emphasis, or wording.

The purpose of the lead in a feature is to draw the reader into the story. While news articles start with the main idea of the story and then move to the particulars, features often start with one of the particulars and move to the general idea. You might start a feature story with an anecdote, a surprising fact or statistic, a comparison of past to present, or a contrast between conflicting facts. The author of the feature story on page 145 reminisces in her lead by describing what she was expected to know in high school. Avoid leading with a famous quotation or a definition of a term, which are usually too dry to keep a reader's attention. And limit your lead to one or two paragraphs.

After the lead, the next paragraph should quickly let the reader know what the article is about. This summarizing paragraph is called the *nut paragraph,* or *nut graph.* It presents the main idea of the article, often containing details like dates, names, and locations. If you read only the lead of a feature article, you won't be sure where the story is headed. In the sample article, the first paragraph suggests several directions the story could take: lowered educational standards, using reference books, or writing a research paper. The next paragraph—the nut graph—shows the article's focus: the tendency of today's technical documents to state the obvious. This is followed by several paragraphs that support the idea introduced there. Paragraphs three through six give examples of technical documents that state the obvious, suggest reasons for the trend, and show why it is wasteful.

Unlike news stories, features end with a formal conclusion. The purpose of the conclusion is to get the reader to remember the story. Often, writers use a circular conclusion—one that echoes an idea mentioned in the story's lead. For instance, you can start telling an anecdote in the

A feature story begins with an attention-getting lead, followed by the "nut paragraph," supporting information, and a formal conclusion.

Writing Tip—Must Manuals State the Obvious?

By Lynne Patnode Nadeau

When I was a compulsive reader growing up in the now-distant 1970s, the average person was expected to understand such research terminology as "preface," "table of contents," "introduction," "glossary," "index." Even "concordance" and "thesaurus" were not considered beyond the reach of average high school students. If we were ignorant of a definition, we assumed that the fault was ours, and we slunk away to the dictionary.

Over the last several months, I've seen a disturbing trend in technical documentation that belies this collective knowledge: we're stating the obvious at every opportunity.

A few weeks ago, just under the header "Glossary," I read: "This section provides an alphabetical listing of terms and acronyms, used in this User's Guide, with explanations." An isolated incident, you say? The very next section, header "Index," explained: "This section provides an alphabetical index of subjects with page number(s) indicating where information on the subject can be found."

What conclusions can we draw from these examples? Are users markedly less knowledgeable than they once were? Does the writer's template require body text after a header, no matter how insubstantial? Or is the writer, like Charles Dickens, paid by the word?

WHO NEEDS IT?

Whatever the reason for this text's existence, I'd bet my firstborn that the users are not reading it. Who turns to an index and then thinks, "I wonder what the heck an index *is,* anyhow . . . "? Somewhere, a writer sweated over these sentences to no purpose. Somewhere, corporate funds are supporting the creation, layout, printing, and translation of those sentences.

To demonstrate just how slippery this slope is, here's my final example from an "About This Manual" section of a different document: "The manual has a Table of Contents which details the structure and headings in the order they are presented." Sounds like an ordinary table of contents to me.

This approach is dangerous. It wastes words, time and money. Worst of all, it condescends to our readers. Wherever and however this started, let's all agree to rage against it so we can spend our time informing users, not patronizing them.

lead and finish it in your conclusion. Some conclusions—like the one in our example—include a call to action, telling readers what to do next. Others include a prediction or a strong quote from a person who was interviewed for the article. Some conclusions contain a vignette that illustrates the changes brought about by the events described in the article. Whichever technique you choose, make sure that your conclusion provides a satisfying ending that doesn't leave your audience confused.

Other Stories

Not every article you may want to run will fit into the standard story structure of news and features. What follows are some alternative formats that might work for your content.

■ **Meeting Reports.** These reports, which can be written as features or news stories, describe events that take place at conferences; presentations; or company, board, and committee meetings. Typically, however, if the meetings are routine gatherings, reporting on them can be dull recitations of the agenda. Instead of insisting upon running full, detailed meeting reports regularly in your newsletter, consider summarizing only the information that is newsworthy. Or, if the meetings cover only one or two actions of importance or interest, such as raising dues, you can cover such actions as part of a news story or in a company "notices" column. Another bit of advice—if you *do* decide to run full meeting reports, don't provide such full coverage that readers will feel there is no need to attend future meetings.

■ **Profiles.** A profile is a feature story that reports on a person's work, achievements, contributions to his field or organization, and/or personality. Highlighting a specific aspect of the person or his experience makes for an interesting article. Profiling him through a story that reads like a resume or biography tends to bore readers.

■ **Reviews.** A review is a feature story that describes and evaluates a book, website, film, or the like. When writing one, be careful not to simply recite the book's table of contents, list the website's pages, or summarize the content of your subject. Highlight the most interesting or important material, and let readers know why they'll find it useful or enjoyable. Be sure to include such information as website addresses, publisher names, and ISBN numbers, so readers can easily access the item being reviewed.

■ **How-To Formats.** Articles that tell readers how to perform a procedure, such as downloading a document from a website or changing a bicycle tire, use a how-to format. They resemble instruction sheets, and usually include a set of numbered steps and/or diagrams that are easy for readers to follow when performing the task.

■ **Lists.** When itemizing the main points of an article, a list format can be ideal. Precede each entry with an icon like a bullet or check mark, or with a number (if numbering is more appropriate for the subject matter). Articles such as "Your Tax Preparation Checklist," "Top Five Graphic Editing Programs," and "Eight Tips for Writing a Resume" all lend themselves to a list format. These types of newsletter pieces are attractive to readers because they are easy to skim.

■ **Q & A Formats.** Formatted with questions (posed by interviewers or by readers looking for information from experts) and answers in alternating paragraphs, the Q & A format works well for interviews, advice columns, and for responses to frequently asked questions.

As you can see, there are a number of different ways to organize the material for your newsletter articles. Varying formats appropriately offers both interest and visual appeal to the reader.

WRITING HEADLINES AND SKIMMING AIDS

Although, ideally, you want all of your articles read from start to finish, research shows that *skimming aids*—the eye-catching elements of an article that readers tend to "skim over"—are read far more than the articles themselves. Headlines, kickers, decks, subheads, pull quotes, and captions are common skimming aids. To stand out, they are typically set in larger type and a different font than that used in the body of the article.

Not only do skimming aids offer information about the article, they also offer the reader different points at which to begin reading. From a visual point of view, they make your pages more organized, attractive, and accessible. If the headline doesn't draw a reader in, a subhead or a photo caption will.

Accuracy is even more important in headlines, pull quotes, and other skimming aids than it is in the text of an article because they are so much more conspicuous. Any libelous statements they contain will be judged more harshly by the courts.

A skimming aid should contain information that originates in the

Typically, readers will scan informative headlines, subheadings, captions, and other eye-catching skimming aids before reading the articles themselves. These elements should be enticing enough to cause readers to want to read the article.

article itself; however, that material should not be repeated in other skimming aids for the same article. Each one should build on the others to give the skimmer a general overview of what the article contains. Common skimming elements are described below. The article "Help Stamp Out Hype" on page 151 shows how they are used in a newsletter.

Headlines

Headlines should always reflect the tone of the article and indicate the information it contains.

The *headline* is the title of an article. A good headline gives enough information to summarize the article, while making readers want to know more. (After all, you want to turn skimmers into readers.) When creating a headline, be sure it isn't misleading and that it doesn't contradict any information contained in the article. Remember that many people will skim only the story's headline, so be sure it doesn't cause any confusion or misunderstanding.

When creating a headline, think about how your audience will react to it. Does the tone of the headline match the tone of the article? You wouldn't, for instance, include a pun in the headline for a disaster story. Also, be sure to avoid using jargon or acronyms that your readers are not likely to understand.

Because of space limitations, headlines follow their own grammatical rules. For example, it's fine to omit articles like "the" and "a" from headlines. Another space-saving technique is to replace the word "and" with a comma. Write headlines in the present tense, even if the event took place in the past (Miller Earns Teaching Award; Panel Discusses Campaign Ethics). For future events, use the word "to" to create the infinitive form of the verb (Board to Vote on Dues Increase at April Meeting; Donnelly to Run for Trustee).

Do not end your headlines with a period, but do use a question mark when the headline is worded as a question. Avoid exclamation points. And whenever possible, use short words in headlines, like those suggested in "Headline-Friendly Synonyms" at right.

Kickers, Decks, Subheads, and Pull Quotes

Kickers, decks, subheads, and pull quotes are additional attention-getting methods for the skimming audience.

A *kicker*, also known as a *standing head, teaser,* and *eyebrow,* is a short line of text located above a headline. Use kickers to label your newsletter's regular columns, such as President's Message, Tax Tips, or Editor's

Headline-Friendly Synonyms

What follows are some examples of short, headline-friendly words that you can substitute for longer ones that don't fit in your headline space. While these shorter synonyms won't necessarily be the words of choice in the text of your articles, you can get away with using them in headlines. Some of the words are just a couple of letters shorter than the ones they replace, but at times that's all you may need to make the headline fit.

Instead of	Use	Instead of	Use
acquire, purchase	buy	infrequent, unusual	rare
agreement	pact	initiative	move
among	amid	leave	quit
approval	nod	legislation	bill
assistant	aide	location	site
campaign, attempt	bid	motivate	spur
celebrate	mark	opinion	view
cheer up	buoy	plan, goal	aim
committee	panel	prohibit	bar
company	firm	promise, pledge	vow
confuse	stump	ready	set
consider, think about	mull, eye	reduction	cut, drop
cooperate, work together	team up	result in	net
criticize	blast, slam, rap	schedule, establish	set
demonstrate	show	speed	pace
highest	top	subside, reduce	ease, ebb
increase	gain, jump, rise	surround	ring

Message. Never use kickers alone; always combine them with a headline. By itself, a kicker like "President's Message" will attract few readers. When combined with a headline like "How to Work Productively and Avoid Layoffs," it will gain plenty of attention.

A *deck* is additional information, usually a sentence or two, that is placed below the headline. Use a deck to highlight additional information from the article that you weren't able to fit into the headline, as seen in the article on page 151. (For years, I had trouble remembering which line was the deck and which was the kicker. Then I realized that a kicker kicks off, or begins, the article. I've been able to keep the terms straight ever since.)

Subheads are headings that appear within the text of an article to introduce a new topic. They should be short—one line, two at most. A *pull quote*, sometimes called a *display quote* or *callout*, is a sentence or sentence fragment that is pulled directly from the article and set in display type in a box or highlighted area within the article. Unlike headlines, decks, or subheads, pull quotes don't summarize information in the article. Instead, they offer a line from the text that is significant and interesting.

Take a look at the article on page 151. Read just the kicker, headline, deck, subheads, and pull quote. Notice how they give you a pretty good idea of what's in the article, even before you begin to read the text?

Captions

A *caption* is an explanatory comment that accompanies a photo or illustration. Its purpose is twofold: to provide information about the picture that is not obvious to the reader, and to entice skimmers to read the story to find out more. A caption should identify who or what is in the photo and when and where it was shot. In addition, it should explain the significance of the event to give some context to the photo.

A caption for a picture portraying more than one person or object should always tell the reader the position of those in the photo, as seen in Figure 6.1 below. To indicate positioning, you can use words like "left" and "right," "rear" and "foreground," "front" and "back," or "clockwise" and "counterclockwise."

For photos that contain unusual subject matter, try to create captions that clearly communicate the images' pertinent aspects to your readers. Let's say you are running an article on your company's president and will be including a photo of him at his surprise office birthday party. In the photo, the staff is dressed in business attire, while the president is shirtless and wearing athletic shorts and sneakers. At first glance, the reader is likely to be wondering why he is dressed that way. Instead of accompanying the photo with a caption that says "Marketing department staff celebrates the fiftieth birthday of President McCarthy, second from left," which does not answer the reader's question (and is also rather dull), provide one that says "President McCarthy was caught off guard—and underdressed—when he

Figure 6.1
This caption below clearly identifies the two women. It wasn't necessary to identify the position of Jim Fossman, since he's the only man in the photo.

Trainer Jim Fossman demonstrates new Orion software to Klassonetics bookkeepers Kathleen O'Hansen, rear, and Melleney Marks, foreground.

Editor's Message ❶

BY CAROL LUERS EYMAN

Help Stamp Out Hype ❷

Translate press releases into objective reporting to increase the credibility of your trade publication. ❸

. . . During a stint as a copyeditor for trade-press newsletters, I became acutely aware of the need to maintain the credibility of editorial material and to distinguish it from advertising. Time and budget constraints often left trade reporters with little more than press releases as source material.

This article offers advice for any of you who find yourselves thrown into the role of trade-press reporter or editor. You'll constantly need to look out for inflated language—hype. You'll need to recognize it in the press releases of others and eliminate it from your own writing.

Beware Superlatives ❺

One of the most glaring marketing tricks is the use of overdramatic language. No company ever announces or releases a product, for example. Instead, *Company X, a world leader in industry Y, unveils* (or *unleashes* or *reveals*) *solutions that deliver the world's fastest widget*. How can we correct this copy?

First, kill the strip-tease metaphors (unveils? reveals?). They don't belong in editorial copy. Second, replace the word "solutions." It's ambiguous, and could refer to software, hardware, courseware, or some combination of the three. It also implies that the item in question will solve one's problem. If it will, use "solution." If you don't have enough information to evaluate the product, don't use the word.

Third, watch for superlatives. If you aren't Consumers Union running a test lab, at a minimum you must change "the world's fastest widget" to "what the company claims is the world's fastest widget."

Eliminate Redundancy ❺

Press releases are full of redundancy, the most common being repetition of the company's name. Marketing writers hope this repetition will appear in editorial copy as well and sway readers into remembering the company name—and ultimately buying the company's products. Use the name sparingly. On second references, substitute "the company" or "it."

One of the most glaring marketing tricks is the use of overdramatic language. ❹

Press releases also tend to repeat lists of product features. A typical introductory paragraph might claim that a projector creates "sharp, stable, realistic images"; a few paragraphs later you'll find something like, "These sharp, stable, realistic images rival those of film." It sounds as if the PR firm wants you to promote a new slogan. Don't do it. Instead, in the latter sentence, say, "The quality of these images rivals that of film."

Conclusion ❺

Keep these basic principles in mind, and your writing should turn out hype-free. Now, if I may break my own rule: *Intercom,* the magazine of the Society for Technical Communication, has just unveiled the world's most comprehensive hype solution!

Kickers, headlines, decks, subheads, and pull quotes communicate an article's main ideas to readers who skim the page.

❶ Kicker

❷ Headline

❸ Deck

❹ Pull quote

❺ Subhead

was lured from his lunchtime workout to a surprise fiftieth birthday party thrown by the marketing department." Not only does this caption tell the readers what they are looking at, it does so in an interesting way. Remember, one of the main purposes of a caption is to provide information about the picture that is not obvious to the reader.

When properly written, headlines, kickers, decks, subheads, and pull quotes, as well as thoughtfully written photo captions, will pique the interest of readers. These skimming aids will also guide them through the pages of your newsletter, leaving even rushed readers better informed.

EDITING YOUR NEWSLETTER

Say That Again?

Drunk Gets Nine Months in Violin Case

Miners Refuse to Work After Death

Arson Suspect Held in Massachusetts Fire

According to Internet lore, the headlines in the margin at left were actually published! Some unfortunate (or unskilled) editor missed their double meanings. Demonstrating that editing means more than spelling names correctly or using proper punctuation, these headlines also show how a poorly edited newsletter can embarrass your company or organization.

It is impossible to review your newsletter only once and catch every error. There are simply too many elements to check. During your first pass, you may remember that you must verify the issue date in the footers, but after reading a few pages, this task may slip your mind. So even professional editors do several levels of editing. For instance, on the first pass, they might check just the issue date on each page. On the next pass, they might verify that all of the articles written for the issue have been placed in the layout. Then, they might look through the newsletter to verify that the proper type styles have been applied to headlines, captions, subheads, and body text. On another pass, they may read the articles for content and grammatical accuracy. And, of course, one pass must be devoted to proofreading for spelling, punctuation, capitalization, and typographical errors (typos).

Ideally, more than one person should edit your newsletter. Never assume you can catch every error yourself. Someone I know, who is otherwise a good speller, found out in her twenties that she had been misspelling the word "surprise" all her life. Many newsletter editors admit that they can always find that one last typo—*after* the newsletter has been published. This is because their minds have had a chance to rest from looking at the newsletter. Rest your mind *before* you publish, rather than after. Put the newsletter aside for a day or at least a few hours before giving it a final going-over.

Talk to any newsletter editor and you'll hear a story about time and energy wasted over one small error. I know one editor who forgot to include her mailing *indicia* (a mark used in bulk mailings in place of a postage stamp) in the layout for one issue. She then had to find a volunteer to stamp the indicia on the 2,500 newsletters before mailing them out. I once changed the date on a newsletter, but forgot to update the issue number (as in Vol. 5, Issue 3). The newsletter's circulation staff received numerous phone calls from confused librarians.

It's not hard to make a mistake that will force you to pay for a second newsletter printing. Save yourself time and money by getting things right the first time. Focusing on different elements of your newsletter during a number of passes, and having a second (or even third) set of eyes to go over the material and layout, are easy methods for catching costly errors.

You can speed up your work by editing electronically. The smoothest process is one in which the editor makes changes directly to the word processing file, and then sends the file back to the author for review. You can also use the online editing feature available in many word processing programs. This marks up changes so the author can approve and then incorporate them into the text with just a few clicks of the mouse.

Editing newsletter pages after they've been laid out can be trickier, especially if you don't have access to the page-layout software used by the layout artist. You can have the layout artist print out a copy of the pages for you to mark up manually. Or he can e-mail you a PDF file of the newsletter, which you can print out and then mark up. Once you've made changes to the copy, you'll have to send the marked-up pages back to the layout artist, who will incorporate the changes.

Editing your newsletter involves three major steps. First, edit the content of the material so that it is clear, accurate, and fits into the available space. Next, edit for consistency of style and usage—a step known as copyediting. Finally proofread for spelling, punctuation, capitalization, and formatting.

The editing phase of your newsletter involves three steps: Content editing—to verify that the copy is clear, accurate, and the right length; copyediting—to maintain consistency of editorial style; and proofreading—to correct spelling, punctuation, and formatting errors.

Editing for Content

The first step in editing your newsletter is to review the articles for content—length, readability, and accuracy. Even small changes in the text can result in big changes to the layout, causing unnecessary extra work for the layout artist. So make sure your copy is as readable and accurate as possible before sending it to be laid out. If any higher-ups have to approve the newsletter's content, this is the time for them to do so.

If you don't understand what an author has written, or you think you've found an error in his work, ask him to clarify the information. Often, if you simply read the questionable sentence out loud to the author, he will see why it's confusing and immediately correct it. If an author questions your edits, explain tactfully why you made the changes, perhaps referencing the authorities you've consulted, like a dictionary or style book. Remember that as editor you have the best perspective for deciding what fits and what doesn't in the newsletter. You know what other stories are running, how they relate, and what your goals are for the issue. You know about schedule pressures and style guidelines. Don't be afraid to assert that authority. On the other hand, be careful not to rewrite your authors' stories in your own voice.

Checklist for Content Editing

The following checklist is designed to prevent any oversights when editing your newsletter articles for length, readability, and accuracy of the content.

Length

☐ Meaning of the article is maintained after cutting.

☐ Other articles do not refer to the material that has been cut.

Readability

☐ Story is well organized.

☐ Sentences in each paragraph relate to a central idea.

☐ Paragraphs are short.

☐ Paragraphs contain transition words and phrases where needed.

☐ Lists are grammatically parallel.

☐ Articles avoid the passive voice.

☐ No dangling or misplaced modifiers.

☐ No redundant phrases.

Accuracy

☐ URLs point to correct website pages.

☐ Company names and locations are correct.

☐ Telephone numbers are correct.

☐ Names are spelled correctly with every use.

☐ Days and dates agree.

☐ Numbers referred to in text add up correctly.

☐ Tenses and time references agree with publication date.

☐ Masthead is up to date.

During this editorial stage, refer to the "Checklist for Content Editing" on page 154. It will help you when editing articles for length, readability, and accuracy.

Length

Editing articles for length should be done first. If you told an author to write 500 words and he wrote 800, there's no sense in cleaning up his grammar in material that may have to be cut. You might consider asking the author to make the necessary word cuts, as he may know best what can be deleted safely. Furthermore, if you make him do the cutting, he'll be more likely to stick to your requested length next time.

If, however, you are going to be making make the cuts, first become familiar with the story's organization. If it's written in inverted pyramid style, indicating that it's a news story, you'll be safe cutting from the bottom up. If it's a feature, look for superfluous information or quotes that do not contribute to the main point of the story. Also look for ideas that are repeated. Often a writer will state an idea and then repeat it in a quote.

After cutting any article, reread it in its entirety to be sure it still makes sense. If the story is too long but contains useful information, consider running it in two or three parts over the course of several issues.

Readability

Once your stories are about the right length, it's time to edit them for readability. You want to make sure the writing is clear and concise. Start by taking a global view: examine the article's organization. If it's a news story, does it lead with the main idea? Do the rest of the facts follow in order of decreasing importance? If it's a feature, does the lead draw the reader into the story? Is it followed by a nut graph? Does it close with a strong conclusion?

Next check the paragraphs. Are the sentences in each paragraph related to one another? Are paragraphs connected by transitional words and phrases that logically guide the reader through the story?

Finally, look at the sentences. Are they well formed? If you find yourself reading a sentence twice, or interpreting it in two different ways, it's probably a good idea to rewrite it. If the article includes a list, do all the listed items follow a parallel grammatical structure? Does the writer minimize the use of the passive voice? Are there any dangling or misplaced modifiers?

Editing articles for length should be the first step in the editing process. Why spend time and energy reworking sentences for readability or correcting grammar in material that may have to be cut?

Once you have pared down an article, be sure to read it in its entirety to verify that it still makes sense.

Accuracy

The final stage of content editing involves checking for accuracy. Pay close attention to details like postal addresses, websites, e-mail addresses, and phone numbers. If the phone numbers you publish are incorrect or have been disconnected, your readers will question the accuracy of the rest of your newsletter. So verify before you publish. Check the spelling of names. Look at a calendar to make sure that days and dates agree (is January 21 really a Monday?). Spot-check the figures in tables to be sure they add up.

A common problem in newsletter writing is the use of future tense for events that happened in the past. This happens when a writer prepares an article about an upcoming event, but the newsletter gets distributed after the event. For example, on November 1, the school principal may give you an article that reads "Report cards will be sent home with students on November 7," forgetting that the newsletter is to be distributed on November 9. Edit the sentence to read, "Report cards were scheduled to be sent home with students on November 7." By making this change, you not only place the event in the past, but if, for some unforeseen reason, the report cards do not go out on the 7th, your sentence, which says they were "scheduled" to go out on that day, is still technically correct.

Finally, be sure to check your masthead, which is an often-neglected area. Verify that your address, phone number, staff list, copyright date, and subscription price are accurate and up to date.

Editing for Consistency

When you're done with content editing, you'll be ready to edit your copy for consistency. This type of editing, known as copyediting, is done after content editing but before layout. To avoid having to ask for multiple revisions of the layout, all of the copy should be as clean as possible before it's placed into your newsletter template.

Copyeditors make sure that a newsletter conforms to the publisher's "style." Use of this word can be confusing in the world of newsletter publishing because of its various meanings. The word "style" can describe a newsletter's design—an artistic or newspaper-like style, for instance. It can also refer to the type of writing used in a newsletter— a formal or informal style. But for copyeditors, the word "style" has another meaning. It's the set of conventions used for spelling, punctuation, capitalization, and certain terms. For example, when mentioning a temperature, does your newsletter print it as "78 degrees Fahrenheit" or "78°F"? Do you spell "barcode" as one word or two? Do you refer to a previous decade as the "nineties," "90s," or "1990s"? None of these choices is right or wrong per se. The right choice depends on your newsletter's style.

Why does your newsletter need its own style? Because it maintains consistency. Writing that is inconsistent detracts from your message. Style guidelines serve several purposes. If you have multiple editors, these guidelines will help them stay consistent. If you work alone, they can remind you how to handle situations that arise infrequently, like formatting a footnote. They can even play the fall guy for you. Let's say an author gives you grief about your edits; you can simply say, "It's not my idea; it's our style."

The simplest way to adopt a style is to use a published style guide, such as *The AP Stylebook* or *The Chicago Manual of Style*. The first is geared to newspaper publishing, but it is also appropriate for most newsletters. *The Chicago Manual of Style*, published by the University of Chicago Press, is more appropriate for academic writing. You might want to adopt it if your audience consists of professors and researchers. Other style guides are listed in the Resources, beginning on page 323.

Unfortunately, not every style decision you need to make will be covered in these guides. You'll have to create and customize your own to fit your particular needs. For instance, your newsletter's style guide should include how you've decided to spell and format certain vocabulary words, symbols, and acronyms that are specific to your audience's field.

How do you choose between two ways of spelling a word, representing a number, or printing a symbol? Think about the usage your readers are most likely to understand and be accustomed to. An audience of physicists will be comfortable with the symbol "μm," but a lay audience will need you to spell out "micrometer" (and tell them what it means). Consider your subject matter and tone. A legal newsletter will contain different vocabulary than a church newsletter.

Part of your customized style guide should be a list of the dictionaries you consult on questions of spelling. Select a general dictionary for common words and a technical, medical, or legal dictionary for specialized terms you use frequently.

Record your custom style decisions, whether in a notebook, in a computer document created for that purpose, or perhaps right on the pages of

Following specific style guidelines for the editorial content of your newsletter will help to maintain consistency in the spelling, vocabulary, punctuation, and formatting choices used in your stories and articles.

the published style guide you use. I haven't provided a checklist for copy-editors, because its contents would be different for every newsletter. But if you find yourself having difficulty catching style errors, create your own checklist that is customized to the style you've adopted.

Proofreading

Proofreading requires a number of passes over your newsletter, with each pass focusing on a different element—accuracy of page numbers and cross references; proper size and alignment of copy and graphics; and correct spelling, punctuation, and capitalization of body copy and skimming aids.

After your articles have been copyedited and placed in the newsletter's layout, you may have to tweak the length of some of your stories. Once you've gotten them to fit, it's time to proofread—the final step in editing your newsletter. As you will see in the following discussion, proofreading involves a number of steps. It is helpful to use the "Checklist for Proofreading" on page 159 during this stage.

In addition to checking for spelling, punctuation, capitalization, and typos, a proofreader must look for common errors that are specific to newsletters. For starters, be sure to check for what I call navigational errors: Do the entries in the table of contents reflect the correct page numbers? Do jump lines ("continued on page 8" or "continued from page 1") state the correct pages? If a story contains a cross-reference telling readers, "See related story, page 6," does the related story really appear on page 6? For that matter, are the pages numbered correctly to begin with?

Next check the issue date, and the volume and issue numbers that appear on the first page. Check the date on headers or footers on inside pages as well. Take a close look at all headlines, kickers, decks, subheads, bylines, and captions. In addition to checking every word for spelling, punctuation, and capitalization, make sure these elements are set in the specified size and typeface, and that the spacing above and below them is correct. Proofreaders tend to overlook these errors, while readers tend to notice them first.

Now look at the layout and graphics—photos, pictures, tables, boxes, and rules (lines). Are they aligned properly (flush with the margin, centered)? Are boxes and rules sized correctly in both their length and width? Do boxes have the correct borders and shading? Are columns, and the white space between them, of consistent widths? Without reading it, eyeball the body text. Is each line properly aligned along both the left and right hand sides? Are paragraphs indented correctly? Is the spacing between paragraphs consistent?

Once you have completed this high-level proofing phase, you can begin to read the text of the newsletter. Watch for spelling, punctuation, and capitalization errors, as well as missing words, repeated words, and

Checklist for Proofreading

The following checklist will help you keep track of the many areas that require attention while proofreading your newsletter.

Navigation

Check for accuracy of page numbers in:

- ☐ Table of contents
- ☐ Jump lines
- ☐ Cross references
- ☐ Headers and footers

Issue Dates and Numbers

Check (on the first page, and in headers or footers) for accuracy of:

- ☐ Issue date
- ☐ Volume number
- ☐ Issue number

Display Type

Check headlines, kickers, decks, subheads, bylines, and captions for:

- ☐ Spacing above, below, and beside
- ☐ Spelling
- ☐ Punctuation
- ☐ Capitalization
- ☐ Hyphenation
- ☐ Typeface
- ☐ Type size

Graphics

Check photos, pictures, charts, graphs, tables, boxes, and rules for:

- ☐ Alignment
- ☐ Size
- ☐ Borders
- ☐ Shading

Columns

Check for accuracy of:

- ☐ Alignment
- ☐ Width
- ☐ Space between

Body Text

Check for accuracy of:

- ☐ Alignment
- ☐ Indentation
- ☐ Paragraph spacing
- ☐ Spelling
- ☐ Punctuation
- ☐ Capitalization
- ☐ Lines preceding or following story jumps

extra or missing spaces between words. Look for awkward line breaks. For example, you don't want to hyphenate the word "amount," since it would leave the "a" alone at the end of the line. As you read, make sure that text continues smoothly from column to column and from page to page. Often, a line will be missing or repeated at the point where a story jumps pages.

When marking corrections on hard copy, proofreaders use a standard set of symbols, which should be understood by your layout artist. For example, the symbol ¶ means to begin a new paragraph, ^ means to insert something, and # means to insert a space. Using these symbols makes it easy to indicate changes in the limited space available on a formatted newsletter page. Your dictionary or style guide may have a chart of these symbols, or you can find them online at *www.m-w.com/mw/table/proofrea.htm* or *www.bartleby.com/61/charts/A4proof.html*.

CONCLUSION

Even the most visually appealing newsletter will quickly lose readers if it doesn't get its point across through good writing. Do your research; write lively, informative articles; and then edit them to a T. If you take the time to write and edit your newsletter articles correctly, you'll find your readers coming back for more.

CHAPTER 7

USING GRAPHICS AND PHOTOGRAPHS

In December, I receive holiday cards from dozens of friends around the country. Often they include letters or notes saying how much their kids have grown or that they're on their way to college. Although I enjoy hearing from my friends, the information they share usually makes little impression on me—unless it is accompanied by a photo or illustration. Show me a picture of Johnny at eighteen years old and sporting a beard, and I'll stop picturing him on a tricycle. Tell me that Elizabeth drew the elaborate reindeer on the front of the card, and I won't forget that she's applying to art school. On the other hand, a card that's all pictures and no text leaves me wanting to know more. For holiday cards—and newsletters—pictures and text need to strike a balance.

Ideally, every page of your newsletter should include at least two or three graphic elements. They can be as simple as the addition of rules (lines), bullets, and boxes, or as complex as custom drawings and professional photographs. Elaborate graphics are more important in a marketing newsletter, which has to grab the reader's attention, than in a professional one. But even a formal subscription newsletter needs some visuals to guide the reader through its pages. As you will see, there are many easy-to-create, attractive graphics that you can place in your newsletter at a minimal cost.

Graphics serve several purposes. First, they clarify what you've written. Photographs, for example, bring life and authenticity to a story. Tables, charts, and graphs supplement statistical data presented in your text and give readers an added tool with which to interpret it. Graphics can also highlight information. For example, you can make a short notice more conspicuous by placing it within a box. Preceding items in a list with

Provide a good balance of text and graphics in your newsletter. Ideally, each page should contain at least two or three graphic elements, which can range from simple rules and bullets to more elaborate drawings and photographs.

symbols, such as bullets or checkmarks, makes them more noticeable and easier to remember. And highlighting a sentence as a pull quote helps convey the flavor of the article's text.

Graphics also help organize your newsletter pages. A few well-placed rules help readers navigate among the columns and articles on the pages. Pictures of various sizes communicate to readers the relative importance of stories. And finally, photos, illustrations, and other graphics add visual interest. Full pages of pure text appear gray and uninviting. They don't signal readers where to look next. Sprucing up pages with a few graphic elements will motivate your readers to jump in and find out what you have to say.

In the first part of this chapter, you'll discover ways to create and use graphics in your newsletter. In the second part, you'll learn how to take photographs and prepare them for the newsletter production process.

GRAPHICS

As you will see, a wide range of visual graphics, both illustrative and decorative, can lend organization and eye appeal to your newsletter pages. This section describes these graphics and explains when to use them and how to create them.

Illustrative Graphics

Illustrative graphics include tables, graphs, various charts, and diagrams. They help clearly communicate certain types of information that can be somewhat complicated to understand when appearing as straight text. Whenever you use these graphics, always mention it in the text of the accompanying article, so readers will know when to refer to them. Also, be sure to accompany such visuals with a caption or heading, so skimmers as well as careful readers can understand them.

Tables

Illustrative graphics—tables, graphs, and charts—help clarify complicated information that appears in articles as straight text.

Tables visually organize detailed information into rows and columns. A schedule of conference sessions, for example, is much easier to understand and refer to when laid out in a table rather than in a paragraph. Tables are also excellent visual aids for comparing different characteristics of multiple items—say, the price, speed, memory, and optional features of five different computer models, or the advantages and disadvantages of print, web, e-mail, and PDF newsletters (as in Table 3.1 on page 51). You can create tables on a spreadsheet or within your word processing or page-layout software.

Graphs, Charts, and Diagrams

Bar graphs, line graphs, and pie charts are three commonly used graphics for easily organizing and illustrating numerical or statistical information, such as polling data, experimental results, and sales trends. Other helpful visuals used in newsletter publications include flowcharts, organizational charts, timelines, and diagrams.

Figure 7.1
Bar Graph
A bar graph can be ideal for comparing statistical information.

Use graphs to illustrate trends over time or to compare data. *Bar graphs,* like the one in Figure 7.1 at right, are useful for comparing information. In this example, it shows the differences between the postgraduate plans of females and males who attend High School A. *Line graphs,* illustrated by the example in Figure 7.2, are

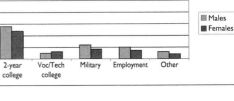

better for showing trends. In this case, it shows (over a five-year period) the percentage of male and female graduates of High School A who attend four-year colleges. No matter which type of graph you use, remember to label both the vertical and horizontal axes.

Figure 7.2
Line Graph
This graph is a good choice for showing trends over time.

Pie charts are useful for laying out statistical data that describe the relationship of parts to a whole—either as proportions or percentages. In Figure 7.3 on page 164, the entire pie represents all of the seniors who attend High School A. Each "slice" of the pie signifies the percentage of those seniors who plan to attend college (four-year, two-year, and technical), join the military, seek employment, or engage in other activities.

If you own a spreadsheet program, you already have the necessary software for producing graphs and pie charts. Once

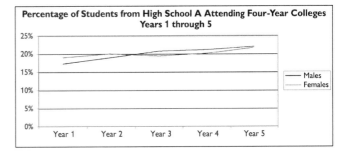

you have entered the data, most of these programs allow you to create these graphics with a few clicks of the mouse.

Flowcharts, which are often used in technical publications to illustrate concepts or procedures, use geometric shapes connected by lines and arrows to show proper sequence of activities in a process. *Organizational charts* use rectangles connected by lines to show hierarchical relationships—often of personnel and/or departments in a large company. Usually these charts are found in corporate or employee newsletters. *Timelines* are linear charts that show a sequence of events over time. They could, for example, be used to show the history of campaign finance legislation in Congress, or the milestones on the way to completing a construction project. Microsoft Visio is a useful graphics program for producing all these types of charts.

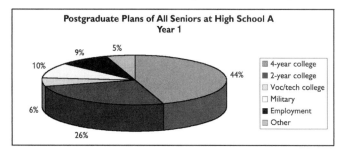

Diagrams are sketches, drawings, or outlines used to point out various parts of an item or to identify its functions. They are also used for demonstrating procedures or showing how something works. For example, a diagram can point out the various architectural elements of a building, or it can illustrate the process of folding a table napkin into a decorative shape. If you are reasonably artistic, look into software such as Adobe Illustrator, Corel-DRAW, or Serif DrawPlus for drawing customized diagrams. If you are not artistically inclined, you can still successfully create diagrams, although more generic ones, with Microsoft Visio.

Figure 7.3
Pie Chart
A pie chart is a good visual graphic for representing the relationship of parts to a whole.

Decorative Graphics

Decorative graphics like clip art, boxes, rules, and dingbats allow you to add graphic interest to pages. They help organize material and draw attention to important items.

Clip Art

Clip art refers to generic pictures that can be purchased on a CD or downloaded, often for free, from the Internet. Some clip art packages also include decorative visual elements such as horizontal rules, bullets, and symbols that are more complex or specialized than those you can create with page-layout software. You can find clip art graphics on just about any subject, such as flowers, animals, cars, and foods. Used prudently, this type of art can help polish your newsletter's message and image quickly and inexpensively. However, when used carelessly or inappropriately, clip art can brand your publication as amateurish and detract from its message.

Keep in mind that clip art images are usually generic, and may not be appropriate for accurately illustrating certain articles. For example, a simple picture of a car may not be specific enough to illustrate a story about the relationship of automobiles to urban sprawl. A picture of the moon won't add anything to an explanation of how a rocket works. Sprinkling the pages of your December issue with holiday icons will not enhance your message; instead, they will look more like computer-generated doodlings that detract from your publication.

On the other hand, when used appropriately, clip art can be quite attractive. I find these graphics especially useful when included with kickers or other headings. Let's say you publish a newsletter for a company that has locations in four different states, and each issue contains news columns from each location. You might integrate a clip art map of the state into the heading of each column. Or if you regularly run a book review column in your newsletter, adding an illustration of an open book or a stack of books next to the kicker can be an effective visual. If you are running an article on a music school, an image of an adult helping a child at the piano could add just the right touch.

I have a cardinal rule when it comes to using clip art in newsletters—never throw it into your layout just for the sake of filling space. White space is preferable to poorly chosen clip art. My advice here is simple: when in doubt, leave it out.

Clip art comes in a variety of styles: realistic or abstract, line drawing or silhouette, conservative or cartoon-like. Select a style that matches your newsletter's topic and tone. A newsletter about Victorian décor, for instance, wouldn't contain modernistic abstract clip art, the same way a publication about fly-fishing wouldn't use conservative clip art depicting people in three-piece suits. Also, when using more than one piece of art on a single page or a two-page *spread* (two pages that face each other), stick with one style. Compare the clip art in the two sets of newsletter pages shown in Figure 7.4 on page 166. Although both spreads contain the same musical instruments, the images in the top spread are squarish with geometric backgrounds, while those on the bottom have loose curvy lines with circular, swirly backgrounds. As you can see, sticking to one style makes for a more unified layout.

Some clip art packages contain a single style while others offer choices. All the clip art in Figure 7.4 came from a single package, which was organized in subject areas such as business, education, people, and travel. Each subject area offered a number of different pictures in different styles—realistic, abstract, cartoon-like, and so forth.

When you place clip art in your newsletter, try shrinking and stretching it until you find a size that looks best. Also evaluate how its shape fits into the layout. Some of the artwork is tall and narrow, some is wide and

"When in doubt, leave it out!" That's my advice when it comes to adding clip art to your newsletter. Avoid using these decorative graphics simply to fill white space on a page. When used inappropriately or overused, clip art will detract from your newsletter.

Figure 7.4

When using more than one piece of clip art on a single page or page spread, stick with a similar style for a more unified look.

On this spread, the illustrations have a squared, geometric look.

On this spread, the illustrations are drawn with circular, curvy lines.

horizontal, and some is square. A wide piece may not work well in a one-column article. A tall, narrow piece might require too much shrinking to remain legible in a quarter-page article.

One advantage of clip art is that it is copyright-free, so when you purchase the pictures, you also purchase the rights to use them in your publication without further permission. For most clip art, these rights allow you to use the images as many times as you like, although you cannot redistribute them. In other words, you can't resell the images as clip art. Before you buy, read the license to make sure your intended use of the material will fit the seller's limitations. Sources for obtaining clip art are provided in the Resources section, beginning on page 323.

Rules

When used properly, rules (lines) help guide the reader's eye along the pages of your newsletter. When placed across the top or bottom of your pages, rules help pull together the left- and right-hand sides of a two-page spread. Horizontal rules placed between stories tell readers when to move their eyes up to the next column. Vertical rules between columns guide the readers' eyes from the top of the page to the bottom. Varying a rule's length and thickness can lend a decorative element to page design as well.

In addition to placing a rule at the top of the page and between columns, the sample newsletter page in Figure 7.5 at right uses rules to set off the kicker from the article's headline, and to separate the author's bio from the end of the article.

Boxes

Placing boxes around your table of contents, masthead, side-bars, tables, and/or calendars will separate them from the rest of the text. Boxes also help highlight short notices that you don't want your readers to overlook, and they can be effective for framing pull quotes. Placing a box around a photo with a light background will prevent the picture from blending into the page.

Page-layout programs allow you to draw boxes and vary the thickness and style of their borders. You can also "fill" the boxes with shaded backgrounds of varying degrees of darkness or color. Simply indicate how dark you want the "fill" to be by entering a percentage in your page-layout program: 10 percent is considered a light fill, while 90 percent is dark. If you're placing text in the box, keep the fill to about 10 percent so the text will be legible; or, you can fill the box with a dark shade and use white letters for the text. Also, be aware that shading appears muddy and uneven on photocopies, so avoid it if you will be photocopying your newsletter.

Although boxes are quite versatile, don't overuse them. Limit their use to one or two on a page. Several boxes placed beside or atop one another will create visual confusion. And be sure to leave a margin of

As decorative elements, rules vary in weight, beginning with very thin "hairlines" and gradually increasing in thickness.

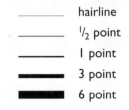

Figure 7.5

On this sample page from *The Ragan Report*, horizontal rules set off the kicker from the headline, and the author bio from the end of the article. Vertical rules separate the columns.

space between the edges of the box and the text within, as well as between the outside of the box and any surrounding text.

Dingbats

Dingbat examples

Dingbats are ornamental characters or symbols that are sometimes used as illustrations or as decorative bullets in lists. Some commonly used dingbats appear in the margin at left. You can also place a dingbat at the end of an article, signifying to readers that the article is over and they don't need to continue to another column or page. Many newsletter and magazine publishers use a small square shaded box (■) for this purpose.

You probably have several sets of dingbats on your computer, stored as fonts. Look for fonts named Wingdings, Webdings, Symbols, Dingbats, or Ornaments. You can see all the symbols included in each of these fonts by selecting "Symbol" from the Insert drop-down menu in Microsoft Word or by using the Character Palette on a Macintosh (see the Macintosh's online help for more information).

Pull Quotes

Creating pull quotes, which are discussed in detail in Chapter 6, is another simple, inexpensive way of adding visual interest to newsletter pages. Pull quotes also make your pages appear more accessible because they break up long passages of text.

Instruction manuals for page-layout programs don't always explain how to create pull quotes, but it's not difficult. First, draw a box, specifying that you want text to wrap around it. Then format the border of the box to the desired width, style, and/or color. Next, specify whether the box is to be clear or shaded (if shaded, specify the percentage of fill). Finally, place the quote inside the box and format it as you like—bold, italic, and so forth. The pull quote in Figure 7.6 on page 169 consists of a shaded box with no borders. The text, while in the same font as the body of the article, is larger, centered, and white, which allows it to stand out against the dark background.

Drop Caps

The drop cap—a noticeably large initial letter of the first word in an article (or a new section of an article)—is another easy-to-create graphical element for adding visual interest to your newsletter. In Figure 7.6, the drop caps, along with the subheads, photos, and a pull quote, help break up the text of the long article into shorter, more inviting chunks. This

Cafe Dining in Paris Proves Relaxing

Duis autem vel eum iriure dolor in hendrerit in vulputate velit esse molestie consequat, vel illum dolore eu feugiat nulla facilisis at vero eros et accumsan et iusto odio dignissim qui blandit praesent luptatum zzril deleniam nonummy nibh euismod tincidunt ut laoreet dolore magna aliquam erat volutpat. Ut wisi enim ad minim veniam, quis nostrud exerci tation ullamcorper suscipit lobortis nisl ut aliquip ex ea commodo consequat.

Duis autem vel eum iriure dolor in hendrerit in vulputate velit esse molestie consequat, vel illum dolore eu feugiat nulla facilisis at vero eros et iusto odio dignissim qui blandit praesent luptatum zzril delenit augue duis dolore te feugait nulla facilisi. Lorem ipsum dolor sit amet, consectetuer adipiscing elit, sed diam nonummy nibh euismod tincidunt ut laoreet dolore magna aliquam erat volutpat.

Ut wisi enim ad minim veniam, quis nostrud exerci tation ullamcorper suscipit lobortis nisl ut aliquip ex ea commodo consequat. Duis autem vel eum iriure dolor in hendrerit in vulputate velit esse molestie consequat, vel illum dolore eu feugiat nulla facilisis at vero eros et accumsan et iusto odio dignissim qui blandit praesent luptatum zzril delenit augue duis dolore te feugait nulla facilisi.

Nam liber tempor cum soluta nobis eleifend option congue nihil imperdiet doming id quod mazim placerat facer possim assum. Lorem ipsum dolor sit amet, suscipit lobortisconsectetuer adipiscing elit, sed diam nonummy nibh euismod tincidunt ut laoreet dolore magna aliquam erat volutpat.

Duis autem vel eum iriure dolor in hendrerit in vulputate velit esse molestie consequat, suscipit lobortis vel illum doorem ipsum dolor sit amet, consectetuer adipiscing elit, sed iam nonummy nibh euismod tincidunt ut laoreet dolore magna aliquam erat volutpat. Ut wisi enim ad minim veniam, quis nostrud exerci tation ullamcorper suscipit lobortis nisl ut aliquip ex ea commodo consequat.

Blandit idoi quiduis autem

Eum iriure dolor in hendrerit in vulputate velit esse molestie consequat, vel illum dolore eu feugiat nulla facilisis at vero eros et accumsan et iusto odio dignissim qui blandit praesent luptatum zzril delenit augue duis dolore te feugait nulla facilisi. Lorem ipsum dolor sit amet, consectetuer adipiscing elit, sed diam nonummy nibh euismod tincidunt ut laoreet dolore magna aliquam erat volutpat.

Nam liber tempor cum soluta nobis eleifend option congue nihil imperdiet doming id quod mazim placerat facer possim assum. Lorem ipsum dolor sit amet, suscipit lobortisconsectetuer

Tesse molestie consequat, vel illum dolore eu feugiat nulla facilisis at vero eros et accumsan et iusto odio dignissim qui duis dolore te feugait nulla facilisi.

Ut wisi enim ad minim veniam, quis nostrud exerci tation ullamcorper suscipit lobortis nisl ut aliquip ex ea commodo consequat. Duis autem vel eum iriure dolor in hendrerit in vulputate velit esse molestie consequat, vel illum dolore eu feugiat nulla facilisis at vero eros et accumsan et iusto odio dignissim qui blandit praesent luptatum zzril delenit augue duis dolore te feugait nulla facilisi.

---

adipiscing elit, sed diam nonummy nibh euismod tincidunt ut laoreet dolore magna aliquam erat volutpat. Ut wisi enim ad minim veniam, quis nostrud exerci tation ullamcorper magna suscipit lobortis nisl ut aliquip ex ea commodo.

Duis autem vel eum iriure dolor in hendrerit in vulputate velit esse molestie consequat, suscipit lobortis vel illum dolore eu feugiat nulla facilisis magna.

Iore eu feugiat nulla facilisis magna.orem ipsum dolor sit adipiscing elit, sed diam nonummy nibh euismod tincidunt ut laoreet dolore magna aliquam erat volutpat. Ut wisi enim ad minim veniam, quis nostrud exerci tation ullamcorper suscipit lobortis nisl ut aliquip ex ea commodo consequat.

Le Traiteur offers lunch as well as late afternoon tea.

dignissim qui blandit praesent luptatum zzril delenit augue duis dolore te feugait nulla facilisi.

Nam liber tempor cum soluta nobis eleifend option congue nihil imperdiet doming id quod mazim placerat facer possim assum. Lorem ipsum dolor sit amet, suscipit lobortisconsectetuer adipiscing elit, sed diam nonummy nibh euismod tincidunt ut laoreet dolore magna aliquam erat volutpat. Ut wisi enim ad minim veniam, quis nostrud exerci tation ullamcorper suscipit lobortis nisl ut aliquip ex ea commodo consequat. Lorem ipsum dolor sit amet, consectetuer adipiscing elit, sed diam nonummy nibh euismod tincidunt ut laoreet dolore magna aliquam erat volutpat.

Ut wisi enim ad minim veniam, quis nostrud exerci tation ullamcorper suscipit lobortis nisl ut aliquip ex ea commodo consequat. Duis autem vel eum iriure dolor in hendrerit in vulputate velit esse molestie consequat, vel illum dolore eu feugiat nulla facilisis at vero eros et accumsan et iusto odio

Nuis autem vel eumin vulputate velit esse molestie consequat, vel illum dolore eu feugiat nulla facilisis at vero eros et accumsan et iusto odio dignissim qui blandit praesent luptatum zzril delenit augue duis dolore te feugait nulla facilisi. Lorem ipsum dolor sit amet, consectetuer adipiscing elit, sed diam nonummy nibh euismod tincidunt ut laoreet dolore magna aliquam erat volutpat.

---

dolor in hendrerit in vulputate velit esse molestie consequat, vel illum dolore eu feugiat nulla facilisis at vero eros et iusto odio dignissim qui blandit praesent luptatum zzril delenit augue duis dolore te feugait nulla facilisi. Lorem ipsum dolor sit amet, consectetuer adipiscing elit, sed diam nonummy nibh euismod tincidunt ut laoreet dolore magna aliquam erat volutpat odio.

Ut wisi enim ad minim veniam, quis nostrud exerci tation ullamcorper suscipit lobortis nisl ut aliquip ex ea commodo consequat. Duis autem vel eum iriure dolor in hendrerit in vulputate velit esse molestie consequat, vel illum dolore eu feugiat nulla facilisis at vero eros et accumsan et iusto odio dignissim qui blandit praesent luptatum zzril

Tesse molestie consequat, vel illum dolore eu feugiat nulla facilisis at vero eros et accumsan et iusto odio dignissim qui duis dolore te feugait nulla facilisi.

Euism od tincidunt

Duis autem vel eum iriure dolor in hendrerit in vulputate velit esse molestie consequat, suscipit lobortis vel illum doconsectetuer adipiscing elit, sed diam nonummy nibh euismod tincidunt ut laoreet dolore magna aliquam erat volutpat. Ut wisi enim ad minim veniam, quis nostrud exerci tation ullamcorper suscipit lobortis nisl ut aliquip ex

Ea commodo consequat. Duis autem vel eum iriure

Ut wisi enim ad minim veniam, quis nostrud exerci tation ullamcorper suscipit lobortis nisl ut aliquip ex ea commodo consequat. Duis autem vel eum iriure dolor in hendrerit in vulputate velit esse molestie consequat, vel illum dolore eu feugiat nulla facilisis at vero eros et accumsan et iusto odio

---

brings up another bit of advice—avoid using drop caps in short articles, as they will overwhelm the text.

Limit drop caps to a maximum of three per page (six per two-page spread). And always check that the drop caps on a spread don't unintentionally spell anything embarrassing or unwanted, like the acronym of your company's competitor or an objectionable four-letter word.

You can create drop caps right in your page-layout software. Usually it's as simple as selecting the letter and having the computer enlarge and format it for you.

Figure 7.6
Pull quotes and drop caps add visual interest and break up the text of long articles.

PHOTOGRAPHS

Photographs add life and vibrancy to any type of newsletter. In a commercial marketing newsletter, professional product photos convey a sophisticated image. In an association newsletter, photos help members get to know one another. Headshots of authors help personalize their writing. Sometimes the subject of a story—a new employee, a renovated building—cries out for a picture.

Your newsletter's budget and purpose will determine whether you hire a professional photographer, take pictures yourself, or purchase photos from an outside source. If you use your newsletter to market your products or services, you'll probably want the sharp images that only a professional can provide. For an expensive subscription newsletter, you'll want the same quality. But in an association newsletter, you can probably get away with reasonably skilled amateur photography (especially if you follow the advice in this section). You can also use a combination of professional and amateur work. Or you might set up a single session with a professional to shoot photos that you'll have occasion to reuse, like head-shots of executives or pictures of your building. Then you can take your own pictures at meetings and other events as the need arises.

The first part of this section discusses the photographic equipment you'll need to "do it yourself," as well as guidelines for setting up well-composed photos. You'll also learn about stock photography and other outside sources for obtaining images. Finally, you'll see how to prepare your photos for print reproduction or online display.

Photographic Equipment

Today's cameras fall into two categories: traditional film and digital. The quality of digital pictures is not always as good as that of traditional photos, but you do have more control over their appearance. Using the image-editing software on your computer enables you to crop (cut down) pictures, correct faulty exposures, adjust sizing, and much more.

Film Cameras

If you choose to use a film camera, you can get good results with either a point-and-shoot or a single-lens reflex camera. *Point-and-shoot cameras* automatically focus pictures and control exposure settings, like apertures and shutter speed. With most *single-lens reflex cameras,* you have the choice of either adjusting these settings manually—giving you more control over your pictures—or having the camera do it for you. If you decide to become more proficient at photography, single-lens reflex cameras also offer the option of buying additional flashes, lenses, and other accessories. They are, however, bulkier and usually more expensive than point-and-shoot cameras. Whichever type of film camera you choose, make sure it comes with a zoom lens that ranges from about 28 or 35 to

70 or 80 millimeters. The zoom lens allows you to take both close-up and distance shots.

In the past, it was important to use black and white film for photos that were to be reproduced in black and white in a newsletter. This is no longer the case. Even if you plan to reproduce your photographs in black and white, you can use color film. When purchasing film, you'll also have to choose a speed, which is marked on the box. Numbers like 200 and 400 indicate film speed—the higher the number, the "faster" the film. A speed of 200 is fine for most purposes, but when shooting in settings like indoor sporting events, where you are photographing fast movement from a distance without the benefit of bright sunlight, use the fastest film you can find.

Digital Cameras

Digital cameras record pictures on a memory card or stick. They don't require film, so you can skip the picture-developing step, and simply transfer your photos from the camera to your computer. You can place digital pictures in your newsletter's page-layout file to send to your printer for reproduction, or you can upload them directly to your web newsletter.

The resolution of digital cameras is measured in pixels. Choose a medium-resolution model for newsletter photography. Most digital cameras offer automatic focusing and have automatic exposure control. Since you'll want to take both close-up and distance shots, choose a camera with an optical zoom rated 3X or higher. (A zoom rated 3X can magnify images up to three times their original size; a zoom rated 8X can magnify up to eight times the original size, and so forth.)

Planning Shots

Whether you're using a professional photographer or taking the pictures yourself, do some advance planning. If you are paying a professional photographer, talk to him before the shoot. Be as specific as you can about the people and events you want captured. This will also ensure that he brings the right equipment for the job. Also, think about whether you can get several jobs done in one day. For instance, if the photographer is coming to shoot a company meeting in the afternoon, perhaps he can take headshots of key personnel in the morning.

Make sure the site for the shoot will be available, and let the photo subjects know ahead of time that you or a photographer will be taking

It is a good idea to give the subjects of a photo shoot advance notice of the event. This will help ensure that they attend, and give them an opportunity to dress and look their best.

pictures at the event. This will help ensure that they attend, and give them the opportunity to dress in the style they prefer. Think about whom you want to photograph with whom, and in what situations. Make a list of the shots you'll need, so you won't forget any.

If you are going to be taking the photos, try to arrive at the event a bit early, so you'll have time to talk to some of the people you'll be shooting and develop a rapport with them. Give them a few minutes warning before you start shooting; they may want to comb their hair or straighten their ties.

When setting up a shot, look at the background. Indoors, a white or neutral background works well. Situate your subjects at least four to six feet from the background. If there are distracting items in view, like a stack of boxes or a hanging plant, you have several choices. If the item is small, you can remove it. If it's large, you can move the people to a different location or shoot from a different angle. You can also have the people move forward, so the distracting item is distant enough that it can be cropped from the photo.

Be aware of any strong vertical or horizontal lines, like the edge of a table, a window frame, or a tree trunk, that will be part of your shots. Don't let these lines cut your picture down the middle. Move up, down, left, or right so that the line is off center.

Knowing how to make people relax is essential for good shots. When taking posed shots, have your subjects repeat a silly word or phrase. Or tell a joke or riddle, as long as it's short and simple enough that everyone will get it quickly. Some people anticipate the flash and automatically close their eyes when having their pictures taken. If you notice this happening, tell your subjects that you are going to count to three and then shoot. The "eyelid shutters" can then force themselves to keep their eyes open.

If you're shooting a small number of people, have pen and paper available to jot down their names. To help you remember who is who, make notes like "girl with striped shirt: Francia Delaney; boy with hat: Armand Jeffries." If you're shooting a large group of people you don't know, submit the developed photo to the person in charge of the group and have him identify the subjects for you.

If possible, try to take a large number of photos in a variety of poses and settings. It takes many shots to come up with just a couple of good pictures. Your page design, for instance, may demand a vertical rather than a horizontal shot, or a shot in which people are looking left and not right. Having a variety of photos from which to choose will make finding the right one easy.

Typically, it takes a number of shots to come up with just a few that you can use. For this reason, during a photo shoot, try to take lots of pictures in various settings and poses. Give yourself a variety of pictures from which to choose.

What follows are tips for shooting typical newsletter photos—head-shots, grip and grins, and group, banquet, and performance shots.

Headshots

Headshots are ideal for capturing a subject's character. For most people, a head-and-shoulders shot is more flattering than a three-quarter or full body shot. But, as your driver's license or passport photo demonstrates, getting a good headshot is challenging. Consider having a professional take these pictures for you, especially if they are of important people or ones you plan to use often. For such cases, a session with a professional photographer can be a good investment.

If you must take headshots yourself, have the subject position his body at a three-quarter angle to the camera, and then turn his head toward his front shoulder, as in Figure 7.7 at right. Shoot the picture vertically, even if you plan to crop it to a square.

Grip and Grins

Photos of people receiving checks, awards, and plaques are common (to the point of being monotonous) in newsletters. Appropriately called "grip and grins," this type of photo usually shows a person receiving an award from another person, while both subjects shake hands and smile for the camera. The good news is there are ways you can make this type of shot more interesting.

Figure 7.8, below, shows two grip-and-grin shots of the same subjects. The photo on the left is a typical one, showing two people shaking hands as they stare into the camera. In it, the subjects seem more interested in the camera than in each other. Also, the doorway, trash can and stool on the right make for a distracting background. In the improved photo on the right, the subjects are looking at each other, rather than at

Figure 7.7
Headshot
For headshots, have your subject turn his body at a three-quarter angle toward the camera, and then turn his head to his front shoulder.

Figure 7.8
Grip-and-Grin Shots
Although the purpose of both shots at left is the same, zooming in on the reaction of the award recipient, and cropping out the distracting background makes the photo on the right more interesting.

the camera, and the focus is on the recipient of the award—and his reaction—rather than on the presenter. The subjects are also standing close enough to each other that the shot was able to be taken vertically, before it was cropped to an appropriate size. Finally, the distractions in the background have been cropped out.

If your goal when taking a grip-and-grin photo is to get a good shot of the plaque or award, as well as the people, forget the handshake. Have the subjects stand side by side, with the recipient holding the plaque in front of his chest.

Group Shots

Making sure that everyone is visible while still creating an interesting shot is your primary goal when taking a group photo.

Taking group pictures can be challenging, but following a few simple guidelines can help you achieve successful results. The primary goal when taking group pictures is to be sure everyone is visible while still creating an interesting shot. For groups of more than ten or twelve, you may have to line up everyone in rows or semicircles to fit into the shot. If they are standing, place the shorter people in front. If the front row is sitting, have the shorter people stand in back to even out the heights of the rows. When shooting people in a semicircle, have the people on your left turn their right shoulders to the camera, and the people on your right turn their left shoulders toward you. Have everyone place their hands at their sides. You don't want some people to appear with their hands behind them and others with their arms folded. If you notice that someone's shirttail is hanging out, rather than singling that person out, make a general suggestion that everyone tuck their shirts in and button their jackets as you discreetly make eye contact with the person you have in mind.

With smaller groups, you can make the picture more interesting by varying their poses and possibly positioning them in such as way as to illustrate why they are together. For example, if you are shooting a group of engineers who designed an automobile, take them outside and situate them around the car. Position some behind it, some in front, others on the bumper, and one leaning on an open door. When taking photos of the members of a local library's book club, you might seat some at a table in front of the stacks, with one or two sitting on top of the table, and others standing beside or behind it.

In a large-group setting like a conference or seminar, when you cannot possibly get everyone into the picture without making them appear so small that they're essentially invisible, consider the following. Focus on one or two people in the group—the presenter with a few members of the audience in the foreground, or an enthusiastic participant raising his hand—and make them the dominant elements in your picture.

Banquet Photos

When photographing people at a luncheon, wedding reception, or dinner meeting, try to do your shooting before the meal is served. If you wait until after the meal, leftover food, empty wine bottles, and dirty napkins strewn across the table will create a distracting foreground for your shot. Also, take care that the table centerpiece isn't blocking anyone's face and that no heads appear to be growing out of the centerpiece itself. At a typical round table that seats ten, you can get a tighter shot by positioning half of the people seated and the other half standing behind them.

When taking photos of people at events where a meal is served—wedding receptions, luncheons, dinner meetings—try to take the shots before the meal. Waiting until after the meal means dealing with a messy foreground of dirty plates, empty wine bottles, and leftover food.

Performance Photos

Once I attended a solo violin concert in a small recital hall that held only about sixty people. As the violinist played, a newspaper photographer approached him and took pictures, moving around and crouching to get shots from several different angles. After throwing the photographer a few dirty looks to no avail, the violinist actually stopped playing and gestured angrily at her with his bow to make her stop.

When planning to shoot a performance, you can avoid such embarrassing situations by taking a few preliminary steps. A week or so before the show, contact the producer or director to find out if taking photos will be permitted during the performance. If not, ask if you can take photos beforehand. Often, such photo opportunities are available during dress rehearsals. This is a great opportunity because costumes and sets will be complete and there's no fear of disrupting a live performance. If, however, you are able to take photos during the actual performance, do not use a flash, which is disruptive to both the performers and the audience.

Getting Permission for Photography

Do you need the permission of the people you photograph before publishing their pictures in your newsletter? It depends. The courts have ruled that photographing people in public places for the purpose of reporting news does not invade their privacy, since people have no reasonable expectation of privacy when they are out in public. Even if you unwittingly publish a picture of two people who are holding hands in the park (but who are also married to other people), or of a person attending a rock concert while playing hooky from work, you haven't

You do not need permission to use photos of people taken in public places for the purpose of reporting news.

violated their privacy. (If, however, you are aware of the touchy circumstance, use common sense, and don't publish the shot.)

You are not, however, free to publish pictures of people in situations that a reasonable person would find embarrassing or highly offensive—for example, an unconscious accident victim who is half-undressed while receiving medical care.

You can also avoid legal problems by making sure the photos you publish are reasonably related to the stories they accompany and to the information in the captions. For example, if you illustrate a story about convicted felons with a picture of a law-abiding citizen, you might be sued for placing the person in a "false light," or for libel.

The courts also recognize the right of individuals to control the commercial use of their likenesses. This means you need permission to use photographs of famous people for commercial purposes, such as in advertising. But you *can* shoot and publish their pictures for news reporting purposes. To avoid the possibility of legal action, ask the subjects of your photos to sign a release form (called a *model release*), such as the one in Figure 7.9. Although this type of form can be signed at any time, typically, it is done at the time the photo is taken. If the subjects are children, have their parents sign the form.

Photography can be banned in courtrooms, museums, military facilities, casinos, and on private property. However, it is permissible to photograph a private building from a public street. But you may need permission from the copyright owner if you want to photograph a copyrighted object, like a painting or a statue. In some cases, shooting commercial photographs on public property requires a permit, which you can obtain from the state or local film commission.

Model Release Form

I, _____,
(name)

hereby grant the use of my photographic image in the *Wildlife Watch* newsletter published by the Hampshire Wildlife Society.

(PLEASE NOTE: If the subject is a child, signature of a parent or guardian is required.)

SIGNATURE:_____

NAME:_____

DATE: _____

Figure 7.9
You can avoid the possibility of legal action by asking the subjects of your photography to sign a release form like this one.

Outside Photo Sources

Don't overlook outside sources for obtaining photos. Some companies and organizations provide them with the press releases they distribute. Contact their public relations departments, which may be able to provide you with pictures of executives, buildings, or products, as well. If you're writing an article about an upcoming presentation by a professional speaker, ask him or his agent for a publicity photo. When writing a book review, download a scanned photo of the book's cover from the publisher's website. (Usually publishers are happy to grant permission for you to do this.)

Stock photography is another good source for pictures. Stock photos are professional shots that you either purchase or rent. The headshot in Figure 7.7 on page 173 came from a collection of stock photography. Like clip art, stock photos come in an extensive range of categories like health, entertainment, people, food, and finance. They are available on CDs or can be downloaded from the Internet. Check out Index Stock Imagery (*www.indexstock.com*), Corbis (*www.corbis.com*), and PhotoDisc (*www.photodisc.com*), or try some of the other stock photography companies listed in the Resources section. You can buy an entire collection, or rent individual photos for one-time use.

Stock photos are far less expensive than custom shots taken by hired photographers. When a deadline is approaching and you need a picture, it's a lot easier to download a stock photo from the Internet than it is to set up a photo shoot. And with stock photography, you can see what the photo looks like before paying for it—a luxury you don't have when using a photographer.

Another advantage of stock photos is that they are taken under ideal light and weather conditions. Keep in mind, however, that although this makes for ideal-looking pictures, such quality can also give your newsletter an unrealistic look. And don't ever run a stock photo in a manner that might cause readers to mistake it for a news photo. For instance, if you're writing a story about last month's company picnic, don't use a stock photo of people at a picnic. Readers may think the people in the photo are company employees or that the park depicted was the site of the event.

Before you buy stock photography, read the license to discover any usage limitations, such as the types of publications in which the photos can appear and how many times they can be used. Make sure that your intended use will fit the seller's limitations.

Preparing Photographs for Production

Before you can use a photograph in your layout, some preparation is necessary. Obviously, if you're using film, you'll have to get it developed.

Stock photos—high-quality professional pictures that come in an extensive range of categories—are available to buy or rent. They are less expensive than custom shots taken by a hired photographer.

For film and digital photos, you may also need to correct exposure problems or crop the photos to remove distracting backgrounds. To spruce up your layout, you may consider adding special effects to your pictures. All of these processes are discussed in this section.

When it is time to develop your film, you can either bring it to a pharmacy or discount store that will send it to a large processing lab, or take it to a small lab that does in-house processing. Keep in mind that you will get better quality prints from a smaller lab, where the technicians have more time to examine them for flaws. A large lab that processes as many as ten or fifteen thousand rolls a day won't be able to give your job that kind of personalized attention. Another advantage to a small shop is that the technicians are on site. You can talk to them about how to improve your photos. If the quality of your prints is flawed, don't assume it's because you made a mistake when you shot them. Discuss the problem with the film technician to see if the pictures can be printed again to correct the problem.

Today, most newsletter editors are choosing to use digital photos in their layouts. The advantage of digital photos is that you can load them onto your computer. Then you can crop them, touch them up, or convert them to black and white using image-editing software like Adobe Photoshop, Microsoft Picture Manager, or Corel Photo Album. It's also much easier to scale digital pictures to the size you want and place them in your layout electronically than it is to do these tasks manually.

Another advantage of using a digital camera is that you don't have to wait for film to be developed—you can preview the photos on the camera's display screen immediately. You can also delete any poor shots, and continue clicking away until you get the exact picture you want. If you'd like, you can even show the photos to your subjects and let them choose the one they like best.

Even if you take pictures with a film camera, processing labs can convert them to digital files. You can also use a scanner to convert printed photos into digital files. If you don't own a scanner, a copy or print shop can scan them for you.

The ability to immediately preview the photos you have taken and delete those you don't want is one of the many advantages of using a digital camera.

Correcting Exposure and Cropping

You wouldn't distribute a newsletter with illegible text, so why would you distribute a newsletter with illegible photos? Just as your articles need editing before they're published, your photographs need editing, too. However, you need to strike a balance between making your photographs clear and altering them until they no longer illustrate the content of the story, or until the results are deceptive. For example, it's considered acceptable to correct or alter basic photographic elements, such as brightness, contrast, and tint for your photos. You can also eliminate certain cosmetic problems, such as red eyespots, which are caused by a camera's flash, and, in headshots, minor facial blemishes. With digital photos, you can make these types of corrections using image-editing software.

It's also acceptable to crop a picture to focus on its main subject or idea, or to cut down an image that is too large for the layout. You can do this manually or through your image-editing or page-layout software. Let's say you've been given the full-shot photo shown in Figure 7.10 at right, but it's too big for your layout. You could shrink it down, but then the girl's face would be so small, it would be difficult to see her expression. Instead, you could crop the image, as shown in the bottom photo. Readers will still get a good look at the girl's expression, and the photo will fit on your page.

You don't want to crop a photo in a way that changes its main idea. Let's say you've taken a picture of a swimmer in a pool. If the purpose of the photo is to show readers how to do the backstroke efficiently, it's okay to crop the lounge chairs on the pool deck from the picture. But if the purpose is to show the luxurious facilities of the health club, you'll want to preserve the chairs. If your story is about traffic jams in the pool caused by overcrowding during lap swims, crop the chairs, but include the other swimmers in the picture.

It is also not acceptable to crop a photo to hide information. For instance, it would be misleading to crop women from the sides of a meeting photo to purposely make it appear as if women were underrepresented at the event. Nor would it be acceptable to delete a woman from the center of the photo, as some photo editing software lets you do. After cropping, reread the article and the photo caption to make sure they don't contradict what the picture shows.

Never publish a photo that is out of focus. A blurry photo doesn't tell readers any story, and it looks amateurish. Finally, use discretion. Think twice before publishing an unflattering photo, like one in which a person is making a quirky face, unless you believe it serves an important journalistic purpose. And to keep yourself out of legal hot water, don't publish photos of people in situations that are highly offensive or that may be embarrassing.

Full shot

Cropped shot

Figure 7.10
Cropping the photo above allows you to enlarge it for a close-up view of the girl's face.

Figure 7.11
Removing the background
of a picture, called
"silhouetting," creates a
surreal effect.

Creating Special Effects

You can spice up your layout by applying special effects to your photographs with image-editing software. For example, you can remove all background behind a person or object to give it the look of a silhouette, as in the bottom photo of Figure 7.11 at left. This effect can be useful for highlighting a picture of a product in a marketing newsletter, or for showing a single person in an association newsletter. Silhouetting does, however, give a surreal look to pictures, so avoid using this special effect on photos that accompany hard news stories.

In addition to silhouetting, there are other special effects you can use to give photos added visual interest. You can, for instance, create shadows behind the pictures or blur the backgrounds. You can also distort images, change colors, or use sepia tones to give photos an old-fashioned, antique look. Altering the edges of photographs is another option. This effect allows you to change the shape and thickness of the edges. You can even blur the edges so the photo appears to fade into the page.

Of course, these and other special effects must be used appropriately. Your decision to use them should depend on whether they fit the tone and design of your newsletter, whether they suit the topic of the article, and whether they meet journalistic standards for accurate reporting.

CONCLUSION

By now you should have a good idea of how to create and use graphics and photos in your newsletter. Following the advice in this chapter will enable you to greatly enhance the quality of the visuals you publish. Even if you thought you lacked the artistic talent to produce an attractive newsletter, you can see how computer software, plus an eye for design, can help you pull it off. The next chapter will help you further develop that eye for design.

PART THREE

Taking It to the Streets
Producing Your Print Newsletter

You've written and edited your newsletter's copy. You've shot the photos and created the graphics, and now you're ready to get your message out. In spite of all the electronic options available these days, you've decided that print is still an effective means for distributing your newsletter. So now your pages need to be designed, laid out, printed, and mailed. As a newsletter publisher, you need to understand the ins and outs of these crucial steps, just as well as you understand the writing and editing process.

The way you present your message is as important as what you say—you must take the same care to assure that your newsletter's design and layout communicate the right message and tone. Whether you or someone else designs it, the results will be a reflection of you. The information in Chapter 8 will help you speak the language of your graphic designer and layout artist and understand their work.

Publishers cannot divorce themselves from the production process—printing and distribution—either. Katharine Graham, the renowned former publisher of *The Washington Post*, learned that lesson well. During a pressman's strike against the newspaper in the 1970s, she spent several months working double shifts beside other executives and white collar employees, doing everything from running the presses to packaging and labeling Sunday papers for mailing.

You may never have to contend with a picket line, but you might have to cope with getting your newsletter printed and distributed in the face of some other unforeseen obstacle. Or you may have to decide whether to "stop the presses" to correct a serious mistake in one of your articles. You'll definitely have to find a way to contain production costs, since printing and postage consume a huge chunk of print newsletter budgets. In fact, if your newsletter is a volunteer effort, all the money you spend may go toward printing and mailing. So becoming familiar with those steps by reading Chapter 9 is essential.

If you plan to distribute your newsletter electronically—via a website, e-mail, or PDF file—you can skip most of Part Three. If, however, you are producing a PDF newsletter, you'll want to read Chapter 8, "Designing and Laying Out Print Newsletters." Most of the principles of page design it presents are transferable to PDF newsletters as well. And the section on "Type Design," beginning on page 201, is valuable no matter what type of newsletter you are distributing.

CHAPTER 8

DESIGNING AND LAYING OUT PRINT NEWSLETTERS

f you've ever built a house (or dreamed of building one), you know that construction projects proceed in two stages. First, an architect designs the house based on the wants and needs of the homebuyer. Out of this work comes a blueprint. During the second stage, the carpenter buys materials and constructs the house according to the specifications of the blueprint. Newsletter production follows a similar process. First, a graphic artist designs the newsletter, based on its intended audience, purpose, and tone, creating a "blueprint"—or template. Then, a layout artist gathers "materials"—copy and graphics—and constructs each issue. Of course, you may be wearing both the design and layout hats, especially if your newsletter has a tight budget.

While the principles of newsletter design and layout are universal, the procedures for carrying them out will vary, depending on the software you use. So you will need to take a training class, seek online help, or read a manual to get started with your particular program. But before getting involved with the minutiae of menus and mouse clicks, read this chapter. It will teach you the goals of newsletter design and show you how to format pages and type to meet those goals. It will also outline a process for preparing layout, and advise you on choosing page-layout software.

Even if you decide to delegate the tasks of design and layout, reading this chapter will give you enough knowledge on this subject to know what you want and be able to explain it to the graphic artist, who does the actual work.

PRINCIPLES OF NEWSLETTER DESIGN

Before getting involved with the details of newsletter design—How many columns should I use? Where do I place artwork? What's the best typeface for a headline?—you need to take a step back and understand what you are trying to achieve with your design. Unlike some graphic design pieces, such as billboards or cereal packages, newsletters require extended reading, and their design must make easy work of it. Your newsletter's design should fulfill the following five goals. It should:

1. Be attractive and easy to read.

2. Draw attention to important information.

3. Provide information through skimming aids.

4. Communicate your chosen tone.

5. Demonstrate editorial stability.

The following material takes a closer look at these goals. While reading them, refer to the newsletter spread in Figure 8.1 on page 187, which serves as an example.

1. Be Attractive and Easy to Read

Your first goal, of course, is to get people to pick up your newsletter and flip through it. To entice them to do so, you have to make it attractive. People generally find certain design elements more attractive than others. Most of us prefer the look of space that is arranged in certain proportions. For instance, we favor rectangles to squares, as you can see by observing the shape of most paintings found in art museums. Newsletters are typically printed on rectangular pages, and divided into rectangular columns and boxes for added visual appeal.

Balance is another appealing characteristic of design. Headlines, photographs, pictures, and boxes on a newsletter page all appear to have different "weights" to the human eye. Large items look heavier than small ones; dark items look heavier than light ones; bold text looks heavier than normal text. People prefer the look of individual pages and two-page spreads that are balanced, not weighted on one side or the other. To appeal to this sense, when laying out your newsletter, you can balance heavy items near the center of a spread with lighter items toward the edges—as if balancing a seesaw. In Figure 8.1, the smaller boxes at the edge of the pages balance the large box of text near the center. And the large, bold headline at the top of each page is balanced by a dark rule at the bottom.

White space on a printed page is another appealing element. It causes the eye to focus on the text and surrounding graphics, and gives an uncluttered look to your pages. White space also helps organize material—items with little white space between them appear to go together, while those with more white space appear separate. For example, on the left-hand page of Figure 8.1, the large amount of white space above the headline of the article at the bottom of the page clearly separates it from the article above.

White space, however, is not appealing when it is created unintentionally. For example, too much space between a headline and a story makes the two items appear unrelated, just as too much space between columns gives them the appearance of floating aimlessly on the page.

Once you've persuaded people to pick up your newsletter, you want it to be easy to read. How wide you make your columns, how closely you space lines of text, the color you choose for paper and type—all of these factors influence your newsletter's readability. In Figure 8.1, the typefaces and their sizes were chosen for their readability. We'll discuss these considerations in greater detail later in the chapter.

> White space is an appealing design element that aids in organizing the material on a printed page, and it helps the eye focus on the text and surrounding graphics.

2. Draw Attention to Important Information

Once you have attracted readers, you'll want to make it easy for them to get the information they need from your newsletter. Your design should draw their attention to the most important items, show them where to start reading, and help them move through the pages.

You can draw attention to important items through their size, weight, and page position. Our eyes tend to follow a common sequence when looking at printed pages. They move from top to bottom and left to right; and from big to small, dark to light, and color to black and white. This means readers will notice a story at the top of the page before they see one at the bottom. They'll look at a large bold headline before the smaller, lighter text of an article. To draw attention to an item that is not in a prime position (say, it's on the bottom or the right side of the page), you can make it darker, larger, or colorful. If it's a headline, you can set it in larger type. If it's a short notice, you can place it in a box. White space also draws attention to darker items that are adjacent to it.

3. Provide Information Through Skimming Aids

Because most readers will skim over your publication before deciding which articles to go back and read, your headlines, captions, subheads, and other skimming aids must stand out. Setting them larger, bolder, and in typefaces that are different from the body text will achieve this purpose.

Today's readers, ever in a hurry, will typically skim through a newsletter first, then go back and read those areas that have attracted their attention. What will attract your readers' attention as they skim? Contrast. Take a look at the pages in Figure 8.1. The headlines, pull quote, subheads, and captions are easy to skim because they contrast with the body text. They are larger, darker, and set in different typefaces or type styles.

To achieve such contrast, you must first create consistency. Let's say a newsletter article contains the address of an important website. To make the address stand out, it is set in bold type. Would the reader spot it faster if it was the only bold item in the article, or one of ten? If it was the only bold item, of course. Bold type, used sparingly, contrasts successfully with the rest of the text.

In addition to skimming your newsletter during a preliminary once-over, readers may want to refer back to what they read earlier. They may, for example, want to find the location of your monthly meeting. Your design can help them find such information by emphasizing it—placing it in a boxed sidebar or table.

4. Communicate Your Chosen Tone

When you developed the idea for your newsletter, you chose a tone—formal or informal, casual or elegant, upscale or cost-conscious. Match the tone you use in your writing and editing to the tone of your design. Symmetrical design, such as a two-column format, conveys a formal tone, whereas an asymmetrical design is more casual. A layout that contains large areas of white space imparts a more upscale tone than does a dense layout. The colors, typefaces, art styles, and paper you choose will convey your tone as well. In Figure 8.1, the conservative tone of this newsletter is reflected in the Garamond typeface, justified columns, and symmetrical boxes along the outer edges of the pages.

5. Demonstrate Editorial Stability

The final goal of your newsletter's design is to demonstrate the stability of your organization. You can do so by giving your publication a unified, consistent look from page to the page, and from issue to issue. If you experiment with different designs on each page or in each issue, readers will become confused. They won't have any visual clues to remind them that this is *your* newsletter. If you're an art lover, you've probably had the experience of walking into a museum gallery and identifying the artist of a painting you've never seen before. If you're a music fan, you can probably recognize different bands or recording artists on the radio before the DJ names them. The design of your pages should identify your newsletter just as strongly as a musical style identifies a composer. In addition, consistent design says, "This newsletter is no fly-by-night operation; it will be around next month, next year, and the year after that."

You achieve consistency by using the same margins, columns, typefaces, and colors on each page. You select styles for boxes, rules, drop caps, and clip art and repeat them throughout. In Figure 8.1, consistently designed borders, rules, and folio boxes unify the pages.

While it's fine to tweak a design once you've begun publication, you don't want to make major changes in each issue. That's why it's so important to spend time learning about design and typography *before* you start publishing. Fortunately, if you're new to graphic design, there are plenty of resources you can turn to for help. We'll discuss them in the next section.

Figure 8.1

This layout illustrates the five goals of newsletter design.

GETTING HELP

As you continue reading this chapter, your head may start to swim as you try to keep straight the difference between picas and points, Pantone and process color. Or you may find that all your other publishing responsibilities don't leave time for you to do your own design or layout. Your involvement may range from just supervising the work of a professional graphic artist to creating a design yourself from scratch. If you do hire a professional, you can still use the information in this chapter to help you speak her language. If you do the work yourself, you can profit from the experience of professionals at little cost by using templates; by collecting design samples; and by consulting books, magazines, and websites about design.

Graphic Designers

Hiring a graphic designer to create the initial design of your newsletter is a sound investment if your budget permits. Remember that design, unlike layout, is a one-time expense. And if the designer creates a software template for your newsletter that includes all the specifications you need for your layout, and gives you a mock-up (a sample issue), you may find that you can handle future layouts on your own.

If you can't afford to get professional help with the design of your entire newsletter, consider getting estimates for nameplate design alone. Professionals have access to expensive illustration software that allows them to customize type and graphics. They can create a unique design for your nameplate to strengthen your newsletter's identity.

Templates

If your budget does not allow you to hire a graphic designer to create a design for your newsletter, consider using a newsletter template, which comes bundled with your page-layout software.

A less expensive way to get a professional newsletter design is by using a newsletter template—a file that comes bundled with your page-layout program. You may also be able to find templates that are sold separately. You can adapt these templates, which are created by graphic designers, to your specific needs. Think of a template as one of those house plans you can order from a home and garden magazine. Templates have pre-designed nameplates, page and column sizes, typefaces, and colors, although you can change these settings. Using them allows you to benefit from the experience of a professional who has made most of the design decisions for you.

On the other hand, you may have difficulty finding a template that suits your newsletter's purpose and tone. And using one does not eliminate the need to learn your page-layout software. For example, the template may not have a style for pull quotes, so you'll have to design one yourself. Or you may have to incorporate your corporate colors into the design. But once you read the rest of this chapter, you should feel more comfortable performing these tasks.

Keep a collection of magazines, brochures, newsletters, and other publications on hand. Browse through them when trying to come up with design ideas.

The Competition

Even experienced graphic artists get some of their ideas by observing the work of others. If you collect sample newsletters, you'll see how other publications have handled design questions. Keep an eye out for free newsletters distributed at retail stores, universities, or conferences. Visit your public library to see which newsletters it carries. Pull them out of your utility bills or bank statements. And save other publications, like magazines and brochures, for typeface, color, and page-layout ideas. Keep a file of these samples, and refer to them when trying to come up with a pleasing design.

Other Resources

Space doesn't allow me to cover all the ins and outs of graphic design in this book. But plenty of books devoted to the topic are available. Look for those written by Robin Williams, Jan White, Roger C. Parker, and Chuck Green. These authors do a good job of making graphic design understandable to laypeople.

You can also look for trade books about your page-layout software. Often these books, available through bookstores or websites, guide you through the process of creating newsletters more specifically than the documentation that comes with the software. Browse through a few to see if they might help you out. Some of these books come with CDs that contain templates.

Subscribing to design newsletters and magazines is another great way for you to stay abreast of design techniques and trends. Try *Dynamic Graphics Magazine (www.dgusa.com)*. Or visit the following two sites— *graphicdesign.about. com* and *desktoppub.about.com*. Both are located on the About.com network, and offer a collection of web articles on design, as well as free e-mail newsletters.

PAGE DESIGN: CREATING A BLUEPRINT

The beginning of this chapter addressed the goals you are trying to achieve with your newsletter design. Now, it's time to answer specific design questions (How many columns should I use? Where do I place artwork? What's the best typeface for a headline?). First, we'll discuss those questions about page design.

When designing a dream house, you must first come up with a floor plan that specifies the size and shape of your rooms. Only later will you get down to the detail level of choosing kitchen cabinets and carpeting. With a newsletter, you start by designing your pages—their size, grid, color, and paper stock—before you design text and artwork.

Determining Page Size

A tabloid format is well suited to newsletters that run long articles and contain large graphics. But because of their size, tabloids don't easily fit into folders or binders, so readers are not likely to keep them.

The standard size of a single newsletter page is 8.5 x 11 inches. This size is the most popular because it fits in standard business envelopes, file folders, and three-ring binders. It is printed on 11-x-17-inch paper, which, when folded in half, produces a four page newsletter. That's why the number of pages in most newsletters is a multiple of four. If your newsletter is six or ten pages long, you'll need a single-sheet insert for the middle two pages, which can be awkward to staple.

You'll also find some newsletters printed as tabloids, as seen in Figure 8.2 on page 191. Each page is usually 11 x 17 inches, although the exact dimensions can vary. This size is reminiscent of a newspaper; in fact, it's often printed on newsprint paper stock. The tabloid format is well suited to newsletters that run longer articles and large artwork. But your readers are less likely to keep a tabloid after they read it, because it doesn't fit into a file folder or three-ring binder.

Another page format, often used for utility company newsletters, is a single sheet, about 6.5 x 11 (or 14) inches. Also shown in Figure 8.2, this type of newsletter, when folded horizontally two or three times, fits into a standard #6 $\frac{3}{4}$ billing envelope.

Before you settle on a paper size for your newsletter, particularly if it's not a standard 8.5-x-11-inch format, find out how much it will cost to print. It's also wise to put together a sample newsletter, folded and stapled as you plan to do, and bring it to the post office to estimate your mailing costs.

Tabloid newsletter   Single-sheet newsletter

Figure 8.2

An alternative to the standard page size of 8.5 x 11 inches is a larger tabloid format, which resembles a newspaper. Tabloid newsletters have space for longer articles and large graphics, but they are cumbersome to store. Still other newsletters are printed on a single sheet, which is usually folded horizontally to fit in a standard billing envelope.

Courtesy of Public Service of New Hampshire.

Setting Up Page Grids

Once you've selected a page size, it's time to decide on a grid. As shown in the example in Figure 8.3 on page 192, a grid consists of nonprinting lines that appear in your page-layout file and define the size and spacing of your columns and margins. It guides you in placing headlines, body text, and graphics. Using a consistent grid within each issue, as well as across issues, is an important way to achieve the design goal of demonstrating editorial stability. Since the vast majority of newsletters are printed on 8.5-x-11-inch paper, that's the size I'll assume you're using as I describe grids in this section.

Columns and Margins

Pull a couple books off your shelf and take a look at the length of each line of text. Chances are they will be less than five inches long. Readability research has determined that the most readable length for a line of type is from 1.67 to 4.5 inches, or about forty to sixty-five characters. This is the reason newspapers are printed in narrow columns, and why trade books like this one have deep margins on the outside of each page.

Figure 8.3
Your page grid defines the
size and spacing of your
columns and margins.

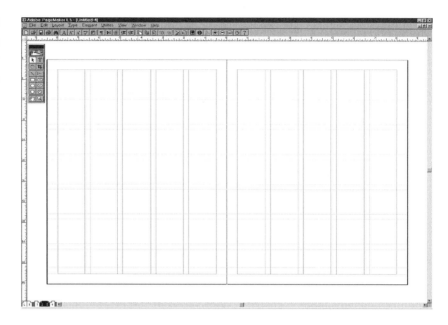

Lines that are too long force readers to shift their eyes from left to right as they read across the page, and make it difficult to find the beginning of the next line as they move down the page. You can create lines of this optimum 1.67- to 4.5-inch length by dividing your newsletter pages into columns.

The number of columns on your pages conveys a tone. A symmetrical, balanced two-column grid gives a conservative impression of being at rest. Three- or five-column grids have a more dynamic look and are also more flexible than two-column grids. As seen in Figure 8.4 on page 193, a two-column format allows you to run your headlines, stories, and pictures across one column or two. In a three-column format, you can run these items across one, two, or three columns.

With a five-column format, you wouldn't run your text in single columns because they are too narrow for readability. Instead, you would combine them. In the five-column example in Figure 8.4, four of these narrow columns on each page are combined to form two wider ones, which contain most of the text. The outer columns on each page, called *scholar's margins,* are devoted primarily to white space. Here, you might place the occasional caption, graphic, or pull quote (as seen in this example). Because white space emphasizes the text it surrounds, scholar's margins help you achieve the design goal of drawing the reader's attention to important information.

How wide should you make your columns? Use wider columns if you will be using larger type, and narrower columns for smaller type. This way, each line will fall within the optimum forty- to sixty-five-character guideline.

You'll also have to specify how much space goes between your columns. This space is measured in *picas*—a unit of measure used by typographers that equals 0.167 inches. Space of one to two picas between columns is about right. And be aware that you can set up your software to show measurements in picas rather than inches. *Ragged right type,* also called *left justified, left aligned,* or *flush left* (type that aligns with the left side of the column only) needs less space between columns than fully *justified type* (type that lines up with both the left and right sides of the column), because most of the words in ragged right type don't reach the end of the column.

Look at the two pages in Figure 8.5 on page 194. The text on the left page is ragged right; on the right page, it is justified. On both pages, the space between columns is one pica. This is fine for the ragged right text,

Figure 8.4
Page Columns
The number of columns you choose for your pages will convey a specific tone and allow for different editorial capabilities.

Two-Column Grid
A two-column grid, which conveys a conservative tone, allows you to run copy across one column or both.

Three-Column Grid
In a more dynamic-looking three-column grid, you can run headlines, stories, and pictures across one, two, or three columns.

Five-Column Grid
In a five-column grid, narrow columns are combined into wider ones for housing text. The outside scholar's margin, which contains white space, can be left blank or include a pull quote or graphic.

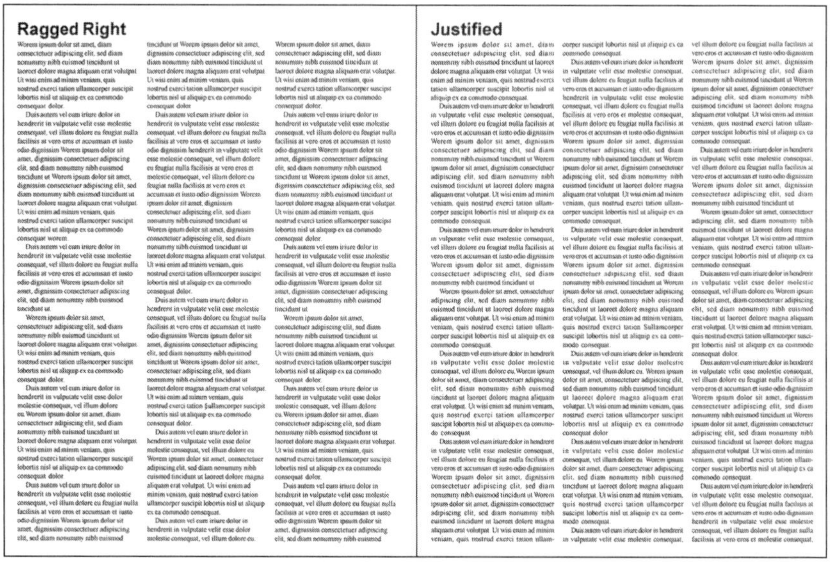

Figure 8.5

The column spacing on both of these pages is equal to one pica, but the justified text on the right could benefit from wider spacing.

but the justified columns on the right could be a bit farther apart. Also, keep in mind that if you decide to draw vertical rules between columns, you will need to add a bit more column space than you would if there were no rules.

In addition to deciding how to divide your space vertically into columns, you must decide how to divide it horizontally. If you set up horizontal gridlines like those in Figure 8.3 on page 192, it will be easy to line up your graphics, headlines, and rules between stories horizontally as well as vertically. You will find yourself dividing horizontal space differently for each issue, depending on the length of your copy and the size of your artwork. That's why there are so many horizontal gridlines in Figure 8.3.

The way you divide space horizontally on the front and back pages of your newsletter will vary somewhat from your inside spreads. On page one, your horizontal nameplate at the top of the page will cause your stories to start lower than they do on other pages. If your newsletter is a self-mailer and does not require an envelope, part of your back page will be devoted to your *mailing panel*—the area for the recipient's address, your return address, and postage. Mailing considerations, such as whether you will be mailing your newsletter flat or folded and how much space is required for the mailing panel, will determine how you set up your horizontal grid on that page. Mailing regulations may also determine where you can place margins on the back page.

When setting up your margins, try one-half inch (three picas) on the top, bottom, and sides to begin with. That amount of space is large enough to meet the minimums required by many printing presses and laser printers, but small enough to leave room for columns of a legible width. If you're using only two columns, you may want to set your margins a bit wider. If you plan to three-hole punch your newsletters so readers can store them in a binder, check the size of the *gutter*—the inside page margin—to make sure there is enough space for the holes to fit without interfering with the text.

Page-layout software makes it easy to experiment with different grids. Set up a two-page spread in your program. Then see how text looks in two-, three-, four-, and five-column grids. Experiment with margin sizes and the space between columns. Print out some samples and have several people look them over for balance, proportion, and readability. Except for the front and back pages, always look at the left- and right-hand pages together as a spread, since that's how your readers will view them.

Using Color

You can achieve several design goals through the use of color. Color can make your newsletter more attractive and help emphasize important elements. Because it contrasts with black ink, color helps readers skim the pages. It also sets a tone for your newsletter—grays, dark blues, and dark greens are conservative; bright colors are casual and friendly; and neon colors have a trendy look.

Your newsletter can gain visual interest through the use of color. In addition to setting a tone and making the pages more attractive, color can help emphasize important elements, like headlines and captions.

No matter how you use color in your newsletter, whether colored ink or paper, use it consistently. Print shops often run specials on certain colors of ink or paper, but don't let these sales tempt you to change colors with the seasons. Choose a color palette and apply it to the same elements in every issue, whether it's boxes, headlines, rules, or drop caps.

You can create two types of color in a printed newsletter, spot and process. We'll take a look at both.

Spot Color

Spot color is so named because, in addition to your black ink, you usually put just a spot of it here and a spot of it there. The color on the pages of this book is spot color. Printing spot color is more expensive than printing only black because, for most printing presses, it means your job has to go through twice—once for black and once for the spot color.

Figure 8.6

In the example below, the ink extends to the top and left side of the page. This effect, called a *bleed*, will add to your printing cost.

Reprinted with permission. Copyright © 2002 Gruner + Jahr USA, publisher of *Inc*. magazine.

Using shades of a spot color will create the effect of having more colors throughout your newsletter, and at no extra charge. Called *tints* or *screens*, these shades are expressed in percentages. In an area tinted at 5 or 10 percent, very little ink gets through the screen onto the printing press, yielding a very light shade of the color. In an area tinted at 100 percent, the full amount of ink reaches the paper.

Common places to use spot color in a newsletter include headlines, subheads, bullets, rules, boxes, captions, and pull quotes. Notice where the spot color is used in this book—chapter headings, subheads, sidebars, and in the border at the top of each page. To increase the legibility of certain colored items, such as subheads, captions, and pull quotes, try setting them in bold.

Some newsletter designs, such as the one in Figure 8.6 at left, include ink that extends all the way to the edge of the paper. This effect, called a *bleed*, requires the printer to use sheets of paper that are larger than your newsletter's page size. The printer then extends the color beyond the edge of the pages and trims the sheets to the correct size. Bleeds add to your printing costs, so get an estimate before incorporating them into your design.

Another design element that can run up your costs involves *tight registration*—exact alignment of different colors. For example, you might want to place a sidebar in a light blue shaded box that is outlined with a black border. Getting the border to line up perfectly around the box without any gaps is tricky and requires more sophisticated printing equipment than is usually available at a quick-copy shop. For this type of job, you will probably need a commercial printer.

The printing industry uses the Pantone Matching System (PMS) for spot color. This system contains over a thousand standard color choices that are each numbered. Your printer can give you a book of PMS swatches, so you can see how the colors look on paper. The better page-layout programs let you select Pantone colors by their numbers and apply them to your text, boxes, and rules.

Some newsletters use a one-color design, in which all text and graphics are the same color—blue, green, or purple, for instance. Printing this type of job is usually more expensive than one that uses only black ink, but it is less expensive than a two-color job. However, it's best to avoid such a design, since text that is printed in color is not as easy to read as black. In addition, your photographs will also be printed in the spot color, which will make them appear muddy and blurred.

Process Color

Process printing is the second type of color reproduction. In this method, also called *four-color printing,* four colors—cyan, magenta, yellow, and black (CMYK)—are used in varying proportions to create other colors. Since this method requires four passes through an offset press, it is even more expensive than spot color. However, if you are not printing large quantities, print shops with digital presses may be able to offer four-color reproduction at a more affordable price than an offset printer. Chapter 9 has more information about digital printing.

Process color is appropriate for upscale newsletters, especially those that include lots of photography. But producing a newsletter using process color can be complex. You will need some extra training to create process color in your page-layout software. And using it will add some time to your production schedule for each issue.

The quality of process color on your final newsletter can vary depending on a number of variables, including the type of paper you use. As with any color print job, be sure to talk to your printer before completing your design.

Shells

If the price of both spot and process color exceeds your budget, you might consider printing shells. Shells are pages on which certain design elements have been preprinted in color; they are used for each issue. To understand this concept better, open up your newsletter and place it flat on the table with the front and back pages facing up. Now identify the color areas on these two pages that will appear in the same place for every issue—perhaps your banner on the front page and the box for your masthead on the back page. Once a year or so, have your printer do a large print run of just the spot color areas on this cover page (which, when folded, becomes the front and back covers). When it comes time to print each issue, the printer will use these shells, adding black ink where it belongs. This way, you can do the expensive two-color print job only once a year, yet every issue will have these colors. In Figure 8.7 on page 198, the top graphic is an example of a preprinted shell, which has received the spot color. In the bottom graphic, text has been printed over the shell.

Figure 8.7
Large runs of preprinted shells can save you money in the long run. When folded, the shell will become the front and back covers of your newsletter.

The sample shell at right includes the spot color that appears in the same location for each issue.

Text is printed over the shell, as seen here.

Back Cover   Front Cover

If you would like to use shells, I recommend waiting until you've published two or three issues and have gotten the kinks out of your design. Otherwise, you may be stuck for a year or so with color in areas that don't work for you. Also, there are several reasons you shouldn't print too many shells. You might, for example, decide to change your design after a year or two. Or the paper you choose for the shells may be discontinued, forcing you to use slightly different paper for the inside sheets. Moisture can also affect the quality of the paper shells if you store them for a long time.

Through catalogs, you can also purchase paper that has preprinted, multicolor graphics, such as rules and borders. These are 11-x-17-inch sheets onto which you can reproduce your newsletter. It can be an inexpensive way to use color on newsletters with small distributions. But before you buy, talk to the copy shop to make sure their machines can handle this type of paper.

Selecting Paper

Paper, also known as *stock,* is another important design component. Take the time to choose your paper several weeks before your newsletter is ready for printing. It may need to be special ordered and can take a few weeks to arrive. The best way to choose paper is by viewing samples and discussing with the printer's customer service representative which type will best suit your needs. Looking at swatch books is a start, but, if possible, ask to view a page that has undergone the same printing method— offset, digital printing, or photocopying—you will be using.

Paper is classified by grade, weight, texture, brightness, coating, and color. I could fill another book with information about these characteristics, but much of it would have little relevance to newsletter design. Instead, I'll focus on five questions you should ask to find out if a paper is right for your newsletter.

Is It Appropriate for My Printing Method?

One of the factors limiting your paper choice is the method by which your newsletter is reproduced. Certain grades, colors, and textures of paper that are made for offset printing presses can't be used in traditional or digital photocopiers. If you want to use paper you found in a catalog or another outside source, make sure the printer's equipment can handle it before buying. Keep in mind that customer-supplied stock may jam some printers' machines. As a result, some printers charge more for the job if you supply the paper.

Will It Make My Newsletter Easy to Read?

For people to be able to easily read text, there must be plenty of contrast between the ink and the paper. A number of characteristics of paper affect its legibility. Color is one. A newsletter printed on anything but white or a very light color like cream or a pale gray is difficult to read. In addition, darker colors can reduce the ability of postal service scanning equipment to properly read addresses and barcodes that are printed on the paper.

Coating—a layer of chemicals and clay that is applied to paper when it is manufactured—also affects the paper's legibility. Paper that has been coated feels smoother to the touch than uncoated varieties. Because it is not porous, coated paper absorbs little ink, so photos and text appear sharper when printed on it. It is particularly suited to newsletters with lots of four-color photography. However, the coating can create a glare that interferes with reading extended amounts of text. Choosing a coated stock with a matte or dull finish can reduce that glare.

Another characteristic of paper that affects its legibility is its *opacity*—how much you can see through it. When you print on both sides of a sheet of paper, you don't want the printing on one side to show through to the other. The grades of paper known as *text* or *book* (sometimes called *offset*) are more opaque than *bond* paper and so more suitable for newsletters.

A paper's brightness also affects its legibility. Brightness is expressed on a scale of 1 to 5 for coated papers, with 1 being the brightest. There is an additional "premium" rating for paper that is brighter than a 1. Brightness for uncoated papers is expressed as a percentage. Choose a coated paper that is rated 1 or premium, or an uncoated paper rated 95 percent or higher.

Paper stock also ranges in texture. Uncoated sheets range from smooth to vellum (rough), while coated stock can be dull or matte (rough), satin (smooth), or glossy (smoothest). Photographs reproduce best on smooth stock. Generally, textured paper does not absorb ink or toner as well as untextured types (particularly with laser printers), so they are more likely to result in smudges or broken characters.

Does It Convey My Newsletter's Tone?

You want to select a paper with a weight, texture, and thickness that contributes to your newsletter's tone. Heavy, coated, and textured papers are expensive and convey an upscale tone. Lighter-weight, untextured, white paper tells readers that you're sticking to a budget. Beige, cream, or gray colored paper is more formal than yellow, pink or lavender.

You (and your audience) may place a priority on the use of recycled and/or recyclable paper. Paper with a high recycled content can be more expensive than regular paper. The selection of weight, grade, and thickness of recycled paper is improving all the time. If you do use this type of paper, be sure to mention that fact in your masthead.

Will It Withstand Mailing?

The mailing method for your newsletter is another consideration when choosing paper. If your newsletter is a self-mailer, you'll need a heavier, more resilient paper to meet postal service standards than if it's mailed in an envelope. If you use a coated paper, make sure the post office will accept it—some glossy-coated papers cannot be used for self-mailers. This is because the ink from the barcodes, which are applied to the mailpiece by the postal service, takes too long to dry. You must also consider how well your paper folds. If you have a lot of pages and a thick paper, the newsletter may be too difficult to fold in half for mailing.

Does It Fit into My Budget?

Be sure to know the cost of any paper you're considering. All the characteristics of paper discussed in this section affect price. Certain grades, such as text, are more expensive than others, like book or bond. Heavier papers cost more than lighter ones. (A paper's basis weight is expressed in pounds. For example, a printer might suggest you use 70-pound text paper. The number 70 refers to how much a ream—500 sheets—of the paper weighs in its standard size. Since the standard sizes vary, depending on the grade of the paper, a 70-pound paper is not necessarily lighter than an 80-pound paper of a different grade.) Coated paper is more expensive than uncoated, and color is more expensive than white. Higher brightness and opacity also add to cost. But, while price is important, don't let it override your primary goal of publishing a newsletter that people will read.

TYPE DESIGN

A youth hockey league is growing so fast that the rink builds a third sheet of ice to accommodate its heavy schedule of games and practices. Communicating with nearly 400 families is a challenge, so the league's board decides to publish a newsletter called *Ice Notes*. One of the hockey moms volunteers for the job. She enjoys learning to use her page-layout software, and dresses up the newsletter by using a different typeface for every article, headline, and subhead. In the stands at the next game, the

Today, most paper stock has at least some amount of recycled content. Paper with a higher percentage can be more expensive than the others, although the price continues to become more competitive. If you use paper with a high recycled content, be sure to mention it in your masthead.

When readers are visually bombarded with too many typefaces, the type speaks louder than the words, making it difficult for readers to determine what to look at first.

parents joked that *Ice Notes* should be renamed *Ransom Notes* because of its excessive number of typefaces.

Using too many typefaces is a common mistake made by people who are new to desktop publishing. So why isn't it good design? Unlike the writer of a ransom note, who wants to remain anonymous, you want your newsletter design to announce your identity. But if every element of your newsletter looks different—if some headlines use the typeface Helvetica and others are in Times Roman, Century Gothic, or Futura; if some articles are set in bold type and others in italics—it won't have a consistent look that people can identify as yours.

Earlier in this chapter, the five goals of good newsletter design were discussed. Drawing the reader's attention to important information through headlines and other skimming aids is one of those goals. However, a page with too many typefaces results in confusion, making it difficult for readers to determine which article is most important. Take a look at the sample page in Figure 8.8 on page 203. Every headline is set in a different typeface. Readers can't tell which article to look at first. On the other hand, if all of the headlines were set in the same typeface, but the most important one was larger than the others and perhaps in bold or italics, readers would be drawn to that one first.

Why should you bother learning how to use type effectively? For starters, your readers will spend more time reading your newsletter if it doesn't cause eyestrain. They'll be able to dedicate more brainpower to processing your messages and fewer to deciphering your words. It's not difficult to learn newsletter typography. If you've grown up reading professionally published books, magazines, and newspapers, as we all have, you can subconsciously recognize good typography. Now you just have to make your subconscious knowledge conscious.

Initially, you may be overwhelmed as you read about the many ways to design your newsletter's type. You might wonder how you will ever remember to apply type-formatting specifications correctly to your newsletter, issue after issue. This is where your computer comes to the rescue. Page-layout programs have a feature called *styles*, which are easy shortcuts for formatting your newsletter's type.

Using the "styles" feature of your page-layout software will help you maintain consistent formatting of the various typefaces and style choices used for the body text, captions, folios, headlines, and other elements of your newsletter— issue after issue.

How do styles work? Once you decide on the typeface and formatting you want for the various elements of your newsletter—body text, headlines, subheads, decks—you can create styles for them in the template. Let's say, for instance, you decide that for your subheads, you want to use the typeface Optima at a size of 12 points. You also want them bold and left justified. You want a 12-point space above them and

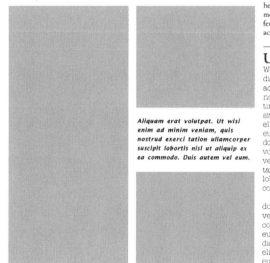

Duis autem vel eum

By John Doe

Worem ipsum dolor sit amet, diam consectetuer adipiscing elit, sed diam nonummy nibh euismod tincidunt ut laoreet dolore magna aliquam erat volutpat. Ut wisi enim ad minim veniam, quis nostrud exerci tation ullamcorper suscipit lobortis nisl ut aliquip ex ea commodo consequat dolor ipsum.

Duis autem vel eum iriure dolor in hendrerit in vulputate velit esse molestie consequat, vel illum dolore eu feugiat nulla facilisis at vero eros et accumsan et iusto odio dignissim Worem ipsum dolor sit amet, dignissim consectetuer adipiscing elit, sed diam nonummy nibh euismod tincidunt ut Worem ipsum dolor sit amet, dignissim consectetuer adipiscing elit, sed diam nonummy nibh euismod tincidunt ut laoreet dolore magna aliquam erat volutpat. Ut wisi enim ad minim veniam, quis nostrud exerci tation ullamcorper suscipit lobortis nisl ut aliquip ex ea commodo consequat.

Duis autem vel eum iriure dolor in hendrerit in vulputate velit esse molestie consequat, vel illum dolore eu feugiat nulla facilisis at vero eros et accumsan et iusto odio dignissim Worem ipsum dolor sit amet, dignissim consectetuer adipiscing elit, sed diam nonummy nibh euismod tincidunt ut dolor adminim.

Onummy nibh euismod

Worem ipsum dolor sit amet, consectetuer adipiscing elit, sed diam nonummy nibh euismod tincidunt ut laoreet dolore magna aliquam erat volutpat. Ut wisi enim ad minim veniam, quis nostrud exerci tation ullamcorper suscipit lobortis nisl ut aliquip ex ea commodo consequat. Duis autem vel eum iriure dolor in hendrerit in vulputate velit esse dolor molestie consequat, vel illum dolore eu.Worem ipsum dolor sit amet, diam consectetuer adipiscing elit, sed diam nonummy nibh euismod tincidunt ut laoreet dolore magna aliquam erat volutpat. Ut wisi enim ad minim veniam, quis nostrud exerci tation ullamcorper susciptis nisl ut aliquip. ✳

Aliquam erat volutpat. Ut wisi enim ad minim veniam, quis nostrud exerci tation ullamcorper suscipit lobortis nisl ut aliquip ex ea commodo. Duis autem vel eum.

VEL EUM IN URE DOLOR

By John Doe

Duis autem vel eum iriure dolor in hendrerit in vulputate velit esse molestie consequat, vel illum dolore eu feugiat nulla facilisis at vero eros et accumsan et iusto odio dignissim Worem ipsum dolor sit amet, dignissim consectetuer adipiscing elit, sed diam nonummy nibh euismod tincidunt ut Worem ipsum dolor sit amet, dignissim consectetuer adipiscing elit, sed diam nonummy nibh euismod tincidunt ut laoreet dolore magna aliquam erat volutpat. Ut wisi enim ad minim veniam, quis nostrud exerci tation ullamcorper suscipit lobortis nisl ut aliquip ex ea commodo consequat.

Duis autem vel eum iriure dolor in hendrerit in vulputate velit esse molestie consequat, vel illum dolore eu feugiat nulla facilisis at vero eros et accumsan et iusto odio dignissim hendrerit in vulputate velit esse

Duis autem vel eum iriure dolor in hendrerit in vulputate velit esse molestie consequat, vel illum dolore eu feugiat nulla facilisis at vero eros et accumsan et iusto odio dignissim. ✳

Ut wisi enim admin

Worem ipsum dolor sit amet, dignissim consectetuer adipiscing elit, sed diam nonummy nibh euismod tincidunt ut Worem ipsum dolor sit amet, consectetuer adipiscing elit, sed diam nonummy nibh euismod tincidunt ut laoreet dolore magna aliquam erat volutpat. Ut wisi enim ad minim veniam, quis nostrud exerci tation ullamcorper suscipit lobortis nisl ut aliquip ex ea commodo consequat.

Duis autem vel eum iriure dolor in hendrerit in vulputate velit esse dolor molestie consequat, vel illum dolore eu.Worem ipsum dolor sit amet, diam consectetuer adipiscing elit, sed diam nonummy nibh euismod tincidunt ut laoreet. ✳

Figure 8.8
Using too many typefaces results in visual "noise." Without a consistent look, your newsletter won't be identifiable as yours.

Greeking
During the design process, to focus attention on the overall appearance of a page, rather than on its specific content, layout artists often use filler text in articles and/or headlines. This filler text (seen in Figure 8.8) consists of Latin, Greek, or nonsense words, and its use is known as "Greeking." It is replaced by the actual text later on.

3 points below (I'll explain these typography terms in a moment). That's a lot of detail to remember (and lots of mouse clicks to make) every time you want to format a subheading. So to speed things up, you can create a style called "subhead," and define it to your software as 12-point Optima bold, left justified, with a 12-point space above and 3-point space below. Once you have created this style and named it, you can click or

Without using the "styles" feature, it's easy to forget small formatting details.

highlight the text of each subhead in your newsletter, click "subhead" from your style menu, and your software will automatically apply all of that formatting you have chosen.

For a typical newsletter, you will need to create about a dozen or more styles—one for body text, another for headlines, and others for subheads, captions, and a number of additional elements that are discussed later in this chapter.

As an added bonus, using styles lets you quickly modify type design throughout the newsletter. Let's say you decide your body text is a little too small—you'd prefer 10-point type to the current 9 point. No sweat. Simply redefine your "body text" style, and the software will automatically change every paragraph of body text to 10 points. The user manual or online help for your page-layout software will give you more details on creating and changing styles.

You are already familiar with the two main categories of typeface used in newsletters—body text and display type. Body text is what you're reading right now—the smaller text used in the body of articles. Display type is the larger type found in headlines, subheads, pull quotes, and other skimming aids. The next section covers character and paragraph formatting for both categories.

As you design your type, experiment with a variety of different formats. On a sample page, place a few articles and headlines, using several typefaces you are considering, and then print it out. Now adjust one or two specifications—say, the size of the type or the spacing between lines—and print it out again. With the help of your colleagues, compare the results. Repeat this process until you are satisfied with the format.

Body Text

Since body text, which is used in the main "body" of your articles, requires extended reading, your goal should be to make it easy on the eyes. The purpose of body text is *not* to attract attention; the article's headline has already taken care of that.

Character Formatting

Character formatting involves the design of the letters, numbers, and symbols—including the choice of typeface, as well as its size and style.

■ **Typeface.** There are two typeface categories: serif and sans serif. *Serifs* are small lines that appear at the edges of letters like "l," "p," and "r."

The body text in this book is set in a serif typeface. On the other hand, *sans serif* typefaces lack serifs (*sans* is French for "without"). The headings in this book are set in sans serif typefaces.

Readability research has shown that serifs act like a ruler, guiding the reader's eye across a line of type. In type that requires extended reading, like body text, serif typefaces are the recommended choice. However, in special situations, you may want to use a sans serif typeface for body text. For example, you can create a nice contrast with the text of other articles by using sans serif body text in a short sidebar, your masthead, or your table of contents.

Some of the serif typefaces that are appropriate for newsletter body text are displayed below. They include Times New Roman, Garamond, Goudy, and Bookman Old Style. Also included are commonly used sans serif typefaces—Helvetica and Arial.

Serif or Sans Serif?
When extended reading is required, serif typefaces are recommended. They are commonly used for newsletter body text. Sans serif typefaces are often good choices for display type, or for the body text in a sidebar or masthead.

(serif)
Times New Roman
Lorem ipsum dolor sit amet, consectetuer adipiscing elit. Donec feugiat orci eget velit. In venenatis. Mauris eget lectus. Donec aliquet. Nullam euismod, felis at eleifend lobortis, turpis urna posuere orci, ut sagittis neque dui nec leo.

(serif)
Garamond
Lorem ipsum dolor sit amet, consectetuer adipiscing elit. Donec feugiat orci eget velit. In venenatis. Mauris eget lectus. Donec aliquet. Nullam euismod, felis at eleifend lobortis, turpis urna posuere orci, ut sagittis neque dui nec leo.

(serif)
Goudy
Lorem ipsum dolor sit amet, consectetuer adipiscing elit. Donec feugiat orci eget velit. In venenatis. Mauris eget lectus. Donec aliquet. Nullam euismod, felis at eleifend lobortis, turpis urna posuere orci, ut sagittis neque dui nec leo.

(serif)
Bookman Old Style
Lorem ipsum dolor sit amet, consectetuer adipiscing elit. Donec feugiat orci eget velit. In venenatis. Mauris eget lectus. Donec aliquet. Nullam euismod, felis at eleifend lobortis, turpis urna posuere orci, ut sagittis neque dui nec leo.

(sans serif)
Helvetica
Lorem ipsum dolor sit amet, consectetuer adipiscing elit. Donec feugiat orci eget velit. In venenatis. Mauris eget lectus. Donec aliquet. Nullam euismod, felis at eleifend lobortis, turpis urna posuere orci, ut sagittis neque dui nec leo.

(sans serif)
Arial
Lorem ipsum dolor sit amet, consectetuer adipiscing elit. Donec feugiat orci eget velit. In venenatis. Mauris eget lectus. Donec aliquet. Nullam euismod, felis at eleifend lobortis, turpis urna posuere orci, ut sagittis neque dui nec leo.

■ **Type Size.** The ideal size for body text is from 9 to 12 points (1 point is equal to 1/72 of an inch or 0.0139). In the serif and san serif examples on page 205, the body text is set in 10-point type, while the subheads are 12 point. The point size is a measure of the length from the top of an upper case letter to the bottom of a lower case letter that has a descender, such as "p" or "y" (a descender is the portion of a letter that descends below its main body). Choose a point size based on its readability, taking into account your readers' ages and possible visual impairments.

Since the width of different typefaces varies, the horizontal space they use also varies, even when they are the same point size. As you can see in the examples, a paragraph of text set in one typeface may take up more lines than the same text set in another typeface. This means some typefaces will allow you to fit more words into your articles than others.

Don't choose decorative typefaces, such as those that resemble script, calligraphy, or handwriting, for your body text. They can be very difficult to read in small sizes, as you can see from the examples at left.

Vivante

Lorem ipsum dolor sit amet, consectetuer adipiscing elit. Donec feugiat orci eget velit. In venenatis. Mauris eget lectus. Donec aliquet. Nullam euismod, felis at eleifend lobortis, turpis urna posuere orci.

Lucida Handwriting

Lorem ipsum dolor sit amet, consectetuer adipiscing elit. Donec feugiat orci eget velit. In venenatis. Mauris eget lectus. Donec aliquet. Nullam euismod, felis at eleifend lobortis, turpis urna posuere orci.

Decorative Typefaces
As you can see, decorative typefaces are difficult to read in body text.

■ **Type Style.** Although it's easy to bold or italicize your body text, do it rarely. Long passages of text set in italics are hard to read, and bold text interrupts the flow. It is, however, appropriate to italicize certain words or phrases, such as titles of books and movies, and foreign words and phrases. Italics also works for short pieces of text like picture captions and author bylines. Bold is sometimes used to emphasize names of people or companies. For example, in the class notes section of an alumni newsletter, you could bold the names of the alumni you are including in the column. This will help readers skim for the names of people they know. In a business newsletter's news briefs column, you might bold the name of each company you mention.

When you want to emphasize an occasional word or phrase, do not underline or set it in all caps. As you can see in the text style examples on page 207, underlining cuts through the descenders of letters, making them hard to read. Using all caps is not a good option either. You see, part of the way our brains distinguish one letter from another is by their sizes and shapes. Lower-case type is easier to read because the shapes of the letters vary more than they do in upper-case type. Some lower-case letters have ascenders that extend to the top of the line, others have descenders, and some have neither. Upper-case letters, on the other hand, are all the same height. To emphasize words in body text, use italics instead.

Reversed type (white text on a black or other dark background) is also difficult to read. Like italics, you can get away with it in small doses. If you use reversed type, set it in a sans serif typeface, increase its size, and make it bold for increased legibility.

Paragraph Formatting

Paragraph formatting involves setting the distance between each line in a paragraph and between the paragraphs themselves. It also entails aligning the text within the columns.

■ **Leading.** Leading (pronounced *ledding*) is the amount of space between each line in a paragraph. Graphic designers measure leading in points. In body text, your leading should be set 1 or 2 points greater than the point size of your type. This means if your type size is 10 points, your leading should be set at 11 or 12 points. A common setting for newsletter body text is 10 on 12, which means the type size is 10 points and the total vertical space allotted for the line is 12 points. The sample paragraphs on page 208 contain 10-point text set on leadings of 11, 12, and 13 points.

You can set your leading a bit higher—2.5 to 4 points greater than the type size—if the line length is long (over 3.5 inches), or if you are using a sans serif typeface for body text. In these cases, you could, for instance, set your leading at 10 on 13, or 11 on 14. The "looser" the leading, the greater the space between lines.

■ **Spacing Between Paragraphs.** There are two ways to indicate that one paragraph of body text has ended and another has begun. Choose one style or the other, but don't use both.

Indenting the first line is the method most commonly used when starting a new paragraph. It is the style used in most books, including this one; newspapers; magazines; and newsletters. If you choose this style for your newsletter, set the indent or tab at one pica (as mentioned earlier in this chapter, a pica is a unit of measure that equals 0.167 inches). Some software automatically sets tabs as much as a half inch, far too deep for a narrow newsletter column.

You can also indicate a new paragraph by leaving a little extra space between paragraphs. However, when using this style, do not simply

Text Styles
Use text styles appropriately. Avoid underlining words or setting them in all caps. Use italics, bold type, and reverses sparingly.

Italicize the names of publications, like *How to Publish a Newsletter*.

Use bold sparingly in body text, perhaps to highlight the names of people or companies, like **Square One Publishers**.

Don't underline text. <u>Underlining cuts through the descenders of letters like "g," "p," and "q" and makes them hard to read.</u>

TEXT SET IN ALL CAPS IS HARDER TO READ than text set in mixed case. Emphasize important information with *italics* instead.

Use reverses in small doses. Increase the type size and use a bold, sans serif typeface.

10 Point on 11 Point

Lorem ipsum dolor sit amet, consectetuer adipiscing elit. Donec feugiat orci eget velit. In venenatis. Mauris eget lectus. Donec aliquet. Nullam euismod, felis at eleifend lobortis, turpis urna posuere orci, ut sagittis neque dui nec leo.

Aliquam lectus eros, mollis et, dignissim et, accumsan sed, nulla. Mauris nec erat. Nam nulla. Class aptent taciti sociosqu ad litora torquent per conubia nostra, per inceptos hymenaeos. Curabitur mollis interdum nibh. Nulla eget ante sed arcu fermentum dignissim.

10 Point on 12 Point

Lorem ipsum dolor sit amet, consectetuer adipiscing elit. Donec feugiat orci eget velit. In venenatis. Mauris eget lectus. Donec aliquet. Nullam euismod, felis at eleifend lobortis, turpis urna posuere orci, ut sagittis neque dui nec leo.

Aliquam lectus eros, mollis et, dignissim et, accumsan sed, nulla. Mauris nec erat. Nam nulla. Class aptent taciti sociosqu ad litora torquent per conubia nostra, per inceptos hymenaeos. Curabitur mollis interdum nibh. Nulla eget ante sed arcu fermentum dignissim.

10 Point on 13 Point

Lorem ipsum dolor sit amet, consectetuer adipiscing elit. Donec feugiat orci eget velit. In venenatis. Mauris eget lectus. Donec aliquet. Nullam euismod, felis at eleifend lobortis, turpis urna posuere orci, ut sagittis neque dui nec leo.

Aliquam lectus eros, mollis et, dignissim et, accumsan sed, nulla. Mauris nec erat. Nam nulla. Class aptent taciti sociosqu ad litora torquent per conubia nostra, per inceptos hymenaeos. Curabitur mollis interdum nibh. Nulla eget ante sed arcu fermentum dignissim.

Leading

In body text, the leading—space between lines—is usually set 1 or 2 points greater than the point size of the type. The copy in the examples above contains 10-point type set on leadings of 11, 12, and 13 points.

press the Enter key twice to add this extra space—it will trap too much white space between paragraphs. Instead, use the paragraph-formatting feature of your software to indicate the amount of space to leave after each paragraph. Start with half the value you set for your leading. This means if your leading is set at 12, add a 6 point-space after each paragraph.

■ **Alignment.** When it comes to aligning body text within columns, you can choose one of two methods—left alignment or justification. As shown in the sample paragraphs on page 209, lines of text with left alignment (called *left justified, left aligned, flush left,* or *ragged right*) are set flush against the left side of the column. Justified text is aligned with both the right and left sides of the column.

Full justification gives a more formal look to your newsletter than left alignment. However, if your columns are narrow (such as when your page grid includes four or more columns), don't use full justification—you will end up with excessive word spacing in many of your lines. Even with wider columns, full justification causes the occasional spacing problem, as seen in the fifth and sixth lines of the fully justified example. This excessive spacing between words will need some fine-tuning to correct. If

Left Aligned

Lorem ipsum dolor sit amet, consectetuer adipiscing elit. Donec feugiat orci eget velit. In venenatis. Mauris eget lectus. Donec aliquet. Nullam euismod, felis at eleifend lobortis, turpis urna posuere orci, ut sagittis neque dui nec leo.

Aliquam lectus eros, mollis et, dignissim et, accumsan sed, nulla. Mauris nec erat. Nam nulla. Class aptent taciti sociosqu ad litora torquent per conubia nostra, per inceptos hymenaeos. Curabitur mollis interdum nibh. Nulla eget ante sed arcu fermentum dignissim.

Fully Justified

Lorem ipsum dolor sit amet, consectetuer adipiscing elit. Donec feugiat orci eget velit. In venenatis. Mauris eget lectus. Donec aliquet. Nullam euismod, felis at eleifend lobortis, turpis urna posuere orci, ut sagittis neque dui nec leo.

Aliquam lectus eros, mollis et, dignissim et, accumsan sed, nulla. Mauris nec erat. Nam nulla. Class aptent taciti sociosqu ad litora torquent per conubia nostra, per inceptos hymenaeos. Curabitur mollis interdum nibh. Nulla eget ante sed arcu fermentum dignissim.

Alignment

Text within columns can be left aligned or fully justified. Full justification typically conveys a more formal tone.

you are new to desktop publishing, it's wise to simplify your page layout by using left alignment.

■ **Hyphenation.** Your hyphenation setting tells your software what to do when a full word cannot fit at the end of a line. If you activate the hyphenation setting, the software will use a hyphen to break the word between syllables. Without the hyphenation setting, the entire word will drop to the next line, leaving excess space, as seen in the first line of the example below. It's best to leave the hyphenation setting on to avoid

Without Hyphenation

Long words, like antidisestablishmentarianism, can cause irregular line breaks in your body text. Use hyphenation to avoid this problem.

With Hyphenation

Long words, like antidisestablishmentarianism, can cause irregular line breaks in your body text. Use hyphenation to avoid this problem.

Hyphenation

Setting text without hyphenation can cause irregular line breaks. Allowing hyphenation corrects the problem.

Editor's Message

Lorem ipsum dolor sit amet, consectetuer adipiscing elit. Donec feugiat orci eget velit. In venenatis. Mauris eget lectus. Donec aliquet. Nullam euismod, felis at eleifend lobortis, turpis urna posuere orci, ut sagittis neque dui nec leo.

Aliquam lectus eros, mollis et, dignissim et, accumsan sed, nulla. Mauris nec erat. Nam nulla. Class aptent taciti sociosqu ad litora torquent per conubia nostra, per inceptos hymenaeos. Curabitur mollis interdum nibh. Nulla eget ante sed arcu fermentum dignissim.

Editor's Message

Lorem ipsum dolor sit amet, consectetuer adipiscing elit. Donec feugiat orci eget velit. In venenatis. Mauris eget lectus. Donec aliquet. Nullam euismod, felis at eleifend lobortis, turpis urna posuere orci, ut sagittis neque dui nec leo.

Aliquam lectus eros, mollis et, dignissim et, accumsan sed, nulla. Mauris nec erat. Nam nulla. Class aptent taciti sociosqu ad litora torquent per conubia nostra, per inceptos hymenaeos. Curabitur mollis interdum nibh. Nulla eget ante sed arcu fermentum dignissim.

Editor's Message

LOREM IPSUM DOLOR sit amet, consectetuer adipiscing elit. Donec feugiat orci eget velit. In venenatis. Mauris eget lectus. Donec aliquet. Nullam euismod, felis at eleifend lobortis, turpis urna posuere orci, ut sagittis neque dui nec leo.

Aliquam lectus eros, mollis et, dignissim et, accumsan sed, nulla. Mauris nec erat. Nam nulla. Class aptent taciti sociosqu ad litora torquent per conubia nostra, per inceptos hymenaeos. Curabitur mollis interdum nibh. Nulla eget ante sed arcu fermentum dignissim.

Opening Paragraphs
As seen in the examples above, you can distinguish opening paragraphs by eliminating the first-line indent, adding a drop cap, or capitalizing the first few words.

such irregular line breaks. Some software also lets you specify the number of consecutive lines that can be broken with hyphens. Since excessive hyphenation looks messy, set this value to just two or three.

■ **Opening Paragraphs.** In most newsletters, the first paragraph of each article looks a bit different from the paragraphs that follow. You can distinguish these opening paragraphs in several ways, as illustrated in the examples above. The most common method is to eliminate the usual paragraph indent, setting the first line flush left instead. In addition, you can add a drop cap to the first word or capitalize the first few words. Many publications, including this book, also eliminate the first-line indent from paragraphs that follow subheads.

Display Type

The elements you set in display type—headlines, subheads, pull quotes, decks—are much shorter than your body text. Therefore, your concern in designing them is less on helping readers get through long passages of text, and more on attracting their attention. How can you make display type stand out? With typefaces, type sizes, and type styles that contrast with body text.

Character Formatting

Character formatting for display type involves choosing the right typeface and setting it in the best size and style.

■ **Typeface.** Although serif and sans serif typefaces are both well suited for display type, sans serif varieties, such as Helvetica, Arial, Frutiger, Futura, Franklin Gothic, and Optima, are used more often. This is because they contrast nicely with the serif typefaces that are usually used in body text.

Limit the total number of typefaces you use in your newsletter to two or three. I recommend a serif, a sans serif, and a decorative typeface. Generally, you would use the serif typeface for your body text and the sans serif for display type, although you might make some exceptions. For example, you might use the serif typeface in pull quotes and the sans serif typeface in sidebars. And, to distinguish your headlines from decks, you might use sans serif for the headline and serif for the deck. Use a decorative typeface (maybe one that appears in your nameplate) sparingly, perhaps just for kickers or page numbers.

Within your two or three chosen typefaces, however, you can create variety and contrast by setting them in different sizes and styles. For example, in headlines, you can use a condensed or narrow version of your typeface to help you fit more words into the allotted space. (Arial, for instance, has a condensed version called Arial Narrow.) For pull quotes, you might use a bold italic version of one of your typefaces. For subheads, you might choose a smaller version of your headline typeface, and simply set it in bold. In Figure 8.9 on page 212, only two typefaces—Times New Roman (serif) and Arial (sans serif)—are used for the various elements on this page, including the headline, byline, pull quote, subheads, and body text. Varying their size, leading, weight, and style creates contrast.

■ **Type Size.** Increasing the size of your type is another way to create contrast between body text and display type. Make your headlines at least 4 points larger than the body text. (Research has shown 4 points to be the smallest size difference that people can readily recognize.) You can

Figure 8.9
Only two typefaces are
used for the headline,
byline, subheads, pull
quote, and body text on
this page. Varying their
size, leading, weight, and
style creates contrast.

Ut wisi enim ad minim ven

*Worem ipsum dolor sit amet, dignissim consectetuer
sed diam nonummy ribh.*

By Jane Q. Doe

Worem ipsum dolor sit amet, diam consectetuer adipiscing elit, sed diam nonummy nibh euismod tincidunt ut laoreet dolore magna aliquam erat volutpat. Ut wisi enim ad minim veniam, quis nostrud exerci tation ullamcorper suscipit lobortis nisl ut aliquip ex ea commodo consequat.

Duis autem vel eum iriure dolor in hendrerit in vulputate velit esse molestie consequat, vel illum dolore eu feugiat nulla facilisis at vero eros et accumsan et iusto odio dignissim Worem ipsum dolor sit amet, dignissim consectetuer adipiscing elit, sed diam nonummy nibh euismod tincidunt ut Worem ipsum dolor sit amet, dignissim consectetuer adipiscing elit, sed diam nonummy nibh euismod tincidunt ut laoreet dolore magna aliquam erat volutpat. Ut wisi enim ad minim veniam, quis nostrud exerci tation ullamcorper suscipit lobortis nisl ut aliquip ex ea commodo consequat.

Duis autem vel eum iriure dolor in hendrerit in vulputate velit esse molestie consequat, vel illum dolore eu feugiat nulla facilisis at vero eros et accumsan et iusto odio dignissim Worem ipsum dolor sit amet, dignissim consectetuer adipiscing elit, sed diam nonummy nibh euismod tincidunt ut.

Onummy nibh euismod

Worem ipsum dolor sit amet, consectetuer adipiscing elit, sed diam nonummy nibh euismod tincidunt ut laoreet dolore magna aliquam erat volutpat. Ut wisi enim ad minim veniam, quis nostrud exerci tation ullamcorper suscipit lobortis nisl ut aliquip ex ea commodo consequat.

Duis autem vel eum iriure dolor in hendrerit in vulputate velit esse dolor molestie consequat, vel illum dolore eu.Worem ipsum dolor sit amet, diam consectetuer adipiscing elit, sed diam

nonummy nibh euismod tincidunt ut laoreet dolore magna aliquam erat volutpat. Ut wisi enim ad minim veniam, quis nostrud exerci tation ullamcorper suscipit lobortis nisl ut aliquip ex ea commodo consequat.

Duis autem vel eum iriure dolor in hendrerit in vulputate velit esse molestie consequat, vel illum dolore eu feugiat nulla facilisis at vero eros

---

*Duis autem vel eum
iriure dolor in hendrerit
in vulputate suscipit
lobortis.*

---

et accumsan et iusto odio dignissim Worem ipsum dolor sit amet, dignissim consectetuer adipiscing elit, sed diam nonummy nibh euismod tincidunt ut Worem ipsum dolor sit amet, dignissim consectetuer adipiscing elit, sed diam nonummy nibh euismod tincidunt ut laoreet dolore magna aliquam erat volutpat. Ut wisi enim ad minim veniam, quis nostrud exerci tation ullamcorper suscipit lobortis nisl ut aliquip ex ea commodo consequat.

Duis autem vel eum iriure dolor in hendrerit in vulputate velit esse molestie consequat, vel illum dolore eu feugiat nulla facilisis at vero eros et accumsan et iusto odio dignissim hendrerit in vulputate velit esse molestie consequat, vel illum dolore eu feugiat nulla facilisis at vero eros et molestie consequat, vel illum dolore eu feugiat nulla facilisis at vero eros et accumsan et iusto odio dignissim Worem ipsum dolor sit amet, dignissim consectetuer

adipiscing elit, sed diam nonummy nibh euismod tincidunt ut Worem ipsum dolor sit amet, dignissim consectetuer adipiscing elit, sed diam nonummy nibh euismod tincidunt ut laoreet dolore magna aliquam erat volutpat. Ut wisi enim ad minim veniam, quis nostrud exerci tation ullamcorper suscipit lobortis nisl ut aliquip ex ea commodo consequat.

Duis autem vel eum iriure dolor in hendrerit in vulputate velit esse molestie consequat, vel illum dolore eu feugiat nulla facilisis at vero eros et accumsan et iusto odio dignissim Worem ipsum dolor sit amet, dignissim consectetuer adipiscing elit, sed diam nonummy nibh euismod tincidunt ut Worem ipsum dolor sit amet, consectetuer adipiscing elit, sed diam nonummy nibh euismod tincidunt ut laoreet dolore magna aliquam erat volutpat. Ut wisi enim ad minim veniam, quis nostrud exerci tation ullamcorper suscipit lobortis nisl ut aliquip ex ea commodo consequat.

Ut wisi enim ad mimim

Duis autem vel eum iriure dolor in hendrerit in vulputate velit esse molestie consequat, vel illum dolore eu feugiat nulla facilisis at vero eros et accumsan et iusto odio dignissim hendrerit in vulputate velit esse molestie consequat, vel illum dolore eu feugiat nulla facilisis at vero eros et molestie consequat, vel illum dolore eu feugiat nulla facilisis at vero eros et accumsan et iusto odio dignissim Worem ipsum dolor sit amet, dignissim consectetuer

Duis autem vel eum iriure dolor in hendrerit in vulputate velit esse dolor molestie consequat, vel illum dolore eu.Duis autem vel eum iriure dolor in hendrerit in vulputate velit esse molestie consequat, vel illum dolore eu feugiat nulla facilisis at vero eros

---

also use headline size to show the relative importance of your articles—
24 to 36 points for your most important articles, 14 to 24 points for those
that are less important.

■ **Type Style.** The sample headlines on page 213 illustrate several styles
of capitalization for display type. They include all caps, initial caps, and
sentence caps.

All Caps:
REMULINK FUNDED TO BUY AMITY SYSTEMS

Initial caps:
Remulink Funded to Buy Amity Systems

Sentence caps:
Remulink funded to buy Amity systems

Capitalization Styles
When set in all caps, the headline takes up extra space and is difficult to read. With initial caps, the first letter of most but not all words is capitalized. With sentence caps, only the first letter of the first word and proper nouns are capitalized.

All caps should be used only for very short pieces of text, such as kickers with one or two words. Why? Because this style is difficult to read and, as you can see from the sample above, it takes up a lot of extra space. With *initial caps,* the first letter of most but not all words in the headline are capitalized. This style is more readable than all caps, but it can be difficult to remember the rules regarding which words should and should not be capitalized. With *sentence caps,* the first letter of the first word is capitalized, and the rest of the headline follows standard capitalization rules.

I prefer sentence caps to initial caps. Initial caps can sometimes blur the meaning of headlines, because this style can make it difficult to distinguish proper from common nouns. To understand this better, take a look at the sample headline with initial caps. It appears that Remulink has been funded to buy a company named Amity Systems. Now read the same headline above with sentence caps. Here, it is clear that Remulink has been funded to buy only some of the systems made by Amity.

Underlining should also be avoided for display type, unless you want to intentionally create a choppy graphic effect. Headlines or subheads that are underlined, or that have rules below them, appear disconnected from the text they introduce. If you want to use rules, place them above the headline or subhead instead.

If you want to use reversed display type (white text on a dark background), do so sparingly. And when you do, follow the same guidelines described earlier for reversed body text—set it bold, increase its size, and use a sans serif typeface.

Paragraph Formatting

Paragraph formatting of display type involves setting the leading, alignment, and hyphenation in headings, subheads, and other display elements.

■ **Alignment.** Fully justified headlines can lead to awkward word spacing, as you can see in the top headline example below. Centering the headline is an option, as shown in the middle headline, but it forces readers to shift their eyes to the right to read the headline and then shift back to the left to start the article. Left alignment, as in the bottom headline, is the recommended option.

Headline Alignment
A fully justified headline causes awkward word spacing. Centered headlines require readers to shift their eyes from the headline to the text below. Left alignment works best.

**Remulink   buys   Amity   systems
in $21   million   deal**
Lorem ipsum dolor sit amet, consectetuer adipiscing elit. Donec feugiat orci eget velit. In venenatis. Mauris eget lectus. Donec aliquet. Nullam euismod, felis at eleifend lobortis, turpis urna posuere orci, ut sagittis neque dui nec leo.

Fully justified

**Remulink buys Amity systems
in $21 million deal**
Lorem ipsum dolor sit amet, consectetuer adipiscing elit. Donec feugiat orci eget velit. In venenatis. Mauris eget lectus. Donec aliquet. Nullam euismod, felis at eleifend lobortis, turpis urna posuere orci, ut sagittis neque dui nec leo.

Centered

**Remulink buys Amity systems
in $21 million deal**
Lorem ipsum dolor sit amet, consectetuer adipiscing elit. Donec feugiat orci eget velit. In venenatis. Mauris eget lectus. Donec aliquet. Nullam euismod, felis at eleifend lobortis, turpis urna posuere orci, ut sagittis neque dui nec leo.

Left aligned

Remulink buys Amity systems

Lorem ipsum dolor sit amet, consectetuer adipiscing elit. Nullam euismod, felis at eleifend lobortis, turpis urna posuere orci, ut sagittis neque dui nec leo.

Remulink buys Amity systems

Lorem ipsum dolor sit amet, consectetuer adipiscing elit. Nullam euismod, felis at eleifend lobortis, turpis urna posuere orci, ut sagittis neque dui nec leo.

Headline Leading

In the example on the far left, too much white space is trapped between the lines of the headline. Reducing the leading, as shown in the other example, solves the problem.

■ **Leading.** The leading initially set by your software will probably leave more space than you want between the lines of your headings. When you create a style for your headings, try to specify leading that is equal to the size of the type. For example, if your headline type size is 18 points, set the leading at 18 points as well. Look at the difference between the two sample headlines above. In the example on the left, too much white space is trapped between the two lines. Reducing the leading, as seen in the example on the right, solves the problem.

Also, be sure to leave more space above a headline or subheading than below it. This will help connect the headline to its article. Remember, too much white space trapped between a headline and the article will make it hard for your readers to connect the two.

■ **Hyphenation and Line Breaks.** The larger your type, the uglier it appears when hyphenated. Headlines should never be hyphenated. In pull quotes that are set smaller, around 12 or 13 points, you can get away with occasional hyphens. And it's fine to set hyphenation on in captions, which are even smaller. Subheads are usually limited to one line, so hyphenation is not an issue.

In headlines and pull quotes, be careful where you break lines. Try to keep the lines even in length and break them at logical places. For instance, the left headline example below is awkward because it separates "Amity" from the word it modifies, "systems." It also looks unbal-

Line Breaks

Avoid awkward line breaks in headlines, as seen in example at far left, and try to keep the lines somewhat balanced, as seen in the other example.

Remulink buys Amity systems

Remulink buys Amity systems

Checklist for Typeface Design

Refer to this checklist when formatting your newsletter's body text and display type. Following these guidelines will result in good type design.

Body Text

Character Formatting

- ☐ Is typeface legible?
- ☐ Is use of decorative typefaces avoided?
- ☐ Is typeface size from 9 to 12 points?
- ☐ Are long italicized text blocks avoided?
- ☐ Is underlining avoided?
- ☐ Is use of all caps avoided?
- ☐ Is reversed text used sparingly and set bold in a sans serif typeface?

Paragraph Formatting

- ☐ Is leading 1 or 2 points greater than the type size? (or more for sans serif typefaces or long line lengths?)
- ☐ Is only one method of separating paragraphs used (first-line indent or line spacing)?
- ☐ Are first-line indents small (one pica)?
- ☐ Is alignment (ragged right or justified) appropriate for the newsletter's tone?
- ☐ Is hyphenation used?
- ☐ Are opening paragraphs distinguished by different typography (no first-line indent; drop cap; upper casing of first few words)?

Display Type

Character Formatting

- ☐ Does display type contrast with body text (through different typeface, type style, or size)?
- ☐ Is number of typefaces limited throughout the newsletter?
- ☐ Are headlines at least 4 points larger than body text?
- ☐ Is reversed type used sparingly and set bold in a sans serif typeface?
- ☐ Is all-cap style used sparingly?

Paragraph Formatting

- ☐ Is headline leading equal or to close to the type size?
- ☐ Are headlines left justified?
- ☐ Is hyphenation avoided in headlines, and used sparingly in pull quotes and decks?
- ☐ Do headlines break at logical stopping points?

anced because the first line is so much longer than the second. The headline on the right keeps these related words together and the line lengths fairly even.

Designing Other Newsletter Elements

In addition to headlines and body text, a newsletter can include a number of other elements—author bios, bulleted lists, bylines, and captions, to name just a few—that you must design. Instead of formatting these elements every time you lay out an issue, I recommend creating a sample of each in your template file. To further simplify the design process, use the same or similar styles for many of these elements. For example, you might choose 9-point Frutiger italic as your style for jump lines, captions, bylines, author bios, folios, and volume and issue number. But your jump lines might be right justified, and your captions might have looser leading than the author bios.

An alphabetical listing of each of these newsletter elements—some of which have been covered in earlier chapters—follows, along with brief descriptions and helpful formatting recommendations. They appear on one or more of the sample pages in Newsletter Elements, beginning on page 222.

Author Bio

An author bio is a short paragraph accompanying an article that gives a bit of information about the person who wrote it. To contrast with the body text, an author bio should be set in italics or in a different typeface. You can also set off this bio from the article by placing a rule above it, or by placing it alongside the article in the scholar's margin.

Bulleted List

Use bullets or numbers for lists that contain three or more entries. This will help make the information stand out, make it easier to remember, and help readers mentally "check off" the items listed. If the order of the items in the list is important, number them. If not, use bullets or dingbats (■ ◆ ❑ are a few commonly used examples). If you decide to use a dingbat, use the same one for all bulleted lists throughout the newsletter.

Byline

A byline, usually found at the beginning of an article, states the name of the person who wrote it—"By Jane Doe," for example. Bylines are usually the same size as the body text, but set in bold, italics, or in a different typeface to make them stand out. Since they are a way of showing appreciation for your writers, make them easy to find. Don't set them vertically, for instance, where readers won't notice them. Although bylines are usually found at the beginning of articles, occasionally, they can be placed at the end. If the same person writes all the articles in a newsletter, don't include a byline with each one—it would be too repetitious. Instead, list the writer's name once in the masthead.

Caption

Captions are short descriptions that accompany illustrations, photographs, and other graphics. They should be set in a type that is the same size or slightly smaller than the body text. To make captions easily distinguishable from the body text, use a different typeface, or set them in bold, italic, or color. Place them below or beside the graphics, and set the text flush left (left aligned)—not centered or flush right.

Deck

A deck is a sentence or two of additional information that is placed below a headline. Set decks at a size that is equal to or smaller than their headlines. Make these two elements contrast by setting one or the other in bold, italics, or in a different typeface. Use left alignment for decks.

Folio

Place page numbers either in the center or on the outside corners of headers or footers. If they appear on the inside corners, readers will have difficulty finding them as they flip through pages.

The page number, name of the publication, and issue date should appear on each page (with the exception of page one). You can place these items, called folios, in a header at the top of the page or in a footer at the bottom. (Some publishers, especially book publishers, use the word "folio" to refer to the page number only.) It isn't necessary to include this information on the first page, because it is already there in the nameplate. If your mailing panel is at the bottom of the last page, you may have to exclude a folio from that page as well, lest it interfere with post office scanning equipment.

When people tear out or photocopy pages of your newsletter and pass them on, having this information in a header or footer tells the recipient where the information originated. Place the page numbers in the center of the header or footer, or on the outside corners. Don't place them on the inside corners, where readers will have difficulty finding them as they flip through the pages.

Jump Lines

Articles that are continued on another page require jump lines, such as "Continued on page 3" or "Continued from page 1," to help readers "jump" to the correct page. On the page where the story is continued, place an abbreviated headline along with the jump line. For example, if the original headline is "Remulink buys Amity systems," the abbreviated headline could say "Remulink."

The jump line itself should be close to or the same size as the body text, but it should contrast. Set it in bold, italics, or a different typeface. Some designers place a rule above or below the jump line. The size of the abbreviated headline should be between the size of your body text and the size of the original headline. Its typeface and type style should coordinate with your other headlines.

Kickers

Usually just two or three words in length, kickers—short lines of text above headlines—should contrast with the headline. They are often accompanied by a unifying graphic that is repeated with each kicker. For example, the two kickers in the *Boston Broadside* newsletter spread on page 223—"The President's Message" and "Society Highlights"—are each accompanied by such a graphic. Other newsletters may use different but stylistically related graphics for each kicker. For instance, a "Book Review" kicker might have a cartoon-like graphic of a person reading, while a "Technology" kicker might have one of a computer.

Logo

A logo—the identifying symbol or trademark—of the company or organization that publishes the newsletter is commonly placed on page one in the nameplate or, occasionally, in the masthead. If your nameplate looks too cluttered with the logo, try moving the logo to the bottom of the page.

Mailing Panel

If you don't use an envelope to mail your newsletter, you'll have to create a mailing panel on the back page for the address label and postage. Remember that this is the first part of your newsletter that readers will see, so identify yourself clearly there. Duplicating your logo or your newsletter's nameplate on the mailing panel makes it clear where the mail came from. Also add your return address and, if you use Standard Mail, your mailing indicia. You might also add your tagline, a teaser about an important article, or another marketing message.

Be sure to place your logo or nameplate on the mailing panel to clearly identify yourself.

To ensure that postal machines can properly scan mail, the postal service has regulations about the amount of blank space that must appear around a mailing label. Chapter 9 provides more information about those regulations.

Masthead

The masthead is where you list your newsletter's staff and other information about its operation, such as mailing address, website, and reprint policy. The most common location for mastheads is on page two or the back page. Be sure to run it in the same spot in every issue. You can place the masthead in a box or a scholar's margin. Typically, it includes the following items:

■ Staff (be sure to include titles, names, and e-mail addresses). Nonprofit organizations may want to list board members, too.

■ Publisher contact information. (Include mailing address, telephone and fax numbers, and website and e-mail addresses.)

■ Copyright notice.

■ Brief description of your newsletter's audience and purpose.

■ Description of your organization.

■ Publication frequency.

■ Reprint policy.

■ Subscription price and address for subscribing.

■ Address-change procedure.

■ ISSN.

■ Contact information for placing ads (if applicable).

■ Recognition of services that have been donated for the newsletter's production.

■ Legal disclaimers. (Check with your organization's attorney or legal department to see if disclaimers, such as "This newsletter is for internal use only and not for distribution to third parties," are needed.)

Since people read the masthead only if they are seeking specific information, like your website address or phone number, you can set it in smaller type than the body text (usually 7 to 9 points).

Nameplate

As discussed in Chapter 2, a nameplate, also called a banner, is the area across the top or side of page one that contains the name of your newsletter. The typeface you use should be legible from several feet away. To decorate your nameplate, you might add boxes, rules, or illustrations.

Newsletters that are published by an individual, such as *Louis Rukeyser's Wall Street,* often contain a picture of the editor in the nameplate. Syndicated marketing newsletters, which are distributed by third parties, sometimes include space for the distributor's photograph. Place your newsletter's tagline, issue date, and volume and issue numbers near or within your nameplate.

Photo Credit Lines

Credit lines are to photographs as bylines are to articles. If your photographers are volunteers, printing credit lines is a good way to thank them. You can place credit lines directly below your photos horizontally, or alongside them vertically. Alternatively, you can give credit in your masthead, particularly if one person does all the photography. Credit lines should be set in smaller type than captions. Typically 6 or 7 points is fine.

Pull Quote

As discussed in Chapter 6, a pull quote, also called *display quote* or *callout,* is a sentence or sentence fragment that is taken directly from an article. Pull quotes should be interesting and significant enough to pique reader interest. They are set in larger type than the body text and positioned within the article itself or alongside it in a scholar's margin. Set pull quotes anywhere from 12 to 18 points. Experiment with bold, italicized, or colored type. Pull quotes are one of the few elements for which reversed type is appropriate. You can left align or center the quote in a box (with or without borders) and add a screen or leave the background clear. Try placing rules above and below a pull quote box that does not have borders.

Sidebars

As discussed in Chapter 4, sidebars are boxed items that accompany news or feature articles, often containing supplemental material or information that refers to or relates in some way to the articles. They might focus on one aspect of a story or provide helpful or pertinent reference information (such as driving directions, a listing of websites, or names of donors or volunteers) that would otherwise interrupt the flow of the article.

Place sidebars in a clear or screened box. If you use a screen, keep it light (no more than 10 percent), so the text that goes over it will be legible. If you are using a spot color for your newsletter, use a light shade of it to screen your sidebars. Body text in sidebars is often set in a sans serif

When adding a screen or tint to a boxed sidebar, be sure it is light enough—10 percent or less—to maintain the legibility of the copy.

Newsletter Elements

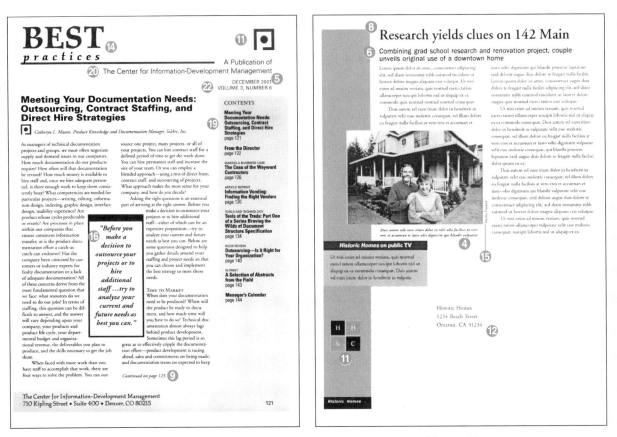

Best Practices

Historic Homes

The newsletter elements discussed throughout the book and detailed in this chapter are found on these sample pages.

Instead of formatting these elements every time you lay out an issue, create a sample of each in your template file. This not only saves time, it also ensures style consistency.

1. Author bio
2. Bulleted list
3. Byline
4. Caption
5. Date
6. Deck

Boston Broadside (2-page spread)

7 Folio

8 Headline

9 Jump line

10 Kicker

11 Logo

12 Mailing panel

13 Masthead

14 Nameplate

15 Photo credit line

16 Pull quote

17 Sidebar

18 Subhead

19 Table of contents

20 Tagline

21 Unifying graphic

22 Volume and issue numbers

typeface that contrasts with the serif typeface of the body text in the main article. Leave a one-pica margin between the text of the sidebar and the box surrounding it.

Subheads

Subheads—short headings that appear within the text of an article— introduce new topics. They are usually the same size or a point or two larger than the body text. For contrast, set subheads in bold or italics, or in a different typeface or color. Use them every few paragraphs in longer articles. Be careful not to isolate subheads at the bottom of a column— make sure at least two lines of text fall beneath them.

Table of Contents

Placing the table of contents in a clear or screened box, or surrounding it with white space, will help it stand out.

For any newsletter that's longer than two pages, include a table of contents to help readers quickly find what they want. Placing it in a box (shaded or clear) or surrounding it with white space will help it stand out. Most newsletters have the table of contents on page one. If, however, your newsletter is a self-mailer, you might want to place it on the back page alongside the mailing panel—it's what readers will see first. Unless the table of contents is on the back page, it shouldn't list your page-one articles. It isn't necessary to include them, since readers can quite well see what's on the same page. It is also unnecessary to include minor filler items.

Tagline

As discussed in Chapter 2, a tagline is the brief line of text that summarizes your newsletter's audience and purpose. Typically, it appears in the nameplate along with the title of the newsletter and logo. Use 9- to 14- point type.

Volume and Issue Numbers

A newsletter's volume number usually corresponds to the number of years the newsletter has been published. Its first year of publication is considered volume 1, second year is volume 2, third year is volume 3. The issue number corresponds to the number of issues that have been published within that year. So January might be number 1; February, number 2; March, number 3. For a bimonthly newsletter, January/February would be number 1 and March/April would be number 2. Some publishers use a school year or fiscal year instead of a calendar year to number their volumes and issues. For instance, a university might number its September issue as number 1, October as number 2, and so forth.

Including volume and issue numbers in your newsletter is not mandatory. But if you expect libraries to subscribe, you must include them, since librarians use them in cataloguing their holdings. And once you've been publishing for more than a couple of years, displaying your volume and issue number shows readers that you're an established publication. Place these numbers on page one adjacent to your nameplate. Use 9- to 12-point type that matches the typeface used for your issue date.

LAYOUT: CONSTRUCTING AN ISSUE

Now that the blueprint for your newsletter is complete, it's time to don your hardhat and begin construction; time to lay out a real issue. You'll start by getting your materials—articles, photos, and graphics—from your editor. You'll apply styles to your text, typeset your punctuation marks, and map your layout. You'll also have to find ways to fit your copy into the space available.

Obtaining Copy and Applying Styles

The first job of the layout artist is to obtain electronic copy—files containing articles, photos, and graphics—from the editor. Except for final proofreading, any copy the editor gives you should be well edited. It should also be unformatted. This means, neither the editor nor writers should apply typefaces, bolding, italics, indents, and the like to their copy. If they do, you'll end up undoing their work anyway. Why? When you import their text into your page-layout software, you will be applying the styles that were created for the newsletter's design. Chances are, if the editor or writer tries to format a headline or body text or a subhead, he'll either forget or be unaware of applicable type specifications. He might know enough to set it bold, but not to set the leading at 24 on 24. But if you use the style feature in your page-layout software, you'll be able to take care of all those formatting specs with a single mouse click.

It's a good idea to set up a system for naming the files you receive for your articles. I like to start the file name with the issue date, followed by keywords from the title or the name of the author. For example, according to my system, "0907 Jones.doc" is an article by Jones written for the September 2007 issue. When that issue has been published, it's easy to identify the file as one you can archive or delete.

As you place each file in your newsletter template, you'll have to

To help identify the electronic files you receive for your articles, set up a system for naming them. I start with the issue date, followed by a keyword or the author's name; however, you might find that a different system works better for you.

apply the appropriate style to every paragraph of text. In a long article with body text interspersed with a few subheads, it can be tedious to click in each paragraph and choose the appropriate style. Instead, I highlight the entire article and apply my body text style to the whole thing. Then I go back and change the headline, byline, and subheads to their respective styles.

Typesetting Punctuation

After you apply styles to your type, take a few minutes to clean it up, using professional typography techniques. You can make most of these changes quickly by using the find-and-replace feature of your page-layout software.

Hyphens and Dashes

A hyphen (-) is used to combine words like "nitty-gritty" and "self-esteem."

An en dash (–) is longer than a hyphen and used to show range between numbers.

An em dash (—) is a long dash used to indicate a strong break or pause within a sentence.

First, remove extra spaces at the end of sentences. Many people type two spaces after a period, question mark, or exclamation point. This creates unattractive, trapped white space in body text, which you can eliminate by deleting the extra space. Also look at the single and double quotation marks (as well as apostrophes). Make sure they are "curly quotation marks," which are shaped differently at the beginning and end of the quote, rather than "straight quotation marks," which should be used only as symbols for inches or feet.

Finally, make sure any hyphens and dashes that appear in the text are used correctly. Of course, to do this, you must know the difference between these punctuation marks. *Hyphens* are the shortest of the dashes and can be found on the keyboard. They are used most commonly to combine words like "nitty-gritty" and "self-esteem." The two other dashes, called em and en dashes, are longer and require you to press a combination of keys that will vary depending on your software. An *en dash* is a short dash that is longer than a hyphen and used to show range between numbers, such as "The recipe calls for 1–2 teaspoons of salt" or "He worked there from 1961–1965." Use the longer *em dash* to create a strong pause or break within a sentence. Em dashes can be used in pairs—to enclose a phrase or word—or they can be used alone to separate the end of a sentence from the beginning. Dashes are often effective within very long, complex sentences. Do not add a space before or after any of these dashes.

Mapping

Before you place your copy on your newsletter's pages, work with the editor to come up with a broad map showing which stories go where.

Sketch out each page of that issue and note where the articles should be placed. A sample map is presented in Figure 8.10 at right.

First, fill in the standing items, like your masthead and mailing panel, that appear in the same spot in every issue. Messages from the editor traditionally run on the second page—a logical spot since they introduce other articles in the newsletter. Calendars are often found on the back page. If your newsletter has a mailing panel on the back page, consider placing the calendar on the page that backs it. This way, if readers want to cut out the calendar, they won't be losing anything important on the back of the page. Select a permanent position for your other recurring columns as well.

Next, from among your news and features, determine which are most important. Put them in the most visible spots—the front and back pages. Place your items of moderate importance at the top of inside pages and continuations of articles at the bottom of inside pages. The editor should allow the layout artist some discretion in placing the inside articles, since it's difficult to predict at the time of mapping exactly how everything is going to fit.

If your newsletter has advertising, you may have to place an ad in a specific position requested by the advertiser. Try not to segregate ads on a separate page, as readers may ignore them. Advertisers will get more response, and be more likely to give you repeat business, if their ads appear near editorial copy. Avoid running ads on page one.

Placing Text and Graphics

Once you have mapped out where your copy should go, you are ready to place copy more exactly on your pages. As we go through some guidelines for placing text and graphics, refer to Figure 8.11 on page 228, which illustrates some of these suggestions.

Your readers should quickly understand which headlines and graphics belong to which stories. To help them, place less space between a headline and its story than between the headline and the story above it. If a story appears above another story, make a clear division between the two, by drawing a rule or extending the headline of the lower story across all columns. Clearly indicate the endings of stories, with a dingbat, a rule, or an author bio.

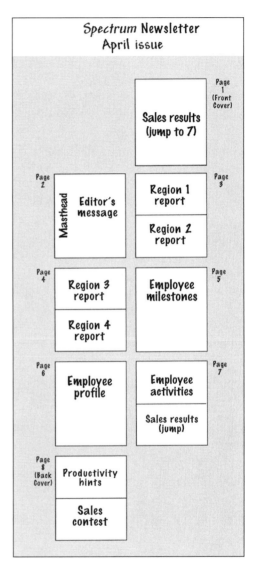

Figure 8.10

Before layout, sketch out a broad map of your newsletter's pages, noting the article placement for that issue. Right-handed pages are odd numbered; left-handed pages are even.

Keep your pages organized by using consistent spacing around all elements. For example, for each story that you start with an 18-point headline, leave the same amount of space between the headline and the byline. Likewise, every time you use a byline, keep the same amount of space between it and the first line of the story. At the bottom of your columns, make sure the distance between the text (or photos) and footers is consistent, and keep the spacing uniform between photos and captions.

Be thoughtful when placing photos and pictures. If you have several photos for one article, try to group them together, rather than interspersing them throughout the text and interrupting your reader. Decide which picture in the group is most important, and make it larger than the others. If you have several headshots of equally important people, set them all the same size.

You can also try placing pictures at the top or the bottom of the article. Align them to horizontal or vertical lines on your grid, as shown in

Figure 8.11

Note the consistent spacing among headlines, blocks of text, and graphics on the two-page spread below.

Figure 8.11 on page 228. If possible, avoid wrapping text around pictures, especially if it creates very narrow columns.

Also avoid placing graphics in the left column directly below a headline, as it confuses the reader as to where the story begins. Since graphics appear heavier than text, make sure you balance those on one side of a two-page spread with those on the other side, as discussed earlier in this chapter. If appropriate, you can also place graphics at an angle to give an informal look and sense of movement to the layout.

Make sure each pull quote appears on the same page as the article it came from. There's nothing more annoying to a reader than having to sift through a page unsuccessfully to find the source of a pull quote.

Avoiding Jumps

Your goal when laying out an article is to place it in its entirety on one page. When a story is continued on another page, a certain percentage of readers will not obey your command to "see page x." Sometimes, however, a jump is unavoidable because a story contains more text than can fit on a single page. Jumps often occur on page one because many editors want more than one story to appear on the front page, which leaves limited space for completing the stories.

If you must jump a story, follow a few rules to keep your readers with you. Always use jump lines, both "continued *on* page x" and "continued *from* page y" along with an abbreviated headline on the second page. Balance the amount of the story that appears on the two pages— place enough on the first page to get readers involved, and enough on the second page to make them feel it was worth the trip. And don't jump a story more than once. Rearrange your layout to make the story fit on the initial pages instead.

> Ideally, an article should appear in its entirety on one page, but sometimes a jump onto two pages is necessary. Place enough of the article on the first page to get the readers involved, and enough on the second page to make them feel it was worth the trip. And never jump a story more than once.

Fitting Copy

Sometimes an article will be too long for its assigned space. If you've trained your writers to use the inverted pyramid style (detailed in Chapter 6), you should be able to cut paragraphs, starting at the bottom of a story, without deleting any important points. Always reread the entire story after doing so, to make sure that any questions posed in the earlier paragraphs are still adequately answered.

When you need to cut several lines from an article, begin by reading through it closely to see if there are any wordy passages you can cut. If

When a paragraph ends in a widow, you can often eliminate this undesirable short line of text by deleting an unnecessary word or words from the paragraph, or by replacing a long word with a shorter synonym.

you need to cut only one or two lines, look for widows. A *widow* is a very short line of text—just a word or a syllable—at the end of a paragraph. You can eliminate a widow by deleting an unnecessary word or words from the paragraph, or by substituting a shorter synonym for a word in the paragraph (replacing the word "company" with "firm," for example).

You can alter the size of graphics to either fill empty space or create additional space for copy. For instance, if you're running an article that includes a picture, you can increase the size of the picture to fill in empty space that remains after placing the text. But don't make the picture so large that it appears more important than it is. If you're running a pull quote, try choosing a shorter or longer passage based on your space requirements, but stick with your usual style. This means, if your pull quotes are always one column wide, don't expand them two columns.

Avoid changing the sizes of drop caps, display type, or body text to meet space requirements. Sticking with the styles you created for these elements maintains unity in your newsletter. Likewise, never adjust leading for the purpose of filling or creating space. Don't be tempted to change your grid—your page margins, column widths, and the space between columns—for this purpose either.

CHOOSING PAGE-LAYOUT SOFTWARE

"What kind of page-layout software do you recommend?" This is one question I can always count on being asked in my newsletter seminars. Since the capabilities of software change with each new version that comes on the market, it's hard to give specific recommendations today that won't be out of date tomorrow. But I can tell you the features you'll need and which categories of software offer them.

When you lay out a newsletter, your primary task is to set up pages. You want your software to let you see how your pages will look when printed. In the software business they call this WYSIWYG (pronounced "wizzy wig"); it stands for "what you see is what you get." You also want the ability to set up a grid—nonprinting lines that you can use to place headlines, text blocks, and graphics within the margins and column guides you have specified.

You also want to be able to set up master pages. Master pages, shown in Figure 8.12 on page 231, are templates of your actual newsletter pages. Page-layout software lets you create left- and right-hand master pages. The left page contains elements that belong on the even-numbered pages of your newsletter, while the right-hand master contains those that belong on the odd-numbered pages. For example, you might place your page numbers in the lower left corner on even-numbered pages, and in the lower right corner on the odd. With master pages, you don't have to recreate your gridlines, borders, and folios every time you add pages to your newsletter. And master pages prevent you from accidentally moving these elements from their proper positions while you manipulate text and graphics on your actual newsletter pages.

Another essential feature of page-layout software is the ability to group—temporarily lock together—text blocks and graphics so you can easily move an entire story, including the headline, byline, body text, graphics, and any other element it contains, from one page to another. Without this grouping ability, when moving the article to a new page, you would have to replicate the effort you put into spacing your headline, byline, article, and graphics.

You also want to be able to place graphics and text precisely where you want them, within minute fractions of an inch. If you plan on using color, you'll want your software to support the type of color you use (process or spot) and allow you to define the colors you need.

If you're planning to publish a PDF newsletter, make sure the page-layout software can create PostScript files, which can be easily converted to

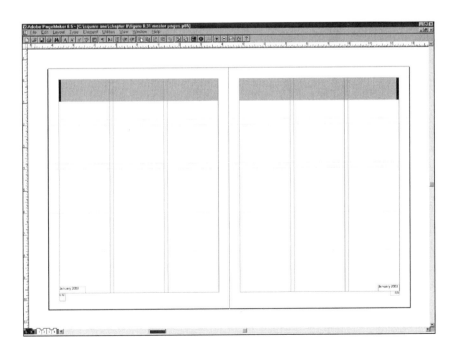

Figure 8.12
Your page-layout software should let you create grids on left- and right-hand master pages.

PDF files. Since Adobe is the creator of PDF, its page-layout software comes with a feature that lets you create PDF files quite easily.

Before purchasing page-layout software, find out if your print shop can handle the type of file you will be creating with it. Most printers prefer to work with the file formats created by professional page-layout programs like Quark XPress and Adobe InDesign. Some cannot accept files from word processing or home publishing software.

If you plan to design your newsletter from a template, see if any are available for the software you are considering. Templates are sometimes bundled with the software, or they can be purchased separately. You will want a good selection of templates—not just one or two—so you can choose a design that is appropriate for your newsletter's purpose, audience, and tone.

Many novices start out using word processing software to lay out their newsletters. Often, this software is already available on their computers. It can also be purchased inexpensively. While such programs claim to have desktop publishing capabilities and, in fact, do allow you to create columns, place graphics, and jump stories from page to page, it is not their primary purpose. Word processing software is more geared to creating letters, memos, reports, and mass mailings. As a result, it can be very difficult to lay out pages using them. Page-layout programs, like Adobe InDesign or Quark XPress, are specifically designed for page layout and help you get the job done much faster. These programs are more expensive than word processing programs, and they take some time to learn. You'll need to either take a class or at least purchase an instructional book with a tutorial CD, to help you learn how to use the program. Your time and effort will pay off in reduced layout time.

If you can't afford professional page-layout software, consider a middle-level program like Microsoft Publisher or Serif PagePlus. They have many of the capabilities of professional packages. Before buying, make sure the program you select can handle all of the needs discussed in this section.

CONCLUSION

The joy of design and layout is that, once you've learned some of the do's and don'ts, you can, with a few clicks of the mouse, markedly improve the look and flow of your newsletter. By implementing the suggestions presented in this chapter, your newsletter will look polished and professional. Expect to receive positive feedback from your readers.

CHAPTER 9

REPRODUCING AND MAILING PRINT NEWSLETTERS

You are now ready to jump the last hurdles in publishing your newsletter: printing and mailing. These steps may seem like afterthoughts to writing, editing, and layout, but both are important and neither is simple. My hope in this chapter is to give you enough background on how the print industry and the postal service work, so you are comfortable communicating your needs to vendors or getting the work done yourself. If I've done it right, you'll stay on schedule and save yourself some money at the same time.

REPRODUCTION

The first time you set foot in a print shop, you might feel the same way a visitor from Mars would feel when trying to buy a car. The Martian would certainly be confused over what he should buy to get around on his new planet . . . a convertible, sedan, pickup truck, or SUV? If he came to you for advice, you would tell him that the best type of vehicle would depend on a number of factors: how much driving he plans to do, how much money he has to spend, whether he wants to impress his friends, and whether he needs to haul around any large equipment, like flying saucers. In other words, it depends on his specific requirements. It's the same with printing your newsletter. Deciding which method of reproduction is best depends on the number of copies you need, the size of your budget, the quality of work your audience expects, the turnaround time you require, and your newsletter's design. It also depends on other options you may need—from three-hole punching and scanning photos to pickup and delivery. This section of the chapter will steer you through all these decisions.

No interplanetary visitor should venture into an automobile show-room until he's received some advice on how to get what he wants from a salesman. Likewise, no newsletter editor should venture into a print shop until receiving some advice on how to work with a printer. So this section is designed to help you choose a shop and develop a good relationship with the staff there, essential if you want your newsletter to go out on time.

Choosing a Method of Print Reproduction

This section presents four ways to reproduce your print newsletter—laser or inkjet printing, photocopying, offset printing, and digital printing. You'll also learn which methods work best for various types of newsletter requirements. Table 9.1 on page 236 presents a summary of these methods.

Laser or Inkjet Printing

Printing out your newsletter from a laser or inkjet printer is a good option when only a few copies are needed. Beyond that, the cost of toner or ink cartridges becomes prohibitive.

Probably the simplest way to reproduce your newsletter is by printing it from the laser or inkjet printer in your home or office. This makes sense if you have to print only a few copies; beyond that, the cost of ink cartridges or toner becomes prohibitive. And if your newsletter is four or more pages, your printer will have to handle 11-x-17-inch paper.

When you use your own equipment, you have control over when the job gets done, but you also have to consider whether you can afford to tie up your printer for several hours, since many home and small-office printers are relatively slow. The quality of the copies will depend on the printer's resolution. While these printers can do a good job with straight black text, the quality of color may not be as good as you need. You may, for example, have trouble exactly matching the corporate colors of your company's logo.

Photocopying

Photocopying is the most economical printing method when the size of the print job requires only a few hundred copies. Beyond that, it becomes more expensive per copy than offset printing, because the toner used by photocopiers is more expensive than offset ink. A quick-copy shop can get your photocopying job back to you in a day or two. If you own a machine, or if you use a self-service machine, you can have your copies even sooner.

What are the downsides of photocopying? For one, photocopiers cannot handle as wide a variety of paper stocks as offset presses. In addition, the quality of photocopied work is not as good as that of offset presses. Photographs and screens do not reproduce well with most photocopiers. However, the newer digital models found in some print shops can produce high-quality photographs and screens. You can think of these machines as giant, high-speed laser printers. Each "copy" they produce is actually an original. For small print runs (under 200 copies) of a black and white newsletter, digital photocopying can be the best choice.

For print jobs that require only a few hundred copies, photocopying is the most economical method.

Digital color photocopiers can produce reasonable quality color output using process color (CMYK). But, as with inkjet printers, the quality of the color may not be adequate for reproducing critical colors like skin tones. Digital color photocopying can be cost effective for quantities up to 5,000.

Offset Printing

Offset printing is what most people are referring to when they talk about getting a job printed. When you use offset, you submit your page-layout file to the shop's prepress operator. The prepress operator sends the file to a machine called an imagesetter, which transfers your document to film. This film is used to create printing plates, which, in turn are placed on the rollers of the offset printing press. During this prepress process, you are able to inspect proofs of your job to make sure it will print correctly. However, if you find errors late in the process, they will be expensive to correct, because the film and/or plates must be recreated.

Offset printing uses ink, not toner. It can reproduce in black and white, spot color, or process color. Of all the printing methods, offset provides the best capability for checking proofs and matching colors, yielding the best-quality printing, whether black and white or color. It also allows you to use the widest variety of papers.

Because of the prepress work required, offset is not economical for printing quantities of less than a few hundred. Offset printing of newsletters using process color does not become economical until your numbers reach a few thousand.

The turnaround time for an offset job, particularly one involving color, is longer than for photocopying or digital reproduction, because of both the prepress work required and the fact that the ink used on offset presses needs some time to dry before the newsletters can be folded. You'll probably have to allow a week or more for your job to be printed. However, you might be able to reduce the amount of time needed for prepress by meeting with the prepress operator beforehand to determine the most efficient way to prepare your files.

Digital Printing

Digital presses eliminate some of the prepress work required with offset printing. Instead of sending your page-layout file to an imagesetter to create film, as is done with offset, some digital presses image the file directly onto the plates that go on the press. Then they print copies using traditional ink. Other digital presses don't even need to create plates; they make the copies directly with toner or a laser beam and electrostatic ink. If you are using the digital method without plates and find a mistake when looking at your newsletter's proofs, correcting it is simpler than with offset—it requires only modifying the digital file. However, with digital printing, the proofs you see won't be as accurate as offset proofs; it won't show exactly how the colors will look on your final printed newsletter.

Because digital presses eliminate some prepress steps, they make it more economical to print small quantities (500 to 2,500 copies), particularly for jobs involving process color. With the digital presses that use tra-

TABLE 9.1.   COMPARING PRINTING METHODS

The table below compares the four printing methods—laser or inkjet, photocopying, offset printing, and digital printing—based on quality, turnaround time, and color availability.

| Printing Method | Assessment Criteria | | | |
	Cost-Effective Number of Copies*	Quality of Output	Turnaround Time	Type of Color Available
Laser or inkjet	Less than 200.	Fair to good.	Few hours.	Process color from some machines.
Photocopying	Less than 200 to 250. Less than 5,000 for process color.	Poor to good. Better with digital photocopiers.	Few hours for in-office equipment; two days or less from print shop.	Process color from some machines.
Offset printing	More than 250 for black and white or spot color. More than few thousand for process color.	Best.	One week or more.	Process or spot color.
Digital printing	500 to 2,500 (or 5,000), depending on type of machine.	Good.	Two days or less.	Process color; some machines handle spot color.

* Quantities are approximate. Always ask your printer what the most appropriate method is for your particular job.

ditional ink, you can economically print as many as 5,000 copies. At higher volumes, the high cost of the toner or electrostatic ink makes the price of digital reproduction prohibitive.

Reduced prepress work, plus the fact that there is no waiting time for ink to dry, means that digital print jobs can be turned around quickly—in just a couple of days. A downside to this type of reproduction is that many of the machines cannot do spot color, which can be a problem if you must match a certain PMS color. Also, you're limited to a narrower selection of paper than with an offset press.

Buying Additional Print Shop Services

In addition to printing your newsletter, your print shop can provide a variety of other services. One is folding. You'll want your 11-x-17-inch sheets folded in half to form 8.5-x-11-inch pages. And you may want them folded further for mailing. In some cases, folding your newsletter in thirds to fit into a standard #10 business envelope, or in half to use as a self-mailer, can reduce your postage. If you have access to a lot of helping hands and money is tight, you can do the folding in-house. You'll have to weigh the savings against the quality of the fold—machine folds will be straighter and flatter than hand folds.

If you don't have a scanner, your print shop can scan your photos for you. They can also three-hole punch your newsletters (also known as *drilling*) so readers can save them in binders. And they can saddle stitch (staple) your newsletters along the fold. Again, you can staple them yourself, but you'll need a special stapler to do so. You can do away with staples entirely, but if you do, you'll probably want to get the newsletters machine folded so the pages lay flat.

Some print shops can also perform mailing services, such as stuffing envelopes, applying address labels, printing addresses directly on the newsletters, and preparing and sorting them for Standard Mail. And many print shops offer pickup and delivery.

Choosing and Using a Print Shop

Although they may list similar services in their Yellow Pages ads, print shops are not all the same. Different printers own different equipment that is suited to different types of jobs. This means the print shop that handles your company's color sales brochure may not be the best one to print your newsletter. Generally, for more complex designs (color, bleeds,

In addition to printing your newsletter, most print shops offer services like saddle stitching, drilling, and machine folding. Some shops also provide mailing services, such as stuffing envelopes, applying address labels, and preparing the newsletters for Standard Mail.

tight registrations) and large quantities, you will need to use a commercial printer. If you use high-quality paper, particularly a coated variety, you'll be better off with a commercial printer. Commercial printers also have higher quality scanners for better reproduction of photos. For offset printing, they use metal (rather than plastic or paper) printing plates, which means better reproduction of photos and screens.

As you compare print shops, you'll want to request price quotes. The cost for print jobs can vary greatly from one shop to another. Get at least three quotes to assure you are getting the best price and service. Use a form like the one on page 239 to make sure you are describing your job exactly the same way to all the printers when getting a quote. (A blank copy of this form is available on page 321.) You may want to ask for more than one quote from each printer to compare, for instance, the cost of using two ink colors as opposed to just one, or the price of using one type of paper over another.

If possible, show your preliminary design to the print shop's pre-press operator and see if she has any advice on how to simplify production or reduce costs. Discuss the workflow you would follow if you did business with the shop—the type of electronic files you would submit, whether you would send fonts and graphics files as well, and how the proofing process works. A fifteen-minute conversation up front can save the prepress operator several hours of troubleshooting (that will add to your bill) later. Also, ask to see samples of other newsletters the shop has printed. Check the quality of the printer's work—are the text and graphics focused and clear? Have the solid areas, such as screened boxes, been printed smoothly and evenly?

As you evaluate print shops, price will be just one factor in your decision. You'll also want to weigh the quality of their work, the turnaround time they promise, extra services they provide (like pickup and delivery), and their location.

In addition to price, you will want to evaluate print shops on such factors as quality of work, turnaround time, location, and the extra services they offer.

Once you've chosen a printer, drop in again and confirm your arrangements. Make a final paper choice and order preprinted shells or envelopes if you need them. Drop off a copy of your production schedule, so they can plan for each issue. Also get into the habit of calling the shop a few days before each deadline to remind them that your newsletter will be ready for them to print soon.

Unless you have major problems with your print shop, stick with it for a while. There is a lot of upfront work involved in changing printers, and you don't want to have to repeat it every couple of months. You'll also find that, over time, you'll get extra attention as a regular customer.

When pricing the printing/reproduction cost of your newsletter, fill out a form like the one below and send it to various printers for different price quotes. A blank form is provided on page 321.

Printing Quote Form

PRINTER

Name: _XYZ Printing_   Contact: _George Anders_
Phone: _(535) 555-1234_   E-mail: _anders@xyzprinting.com_

CUSTOMER

Newsletter: _Wildlife Watch_   Editor: _Karen Jovonavitz_
Phone: _(535) 555-4321_   E-mail: _karen@wildlifewatch.com_

DETAILS

QUANTITY

Pages per issue: _8_   Issues per year: _6_   Copies per issue: _2,500_

PAPER STOCK

Grade: _Text_   Weight: _70#_   Color: _White_   Finish: _____   Brightness: _98%_
Brand: _Smithson_   Trim size: _8.5 x 11 inches, printed on both sides_

INK COLOR

✓ Black
✓ Spot PMS # _507 U_   PMS # _____
____ 4-color process (CMYK)
____ 4-color process + spot / PMS # _____
____ Shells / Quantity: _2_

PHOTOS

✓ Scan / Quantity: _2_

PROOFS REQUIRED

✓ Laser   ____ Color key   ____ Blueline   ____ Digital   ____ Matchprint   ____ Press proof   ____ Contact

BINDERY REQUIREMENTS

✓ Fold: _fold 2 times down to 8.5 x 5.5 inches_
✓ Collate
✓ Saddle stitch
____ 3-hole drill

SHIPPING

✓ Deliver to mail house _12345 Main Street, Boston, MA_
     (address)
____ Deliver to customer _____
     (address)
____ Customer to pick up
____ Other _____

PRICE QUOTE

Price per issue: $_____   Turnaround time required: _____
Payment terms: _____

Your work is likely to get priority on the press, you will be alerted if something in an issue appears to be out of the ordinary, and the printer is apt to make amends if a mistake is made on your job.

If you publish a nonprofit newsletter, you may be able to find a printer who will donate paper, printing, or the entire job to your organization. Or you might ask a local business to donate the use of its photocopying equipment. Be sure to mention such donations prominently in each issue of your newsletter.

MAILING

Preparing hundreds or even thousands of newsletters for mailing can be a daunting task. Fortunately, it's one for which help is often easy to find. For many associations or nonprofit organizations, preparing a newsletter for mailing is an occasion for a party. They often find volunteers—children as well as adults—to stuff, seal, and sort with promises of pizza and good company.

Hiring a mailing service to stuff and fold envelopes, add addresses, and apply postage can actually save money when sending out hundreds of newsletter copies.

For some organizations that mail over 200 to 500 copies of each issue, hiring a mail house to stuff envelopes, print addresses, and apply postage can actually save money. The mail house may be able to prepare the mailing in accord with US Postal Service regulations that net reduced postage, and those savings are often enough to pay the mail house bill. Or, to realize the full savings of reduced postage rates, you can prepare mailings yourself. Even if your mailing has fewer than 200 to 500 pieces, it's to your advantage to design your newsletter or envelope for quick processing by the post office, to assure quick and accurate delivery.

What follows is a summary of US Postal Service guidelines for obtaining reduced postage rates. The full requirements are complex and rates change frequently, so you'll have to consult with the postal service or a mail house—not just before your first mailing, but before completing the design of your newsletter's mailing panel or envelopes. The section "Resources for Getting Help with Mailing," beginning on page 244, will point you in the right direction for assistance.

First Class and Standard Mail

Most newsletters that are distributed through the post office are mailed as either First Class or Standard Mail. The services provided for these two types of mail vary according to speed, weight limits, forwarding and return options, and sorting requirements.

Speed

First Class Mail is transported between postal facilities by air if the distance is great, while Standard Mail is sent via ground transportation. Depending on the destination, Standard Mail can sometimes take ten days to two weeks for delivery; however, when sent within your state, it usually takes less than ten days. These differences in speed can be important if your newsletter contains time-sensitive information, or if you have a large number of out-of-state subscribers.

Weight Limits

With First Class Mail, rates increase once the newsletter's weight exceeds 1 ounce. Each additional ounce means added cost. With Standard Mail, the rate does not increase until the newsletter exceeds 3.3 ounces. So if you publish a lengthy newsletter, insert flyers, or use heavy paper, take this difference into account when comparing First Class and Standard Mail rates.

Forwarding and Return Options

With First Class Mail, your newsletter will be forwarded for twelve months, free of charge, to anyone on your mailing list who moves. During the following six months, the mailpiece will be returned to you with the person's new address (if available). After that, it will be returned with the reason for nondelivery noted.

There is no free forwarding with Standard Mail, and any undeliverable newsletters are disposed of by the postal service. This makes it difficult to keep an updated, cost-effective mailing list. You can, however, add what the postal service calls "ancillary service endorsements" to the mailpiece—a variety of optional forwarding and address-correction services. Included among these options are "Address Service," "Return Service," "Change Service," and "Forwarding Service." Of course, each option carries an additional fee, but in return, will enable you to maintain a current mailing list. And an updated list will save you money (often a considerable amount) in the long run. It will prevent you from literally throwing away money both on postage for future mailings and on the cost of the newsletter itself.

Sorting Requirements

First Class Mail is more expensive than Standard Mail. Presorted First Class Mail, in which you sort and deliver your newsletters to the post

First Class Mail is transported by air, while Standard Mail is sent by ground transportation and can take up to two weeks for delivery. If your newsletter contains time-sensitive material, these differences in speed can determine the mailing method you choose.

Standard Mail bulk rates are designed to save the post office time and money. They encourage the creation of mailpieces that are easily read by post office scanning equipment and easily sorted by its machines.

office according to certain requirements, is less expensive than regular First Class. Standard Mail, which also requires sorting and delivery, costs even less, and Standard Mail Nonprofit is the least expensive of all. (See "Obtaining Nonprofit Postage Rates" on page 243 for additional information.)

If you choose First Class Mail and your mailing consists of at least 500 pieces, you have the *option* of receiving a discount by preparing your mail to qualify for bulk rates. If you choose Standard Mail, which requires a minimum of 200 pieces, you are *required* to prepare your mail to qualify for bulk rates. The postal service adopted these reduced bulk rates to save itself time and money. Bulk rates encourage people to design their mailpieces in a manner that is easily read by post office scanning equipment and easily sorted by its machines. So the more work you do to prepare your mailing, the more money you can save.

For bulk rates, you must sort your mail by such characteristics as the area distribution center, the ZIP code, or, in some cases, the carrier route. You must also place it in special trays labeled to meet postal service requirements. In some cases, a minimum number of pieces within ZIP codes is required. Your stuffed envelope, or the newsletter itself, if it's a self-mailer, must meet certain restrictions for length, width, and thickness. Every piece you mail must be identical (you cannot, for example, insert a flyer into some newsletters and not others). Bulk rates also require certain guidelines for formatting and placement of addresses. If it is a self-mailer, your newsletter must be sealed in a certain manner, using wafer tabs, not staples. You must obtain a bulk rate mailing permit and pay an annual mailing fee.

A further way to save money on postage is by preparing your newsletter so that it can be handled by the postal service's automated equipment. To qualify for this special automation rate, the mailing must first meet all of the requirements for bulk rates. In addition, each piece of mail is required to have a barcode that contains information about its destination.

Whoa! I just read over the last few paragraphs, and I'm afraid I may have scared you away from bulk rates entirely. Not my intention! Like any unfamiliar project, getting started with bulk mail will require you to do some planning, ask some questions, and adopt new practices. But it's not as hard as it might sound. And the postal service is more than willing to help you, as you will see in "Resources for Getting Help with Mailing" on page 244. Just be sure to give yourself several weeks—before your mailing deadline—to get started.

Periodicals Mail

Periodicals mail, most commonly used for magazines and newspapers, has rates that are even lower than Standard rates. It's possible for newsletters to qualify for these rates, but the requirements are difficult to meet. In addition to meeting the criteria described in the previous section for bulk rates, other restrictions apply. For instance, your newsletter must be requested or subscribed to by a certain percentage of its readers. (If a large percentage of your newsletter is distributed at conferences or trade shows, it is not eligible for Periodicals mail. Nor is this rate an option for a free marketing newsletter.) Your newsletter must be published on a fixed schedule, at least quarterly. (If you have trouble sticking to your production schedule, Periodicals mail is not for you.) You must also publish from a business office, keep certain records to show that you meet the eligibility requirements, and, to top it off, you are subject to audits for compliance. For most newsletter publishers, First Class and Standard Mail are better choices.

Like Standard Mail, Periodicals mail offers lower nonprofit rates to eligible groups. For more information on Periodicals mail, search for Handbook DM-204 at *www.usps.gov.*

Obtaining Nonprofit Postage Rates

If you use Standard Mail or Periodicals mail, you may be eligible for nonprofit postage rates, which can significantly reduce your costs. Organizations that are eligible may include religious, educational, scientific, philanthropic, agricultural, labor, veterans, and fraternal organizations. National and state political committees, as well as voting registration officials, may also be eligible; but usually business leagues, chambers of commerce, social and hobby clubs, and some political organizations are not. The postal service also enforces rules concerning the type of mail that can be sent at nonprofit rates. For instance, insurance and travel promotions are restricted, and credit card ads are prohibited.

To apply for nonprofit rates, you must fill out Form 3624, *Application to Mail at Nonprofit Standard Mail Rates.* You will also have to submit supporting documentation, such as your articles of incorporation and an IRS letter of exemption from payment of federal income tax. Additional documentation may be required as well. There is no fee to apply for nonprofit rates, although you do have to pay annual mailing and permit fees.

After submitting your application, you must pay regular Standard Mail rates while waiting for approval. Once approved, however, you can request a refund of the difference between the regular and nonprofit rates that were incurred during the waiting period.

For more information on qualifying for nonprofit rates, request the US Postal Service's Quick Service Guide 703, *Standard Mail—Nonprofit Eligibility,* or Publication 417, *Nonprofit Standard Mail Eligibility.*

Resources for Getting Help with Your Mailing

Take advantage of the postal service's many useful publications, online courses, and on-site design analysts to help with all of your mailing needs. These free offerings cover topics from designing mailpieces and preparing them for mailing to obtaining necessary permits and applying barcodes.

If you don't have the time or ability to meet all the requirements for discounted postage yourself, you can still save money by using a mail house. Mail houses, also known as *letter shops*, have machines and software for everything from printing barcodes and verifying ZIP codes to stuffing envelopes. They are well versed in US Postal Service regulations and can give you advice on how to reduce your mailing costs. While they do charge fees for their work, it is often less than the amount you will save on postage by using them.

The post office offers a wealth of free information for those getting started with business and nonprofit-organization mailings. Start by taking its short online course called Business Mail 101, available by visiting *www.usps.gov*. This course includes user-friendly explanations of bulk and other classes of mail, a decision tree to help you determine if bulk rates will work for you, checklists for mailers, and more.

Next, take a look at some of the postal service's publications. You can obtain them from the following online site: *pe.usps.gov*, or by contacting your local post office. You'll find the following most useful:

■ *Ratefold* (Notice 123) presents charts summarizing rates for all types of mail.

■ *Getting Started with Standard Mail* (Publication 49) explains everything about Standard Mail, from how to create mailpieces to how to obtain mailing permits.

■ *Designing Letter Mail* (Publication 25) presents the guidelines for designing letter-sized mailpieces, addressing them, and applying barcodes.

■ *Ancillary Service Endorsements* (Quick Service Guide 507d) provides an overview of additional services offered by the post office, including options for handling undeliverable mail.

Finally, make use of the postal service's MERLIN program, which is designed to help improve the quality of your mailpiece. Through it, you can get in touch with a mailpiece design analyst (MDA), who will work with you, free of charge, to help design your piece and verify that it qualifies for a discount mailing rate. An MDA can also arrange for a small sample test run of your mailpiece to see if it has any quality problems before completing a full print run. Providing help with barcoding and other technical matters is another service offered by MDAs. To locate an analyst near you, check with your local post office, or visit the MERLIN website at *www.usps.gov/merlin*. Click on the "Get Help with MERLIN" link, and then click on "Find a Mailpiece Design Analyst."

CONCLUSION

If you are a savvy editor, you will place your own name on the mailing list to get a copy of the newsletter along with your readers. This is a way to verify that the newsletter really did get mailed, to find out how long it takes to arrive, and to get an idea of how it holds up physically in the mail. Some editors are reluctant to read their newsletters at that point, sure that they will find one final typo. But I say, take the leap, look it over, and take pride in the results of all your hard work. If you do find that typo, take it in stride, and think about how to prevent it from happening next time.

If you plan to distribute a web, e-mail, or PDF version of your newsletter in addition to print, it's time to turn to the applicable chapter (or chapters) in Part Four.

PART FOUR

LAUNCHING IT ONLINE
PRODUCING YOUR ELECTRONIC NEWSLETTER

So you're fed up with the high prices and long delays that go with printing and mailing your newsletter. You've sworn never to produce a hard copy of your publication again. Instead, you are going to publish an online version. Or maybe you still need to publish in print, but you want to add a web, e-mail, or PDF version as well.

If you are not sure which online format to use—website, e-mail, or PDF—the chapters in Part Four are ready to help. They present overviews as well as detailed information on writing, editing, designing, and laying out each of these online options. Each chapter covers testing and distribution methods, and offers helpful advice on the software you will need to get the job done. Once you have familiarized yourself with the various online formats, it will be easy to make an informed choice.

If, however, you already know which format (or formats) you want to use for your publication, you can focus on only the chapter (or chapters) that specifically applies. Whichever type of newsletter you choose, the information in Part Four is designed to carefully guide you in successfully launching your online publication.

CHAPTER 10

PRODUCING WEBSITE NEWSLETTERS

If your organization has a website up and running, the easiest way to convert your print newsletter to an online version may be to simply add it to the site. You can add a link from the site's home page to the main page of your newsletter. From there, readers can choose to read the current issue or one of your back issues. When choosing an issue, they can see its "front page" as well as links to other articles.

If your organization doesn't have a website, you'll have to find an Internet service provider (ISP) to host the site. This could be the same ISP you are using for e-mail and online surfing—most offer some free storage space to their customers. But, unless you want to make your readers remember a lengthy and confusing website address for your newsletter (such as *www.provider.com/users/wildlifewatch*), you'll also want to register your own domain name (*www.wildlifewatch.com*).

Web newsletters have several advantages. Distribution is faster and cheaper than print versions. You can lay them out more quickly than print or PDF newsletters. You can format them attractively, and even add color without added cost. They also increase traffic to other parts of your website.

In this chapter, you will learn how to adapt your writing and editing processes to a website newsletter. You will also discover how to design and lay out web pages, how to test and proofread them, and what to look for when selecting web-development software.

WRITING AND EDITING WEB NEWSLETTERS

Jakob Nielsen, who is an expert on making the Internet easy to use, has researched how people read web pages. Many of his findings are found on

Because reading from a computer screen is not as comfortable as reading from a printed page, online newsletters should contain short articles with many subheads. To help readers navigate through the material easily, they should also have hyperlinks (links), which allow readers to jump from one area of the paper to another with a simple click of the mouse.

his web page, "The Alertbox: Current Issues in Web Usability" (*www.useit.com/alertbox*). Nielsen found that people take 25 percent longer to read online articles than print versions. He also noted that readers are uncomfortable reading from a screen. Why? When people read from a computer screen, their eyes are usually angled straight ahead or upward; with print material, they angle down. Also, a person's eyes are usually further from the screen than from printed material.

Nielsen's findings indicate that you have to put forth special effort when writing a web newsletter, so that it's easy for your audience to read. Fortunately, Nielsen also came up with the following guidelines for doing so:

- Write less.

- Use headlines and subheads.

- Use hypertext to your advantage.

- Follow the inverted pyramid style.

Most of these suggestions echo the newsletter writing style you learned about in Chapter 6. So adapting newsletter writing from print to the web is easier than adapting other types of writing to online uses. The following section discusses Nielsen's suggestions further, and offers some special considerations for editing web newsletters.

Writing Less

Nielsen and many other web designers suggest writing only half as much text for a web article as you would for a print version. Short articles mean there will be less scrolling and less eyestrain. You will want to make reading your newsletter as comfortable as possible, especially if your audience is not particularly motivated—for example, they are people you are soliciting for donations who have not shown strong interest in your cause.

But even though "write less" has become a mantra for web writing, there are times when you will want to make exceptions. If your audience is highly motivated to read your newsletter, it will appreciate in-depth articles. For example, an audience of nurses would appreciate complete advice and cautions on operating a new medical device. Patent lawyers, paying hundreds of dollars a year to subscribe to a bar association newsletter, would find value in extensive coverage of a major Supreme

Court decision on intellectual property rights. However, you can provide that in-depth information without straining your readers by using the web's hypertext structure (linking ability) to your advantage. More about this later.

Using Headlines and Subheads

Web surfers, even more so than print readers, like to skim and scan, picking and choosing what to read more closely. They appreciate *meaningful,* not clever, headlines—headlines that allow them to make informed decisions on whether or not to read the articles. As Nielsen notes, web headlines are often displayed outside their original context. This means that the headline of your article may appear on a list of web pages found by a search engine. Or it can be displayed in a reader's "favorites" list (bookmarks) in his or her web browser. In such contexts, the headline won't be surrounded by the photos, graphics, and blurbs that give it context and additional meaning, as it does when appearing on your web page. For example, a clever-sounding headline like "We're in the Money" listed on a search engine doesn't tell the reader who has money, where they got it, and how much of it there is. But a meaningful headline like "Wildlife Society Donations Rise 40 Percent in First Quarter" answers those questions and is far more useful to the reader.

When it comes to article headlines, always choose "meaningful" over "clever." When scanning the pages of a newsletter, readers appreciate headlines that clearly indicate the information they will find in the articles.

Because of the tendency of web surfers to skim and scan, use skimming aids like subheads, decks, pull quotes, and captions in web newsletters even more than you do in print versions. Check back to Chapter 6 for advice on how to write them. Later in this chapter, you'll learn how to design display type for skimming aids to make them stand out on a page.

Using Hypertext to Your Advantage

The Internet is composed of *hypertext*—a collection of documents (web pages) containing cross-references (links) to other pages. Knowing how to use this linking ability correctly will make your newsletter easy for readers to navigate and read.

On some sites, you'll find that, rather than adapting their writing for the web, authors simply split long articles into multiple web pages to make them appear shorter. This practice can be annoying to readers for two reasons. First, they have to wait multiple times for pages to download, instead of just once. Second, if they want to print the article, they have to go to multiple pages and print each one separately. As an alternative to splitting articles based on length, Nielsen suggests dividing the article by subject matter, with each page covering a specific topic. This way, readers can visit just the pages that interest them. For example, you can put background or historical information on one page, technical explanations on another page, and the main ideas of the story on yet another page. This approach is similar to using sidebars in print newsletters.

Let's say you're writing an article about amendments to the Endangered Species Act that are being debated in Congress. You're concerned because the text is so long that it requires readers to scroll three times down the screen, so you're tempted to split the material into thirds to create three web pages. Instead, shorten the article by placing background and technical information on separate pages that are referenced with underlined links, as seen in the following example:

Using underlined links (as seen at right) helps keep article length short. It also gives readers the option of linking to a page that contains additional material of interest.

Previous Congressional debate on the Endangered Species Act has always been contentious. Congressional committee staffers crafted the wording of the amendment over a period of two years.

Clicking on the first link would lead to a page containing a summary of earlier House and Senate debate on the act, accommodating readers who need historical information. Clicking on the second link would bring readers to a page containing the exact wording of the current amendment—of interest to some but not most readers.

Don't overuse linking. For instance, if background or technical information is just a sentence or two long, include it in the main article. Readers don't like to download a separate page for such brief material. Also, an excessive number of underlined links becomes distracting for readers, forcing them to make decisions each time they see one and reducing their ability to concentrate on the contents of the current page.

You can also make your links easy to use by making them descriptive. You've probably experienced the frustration of clicking on a link, waiting for a new page to download, and then discovering that it didn't contain the information you expected to find there. Spare your readers the same aggravation by using phrases, rather than single words, to describe your links. In the example above, the first link is assigned to the rather lengthy phrase, "Previous Congressional debate on the Endangered Species Act" because it clearly states the topic of the linked page. If just "Endangered Species Act" were underlined, readers might click on it expecting to find the text of the law itself, instead of information about Congressional debate on it.

In a website newsletter, descriptive links are particularly helpful in your table of contents or front page. Take a look at the headlines in the two center columns on the front page of the *American Bowling Congress* newsletter in Figure 10.1 at right. In addition to being relatively long, each linked headline is followed by a descriptive sentence or two about the story. Readers who follow these links can be fairly confident of the type of material they will find there.

Another way of communicating more information about a link without forcing your reader to go to the linked page is to have a short message display when the reader moves the cursor over the linked text. For example, if you display the sentence "Next year's conference, featuring keynote speaker Jane Blikowicz, will be held at the Essex Hotel," when a reader moves the mouse over "Jane Blikowicz" a small message can pop up saying "Biography of Jane Blikowicz" or "List of Jane Blikowicz's publications," depending on where the link leads.

In your newsletter, you'll also want to include links to other websites that readers can visit for more information. You don't, however, want to lose your readers to another website while they're in the middle of reading your article, so it is best to place such external links at the end of an article. And word these links in a way that lets readers know that clicking on them will cause them to leave your site. For example, it's better to label a link "The US Department of the Interior's list of endangered species" than "list of endangered species," which the reader might think will take them to another page on your site.

Another way you can use hypertext to your advantage is by including forms in your newsletter. This gives readers an easy way to respond to your articles, to request print information about your products, or to ask for a call from a sales representative. You can even create an e-commerce page that lets them buy a subscription or another product you sell.

Finally, whenever you mention an e-mail address on a web page,

Figure 10.1
Each of the linked headlines on the front page of the *American Bowling Congress* newsletter includes an introductory sentence or two.

This image courtesy of *www.bowl.com* and the American Bowling Congress.

make it a link, so readers can click on it to send the person a message. "Contact Alicia Fried" is a useful link because it does two things. One, it tells readers the name of the person associated with the e-mail address, so they can start the message with "Dear Alicia." Two, it provides a "mailto" link that they can click on to create a message with Alicia's e-mail address automatically entered in the To field. Many newsletter publishers shy away from displaying actual e-mail addresses on their web pages for fear that search software used by spammers will find them and add them to their mailing lists.

Following Inverted Pyramid Style

Using the inverted pyramid style for online articles is recommended because it places the most important information at the beginning. This means readers do not have to scroll down the screen to find it.

In web newsletters as in print versions, writing news stories in inverted pyramid style is essential to getting your point across quickly. This style works well for two reasons: it puts the main ideas of the story near the top of the screen, so readers don't have to scroll to find them. It also enables you to write short articles while still communicating your main idea. Start with a one- or two-sentence lead paragraph that explains the "who, what, when, where, why, and how" of the story. Follow with details and less-crucial points. For more information on the inverted pyramid writing style, see the "News Stories" section in Chapter 6.

Editing Web Newsletters

It's easy to fix an error in a web newsletter, isn't it? If you misspell a word or give the wrong date for a meeting, you can just edit the file and the mistake will be gone, right? You might think errors in web newsletters are not as big a problem as errors in a print newsletter. Unfortunately, it's not that simple.

Yes, you can correct the file. But, as you will see later in this chapter, when your newsletter is ready for viewing, you will be sending an announcement to subscribers. Most subscribers will view or print the newsletter as soon as they receive the announcement. They won't refer back to it a week later, after you've made the correction. They might write the wrong date for the monthly meeting on their calendars and never return to the website to notice the change. This means you have to be just as conscientious in editing your web newsletter *before publication* as you are for a print version.

Once you have written all your copy, check that the writing is clear, organized, and accurate. Use the "Checklist for Content Editing" on page

154 in Chapter 6 to make sure you have covered all the bases. Also check that the writing meets your organization's usage style, based on your style manual. But wait until *after* you have laid out your web pages to proofread your newsletter.

DESIGNING WEB NEWSLETTERS

In the "Principles of Newsletter Design" section of Chapter 8, you learned the five goals for a print newsletter's design. The design should:

1. Be attractive and easy to read.

2. Draw attention to important information.

3. Provide information through skimming aids.

4. Communicate your chosen tone.

5. Demonstrate editorial stability.

These principles apply equally to a web newsletter's design. However, keep in mind that the best way to implement these principles in a print version may not necessarily be the best way to implement them on the web. In this section, I'll point out some of the similarities and differences between print and web design; show you how to design web pages and type that are readable, attractive, and convey your chosen tone; and discuss how to use headlines, subheads, and decks to draw attention to important information and facilitate skimming.

Because many people are suspicious of the credibility of information they find online, it's especially important to use your design to demonstrate editorial stability. Consistent design across the pages of your newsletter (as well as between issues) goes a long way toward conveying this stability, as do professional photos and graphics, and an easy-to-find masthead.

When you produce a print newsletter, you know exactly what your readers see on the page. With web pages, you don't have as much control—readers may see slightly different formatting, depending on which browser (such as Internet Explorer, Netscape, or Mozilla Firefox) they use. This means, for example, you can specify typefaces for your web newsletter, but readers who don't have those typefaces on their computers will see different ones. Also, readers can set their browsers to override the size you specify for the text of your newsletter. They can suppress the display of your graphics, or change the formatting of text

Conveying your newsletter's stability is especially important for online versions because people tend to question the credibility of the information they find online. Professional graphics and photos, an easy-to-spot masthead, and a consistent design across the pages of your newsletter are a few ways to convey this stability.

When hiring someone to help design your website newsletter, be sure the person has both the technical skills to implement the features you need and the graphic expertise to create attractive pages that are user friendly.

links from the typical blue underline to any color that catches their fancy. They can also decide how large to make their browser windows, which means they may not see your entire screen at one time. So you can create a pleasing design, but keep in mind that some people may see it differently.

Is there anywhere you can turn for help in designing your web newsletter? There are many options. If you have a healthy newsletter budget, you might choose to hire a professional web designer. Remember, however, that there is a difference between a web designer and a web developer. Be sure the person you choose has both the technical skills to develop web pages with the features you need, and the graphic design skills to make it attractive and user friendly. (This might eliminate your boss's teenage son from the list of candidates for the position.) To save some money after the initial design has been developed, have the designer train you to create the pages yourself.

If you use page templates, it is not necessary to hire a professional to create a good-looking web page. Web-development software often has these templates bundled with the program. A number of companies that offer website hosting services provide templates as well. Templates include a suggested page design with graphical navigation buttons for links, as well as complementary typefaces, color schemes, and background graphics.

Don't be shy about surfing other online newsletters for design ideas. While you can't copy their designs outright, you may find a typeface, a table of contents design, or a color scheme that you like. Visit the sites of large companies, universities, or nonprofit organizations. Look for links to their newsletters on their home pages, or enter "newsletter" into the site's search engine. If you are affiliated with a chapter of a larger organization, look at the newsletter sites of other chapters for ideas. And don't forget to talk to your own webmaster before developing your newsletter design. It may be possible to fit your newsletter into the page template of your site's current design and avoid reinventing the wheel.

Finally, you can consult websites, books, newsletters, and magazines for advice on creating attractive, easy-to-use web pages. Check the Resources, beginning on page 323, for suggestions.

Page Design

The best way to approach designing your newsletter's web pages is from the top down. In other words, you want to start by coming up with a consistent system of placing recurring elements on each page. Your recurring elements will be, at the very least, your nameplate and the table of contents. Most web newsletters have the nameplate at the top and the table of contents either below it or in a column on the left. For example, in Figure 10.2 below, the nameplate (International Programs Newsletter) is at the top of the page; the table of contents (Inside This Issue) is below the photo. The entire newsletter is embedded in the March of Dimes website, which is why you see additional links at the very top and left side of the page. Other items to include on each page are a copyright notice, a link to your home page, and a link to your contact information.

Figure 10.2

A typical web newsletter design includes a nameplate across the top, a table of contents (located beneath the photo in this example), and a single, narrow column of text.

Placement of the navigation buttons in a column on the left side of the page, as in Figure 10.2, is common in web newsletters. You can also place them horizontally across the top of the page, or vertically on the right side. But if you place them on the right side, readers may have to scroll over to find them. What's most important is to place these buttons in the same location on each page.

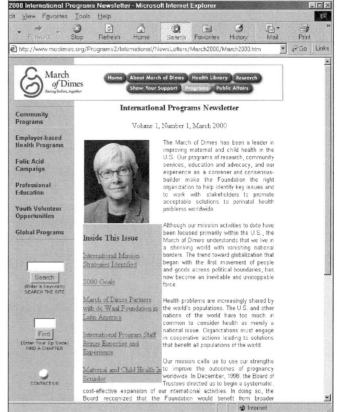

The underlying page grid of this figure is also a typical one. The width of the text is approximately sixty-five characters, which, as you learned earlier, is the maximum number most readers can process without having to shift their eyes from left to right. It is best to limit the width of text columns to 350 to 500 pixels, which roughly translates to forty to sixty-five characters.

Web newsletters usually have just one column for text. Don't try to recreate a typical print-newsletter layout on the screen by running text in three columns. Readers will object because they will have to scroll down to finish reading a column, and then scroll up to the top to continue with the story.

If you accept advertisements in your newsletter, you can place them vertically in a left- or right-hand column, or horizontally at the top or bottom of the page. Don't place ads in the column you use for text; they will interrupt the flow of the article and confuse readers. Also, remember that readers won't always see banner or pop-up ads: some people have installed software to block pop-ups; others might scroll down the page before a banner ad has been downloaded and displayed.

Another task in designing your web newsletter pages is choosing colors. Since newsletters require extended reading, legibility should be your first concern. Always stick with dark text on light backgrounds, which is much easier to read than light on dark. Avoid using patterned or textured backgrounds, which are distracting for the reader. And limit the number of colors you use for text and background, to give your pages a unified look.

There are several ways to further improve a reader's experience with your web newsletter. First, make your pages quick and easy to download. Learn how to reduce the size of graphics files, and avoid using music, sounds, animations, or movies that subject your readers to long waits while they download. Not only can these "added attractions" prove to be annoying, sounds and music can be disruptive or embarrassing for those who read your newsletter at work.

Another favor you can do for your readers is to provide a link to a separate web page that contains the entire text of your newsletter, formatted with a column width of about sixty-five characters. You can call this your "printer-friendly version." When readers go to this page, they can print the entire newsletter with one click of the print button, rather than having to go to each story and print it individually.

Type Design

When you design type for your website newsletter, always keep in mind the five goals of newsletter design, discussed earlier in this chapter. Your type design should contribute to all of these goals. As mentioned previously, you don't have quite as much control over the appearance of your type on a web page as you do on paper. For example, if your readers don't have the typeface you specify in your HTML, or Hypertext Markup Language (the computer language used to define the structure, formatting, and layout of most web pages and some e-mail messages), they will see a different one. But you *can* maintain some control over the appearance of the typeface they see in this situation, by specifying in your HTML code not only a suggested typeface name (Arial, Verdana, Georgia, and so forth) but also whether it should have serifs. (Serifs, as discussed in Chapter 8, are small lines that appear at the edges of letters

Many of the guidelines for designing body text and display type for print newsletters (detailed in Chapter 8) also apply to web versions.

like "l," "p," and "r." The body text in this book is set in a serif typeface. Typefaces without serifs, such as those used in the headings of this book, are called sans serif.) If you specify "Verdana" *and* "sans serif," for instance, and the reader doesn't have Verdana, the browser will display another sans serif font.

Although you can also specify a point size for the type on a web page, you might want to avoid doing so. Web browsers allow readers to change the text size, using designations like largest, larger, medium, smaller, and smallest. Many readers like being able to increase the size of type if they have trouble seeing it; others appreciate the option of fitting more text in a window by reducing the type size. What you *should* specify is the relative size of type, making subheads larger than body text and headings larger than subheads.

serifs r

Serif Typeface
The edges of letters have small lines.

r

Sans Serif Typeface
The edges of letters have no lines.

Body Text

You'll want your body text—the main portion of your articles—to be the most readable of all the text on your pages. Although serif text is suggested for the body text of print newsletters, most experts suggest using sans serif typefaces for body text on a computer screen. Their argument is that the resolution of type on a screen is much lower than the resolution of type on a printed page, and that the "feet" of serif typefaces interfere with readability. But some research suggests that it is more important to use a familiar font, whether serif or sans serif, and not to switch between them within body text. If you want to use a serif font, try Georgia, which was designed specifically for web pages, or the familiar Times New Roman. Sans serif typefaces commonly used on websites include Verdana, Tahoma, Arial, and Helvetica. Examples of these fonts are on page 260.

Choose black or another dark color for body text. For links within body text, stick with the default formatting: blue and underlined, with the text changing to purple when the link has been visited. If you vary from this standard color format for links, readers may become confused, unable to remember which color means a link has been visited and which means it has not. And do not underline text that is not a link. Use italics or bold type instead.

On a web page, you have minimal control over the formatting of your paragraphs. Lines can end in different spots, depending on how large or small readers choose to display the text, and how large they make the browser window. But you can and should leave a line of white space between paragraphs. And use bulleted or numbered lists for three

(sans serif) **Verdana**	(sans serif) **Tahoma**	(serif) **Georgia**
Lorem ipsum dolor sit amet, consectetuer adipiscing elit. Donec feugiat orci eget velit. In venenatis. Mauris eget lectus. Donec aliquet. Nullam euismod, felis at eleifend lobortis, turpis urna posuere orci, ut sagittis neque dui nec leo.	Lorem ipsum dolor sit amet, consectetuer adipiscing elit. Donec feugiat orci eget velit. In venenatis. Mauris eget lectus. Donec aliquet. Nullam euismod, felis at eleifend lobortis, turpis urna posuere orci, ut sagittis neque dui nec leo.	Lorem ipsum dolor sit amet, consectetuer adipiscing elit. Donec feugiat orci eget velit. In venenatis. Mauris eget lectus. Donec aliquet. Nullam euismod, felis at eleifend lobortis, turpis urna posuere orci, ut sagittis neque dui nec leo.
(sans serif) **Helvetica**	(sans serif) **Arial**	(serif) **Times New Roman**
Lorem ipsum dolor sit amet, consectetuer adipiscing elit. Donec feugiat orci eget velit. In venenatis. Mauris eget lectus. Donec aliquet. Nullam euismod, felis at eleifend lobortis, turpis urna posuere orci, ut sagittis neque dui nec leo.	Lorem ipsum dolor sit amet, consectetuer adipiscing elit. Donec feugiat orci eget velit. In venenatis. Mauris eget lectus. Donec aliquet. Nullam euismod, felis at eleifend lobortis, turpis urna posuere orci, ut sagittis neque dui nec leo.	Lorem ipsum dolor sit amet, consectetuer adipiscing elit. Donec feugiat orci eget velit. In venenatis. Mauris eget lectus. Donec aliquet. Nullam euismod, felis at eleifend lobortis, turpis urna posuere orci, ut sagittis neque dui nec leo.

Online Typeface Choices

On computer screens (unlike print publications), sans serif typefaces like Verdana, Tahoma, Arial, and Helvetica tend to be easier to read than those with serifs. If, however, you prefer a serif font, Georgia (designed specifically for web pages) and Times New Roman are good choices.

or more items. They are easier to scan than dense paragraphs. For added interest and clarity, try setting the bullets themselves in color.

Display Type

Your display type—the type you use for headlines, subheads, decks, and other skimming aids—attracts attention to your newsletter and helps your readers skim through it. Make your display type stand out. It should be larger than body text, bold, and possibly set in a different color. You might want to use a different typeface from your body text as well. Select one that communicates your newsletter's tone—casual or formal, trendy or traditional. To communicate unity and editorial stability, limit the total number of typefaces on a page to two or three.

Use display type frequently. Place a meaningful subhead every three to four paragraphs. Subheads should be closer to the body text following them than to the body text that precedes them. Avoid centering headlines and subheads, and don't set them in all caps. Capitalize them as you would a standard sentence instead.

Masthead Design

As in print newsletters, your masthead should appear in each issue of a web newsletter. You can link it to the table of contents. The items to include in your masthead are usually the same as those for print versions, presented on page 220 in Chapter 8. However, some information—a list of board members, your contact information, or a description of your organization—may already appear elsewhere on your website. If so, you may choose not to include these items in the masthead of your web newsletter.

Since space isn't as limited in web newsletters as it is in print versions, you might consider including brief biographies or even photographs of the people listed in your masthead. You may also want to provide their contact information.

Designing Other Elements

For ideas and recommendations on designing additional newsletter elements, such as photo captions, bylines, photo credit lines, and author bios, take a look at the material on "Designing Newsletter Elements" in Chapter 8. As a general rule, for each of these items you'll want to use type that contrasts slightly with your body text. Most designers achieve this by setting them in bold or italics, or by using different typefaces or colors. Keep the size about the same as that of your body text, with the exception of photo credit lines, which should be set a bit smaller.

LAYING OUT WEB NEWSLETTERS

When you're ready to produce an issue of your web newsletter, gather your material—article text, photos, and other graphics—from your writers, photographers, and artists. Be sure your writers know not to format the text (with typefaces, italics, line spacing, and the like) before sending it to you, since you will end up redoing most of the formatting yourself. Decide which articles are most important and which ones fit into regularly run columns, like the president's message, news briefs, or regional reports. In your table of contents, create a link for each article, always listing the most important articles first and the regular columns and masthead toward the end. Unless you have a cover page for your

Be sure to tell your writers not to spend time and effort formatting the text of their articles with various typefaces, font styles, and line spacing before sending them to you. Once the material is turned in, it will have to be reformatted to conform to the publication's chosen style.

newsletter, make sure that your most important story is the one readers see first when arriving at the site.

Place the articles and graphics into your newsletter's template file, and format them according to your chosen design. Read every word of the text, checking spelling, grammar, punctuation, and capitalization.

While you are in the process of creating your newsletter files, be sure to keep them on the hard drive of your computer, not on your web server. If they are on the server, people may find them through a search engine, which means they can view the files before they have been finalized.

TESTING WEB NEWSLETTERS

File transfer protocol (FTP) is a method of copying files to and from the hard drive of a personal computer to a file server, regardless of the operating systems involved. This method is especially useful for transferring very large files.

When it comes time to do final testing of your newsletter, you'll have to send the HTML files to your web server. To send the files, you might be able to simply e-mail them to your company's webmaster, who can post them. If you don't have a webmaster, you will have to transfer the files to your website in a manner that is similar to the way you transfer other web pages you create. You can use a type of program for uploading files known as FTP (file transfer protocol) software to send the files, or possibly web-development software. Your web-development software may refer to this step as "publishing" the newsletter. The service that hosts your website can give you any specifications you might need for sending the files, such as a user ID, password, and the names of the "host" (computer) and the directory to which you should send the files. It's a simple process once you know the necessary specifications. When your newsletter is up and running on your website, you'll be able to access it from a number of different computers to test it.

You could spend hours or even days trying to get your website newsletter to look right in every conceivable hardware and software combination that your readers might be using. But before you pull an all-nighter doing so, first try to determine which hardware and browsers are most popular with your readers, and then test your newsletter on those. If your readers are average home or office computer users, they probably use Windows and Internet Explorer (either the current or the second most-current version) on PCs. A small percentage may use Macs. But if your readers are hobbyists or technical people, they may run their computers on Linux and use a different browser like Mozilla Firefox. If they are all employees of your company, which provides a specific version of Internet Explorer on PCs using a T-1 line, your job is obvious—simply test your newsletter on that type of system. If you are not sure of the hardware and browsers your readers use, do an online search for current statistics on browser and operating system usage. You'll be able to determine the ones that are most common, and then use that information as a starting point.

Don't forget to test your newsletter on different types of Internet connections. If you have high-speed Internet access, be sure to test your pages on a slower connection to see if download times will be acceptable for those readers who use the slower method.

If you don't have access to a variety of hardware and software in your office or home, try viewing your pages at the public library or on the computer of a relative or friend. You might ask one or two colleagues to take a look at the newsletter and let you know if they find any "bugs" before you go public with it. Once you get a sense of what works on which types of hardware and software, and as long as you don't use any new formatting that you haven't tested on other machines, you may not have to test your newsletter as extensively for every issue.

When editing and testing your website newsletter, you'll find it helpful to refer to the checklist on page 264. You may want to make a separate copy for each browser, operating system, or Internet connection on which you test your newsletter.

Checking Navigation

It is very important to test every link or navigation button found in your newsletter. Be sure that each is labeled correctly and goes to the right page. Do this for both the links that stay within your website and those that link to others. For text links, make sure the color of the link text changes once it has been followed. Also, make sure that whenever you click on an e-mail link, a new, blank e-mail message that is addressed to the appropriate person appears.

Next, check that all of your graphics are displayed properly. If you haven't placed your graphics files in the right folders on your web server, or if you have forgotten to move them to your server, they won't show up. Instead, the browser might display an icon indicating a missing graphic, the name of the graphics file, or some alternate text you may have specified.

If your newsletter includes a response form, fill it out and submit it. You can then check to be sure that the information was captured by your database or sent to the proper e-mail address.

In addition to checking your web newsletter on computers with different hardware and browsers, see how well it downloads using both slow and high-speed Internet connections.

Checklist for Proofreading and Testing Website Newsletters

The following checklist is designed to help you keep track of the various elements found on your web newsletter. During the testing stage, you may want to fill out a separate form for each browser, operating system, or Internet connection you use.

Testing Environment

Browser Tested: _____

Browser Version: _____

Operating System: _____

Hardware: PC _____   Mac _____

Type of Internet Connection: _____

Navigation

Test each of the following items, making sure they produce the expected results. Check that text links change color after you follow them.

☐ Table of contents links

☐ Other links to web pages

☐ E-mail links

☐ Graphics

☐ Response forms

Elements

Be sure the following items appear on the appropriate pages:

☐ Articles

☐ Nameplate

☐ Logo

☐ Masthead

☐ Issue date

☐ Volume and issue numbers

☐ Copyright notice

☐ Links to home page and masthead

Type and Formatting

Check both body and display type for correct:

☐ Typeface

☐ Size

☐ Style

☐ Color

Also check for correct:

☐ Spelling

☐ Capitalization

☐ Punctuation

☐ Special characters

☐ Spacing between paragraphs

Graphics

Check photos, pictures, charts, graphs, tables, boxes, and rules for:

☐ Alignment

☐ Size

☐ Borders

Columns

Check for proper:

☐ Background color

☐ Alignment

☐ Width

☐ Borders

Checking the Elements

Be sure your newsletter includes all of the essential elements. Refer to your article tracking log (see page 82) and verify that all of the material that was scheduled to appear in the issue has been included. Also, check that your nameplate, logo, issue date, and volume and issue numbers appear as specified in your design, preferably on every page. Make sure that every page includes a link to your home page and a copyright notice. Finally, check that you have included a link to your masthead.

Checking Type

Look at the sizes, styles, and colors of your typefaces, as well as the spacing between paragraphs. When checking the typefaces, keep in mind that different browsers and operating systems may display type differently. Realize that discrepancies between what you expect and what you actually see may not be in your power to change. What you *must* be sure of is that all variations are readable.

Also, look closely at punctuation marks and special characters. During the process of converting your text into HTML, they may become garbled. For example, there is an HTML code ( ) that specifies a nonbreaking space. When a browser sees this code, it is supposed to display a space and keep the words before and after the space on the same line. Some browsers display it correctly, but others display the code " " instead of a space. Similar problems can occur with quotation marks, dashes, copyright symbols, ampersands, and the like, so check these types of special characters and punctuation marks carefully.

Checking Graphics

When checking the navigation of your newsletter, you verified that all graphics displayed properly. You must also make sure photos, pictures, charts, graphs, tables, boxes, and rules are formatted correctly. Are they aligned properly (flush left, centered, or flush right)? Is each element appropriately sized? If borders are used, are they the right type?

After verifying that all of your newsletter's graphics—photos, charts, boxes, rules—display properly, make sure they are also formatted correctly.

Checking Columns

Finally, check the columns on each page for proper width and alignment. If there are borders between columns, have they been formatted correctly? Also, check that the columns containing such items as navigation buttons, text, and/or ads have the correct background color.

As with print newsletters, there are many elements in a web newsletter that require your attention during the proofing/testing phase. Following the checklist on page 264 will prevent you from overlooking any of these important items.

SELECTING SOFTWARE

To create your website newsletter you will need web-development software, which is sometimes called a "web-authoring tool," an "HTML editor," a "web-page editor," or a "site builder." This type of software allows you to transform text and graphics into web pages.

The cost of web-development software can run several hundred dollars, but many computers come with one of these programs, such as Microsoft FrontPage. And most Internet service providers, like EarthLink and AOL, allow you to use their web-development software if they host your website. So before investing in a software program, find out what you already own, or visit your Internet service provider's home page to see what it offers.

Before purchasing costly web-development software, check with your Internet service provider. Many ISPs will allow you to use their software if they host your website. Also, be aware that many computers come with these software programs.

If you are completely new to web page creation, I recommend using software that comes with "wizards," which help guide you through the process. Wizards ask you questions about how you want your web pages to look, and then help you create them based upon your answers. Usually wizards let you choose among a number of templates that contain page layouts, navigation buttons, and pre-designed color schemes. Most ISP web-development software comes with wizards and templates, as do many other software packages. Just be sure to verify this before buying.

If you want greater control over the look of your web newsletter—perhaps you are a graphic designer and want creative freedom, or maybe your organization or company wants the newsletter to fit a unique design—you will need a more sophisticated software program, such as Microsoft FrontPage, Macromedia DreamWeaver, or Adobe GoLive. These programs give you control over colors, page layout, fonts, and so forth.

Another way to create web pages is to use software that automatically converts a document designed for print into an HTML file. Microsoft Word and Publisher, as well as Corel WordPerfect, have features that let you *convert* (or *export* or *save as web page*) print documents to HTML with a few clicks of the mouse. But before committing to this method of creating web pages, I suggest that you do some testing. With this method, you don't have as much control over the formatting as you do with web-development software. It can, however, be useful for quick jobs when fancy design is not a priority.

If you are plugging your newsletter into your company's existing website design, talk to the webmaster about how to create pages. The company may have special software that lets you easily enter updates, while maintaining the uniform graphic design of the rest of the site.

When choosing software, don't forget to take into account the time it will take you to learn to use it. Consider using software that resembles other programs you are familiar with. For instance, Microsoft FrontPage is similar to other Microsoft Office products—Word, Excel, PowerPoint—so if you use those programs, you are likely to find FrontPage relatively easy to use. Likewise, if you are accustomed to using Adobe PageMaker or InDesign, you might choose Adobe web-development software to reduce your learning curve.

Finally, when selecting a program, find out if it comes with a manual or online help. If you can't get answers to your questions in the manual, can you go to the bookstore and pick up a book on how to use the software? Can you find other users—colleagues, friends, family, or participants in Internet discussion groups—to help you when you have problems? If you are using software on an ISP's server, find out if online help and twenty-four-hour technical support are available.

For more information on web-development software, check the Resources, beginning on page 323.

DISTRIBUTING WEB NEWSLETTERS

You have tested your web newsletter and are now ready to go public with it. Your next step is to set up a link from your home page to the new issue. If you maintain archives of past issues, it is also time to create a link to the previous issue from your archives page.

If your newsletter is only available through paid subscription, or if you want to restrict access for other reasons, you will want to require the reader to enter a password to view the newsletter. Your webmaster or Internet service provider will show you how to implement password protection for your newsletter.

Since you can't assume your readers will remember to visit your website regularly to read the latest issues of your newsletter, you will have to let them know it's there. The quickest and cheapest way to do

One factor to consider before choosing a web-development program is the amount of time it will take you to learn it. It's best to go with a program that is similar to one you are familiar with. This means, if you are comfortable with Microsoft programs, it's probably a good idea to go with that company's web-page software.

this is to send out an e-mail message announcing it. Include the table of contents, perhaps with a sentence or two summarizing each article.

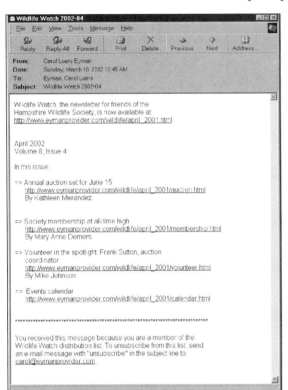

Also provide a link, such as the one shown in Figure 10.3 at left, that will take your readers directly to the main newsletter page. Even better, you can link every item listed in the table of contents to its corresponding article. Simply place the address of each page below the headline in the table of contents.

To send out these announcements, you will need to maintain a list of your subscribers' e-mail addresses. You'll also have to develop a process for adding and deleting subscribers. In Chapter 11, the section on "Distributing E-Mail Newsletters," starting on page 279, explains how to manage e-mail distribution lists.

Figure 10.3

This e-mail announcement of *Wildlife Watch* web newsletter provides a convenient link directly to the publication. It also includes links to each of the items that are listed in the table of contents.

CONCLUSION

Once you have completed your newsletter and have launched it online, take a breather before getting wrapped up in your next issue. Reflect on the publication you have just produced. Did it meet your expectations? Did the publishing process go smoothly, or would you make some adjustments for your next issue? This downtime you have between issues is perfect for a postproduction meeting with your staff (called a *postmortem*). Use this time to iron out any problems with the publication, rather than trying to do so during the middle of the production cycle, when you are pressured by impending deadlines.

If you are interested in publishing an e-mail or PDF newsletter in addition to your web version, the next two chapters will offer you helpful guidance.

CHAPTER 11

PRODUCING E-MAILNEWSLETTERS

Since the mid-1990s, I have found myself getting less and less work done by talking on the telephone or writing letters. It's not that I'm accomplishing less; I'm simply substituting e-mail for phone calls and correspondence. I send e-mail to set up appointments and run committees. I receive e-mail from organizations reminding me about upcoming meetings, from students handing in writing assignments, and from my son asking me to puh-*leeze* bring the homework he forgot to school . . . right away. When I boot up my computer, my e-mail program is always the first one I open, and it remains open until I shut the computer down for the night. As e-mail permeates both my professional and personal lives, receiving newsletters this way makes more and more sense for me. If a newsletter article tells me that I can find further information on a website, or that I can reply to this or that e-mail address, I can get those tasks done more efficiently if I'm already online when I'm reading it.

E-mail newsletters are ideal for news that needs to get out quickly or frequently, like stock numbers, sports scores, or last-minute notices. E-mail newsletters are delivered directly to your readers' electronic inboxes, and readers need minimal computer skill to open them. For most subscribers, accessing one is as simple as clicking the mouse on a new message.

You can create an e-mail newsletter in two formats: text and HTML. A text e-mail newsletter consists of just what its name advertises: plain text. Sometimes, you might hear this called "ASCII text" (pronounced AZ-kee). As seen in Figure 11.1 on page 270, text e-mail newsletters are very basic—they don't contain graphics or even formatting like bold or italics. They can, however, include links to websites or e-mail addresses. They can also contain ads, which must be in straight text format as well, but cannot

269

```
-------------------------------------------------------
                    WILDLIFE WATCH
        News for friends of the Hampshire Wildlife Society
July 2001                              Volume 8, Issue 7
-------------------------------------------------------

You are receiving WILDLIFE WATCH because you requested a
subscription. If you wish to unsubscribe, send a blank
e-mail to wildlife@eymanprovider.com with the word
"unsubscribe" in the subject.

-------------------------------------------------------

IN THIS ISSUE

-------------------------------------------------------

    => Annual auction set for August 15
       By Kathleen Merandez
    => Society membership at all-time high
       By Mary Anne Demers
    => Volunteer in the spotlight: Frank Sutton, auction
       coordinator
       By Mike Johnson
    => Events calendar

-------------------------------------------------------

ANNUAL AUCTION SET FOR AUGUST 15 By Kathleen Merandez

-------------------------------------------------------

The Hampshire Wildlife Society's fundraising auction has
been scheduled for Saturday evening, August 15. At the
annual event, participants bid on products and services
donated by local businesses, with proceeds benefiting the
Society. The auction, which in past years has funded up to
50% of the Society's budget, will be held at the Hampshire
Country Club. Cocktails and viewing will begin at 6 pm,
dinner at 7 pm, with the auction starting at 8 pm. For

-------------------------------------------------------
```

include graphics. You can lay out a text e-mail newsletter quickly with little graphic design skill, and anyone with an e-mail account can open and read them.

HTML e-mail newsletters, on the other hand, can contain graphics, color, and varying typefaces and type styles. In a sense, this type of e-mail newsletter, seen in Figure 11.2 on page 271, is a web page within an e-mail message. HTML e-mail can contain links to websites and e-mail addresses, as well as to locations within the newsletter itself—from a table of contents to an article, for instance. It can also contain response forms, allowing the publisher to obtain reader feedback or even display an online store. HTML e-mail newsletters yield better response rates than text e-mail newsletters. Advertisers like them because they can display graphical banner ads and because the publisher can track how many readers opened the newsletter.

If you are not familiar with e-mail newsletters, go online and subscribe to some. It's easy enough to find free newsletters on just about any topic. Simply go to a search engine or directory like Google or Yahoo! and do a search using the keywords "free newsletter" along with your topic of interest ("woodworking," "lacrosse," or "marketing," for example). When you find a newsletter that interests you, follow the instructions for subscribing. If possible, subscribe to both the text and HTML formats. Receiving, opening, and reading these newsletters will help you understand the experience of your own readers.

You may ask why anyone would produce a straight text e-mail newsletter when they can create a far more attractive one with HTML e-mail. There are several reasons. With text e-mail newsletters, you don't have to worry much about the type of e-mail program or service your reader is using (Outlook, Mozilla Thunderbird, or Yahoo! Mail, for example). A small percentage of your readers may still use text-only e-mail programs that do not correctly display HTML e-mail messages. The formatting for text e-mail is so simple, any e-mail program can read it.

In addition, the type of Internet connection your readers have can affect the ease of receiving HTML e-mail. For example, those with slower dial-up Internet service may resent the fact that your HTML e-mail newsletter is about twice the file size of a text newsletter. Internet users with dial-up connections may try to limit the time they spend online, either to avoid long-distance charges or to free up their telephone lines. If these users go online to download e-mail and then go offline to read it, they won't be able to see any graphics you have linked to your website.

Another reason readers may reject HTML e-mail, either automatical-ly or by manually deleting it, is fear of computer viruses. Because HTML messages often contain graphics, they sometimes appear flagged in a receiver's inbox, indicating they have attachments. And computer users are trained never to open an attachment from someone they don't know and trust—which might be you, especi-ally if you don't publish often and they aren't accustomed to seeing your name in their inboxes. On the positive side, savvy Internet users nowadays use antivirus software, which greatly reduces any risks presented by HTML e-mail.

And finally, personal preferences play a part in the HTML/text e-mail debate. Some people prefer to read their e-mail on a handheld device like a BlackBerry, which may not clearly display HTML messages. Others like to enlarge or reduce the font size in e-mail, which is not always possi-ble with HTML messages.

So which format is best? Often the answer is both. Many e-mail newsletter publishers allow their readers to make the choice. If you use an online distribution service, it can send your newsletter in a format called "multipart MIME," which contains both text and HTML versions, and displays correctly in your reader's chosen format.

But if your goal is to produce your newsletter as quick-ly as possible, publish in text only. Then you won't have to take the time formatting type and graphics, as you would with HTML. On the other hand, if you prefer HTML and want to skip the step of creating a text ver-sion, today you can be confident the vast majority of people can read it.

The next section provides guidelines on writing and editing e-mail newsletters. Later in this chapter, you'll learn how to create, test, and dis-tribute them. If you plan to publish an HTML e-mail version of your newsletter, then in addition to reading this chapter, be sure to read Chap-ter 10, "Producing Website Newsletters." Many of the principles that apply to website newsletters also apply to HTML e-mail versions.

WRITING AND EDITING E-MAIL NEWSLETTERS

Many subscribers will read your e-mail newsletter right on the comput-er screen instead of printing it out. Since it is more difficult to read text

Figure 11.2
An HTML e-mail newsletter can contain graphics, color, and a variety of typefaces and type styles.

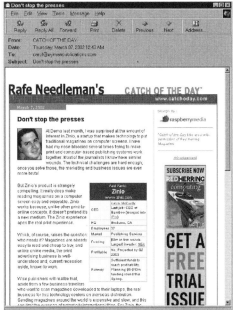

on a screen than on paper, you will want to keep your newsletter writing brief and concise. Use short sentences, paragraphs, and articles. Limit the length of the entire newsletter to 1,000 to 1,500 words—three or four articles—an amount that people can read in just a few scrolls down the screen. For a daily newsletter, write even less. Make your headlines clearly descriptive of the content of the articles, and use lots of skimming aids.

Run your most interesting article at the top of the newsletter to catch your reader's attention right away. Remember that your newsletter may be competing with dozens of other messages in readers' inboxes that morning. Make your lead story demonstrate right away why they shouldn't delete this one. To get them to read the rest of the newsletter, place a popular recurring column or department at the end of each issue. As readers get used to its being there, they'll make a point of scrolling down to it, giving them at least a glance at all your content.

Once you have written all the copy for your e-mail newsletter, check that the writing is clear, organized, and accurate, and that it meets your organization's usage style. In other words, perform content editing and copyediting as described in Chapter 6. Use the checklist on page 154 as a guide. Do not proofread the material until you have created the e-mail message—a step that is explained in the following section.

CREATING E-MAIL MESSAGES

Once you have written the text for your newsletter, you can place it into an e-mail message to send to your readers. But the method of doing so depends on whether your newsletter is in text or HTML format.

Creating Text E-Mail Messages

As I described earlier, text e-mail messages contain plain text without any formatting. You can create such messages using a word-processing program or a *text editor*. Notepad, which comes with Windows, is an example of a basic text editor. But you will probably find it easier to use a slightly more sophisticated program like TextPad, which offers useful features like spell check, word count, and find-and-replace. You can also use WordPad, which comes with Windows, and TextEdit, which comes with Macintosh operating systems.

If you use a word processor like Microsoft Word, you'll have to change some of its settings so that it doesn't convert characters like the inch symbol (") to a typographer's quotation mark (" or "), ordinals (2nd) to superscript (2nd), fractions (1/2) to fraction characters ($\frac{1}{2}$), and the like. Such special characters will appear as gibberish to some of your readers. You'll also need to save the document as "text only" and check it carefully for special characters.

Creating your newsletter will be easier if you set up a template. The template can be a text file that includes items that belong in every issue, like your nameplate and masthead. When composing each new issue, open the template in your text editor, save it as a new file (to leave the template intact), and type the articles into the appropriate spots. Then copy the entire text of the newsletter, and paste it into a new e-mail message. In your e-mail software, make sure that the default method for "creating mail" and for "sending mail" is set to plain text and not HTML.

Formatting

One way you can make your text e-mail newsletter easier to read is by limiting the length of each line of text to a maximum of sixty-five characters. As with print newsletters, this is the maximum line width that most people can read without shifting their eyes from left to right. Simply setting the word wrap at sixty-five characters as you type won't necessarily make your lines end at this number of characters for all readers. So you will have to press the Enter key (to force a "return" and begin a new line) when you reach the sixty-five character point in each line. To be able to see where sixty-five characters end, place a temporary horizontal line at the top of your newsletter template like this one:

Using a Horizontal Guideline

While typing out your newsletter, using a horizontal guideline that is sixty-five characters long will help you keep the line lengths uniform in appearance.

```
1 2 3 4 5 6 7 8 9 0 1 2 3 4 5 6 7 8 9 0 1 2 3 4 5 6 7 8 9 0 1 2 3 4 5 6 7 8 9 0 1 2 3 4 5 6 7 8 9 0 1 2 3 4 5 6 7 8 9 0 1 2 3 4 5
            10                  20                  30                  40                  50                  60
```

Using this line as a guide while typing out your newsletter will assure that your readers see sixty-five-character lines of reasonably uniform length. (Be sure to delete the line from your final copy.) There is, however, one provision—the guideline must be displayed in a *monospace* typeface. This kind of typeface has an equal amount of horizontal space for every character, whether it's a wide one, like the letter "m," or a narrow one, like the letter "l." The most commonly used monospace font is Courier. The opposite of a monospace typeface is a *proportional* typeface, which allots a different amount of space for each character, depending on its width. Times Roman, Helvetica, and Arial are examples of proportional typefaces.

To emphasize a word or phrase in a text e-mail newsletter, enclose it in asterisks, ***like this***. Don't use bold or italics. If you do, your newsletter may turn into an HTML format.

In a text e-mail newsletter, type spaces at the beginning of a line to indent it. Do not use the tab key. For some readers, the tab may be set at five spaces, for others, it may be set at twenty-five spaces. This means you cannot predict how much your tabbed text will be indented, so you must type the spaces instead.

Making headlines stand out in text e-mail newsletters presents a challenge, because you can't specify typefaces and type sizes. But you can create contrast in other ways. You can type your headlines in all caps, leaving blank lines above and below them. You can also type lines of separating characters above and below the headline, like this:

Headline Formatting

Typing out a text e-mail headline in all caps, and then placing it between lines of special characters (dashes in this example) will help set it apart from other copy on the page.

```
─ ─ ─ ─ ─ ─ ─ ─ ─ ─ ─ ─ ─ ─ ─ ─

ANNUAL AUCTION SET FOR AUGUST 15
        By Kathleen Merandez
─ ─ ─ ─ ─ ─ ─ ─ ─ ─ ─ ─ ─ ─ ─ ─
```

You can even exercise a bit of creativity by choosing and combining separating characters like addition signs, asterisks, hyphens, or equal signs. Any character you see on your keyboard will work.

Whenever you point readers to a website, be sure to include the URL (address) so your reader will see a clickable link. For example, you might say "Visit the Writers' Roundup website at www.writersroundup.com" And don't put any punctuation around the URL, such as a period at the end or brackets before or after it. These marks sometimes break the link.

Standing Elements

Because many readers are suspicious of the source of e-mail messages, you'll want to establish your credibility by including information in your newsletter that clearly identifies it. Standing elements like a nameplate, table of contents, and masthead will take care of this.

Your nameplate belongs at the top of the e-mail message, as seen in Figure 11.3 on page 275. As discussed in Chapter 2, a nameplate should include the newsletter's name, tagline, and issue date. Also include the volume and issue numbers.

The second standing element you'll need is a table of contents that lists all articles in the order in which they appear in the newsletter. Make each headline descriptive so the reader knows what's coming. You might want to include the byline for each article in the table of contents, too.

A third standing element is the masthead, which provides additional information for identifying your publication. As in print newsletters, your masthead should appear in each issue of an e-mail newsletter. The items it should include are generally the same as those for print versions, presented on page 220 in Chapter 8. (Note that the masthead of a commercial e-mail newsletter is required by law to include the sender's physical postal address, as well as an indication that the e-mail is an advertisement. More information on this law is included in the "Avoiding the 'Spammer' Label" section of this chapter.) As long as you identify yourself with a nameplate at the top of your newsletter, you can place your masthead at the bottom. Readers who need the information will know enough to scroll down and find it.

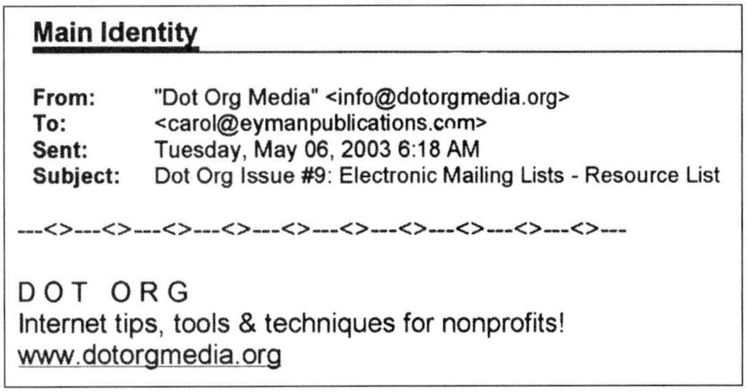

> **Main Identity**
>
> From: "Dot Org Media" <info@dotorgmedia.org>
> To: <carol@eymanpublications.com>
> Sent: Tuesday, May 06, 2003 6:18 AM
> Subject: Dot Org Issue #9: Electronic Mailing Lists - Resource List
>
> ---<>---<>---<>---<>---<>---<>---<>---<>---<>---<>---
>
> D O T   O R G
> Internet tips, tools & techniques for nonprofits!
> www.dotorgmedia.org

Figure 11.3

Place your nameplate at the top of a text e-mail newsletter, as shown in this example from Dot Org Media.

Dot Org Media is a content publishing and syndication service that offers a free e-mail newsletter, Web content, and special reports on selected topics such as ASPs, online advocacy, fundraising, and Internet strategy. We present case studies, effective practices, techniques and tools to help nonprofits maximize their Internet presence. Dot Org Media is a coproduction of Marc Osten at Summit Collaborative and Michael Stein. Back issues and more information: www.dotorgmedia.org.

Creating HTML E-Mail Messages

If you have chosen to produce an HTML e-mail newsletter, you can create the material in a web-page development program, and then copy and paste it in an e-mail message. You can also create your newsletter directly in your e-mail program. As another option, you can use an e-mail list-hosting service and create your newsletter in one of the online templates that many of them provide. (You'll find more information about using list-hosting services in the "Distributing E-Mail Newsletters" section of this chapter.) These templates are often accompanied by "wizards," making them quite easy to use. However, if you use this option, you will sacrifice some control over your formatting.

Because HTML e-mail newsletters are so similar to web newsletters, the information in Chapter 10, "Producing Website Newsletters," is important, especially if you do not use a list-hosting service's template. The chapter explains how to write, design, lay out, and test a web newsletter. It also offers advice on choosing web-page development software.

A number of basic guidelines are specific to HTML newsletters (as opposed to web pages). For starters, you will please your readers by keeping the size of your HTML file small—less than 40 KBs (kilobytes).

Why? The file will download and open quickly, and take up a small amount of storage space in their inboxes. If your newsletter's content is too large to fit into a file of this size, try running only summaries of the articles in the e-mail message, with links to the full text on your website.

When creating the e-mail message for your newsletter, it is important to make sure your e-mail program is set up to send messages in HTML format. Check your program's online help or instruction manual to learn exactly how to do so.

Finally, avoid creating confusion on the part of readers who may subscribe to your newsletter in HTML format without realizing that their e-mail programs are not set up to read it. For them, your message will appear as plain text interspersed with lots of confusing HTML codes. To help these readers out, you can place a comment line at the beginning of your HTML code directing them to your website, where they can view the newsletter or change their subscriptions to text format. For example, this comment line might appear as the following:

For the sake of readers who have incorrectly subscribed to an HTML version of your e-mail newsletter, place a message such as the one at right in every issue. It will enable the readers to switch their subscriptions to a text format.

```
<!— If this e-mail message has formatting errors,
please go to www.eymanprovider.com/wildlife to view
the newsletter on our website. While you are there,
please change your preferred subscription format
to text.—>
```

Readers whose e-mail programs cannot read HTML will be able to read this message and follow its instructions. In e-mail programs that *can* display HTML correctly, the characters (<!— and —>) that appear before and after the text of this comment will make the comment invisible. This is just what you want, since those readers who *can* see the HTML version do not need to see this message.

TESTING E-MAIL NEWSLETTERS

Once you have written your articles, edited them for content, copyedited them, and placed them in an e-mail message, it is time to test and proof-read your newsletter.

For Text E-Mail

Before distributing your text e-mail newsletter, you must proofread the final copy. You will also need to test it, to make sure your readers won't

Checklist for Text E-Mail Newsletter Proofreading and Testing

Use this checklist for proofreading and testing text e-mail newsletters.

Navigation

Test each of the following types of links, making sure they produce the expected results. Check that they change color after you follow them.

☐ Web page links

☐ E-mail links

Standing Elements

Be sure you have included the following items:

☐ Nameplate

☐ Table of contents

☐ Masthead

☐ Articles

Type and Formatting

Check text for correct:

☐ Line length

☐ Spacing between paragraphs

Be sure text *does not* contain:

☐ Special characters

☐ Bold or italics

Proofreading

Check for correct:

☐ Spelling

☐ Capitalization

☐ Punctuation

have any problems displaying, reading, or using it. Use the checklist above to guide you through this proofreading and testing stage.

The first step when testing your newsletter is to send the message to yourself. This way, you can verify that it has been sent properly, and you can also see how the page looks. Also, especially when you are testing your first issue, send the message to a few other people—preferably those who use different e-mail software from yours. For example, if you use Microsoft Outlook, try sending the message to someone who uses Mozilla Thunderbird. You can also set up a free e-mail account at a site like *www.yahoo.com* or *www.juno.com* and then send the newsletter to yourself there, as well. This will give you an idea of how your newsletter looks in even more e-mail programs. Sending out these first "tests" will help you identify any problems that may occur with special characters, formatting, and/or line lengths.

Next, test every link in your newsletter—for both web pages and e-mail addresses. Click on each web link to verify that it takes you to the right page. When you click on an e-mail link, be sure it displays a blank e-mail message screen that is addressed to the appropriate person.

Make sure you have included your newsletter's standing elements—nameplate, table of contents, masthead, and articles—and that they contain all of the necessary information. Go through your article tracking log to verify that all of the articles you intended to publish have, in fact, been included in the newsletter.

Next, check the type for proper formatting. Verify that the line length is sixty-five characters or less, and that there is adequate spacing between paragraphs, as well as between headlines and articles. Take a look at the typeface to verify that you have used the right one. There should not be any special characters, nor any bold or italicized text. Proofread carefully for spelling and capitalization. Also look closely at punctuation, like quotation marks and dashes, to confirm that they display properly.

Once you are confident that you have corrected all of the errors in your newsletter, you can jump ahead to the section on "Distributing E-Mail Newsletters," beginning on page 279. If you are also sending an HTML version, the following section contains important information you will need.

For HTML E-Mail

Before you can distribute your HTML e-mail newsletter, you will need to proofread the final layout closely. You must also try to discover if your readers will have any problems displaying, reading, or using it. This process of testing an HTML e-mail newsletter is very similar to that of testing a web newsletter. In Chapter 10, the section "Testing Web Newsletters," beginning on page 262, has guidelines and a checklist that you can use to test your HTML e-mail newsletter. The only difference is that instead of testing your newsletter in several different browsers (as recommended with web newsletters), you will want to test it in several different e-mail programs.

Just as you would when testing a text e-mail newsletter, send the HTML message to your own e-mail address, as well as to a few others who (preferably) use different e-mail software than yours. If, for instance, you use Microsoft Outlook, try sending the message to someone who uses Mozilla Thunderbird. Set up free e-mail accounts for yourself at a site like *www.yahoo.com* or *www.juno.com* and send your newsletter to yourself there, too. This will give you an idea of how your newsletter looks in additional e-mail programs. Ideally, to further test your newsletter, try downloading it on both Windows and Macintosh computers, using both fast and slow Internet connections. Once you have completed this testing stage, continue to follow the guidelines in Chapter 10 to verify that the links work properly and the formatting is correct.

DISTRIBUTING E-MAIL NEWSLETTERS

No matter which type of electronic newsletter you publish—web newsletter, text or HTML e-mail, or PDF—you will find this section useful. E-mail newsletter publishers will find the information helpful for distributing the newsletter itself, while PDF and web publishers will find it helpful for distributing e-mail announcements of their issues.

Most of the work required for distributing electronic newsletters involves managing subscriptions—processing new requests, renewals, and cancellations. If you charge for subscriptions, you will also have to create a system for maintaining account information.

First, you will have to decide whether you are going to distribute the newsletter and manage subscriptions yourself (with or without distribution software), or have a list-hosting service do it for you. To help you decide, let's take a look at the work involved in regularly distributing a newsletter (or an announcement of one) to a large group of subscribers.

Most of the work involved with distributing electronic newsletters relates to managing subscriptions. To begin with, you have to provide a way for people to request subscriptions—either through e-mail or by filling out a form on your website. If you charge for subscriptions, you will have to collect credit card information and possibly demographic data if you sell advertising. If you publish your newsletter in both text and HTML formats, you will want your readers to indicate which format they want. You must process these subscription requests, which means adding subscriber addresses to your mailing list, and replying with messages confirming their requests. Once the subscriber has responded to the confirmation message, you will be sending out an introductory message, which typically includes basic information about your newsletter, including publication frequency, how to contact you, and how to unsubscribe. In addition to processing subscription requests, you will also have to process the requests of those who want to unsubscribe to your newsletter. This involves removing the names from your mailing list, and then responding with confirmation messages.

When managing a subscription newsletter, you will undoubtedly have subscribers who change their e-mail addresses. It is important for you to provide a way for them to easily make this change, without forcing them to unsubscribe their old address and then re-subscribe with the new one.

List software can handle these tasks automatically with programs called *autoresponders*. Autoresponders automatically send out a specified reply message to any e-mail that is sent to a certain address. For example, after a person sends an e-mail to the subscription address provided by a newsletter publisher, or signs up for the publication through a form on a website, an autoresponder could reply with a message that says, "Thank you for subscribing to Writers' Roundup. You are subscribed as carol@eymanpublications.com. Please reply to this message to confirm your subscription request."

You will also have to deal with *bounced mail*—messages that don't get delivered because the subscribers have forgotten to inform you of an e-mail address change. You'll have to remove these addresses from your list. You may also have to figure out how to prevent your readers' Internet service providers from rejecting your newsletter as spam or unsolicited e-mail. This can happen when you send a message to a large number of addresses at a single Internet service provider.

Be aware . . .
when sending an e-mail message to a large number of addresses at a single Internet service provider, the messages might be viewed as spam or unsolicited e-mail and automatically rejected. Using list software can help bypass this problem.

So, can you handle this work yourself, or should you farm it out to a list-hosting service? If your mailing list is small, just a few hundred subscribers, it's possible to distribute and manage your newsletter yourself with marginal effort. As your list grows, however, the time required to manage it and deal with technical glitches in distribution will multiply. At that point, you will probably find it best to have a list-hosting service take over.

Your budget will also influence your decision on using a list-hosting service. Handling your distribution list manually doesn't cost anything more than the price of the e-mail software and Internet service, which you probably already have. Or, you can go one step further and use free list-handling software and a free list-hosting service. But the larger your list and the more frequently you publish, the more cost-effective it becomes to invest in higher-end, more-sophisticated software or a paid list-hosting service.

Let's look first at some of the mechanics of distributing your newsletter yourself, and then at the mechanics of hiring a list host.

Do It Yourself

If you have only a small number of subscribers, the address book feature in your e-mail program can help you with newsletter distribution. Most address books let you create a "list," or "group," or distribution list, of addresses. Once you put all your subscribers into a group, you can tell your e-mail program to send a particular message—your newsletter—to the entire group, instead of having to type out each individual sub-scriber's address. A word of advice: When sending out a group e-mail, don't place the addresses in the To field. Instead, place them in the BCC (blind carbon copy) field. Addresses in the BCC field cannot be seen by the recipients, while those in the To field can. This preserves the privacy of your subscribers, who won't want their e-mail addresses available to others.

I send out a brief monthly newsletter to about 120 members of a parent group that I belong to. For this, I have created a group in my Microsoft Outlook Express address book that includes the e-mail addresses of all the members. This makes distribution easy. I simply type the name of the group in the BCC field of the e-mail message screen, and all of the addresses it contains are automatically entered.

This method works well for the newsletter of this small parent group—the number of requests to subscribe and unsubscribe is small, except for a flurry of activity at the beginning of each school year. And because the list remains small, only four or five addresses bounce when I distribute each issue. An automated distribution system probably wouldn't save me much time with these tasks; it would, however, take a chunk of time and/or money to get it going.

If the volume of activity on my list was a bit higher, I might try to automate it somewhat by using a trick offered by Chris Pirillo, author of *Poor Richard's E-Mail Publishing*. He suggests using the signature feature of your e-mail program as a sort of autoresponder. Here's how. Many e-mail programs let you create multiple signatures for your mail. For example, you could have one signature that says "John Arroyo, Director of Marketing, ABC Consulting Service" and another that says "John Arroyo, Scoutmaster, Pack 83." When you type a message, you can select the signature you want to use. The program will insert the signature, so you don't have to type it. To use this feature to automate your subscription management tasks, you can create one "signature" that, rather than containing your name and title, contains the message you send to confirm new subscriptions. Another signature could contain the message you send to confirm unsubscribe requests; another could contain a standard response to a request for back issues, and so forth.

As the size of your list grows, you might decide to use list software to truly automate your distribution tasks. List software can take over the subscription management tasks just described. It can also provide features, such as the ability to place a line in your message saying, "You are subscribed to this newsletter as [e-mail address]." This helps readers

To preserve the privacy of subscribers when sending out a group e-mail, rather than placing the addresses in the To field, place them in the BCC (blind carbon copy) field where they cannot be seen by the other recipients.

with more than one e-mail address know which one to unsubscribe if they no longer want your newsletter. (Often, these readers forget which e-mail address they used to subscribe, and they will send you an unsubscribe request referencing the wrong e-mail address. Then they become irate when they continue to receive the newsletter.)

As mentioned earlier, some Internet service providers, in an effort to eliminate spam, may reject an e-mail that is sent to a large group of addresses. List software can bypass this problem by sending out your newsletters individually or within small groups.

Another task that can become cumbersome with large lists is checking for duplicate addresses. Some people may forget that they have already subscribed to your newsletter and subscribe again. As a result, you will be sending them duplicate copies of the publication. This is another area in which list software is advantageous. It will check to see if the address is already on the subscription list; if so, it will not be added again.

A number of programs are powerful enough to handle large lists; among them are Lyris ListManager and L-Soft Listserv. Often, companies that produce such higher-end software also offer simpler, less-expensive or even free versions to use with smaller mailing lists. Some companies may give you a choice of purchasing their software and administering it yourself, or hiring them as a list host, in which case they will administer it for you.

List Hosting

If your distribution list is too large to manage yourself, even with the aid of list-hosting software, consider hiring a professional list-hosting service to take over. Then all you have to do is send a message containing your newsletter or newsletter announcement to the service, who will take over from there.

Let's say your newsletter's distribution list is growing robustly. You're pleased with your success, but you don't have the knowledge or the time to learn how to use list software. Maybe your list isn't huge, but you're busy running a business that entails much more than publishing a newsletter. Or perhaps you are getting a lot of bounces because your readers' ISPs are detecting your newsletter as spam. In these cases, you would do well to hire a professional list-hosting service, also known as a *mailing list service*, to handle distribution for you. Then your role in sending out each issue will be reduced to a simple task—sending an e-mail message containing your newsletter or newsletter announcement to the list service. The service will take over from there. Depending on your needs, you can use a paid or free service.

There are thousands of list-hosting services from which to choose. Among the basic, less-expensive services are Constant Contact, Your

MailingList Provider, Microsoft List Builder, and Vertical Response. For large lists that need more sophisticated services, SparkList and Lyris are recommended choices. IntelliContact provides services for all sizes of mailing lists.

When you pay for a list-hosting service, you can expect to benefit from some or all of the following services:

■ Templates and wizards for creating HTML e-mail newsletters.

■ Scheduled delivery of your newsletter at the time of distribution you choose.

■ Reports on the number of subscribers, number of messages distributed, bounced addresses, number of messages opened by readers, and the like.

■ Removal of bounced addresses and duplicate addresses from the list.

■ Twenty-four-hour customer service and technical support.

■ Security against outside access to your mailing list.

■ Ability to back up your list.

■ Communication with large Internet service providers to resolve problems with spam filters.

■ HTML code to create a form on your website that allows readers to subscribe.

> No matter which type of list-distribution service you use, always get a backup copy of the file that contains your subscriber list. Keep it stored at your site and have the service update the list frequently.

Technical support is essential if you distribute a paid newsletter, if you sell advertisements, or if your newsletter is a marketing tool for your business. Problems with your newsletter's distribution—undelivered issues, multiple copies sent to one subscriber, and the like—exacerbated by inadequate technical support from your list-hosting service can destroy your image and cost you subscribers.

If you can't afford a list service, you can still get help with list distribution. If you are affiliated with a college, university, or other large institution, you may be able to use its list-hosting and management services without charge. If you have no such affiliation, look into other free services like Topica (*www.Topica.com*) and Yahoo! Groups (*www.groups.Yahoo.com*). These services usually come with conditions—inserting advertisements into your messages is the most common. But many small associations, nonprofit organizations, and hobby groups find this an acceptable trade-off.

Whatever type of service you use, always be sure to get an electronic backup copy of the file containing your subscriber list. Store it at your site, and have the service update it frequently.

Be sure to check out several list-hosting services before selecting one. In addition to cost, compare the features and customer service each one offers. For a complete picture of the service, be sure to ask the questions found in "Assessment of List-Hosting Services" on page 287.

Avoiding the "Spammer" Label

Every publisher of e-mail newsletters must understand that all readers detest unsolicited e-mail, known as *spam*. Downloading, sorting through, and deleting spam is time-consuming, expensive, and just plain annoying. In 2003, Congress passed the CAN-SPAM (Controlling the Assault of Non-Solicited Pornography and Marketing) Act. This law targets e-mail whose primary purpose is to advertise or promote a commercial product or service. (E-mail that deals with an agreed-upon transaction or updates a customer in an existing business relationship, while it may not contain false or misleading routing information, is otherwise exempt.) Basically, the CAN-SPAM Act:

■ Bans false or misleading information in an e-mail header, such as the To and From fields.

■ Prohibits deceptive subject lines.

■ Requires e-mail recipients to be given the option of removing their names from the mailing list.

■ Requires commercial e-mail to be identified as an advertisement, and to include the sender's physical postal address.

One way to prevent your online newsletter from being mistaken for spam is by clearly identifying the name of your company or organization in the From field of your e-mail message. In the Subject field, display the newsletter's name or headline of the lead article.

You can visit *www.ftc.gov/bcp/conline/pubs/buspubs/canspam.htm* for additional details of the CAN-SPAM Act. It's important to keep in mind that although this act prohibits sending commercial e-mail only to those who have opted *out*, responsible e-mail publishers *never* distribute their newsletters to people who have not opted *in* (requested them). Unfortunately, even requested newsletters are sometimes deleted because the recipients think they are spam, or their Internet service providers block them. This is why publishers must know how to prevent a message from looking like spam.

Your readers will be more likely to open your newsletter if they can easily recognize it as one they have requested. There are several ways you can help. First, make sure the information in the From field in their inboxes clearly and truthfully identifies you. E-mail programs let you specify (often under "options" or "preferences") a name to display in this field. If you don't specify anything, your readers will see only your e-mail address, and if they don't recognize it, chances are they will delete the message. Displaying your name in the From field may not work either, unless you're sure people know who you are. Your best option is to use the name of your company or organization, or the name of the newsletter itself.

Another way to identify your newsletter is by carefully writing an appropriate message in your Subject line. (As just mentioned, deceptive subject lines for commercial e-mail are prohibited.) I recommend displaying your newsletter's name or the headline of your lead article there. It is also important to be aware that readers view promotional or enticing language in the subject line—"Free offer!" "Sign Up Today!" "Information You Need Now!"—as an indication that the message is spam. They also view subjects that include words like "sex," "girls," "free," or "money" the same way.

Elaine Floyd, author of *Quick & Easy Newsletters*, suggests creating a subject line that includes your newsletter's name, a space, and then the date in year-month format. When readers sort their e-mail by subject, all your newsletters will display in chronological order. For example, the first three months of *Wildlife Watch* in 2007 would appear as follows:

```
Wildlife Watch 2007-01
Wildlife Watch 2007-02
Wildlife Watch 2007-03
```

You can also help readers identify your newsletter by publishing it regularly. If you publish infrequently, less than once a month or so, readers may not remember who you are and will likely delete your message.

Within the body of your newsletter message, clearly identify the publication—at the top—with your nameplate. You should (and if your newsletter is commercial in nature, you must) tell your readers how to unsubscribe. The following message serves as an example:

```
You are subscribed to this newsletter as
[insert recipient's e-mail address]
To unsubscribe, click here or send a blank
e-mail to [insert appropriate e-mail address]
```

The Subject fields of e-mail messages that contain promotional phrases like "Free Offer" and "Today Only," or suggestive words like "sex," "free," and "money," are likely to be viewed as spam—and are also likely to be deleted.

To Unsubscribe . . .
Within your e-mail newsletters, be sure to tell your readers how to unsubscribe. The message at left serves as an example.

When you receive a subscription request, send a message to the subscriber informing him that you have received the request. Also instruct him to verify the request by replying to your message. Once he responds to that message, you can reply with an introductory message about the newsletter itself—how frequently it's distributed, how to unsubscribe, and whom to contact with questions. This extra step solves the problem of fulfilling fraudulent subscription requests, in which people subscribe others without their permission.

The suggestions above will help you get your readers to open and read your newsletter. But you will also want to take some steps to make sure your newsletter isn't blocked from your readers' inboxes to begin with. As problems with unsolicited e-mail have increased, Internet service providers have instituted procedures to prevent spam from reaching their customers. Many ISPs screen incoming mail for spam-like characteristics. When they detect such characteristics, they either block the message or send it to their customers' bulk mail folders (which customers usually ignore). The ISPs try not to make public their techniques for detecting spam because they don't want spammers to figure out how to outwit the filters. But there are a few ways you can help your legitimate messages get through.

First, if you use HTML e-mail, don't include any Javascript code in the message. Javascript is a language that can be used to run programs from your HTML e-mail newsletter. Unfortunately, it can also activate viruses, so some spam filters reject any message that includes it.

Javascript—a language that can be used to run programs from your HTML e-mail newsletter—can also activate computer viruses. Many spam filters reject messages that include it. For this reason, if you use HTML e-mail, don't include Javascript code in the message.

Second, review the bounced messages you receive when distributing your newsletter. See if you can find a pattern in the addresses. If a large number is from one ISP, try to find out why. Some ISPs block any message that is sent to more than 100 or 200 users of their service, even if it was requested. You might have to send out your newsletter in smaller batches to get around this type of filter. The software you use to distribute your newsletter may be able to do this, or your list-hosting service can handle it for you. Contacting the ISP that is causing your newsletter to bounce is another possible option for resolving the problem.

It's also a good idea to inform your own ISP, website host, e-mail server, and list-hosting service that you are distributing an e-mail newsletter to people who have requested it. If your subscribers think you are sending spam, they may complain to these companies before contacting you. You will have more credibility denying the charge if you've previously informed everyone of your publishing activities.

If you use a list-hosting service, you also run the risk of having your

Assessment of List-Hosting Services

When deciding on a list-hosting service to handle the distribution of your newsletter, be sure to ask the following questions:

General

1. How long have you been in the list-hosting business?

2. Can you supply references from other customers?

3. What do you charge?

4. When is your technical support available? Do you provide support via telephone, e-mail, or online chat?

Capabilities

1. Can I administer my list through e-mail commands only, or through a web form as well?

2. Can I use mail merge commands? (For example, can I add a line in my newsletter that says, "You are subscribed as *carol@aol.com*"?)

3. Can I send you my newsletter in advance and have it distributed later at a designated time?

4. What type of delivery reports do you provide?

Capacity

1. What's the maximum size distribution list you can handle? How big is the largest list you currently handle?

2. How long will it take to deliver my newsletter?

Security Policies

1. How often will you back up my list? Can I get my own backup copy?

2. How will you assure privacy/security of my list?

3. Do you allow any of your customers to distribute unsolicited mailings?

---

list used by another party to distribute spam. Before choosing a service, find out what measures it takes to preserve the security of your list so that it is never sold or stolen. It's a good idea to create an extra e-mail address for yourself (one that doesn't clearly identify you) and put it on your distribution list. Don't use this address for any other purpose. If you receive e-mail other than your newsletter at this address, you'll know that your list has been misused.

Archiving Back Issues

Many publishers maintain a page on their websites for subscribers and potential subscribers to access back issues of their newsletters. If you charge for subscriptions, you can post a sample issue for nonsubscribers, but make additional issues available to subscribers via a password. If your newsletter is free, it's nice to post as many issues as possible. These

Blogging
Another Way to Talk to Readers

The word "blog" is a shortened version of "web log." What started out as personal journals posted on the websites of individuals, blogs have evolved to include news and opinions on all sorts of topics. As a newsletter publisher, you can post articles to a blog quite easily by using blogging software. It is also simple and convenient for people to write comments about what you have published and post them to your blog, where you—and the rest of your readers—can see them. This kind of reader feedback and interaction is invaluable because it keeps your newsletter responsive to the interests of your audience. You will, however, want to monitor reader comments to avoid posting potentially libelous remarks. Spam can also be a problem for blogs, but automated filters are available to keep this to a minimum.

archives will be even more useful to your readers if you provide a search engine, so they can easily find the desired information.

CONCLUSION

As I suggested at the end of the last chapter on web newsletters, once you have sent out your newsletter, take a break before starting work on the next issue. Give yourself a chance to assess the issue you just completed, and work out any kinks for future issues. Between publications, rather than in the midst of deadlines, is a good time to meet with your staff to iron out any problems in your publishing process.

If you plan to publish a PDF issue of your newsletter in addition to the e-mail version, it's time to move on to the next chapter, "Producing PDF Newsletters."

CHAPTER 12

PRODUCING PDF NEWSLETTERS

D o you want to distribute your newsletter online without sacrificing the attractive design of your print edition? Would you like to publish a newsletter that can be read on any computer operating system, using software that anyone can download free on the Internet? Oh, and do you need a reasonably sized newsletter file that does not take an eternity to download? Then PDF (portable document format) is the newsletter format for you.

Because PDF faithfully reproduces the formatting of printed documents, it has become a common file format for distributing documents on the Internet. It can be read on virtually all types of computer operating systems, such as Windows, Macintosh, and Linux. Adobe has distributed hundreds of millions of copies of Adobe Reader—the application software needed to read PDF files. Anyone who doesn't have the program can visit *www.adobe.com* and download it for free.

The process of producing a PDF newsletter is similar to the process of producing a print version. After writing and editing your articles, you must lay them out using a page-layout program. As you can see from Figure 12.1 on page 290, a PDF newsletter looks just like a printed one. It can include graphics, multiple columns, color, a variety of typefaces and type styles, and most any kind of formatting. But instead of sending your page-layout file to a print shop, as you would for a print newsletter, you use special software to convert it to PDF. After the conversion—a simple process that takes just a few minutes—you can post the PDF newsletter file on your website and send readers an e-mail to let them know it's there.

If you are not familiar with PDF newsletters, you can view some online. It's simple enough to find free newsletters on just about any topic.

Figure 12.1

A PDF newsletter looks just like a print publication, with graphics, multiple columns, color, a variety of typefaces and type styles, and most any type of formatting.

Traffic congestion: is it a war or a team effort?

Simply go to a search engine or directory like *www.google.com* or *www.yahoo.com,* and do a search, using the phrase "PDF newsletter" plus your topic of interest, such as "cats," "softball," or "parenting." When you find a web page for a PDF newsletter, follow the viewing instructions. If possible, request a free subscription, so you will receive announcements of future issues. Opening and reading these PDF newsletters will help you understand the experience of your own readers.

The widespread use of PDF has allowed immediate availability of documents that otherwise would take a week or more to request and receive by postal mail. As an added bonus, they are free. While this has obvious advantages for readers, it is of equal benefit to the publishers of documents— software companies, for instance, can save big bucks by eliminating the printed manuals for their products and delivering them as PDF files on their websites instead.

I must admit, however, that sometimes I feel a twinge of irritation when companies deliver documents in PDF format. Whether it is a product brochure or a company newsletter, in effect, the company is transferring the effort and expense of printing from their pockets to mine. And in spite of retaining its original formatting, the final product has its downside. When I print a PDF newsletter, I get 8.5-x-11-inch separate sheets of paper that are printed on one side, instead of the nice packet of folded and stapled 11-x-17-inch sheets I get with the printed newsletters I receive in the mail. Also, the graphics don't reproduce as well on my desktop printer as they do when they are professionally printed. And although a PDF newsletter may have been produced in color, if I print it out, I am likely to do so in black and white to save money on color ink. Often, I find myself skimming a PDF newsletter on-screen and printing only the pages that interest me most.

My receptiveness to a PDF newsletter often depends on the classification of the publication. If it comes from an association with a small budget, usually I just shrug at the minor inconveniences of PDF because I realize that online distribution keeps my dues low or frees up the group's money for other projects. And I'm sure that if I worked in an industry in which my livelihood depended on getting up-to-the-minute information from a professional newsletter, the speed of PDF distribution would override any concern I had about do-it-yourself printing. On the other hand I would be unhappy if a consumer newsletter I paid for became unavailable in print. And I wouldn't spend my time printing and reading a marketing newsletter that was distributed as PDF, whereas I might read or skim a few pages if it came in the mail.

Every newsletter format has its advantages and disadvantages. If low distribution cost, speedy delivery, and attractive appearance are important to you, PDF is a wise choice.

WRITING AND EDITING PDF NEWSLETTERS

The best writing style for a PDF newsletter depends on whether your audience will be printing it out or reading it on-screen. If you believe they are more likely to print it out, write the articles just as you would for a print newsletter. If, on the other hand, you feel your audience is more likely to read the publication on-screen, write shorter articles. Also, since it takes people longer to read on-screen material, limit the number of pages in each issue.

Once you have written all the copy, check that the writing is clear, organized, and accurate. Make sure it meets your organization's usage style. In other words, do the content editing and copyediting described for print newsletters in Chapter 6, and use the checklist on page 154 as a guide. Once this is done, you can lay out the newsletter.

DESIGNING AND LAYING OUT PDF NEWSLETTERS

The process of designing and laying out a PDF newsletter is essentially the same as that described in Chapter 8 for a print newsletter. Using page-layout software, like Quark XPress, Adobe InDesign or PageMaker, or Microsoft Publisher, follow the guidelines in Chapter 8 to design and lay out your PDF newsletter.

For the most part, a PDF newsletter contains all the elements that are included in a print version, such as nameplate, tagline, masthead, folios, table of contents, and so forth. But if you are creating both a print and a PDF version of your newsletter, you might have to make some minor modifications to the print version so it is adaptable for PDF. For example, let's say you can't afford to use color in your print newsletter. Fortunately, adding color to the PDF version will cost you nothing. First, make a copy of the page-layout file. On this copy, change any type and graphics to the desired color, and then convert this file to a PDF (converting files is described in the next section).

If you use preprinted shells for the front and back covers of your

Viewing a PDF file requires Adobe Reader, a free downloadable program from Adobe Systems.

One drawback to reading a PDF newsletter on-screen is that the print is small. If you zoom in enough to make the copy large enough to read, you cannot view the entire page at once. This results in lots of scrolling up, down, and across columns, and is one reason many people print out this type of newsletter before reading it.

print newsletter (as described in Chapter 8), you will also have to make a copy of your page-layout file to use for your PDF version. For example, look back at the top spread of Figure 8.7 on page 198. The shaded boxes, the rules, and the words "Writers' Roundup" in the nameplate would not normally appear in a page-layout file for this newsletter, because they are already printed on the shells. This means you would have to place the boxes, rules, and nameplate in the copy of the page-layout file before converting it to PDF

I think you will find that most readers who receive a PDF version of your newsletter will print it out before reading it. The problem with reading a PDF newsletter on-screen is that if you zoom in enough to make the type large enough to read easily, you cannot see the entire page. This means you have to do lots of vertical and horizontal scrolling, making it easy to lose your place when you get to the bottom of a column and have to scroll up to the top again. So keep in mind that your page design should be easy to print, and easy to read from a printed copy.

One way to make your newsletter easy to print is by sticking to the standard 8.5-x-11-inch page layout, and avoiding tabloid or legal-size layouts. Keep in mind that few computer printers accept tabloid-size paper, and although most computer printers can accept legal-size paper, many readers won't have any on-hand.

It is also important to remember that readers will probably print out your PDF newsletter on just one side of the paper. This means that when reading it, they will see only one page at a time, not the two-page spread of a print version. So to make the PDF version easy to follow, don't refer to articles or illustrations by saying, "See related story, opposite" or "See table on facing page."

You may also have to add jump lines ("continued on page 3") to your PDF version. Let's say, for instance, an article is continued from a left-hand page to the opposite right-hand page. Since readers can easily see the continuation of the article in the print version, a jump line may not be warranted. However, in the PDF version that is printed on single sheets, readers *will* need that jump line to guide them to the rest of the article.

An advantage of using PDF is that you don't have to worry about fitting your copy into a number of pages that is divisible by four, as you do with print newsletters. (As you learned earlier in the book, print newsletters are typically printed two-sided on 11-x-17-inch sheets. When these sheets are folded in half, each one forms four 8.5-x-11-inch pages.) A five- or six-page PDF newsletter doesn't look any more unusual than one that is four or eight pages.

If for some reason you think your readers will prefer to read your newsletter on-screen, you'll want to modify your design to improve its legibility. Use a type that is 1 or 2 points larger than you would use for print; 11- or 12-point type is recommended. Choose a screen-friendly typeface, such as Georgia, Verdana, or Tahoma. To help readers keep their places, try to avoid jumps from one page to another in a single article. And if you have the time, convert e-mail addresses and website addresses into clickable links. If your newsletter is longer than four to six pages, you might want to convert jump lines and the table of contents into links as well. (See "Creating Links in PDF Files" on page 294.)

Once you have the newsletter completely laid out, proofread it thoroughly. Use the "Checklist for Proofreading" on page 159 to help you catch any typographical errors. When you're done, you're ready to go on to the next step, converting your page-layout file to PDF.

If you believe your readers prefer to read PDF newsletters on-screen, you can improve the publication's legibility with a few design modifications. Set the type a bit larger than you would for a print version, choose a screen-friendly typeface, keep articles on one page, and convert websites and e-mail addresses into clickable links.

CONVERTING PAGE-LAYOUT FILES TO PDF

Now that you've written, edited, laid out, and proofread your newsletter, you're ready to turn it into a PDF file, which your readers can download or open online. Creating a PDF file from a page-layout file involves two steps:

1. Converting the page-layout file to a new file in a format called Post-Script.

2. Converting, or *distilling*, this PostScript file to a PDF file.

Fortunately, most PDF-creation software combines these steps into a single, simple procedure that you run from your page-layout software. Let's say, for example, you lay out your newsletter in PageMaker, and you have Acrobat Distiller software for converting your newsletter to PDF. In PageMaker, you can simply select "Export" and then "Adobe PDF" from the File menu, complete a few dialog boxes, and then sit back for a moment while Distiller creates your PDF file for you.

You may already have Acrobat Distiller or some other PDF-creation software installed on your computer, especially if you own other Adobe software, such as PageMaker or InDesign. Take a look at the menus in your page-layout software for an option like Export, Create Adobe PDF, Publish to PDF, or Convert to Adobe PDF. These options are often found on the File menu. Alternatively, you may find a menu named "Adobe," or a button on the toolbar with which you can convert your file.

Sometimes, as mentioned earlier, the conversion requires two-steps.

Creating Links in PDF Files

PDF newsletters can contain links (also called *hyperlinks*), both to locations within the newsletter and to websites or e-mail addresses. For example, in Figure 12.2 on page 295, the newsletter *Dateline Houston* has links from its table of contents on page one to the articles that are included in that issue. In addition, the editors have created bookmarks that are located on the far left of the screen. Clicking on the bookmarks is another way for the reader to go to each article. When clicked on, the website addresses in *Dateline Houston* bring readers to those sites. In addition, each e-mail address is formatted to display a blank e-mail message with the chosen address. Another type of link you can create in a PDF newsletter is from a jump line to the remainder of the article on another page.

The exact instructions for creating these links will vary, depending on the software you use to lay out your newsletter and to convert it to a PDF file. But the concept behind creating links is the same, regardless of the software.

To activate the links in your newsletter's page-layout file, you must tell the program which text or graphic in your newsletter is the *source* of the link (the place the reader must click) and which website, e-mail address, or newsletter location is its *destination* (where the reader will end up after clicking on the link). The instructions that come with your page-layout software will explain how to specify these sources and destinations.

When using PDF-creation software to convert your page-layout file to a PDF file, you must specify that you want it to automatically convert the links from the page-layout file into links or bookmarks in the PDF file as well. (Less-sophisticated PDF-creation software doesn't have this ability.) You may also be able to specify how you want those links to look in the PDF file—underlined, highlighted, outlined, and so forth. The instructions for your PDF-creation software will provide specific information on how to do this.

One more word of advice: If you decide *not* to link the websites and/or e-mail addresses that appear in your PDF file, make sure they don't look like links to your readers. This can happen, for example, if you use Microsoft Word to lay out your newsletter. Word automatically converts websites and e-mail addresses to a blue, underlined format that is clickable in the Word file, but may not remain clickable after you convert the file to PDF. They do, however, still appear blue and underlined in the PDF file, and can cause readers to think something is broken when they click on the link and nothing happens.

Links help your reader navigate through your PDF newsletter, so it's worth your time to learn how to create and activate them.

In this case, you would select Print from the File menu in your page-layout software, choose "Acrobat Distiller" as your printer, and print the file. No hard copy is actually produced when you use the Acrobat Distiller printer. Instead, your document is "printed" to a new file in PostScript format. You would then have to use PDF-creation software to convert the PostScript file to a PDF file.

If these options do not appear in your page-layout software, you will

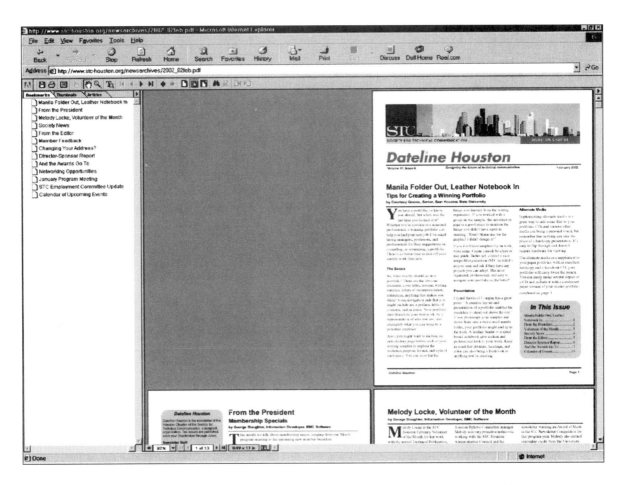

Figure 12.2

In *Dateline Houston*, readers can click on the items in the table of contents (in the "In This Issue" box at the bottom right corner of the first page), or on the bookmarks (located on the far left side of the screen) to jump to the articles found within the issue.

Courtesy of the Society for Technical Communication, Houston Chapter.

have to find another way to convert your files. One way is to purchase the Acrobat package from Adobe. (Remember that the Adobe Reader alone, which you may already have, can display PDF files, but it cannot create them.) If you purchase the full Acrobat package, you will be able to convert your files to PDF and benefit from some additional features, as well. For example, you will be able to share your newsletter drafts online with your reviewers and proofreaders (assuming they also have Acrobat), and they will be able to insert digital "comments" into your drafts. You will also be able to select from certain options that help control the size of your PDF file.

While publishers in large organizations might need these options in their PDF-creation software, smaller publishers often prefer simpler, less expensive software that doesn't require them to understand and specify so many settings. If you fall into the latter category, go to Planet PDF (*www.planetpdf.com*), where you will find a list of PDF-creation software packages, as well as links to the websites of their distributors. Planet PDF also lists some of the available services that let you convert your newsletter to a PDF file online without downloading or purchasing any software. Adobe (*www.createpdf.com*) and PDF Online (*www.gobcl.com*) both offer such services.

Before purchasing any type of PDF-creation software or service, find out just how much you are able to control the settings when creating your PDF file. Even if you don't need a package as sophisticated as the full version of Acrobat, you will definitely want the ability to *embed* (include) fonts, so all typefaces appear correctly in your PDF file. You may also want to be able to compress any large graphics files, and to convert website addresses, e-mail addresses, and table of contents entries into links.

Once you have purchased and installed PDF-creation software, consult the software manual or online help to learn the exact procedure for converting your newsletter to PDF. If you use an online service to do your conversion, the instructions will be provided on the service's website.

TESTING PDF NEWSLETTERS

After converting your newsletter to PDF, you will need to test it before distribution. Testing must be done from two places—first, from your hard drive (known as *local testing*), where you will iron out any preliminary wrinkles, and then from your web server.

Local Testing

To test your newsletter locally, open it and review it in Adobe Reader. Since you should have edited and proofread the newsletter *before* converting it to PDF, the purpose of this local testing of the file is not so much to find misspelled words or punctuation errors, as it is to make sure that the PDF conversion retained the formatting of the original page-layout file. It is also to verify that any links you may have included within the newsletter are working. However, if you did miss a few typos in your original proofreading, you will have a chance to correct them now.

During this testing stage, use the checklist on page 298 to make sure you have done a thorough job. First, test to make sure your readers can navigate through the newsletter properly—this means you must click on any links to websites and e-mail addresses to make sure they are working properly. Also check any internal links, such as those found in the table of contents or in jump lines, to verify that they bring you to the right locations.

Next, look over your newsletter's columns, display type, body text, and graphics to verify that they are formatted correctly. In particular, make sure that the text flows as you expected it to—that columns and lines end and begin where they did in the original file. Also check that your type and graphics display as they did in your original file.

This testing will reveal two types of errors. The first results from laying out or formatting something incorrectly in your original page-layout file. For example, you may notice that a headline that should be bold is not. Chances are you forgot to bold it in the original page-layout file. To correct this type of error, you will have to re-open the page-layout file, bold the headline, and convert the file to PDF again. Because converting files to PDF ordinarily goes very smoothly, you will find that most errors are caused by this type of page-layout oversight.

The second type of error—one that results from using the wrong settings when converting your file to PDF—is much less common. For example, you may find that the text you wanted set in Palatino is displayed in Times Roman. You check the page-layout file and find that you did indeed specify Palatino there. This means you don't have to make any change to the page-layout file, but you *do* have to change the settings in your PDF-creation software to embed fonts. You must then convert the page-layout file to PDF again.

If you cannot figure out why there is a discrepancy between your print and PDF versions, don't just compare the printed copy to the PDF version. Be sure to also open the page-layout file and check for irregularities in how you have formatted the text or graphic in question. If you still cannot figure out how to correct the problem, consult the manual or online help for your PDF-creation software. Or go to *www.adobe.com*, *www.planetpdf.com*, or *www.pdfzone.com*. You can search through collections of articles on any of these sites to find assistance with the particular problem you are encountering. Or you can use one of their online forums or discussion groups to get answers. These sites will probably recommend changing something in your page-layout file, or altering a setting in your PDF-creation software. Make the changes they recommend and then repeat the process—convert your source file to PDF, and check the result until it displays correctly.

After a file is converted to PDF, you must verify that it has retained the correct formatting. Also check that any links included in the file are working properly.

Web Server Testing

Once you are satisfied with the results of your local testing, it's time to send your PDF file from your computer to your web server for more testing. To send the file, you may need to simply e-mail it to your company's webmaster, who can post it. If you don't have a webmaster, you will have to transfer the files to your website in a manner that is similar to the way you transfer other web pages you create. You can use a type of pro-

---

Checklist for Testing PDF Newsletters

Use the following checklist during local and web server testing of your PDF newsletter.

LOCAL TESTING

Navigation

Test each of the following links, making sure they produce the expected results:

- ☐ Website links
- ☐ E-mail links
- ☐ Table of contents links
- ☐ Jump lines to and from continuation pages

Columns

Check for proper:

- ☐ Alignment
- ☐ Width
- ☐ Space between
- ☐ Line length

Display Type

Check headlines, kickers, decks, subheads, bylines, and captions for correct:

- ☐ Spacing above, below, and beside
- ☐ Typeface
- ☐ Type size

Body Text

Check for correct:

- ☐ Alignment
- ☐ Indentation
- ☐ Paragraph spacing

Graphics

Check photos, pictures, charts, graphs, tables, boxes, and rules for proper:

- ☐ Alignment
- ☐ Size
- ☐ Borders
- ☐ Shading

WEB SERVER TESTING

Links

Test each of the following links, making sure they produce the expected results:

- ☐ Link from your website to your PDF newsletter
- ☐ Links from your newsletter to other websites
- ☐ E-mail links in your newsletter

gram for uploading files known as FTP (file transfer protocol) software to send the files, or possibly web-development software. Your web-development software may refer to this step as "publishing" the newsletter. The service that hosts your website can give you any specifications you might need for sending files, such as user ID, password, and the names of the "host" (computer) and the directory to which you are sending the files. It's a simple process once you know the necessary specifications.

Note that, unlike web newsletters, which can look different depending on the browser used to view them, PDF newsletters look the same to everyone. This is because all readers use the same software—Adobe Reader—for viewing. So, assuming you carefully reviewed your newsletter during local testing, you don't need to look for errors in formatting, type, and graphics when you test the newsletter on your web server.

Once you've transferred your PDF file to your web server, create a link from your website to the new issue. Click on it and make sure the newsletter opens in Adobe Reader. Also double-check that any links to websites and e-mail addresses within the newsletter still work when it's posted on your web server. If everything functions as planned, you're ready for distribution.

DISTRIBUTING PDF NEWSLETTERS

Once you have thoroughly tested your PDF newsletter, you are ready to go public with it. In the previous section, you created a link from your website to the latest issue. This link will be used primarily by people who surf to your website, but who are not subscribers to your newsletter. If your newsletter is available only through paid subscription, or if you need to restrict access for other reasons, you will have to modify the link so it requires readers to enter a password after they click it. Your webmaster, Internet service provider, or website host will help you implement this password protection.

The page or pages on your website that contain the link to your newsletter should state that the file is a PDF. Most people will have opened PDF files in the past. But if your audience is not computer literate, you should also mention that they will need Adobe Reader to open

Figure 12.3

This e-mail announces the availability of a PDF newsletter. It includes a link to the issue and a table of contents.

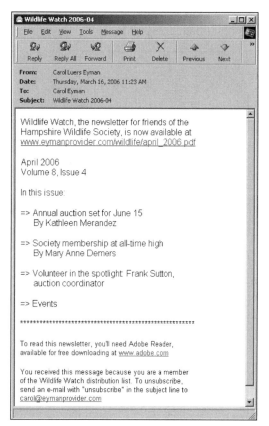

the file. Provide a link to the Adobe website (*www.adobe.com*), where they can download Reader for free.

The last step in distributing your PDF newsletter is to send subscribers an e-mail announcement, letting them know it is available. As seen in the sample announcement in Figure 12.3 on page 299, it's a good idea to include the issue's table of contents and perhaps bylines or short summaries of each article. Your announcement should also provide a link to the newsletter, mentioning that it leads to a PDF file. (Some publishers also note the size of the PDF file to give readers an idea of whether it will take a long time to download.) When subscribers click on the link, their web browsers should automatically open the newsletter in Adobe Reader.

Do not distribute your PDF newsletter as an attachment to the e-mail message. There are a number of reasons this is not a good idea. To begin with, computer novices in your audience may not understand how to open an attachment. Their computers may ask them which program to use to open it, and they may not know which one to choose. Another reason is that some readers will refuse to open the attachment for fear it contains a virus. And finally, if you are distributing your PDF newsletter internally (such as to company employees), you could possibly overload the company network by simultaneously sending the message to all of the employees.

To send out your e-mail newsletter announcements, you will have to maintain a distribution list that contains the e-mail addresses of your subscribers. You will also need a system for adding, changing, and deleting names on this list. The section on "Distributing E-Mail Newsletters" in Chapter 11 will help you with the upkeep of this mailing list.

CONCLUSION

Take some time to evaluate the PDF newsletter you have just produced. Gather your staff together for a meeting (called a *postmortem*) to evaluate the issue. Did it meet your expectations, as well as those of your readers? Did the writing, editing, layout, conversion, testing, and distribution go smoothly, or does your process need some adjusting? The time right after the issue is completed, when you have a little breathing room before starting the next issue, is best for ironing out any production problems.

CONCLUSION

SUSTAINING YOUR SUCCESS

Most of us hate doing our taxes. The thought of sorting through paperwork, decoding IRS instructions, and writing a fat check is enough to make anyone dread the approach of April 15th. Yet, even if Uncle Sam weren't breathing down your neck for his Form 1040, you would have to concede that there is value in reviewing your finances once a year. It is an opportunity to analyze where your money has gone and consider how to spend it in the future.

A periodic review is valuable for your newsletter as well. At least once a year, carve some time out of your regular schedule to step back and evaluate your work. Meet with your staff, board of directors, or editorial board in a place that is away from the usual office—in a hotel meeting room, at someone's home, at a conference. Ask participants to prepare for the meeting by compiling statistics on such topics as the number of new and renewed subscriptions or memberships, the number of visits made to your web newsletter, and the responses to reader surveys. Also have them jot down what they have learned from talking to newsletter readers and pertinent industry leaders over the past year.

At the meeting, analyze what this information reveals about your success in reaching your newsletter's purpose and the goals of your business or organization. Then discuss possible ways to improve your performance over the next year. How well have you covered topics of interest to your audience? What new topics should you begin covering in the coming months? Do you foresee any changes in the coming year (in your audience, the economy, technology) that will require you to shift your editorial focus, alter your marketing strategy, or adopt a different distribution format? Have you been able to keep your expenses within your budget and meet your revenue targets? Could you make procedural changes—in scheduling, staffing, or the production process—that would improve the quality of your newsletter and simplify its publication?

If your newsletter has low renewal rates, consider if it is adequately addressing the trends and issues in your field. Plan to stay in tune with your audience better. Interact with them at conferences, trade shows, and seminars. Ask them what new lines of business or research they are pursuing; find out what trade journals they are reading, websites they are visiting, and television programs they are watching. Make sure that notable people in your industry are receiving copies of your newsletter. Consider forming an editorial advisory board composed of leaders in your field.

Another key to retaining readers is providing responsive customer service. Be receptive to your readers' suggestions and complaints, even if the problems they report are not of your making. Act promptly to set the situation right. When readers cancel or fail to renew their subscriptions, give them a call or send them an e-mail to find out why.

Lack of reliability is another common reason for a drop in readership. In addition to expecting consistent high quality, readers want to be able to count on a newsletter that is published regularly, with issues that are about the same length and similar in appearance. Be wary of eliminating regular columns that readers may have looked forward to reading.

An overhaul of your design may be the key to reviving your newsletter. A new design can catch the attention of current readers and attract new ones. Design changes are best implemented all at once, rather than piecemeal over the course of several issues. Whenever you make large-scale changes, run an editor's message to keep your readers informed of what you're doing and why.

Your annual review may show that readership is robust but your revenues are still disappointing. If this is the case, you may want to boost your income by selling ancillary products. You already have the mechanism to market them—by advertising in the newsletter itself or in inserts. You will find it simplest to develop products that draw on your current assets. For example, you can publish special reports or annual industry reviews to sell or use as subscription premiums. These can draw on, as well as supplement, the content you have already published in your regular issues. You can also leverage the investment you have made in compiling your subscription mailing list by renting it out, either on your own or through a list broker.

You can also offer a directory of professionals, companies, publications, or products in your field, either as a print publication or as a searchable online database. Depending on your market, you can earn income by selling the directory, charging for listings, or selling advertising in the directory.

Selling books is another way of supplementing your income. Your editorial staff can use its expertise to write books that target your newsletter's audience. Or you can earn commissions by selling relevant books published by outside companies.

Sponsoring events can greatly increase the visibility of your publication and add to your list of subscription prospects. Seminars and conferences can be successful if your market is one of professionals, such as physicians, real estate brokers, teachers, and lawyers, who are required to earn continuing education credits to maintain their licenses. Seminars and conferences also work well in industries that are constantly changing because of technological advances or new laws and regulations.

The Internet offers a host of opportunities for selling ancillary products. You can earn royalties by having your articles stored in online subscription databases like Lexis Nexis. On your website, you can sell back issues of your newsletter, archived articles, or special reports. You can host a bulletin board or discussion group just for subscribers that will increase their loyalty to your newsletter. Or you can host online chats with leaders in your field.

Developing ancillaries, like any line of business, can be financially rewarding, but it can also present risks to both your balance sheet and reputation. Don't underestimate the additional labor and expenses involved in producing such products. You can't, for example, expect your editors to write books without relieving them of some of their regular duties. Remember that the quality of any ancillary product is a reflection of your main business—it should have the same high standard that is characteristic of your newsletter.

As a newsletter publisher you should not only keep abreast of trends in your newsletter's subject area, but also in the publishing industry itself. Ever-improving technologies are constantly enticing people to embrace new distribution methods for the written word. With the latest advances, you can format your newsletter to be read (or heard) on a cell phone or MP3 player. The growing popularity of RSS (Real Simple Syndication) feeds can let you broaden your newsletter's reach while simplifying your distribution process at the same time. Keeping your finger on the pulse of progress will help maintain the effectiveness of your publication.

Well, you have come full circle. At the beginning of this book, you came up with an idea for your newsletter and defined its audience, purpose, and content. You established your publishing operation and set out to find readers. You have learned ways to improve your writing, editing, and design skills. And after boning up on the nuts and bolts of print and electronic distribution, you turned out a finished product. Now, if you assess your progress toward achieving your purpose and meeting your audience's needs, you will be well on the way to sustaining your success.

GLOSSARY

Words that appear in *italic type* are defined within this glossary.

active voice. A sentence construction in which the subject performs the action expressed in the verb. "The car hit a tree" is written in active voice; "The tree was hit by a car" is written in *passive voice.*

agreement. A contract or a letter of agreement between a publisher and an outside contributor (freelance writer, layout artist, photographer) to the publication. Typically, this agreement states the purchase conditions of the material or service, often including such matters as deadlines and payment details.

alignment. The manner in which lines of text in a paragraph line up with the sides of the column. Alignment can be *left justified,* right justified, fully justified, and centered.

all caps. A capitalization style in which all of the words are set in upper case. See also *initial caps* and *sentence caps.*

ancillary product. A bonus offer, such as a special-interest report, seminar, or directory, that is offered to the reader. Ancillary products are often intended to generate income or increased readership.

ascender. The portion of a lowercase letter, such as an "h" or "d," that extends above its main body.

ASCII format. A file format containing only plain text with no boldface, italics, or other formatting options. It can be read by most software programs.

association newsletter. Produced by an organization or association, this type of newsletter is designed to keep members informed about the group's news and activities, while fostering a sense of community.

author bio. A short description of a writer's credits, often including educational degrees, previous publications, and occupation.

automation rate. A discounted postage rate for mailings with barcodes that can be read by US Postal Service scanning equipment.

autoresponder. An e-mail program that automatically sends a specified response message to any e-mail that is sent to a certain address.

banner. See *nameplate.*

banner ad. Usually a rectangular graphic, this type of advertisement commonly runs across the top or along the sides of web pages and *HTML e-mail newsletters.* In many cases, clicking on a banner ad can take you to the advertiser's website.

bleed. A printing method in which ink extends (bleeds) to the edge of the page.

body text. Passages of writing that make up the body of a story or article.

bulk rate. A discounted postage rate for mailings that meet US Postal Service requirements for volume and preparation.

bullet. A *character*—usually a filled circle—that is typically used to set off items in a list.

bulleted list. A list in which each entry is formatted as a separate paragraph and preceded by a *bullet, dingbat,* or other special *character.*

byline. The author's name as printed at the beginning or end of an article.

camera-ready copy. Artwork and text that are ready to be photographed for reproduction.

caption. An explanatory comment that accompanies a photo, illustration, chart, or other graphic.

casual writing. A style of writing that suggests no distance between writer and reader. This is done through the use of first and second person pronouns, informal sentence structure, slang, and colloquial expressions. Casual writing style is often used in newsletters.

character. An individual letter, number, punctuation mark, or symbol.

character formatting. The designing of letters, numbers, and symbols through *typeface, type style,* and type size choices. See also *paragraph formatting.*

circulation basis. The method through which a periodical is distributed—subscription (for a price) or nonsubscription (free or included as part of a paid membership).

classification. A newsletter category based on why it is being published and to whom it is directed. Newsletter classifications include professional, association, consumer, and marketing.

clip art. A collection of copyright-free drawings and other graphics.

clipping service. A service that distributes (via web page, e-mail, fax, or print) news articles related to a specific topic.

CMYK. An acronym for cyan, magenta, yellow, and black—the ink colors used to produce *process color.*

coated paper. Paper that has been coated with a layer of chemicals and clay, giving it a smoother feel than uncoated paper. It is well suited to *four-color printing.*

compiled list. A mailing list gathered from sources such as telephone and industry directories, association members, conference and seminar attendees, and public records. Because they typically draw fewer customers than *response lists,* compiled lists cost less to rent.

condensed typeface. A typeface variation in which the width of the letters has been reduced, resulting in a narrower look. It is used primarily in headlines, where the text needs to fit in a small space.

consumer newsletter. Informative newsletter that covers a general or specialized topic of consumer interest. Typically, those of general interest carry relatively low subscription rates, and are free if distributed online.

content. All of the text and graphics that make up a publication.

content editing. The review and revision of a story or article for its organization, length, readability, and accuracy.

copy. The actual words (text) of an article or other piece of writing.

copyediting. The review and revision of an article for conformity with the publisher's chosen *style* for spelling, punctuation, typography, and word use.

copyfitting. The process of estimating the amount of copy (based on *typeface* and type size) that will fit into a given space in a publication.

copyright. The legal overall right granted to an author or publisher for ownership of a written work. Under this ownership comes a number of specific rights, including the exclusive rights to print, sell, distribute, and translate the work.

credit line. A line of text citing the source of a photo, illustration, or other graphic.

crop. To eliminate the outer edges of a photograph or other graphic to improve its appearance and eliminate extraneous material. Cropping can be done manually or in an image-editing or page-layout program.

data card. A sheet that provides the size, price, source, demographic profile, and other *mailing list* details.

deck. A highlighted sentence or two located below the *headline* of an article that provides some detail of the article's contents. A deck is set in a smaller point size than the headline but larger than the *body text*.

descender. The portion of a lowercase letter, such as "p" or "y," that extends below its main body.

digital camera. A camera that records photographs as electronic files, which are usually loaded onto a computer for printing or for use in e-mail messages, web pages, and other documents.

digital printing. A catch-all term for printing methods in which certain prepress steps are eliminated. With some digital presses, printing plates are created directly from a page-layout file or camera-ready copy without creating film first. With other digital presses, neither film nor plates are created, and the page is produced with toner or with a laser beam and electrostatic ink. See also *offset printing*.

dingbat. An ornamental *character* or symbol, such as an asterisk, flower, or *bullet* that can be used to precede entries in a list, to signify the end of an article, or to decorate a page.

direct mail. An advertising method through which sales literature is mailed directly to potential customers.

direct mail piece. The sales literature packet that is distributed in a *direct mail* campaign. It often includes a sales letter, brochure, *lift letter*, reply card, and return envelope, among other items.

display ad. An advertisement that usually contains graphics and *display type*. It is typically larger than a classified ad, which contains only text.

display quote. See *pull quote*.

display type. Type used for *headlines, subheads, pull quotes,* and other highlighted elements on a page. It is usually larger than the *body text* and set in boldface, italics, or color to create contrast and make it stand out.

distribution format. The method, print or electronic, by which a publication is circulated to its readers.

domain name. The string of *characters* that identifies a website, such as whitehouse.gov or amazon.com.

drilling. The punching of holes in printed sheets to allow their insertion in a binder.

drop cap. An enlarged initial letter, often used in the opening paragraph of an article. This letter lines up with the top of the paragraph and drops down one or more lines below the baseline.

editor. A catch-all term referring to anyone involved in the production of the nonadvertising copy and graphics of a publication. A newsletter staff can include a managing editor, production editor, contributing editor, copyeditor, and proofreader.

editorial content. Term used to describe the copy and graphics prepared by a publication's editorial staff, and to distinguish it from advertising content.

editorial calendar. A publication's internal schedule in which the *editors* lay out their themes and topics for the coming year's issues.

editorial posture. The stance that a newsletter's writing takes on the topics it covers.

em dash. A long dash (the width of the letter "m") that is used to create a strong pause or break within a sentence. Em dashes can be used in pairs—to enclose a phrase or word—or they can be used alone to separate the end of a sentence from the beginning.

en dash. A short dash (the width of the letter "n") that is longer than a *hyphen*, and used to show range between numbers, such as "The recipe calls for 1–2 teaspoons of salt."

eyebrow. See *kicker.*

e-zine. An e-mail newsletter or magazine.

fact check. The act of verifying the quotes, statistics, and other information that appear in an article before it is printed.

fair use. A provision in the *copyright* law that allows for limited copying of published works without permission. Because the law is subject to different interpretations, it is generally best to avoid quoting from copyrighted material without permission.

feature story. An article that covers people, places, or events from a special point of view or angle. It is usually less time-sensitive than a *news story.*

filler article. A short article specifically designed to fill space on a page.

file transfer protocol (FTP). A method of copying files to and from the hard drive of a personal computer to a file server.

First Class Mail. A class of mail defined by the US Postal Service that is generally more expensive than other classes. It is delivered faster and does not require sorting, preparation, or a minimum number of pieces. See also *Standard Mail* and *Periodicals mail.*

fixed cost. Expenses incurred over a specified calendar period—usually one year—that do not vary. Rent, utilities, and insurance are examples of fixed costs. See also *per-issue cost* and *startup cost.*

flush left. See *left justified.*

folio. A page number in a publication, often printed in a header or footer that also contains the issue date and name of the publication.

font. A specific *typeface* of a particular size and style. For example, "12-point Helvetica bold" is a font, but "Helvetica" is a typeface.

formal writing. A style of writing in which the writer keeps a distance from the reader through the use of formal vocabulary, third person pronouns, and strict adherence to grammatical rules.

four-color printing. See *process color.*

franchised newsletter. See *syndicated newsletter.*

FTP. See *file transfer protocol.*

graphic artist. A person who designs the placement of print and graphics in print or online publications.

graphics. Illustrations, photos, drawings, graphs, charts, and other pictorial elements.

grid. The nonprinting lines in a page-layout file that define the size and spacing of columns and margins. Grids are used for placing graphics, *headlines,* and *body text* on a page.

gutter. The inside margins of two facing pages on a printed document. On left-hand pages, the gutter is the right margin. On right-hand pages, the gutter is the left margin.

headline. The title of an article.

house ad. An advertisement that promotes the publication in which it appears.

house list. A *mailing list* compiled by a company or organization for its own use. House lists include current customers; people who have requested information; people whose subscriptions have expired; and suppliers, vendors, and employees.

HTML. See *Hypertext Markup Language.*

HTML e-mail newsletter. A newsletter distributed via e-mail that is created using HTML coding, and can include graphics and text formatting.

hyperlink. A word, phrase, or graphic in a computer document or on a web page that, when clicked, brings the reader to another page or section within that document. In addition, hyperlinks can bring readers to a new document, to a web page, or to a blank pre-addressed e-mail form. Also called *links.*

hypertext. Electronic pages containing linked text, images, sounds, or other elements.

Hypertext Markup Language (HTML). The language used to define the structure, formatting, and layout of most web pages and some e-mail messages.

independent contractor. A worker who is not an employee of a company (or other hiring party), but who provides a service or goods under terms specified in an agreement or contract. Independent contractors are subject to different tax regulations than employees.

informal writing. A style of writing, often used in newsletters, that puts very little distance between reader and writer. It commonly uses first and second person pronouns and occasionally contains contractions.

initial caps. A style used in display type in which only the first letters of certain important words (as defined by the publisher's style guide) are set in upper case. See also *all caps* and *sentence caps*.

International Standard Serial Number (ISSN). A number issued by the Library of Congress that uniquely identifies a periodical, regardless of the country or language in which it is published. The ISSN usually appears in the periodical's *masthead*.

inverted pyramid. A writing style for news stories in which the most important information appears first and the least important appears at the end.

ISSN. See *International Standard Serial Number*.

issue number. A number that represents how many editions of the newsletter have been published in the current year or volume. It usually appears in the newsletter's *nameplate* and may also appear in the *masthead*. See also *volume number*.

jump. To continue an article or story from one page to another.

jump line. A phrase that indicates the page *on which* an article is continued ("Continued on page 8") or the page number *from which* the article is continued ("Continued from page 8").

justify. To align type with the left, right, or both sides of a column.

kicker. A short line of text located above the *headline* of a regular column, such as President's Message, Tax Tips, and Editor's Message. Kickers are always

used in combination with a headline. Also called *standing head*, *teaser*, or *eyebrow*.

layout. The arrangement of text and graphics in a print document or on a web page.

layout artist. A person who places and formats the text and graphics in a publication according to the specifications of a design *template*. Many layout artists are also *graphic artists*. Also called *production manager* or *production editor*.

lead paragraph. The opening paragraph of an article or story, often called simply *the lead*.

leading. The amount of space, measured in *points*, between lines of text. Pronounced *ledding*.

left aligned. See *left justified*.

left justified. A style in which lines of text in a paragraph align with the left side of the column. Also called *left aligned*, *flush left*, and *ragged right*.

letter shop. See *mail house*.

libel. A written statement that damages a person's reputation, character, or good name. The statement can appear in a letter, in an article, or even in a posting on an e-mail list or online bulletin board.

lift letter. A letter, usually signed by the company president or the *publisher*, that supplements the sales letter in a *direct mail piece*. Lift letters tend to "lift" the response rate of the mailing.

link. See *hyperlink*.

list. See *mailing list*.

list broker. A person who rents and/or sells lists of names and addresses for *direct mail* campaigns.

list host. See *list hosting service*.

list hosting service. A company used by e-mail publishers to distribute online publications to large lists of recipients. This type of service also manages those lists. Also called a *list host* or *list server*.

list manager. A person who handles the rental of *mailing lists* for the list owner.

list server. See *list hosting service.*

list owner. The originator of a *mailing list.*

mail house. A company that prepares pieces for mailing. Services offered can include addressing, sorting, barcoding, verifying addresses and barcodes, stuffing envelopes, and applying postage. Also known as a *letter shop.*

mailing list. A collection of names and addresses of people who make up a target audience for a *direct mail* campaign. Also the e-mail addresses of subscribers to an online publication.

mailing panel. The section of a self-mailer newsletter (usually the back) for placement of the recipient's mailing address, the publication's return address, and the postage.

managing editor. The coordinator of a publication's various departments—editorial, art, and typesetting—whose job is to maintain a smooth production process and meet deadlines.

mapping. The process of assigning the general placement of articles and graphics in an issue of a publication.

marketing newsletter. A type of newsletter for promoting a product, service, cause, or organization. It serves as a soft marketing piece—to show that the company, organization, or politician is doing a good job, or to increase demand for its products through informational articles.

master page. A nonprinting page in a page-layout file that contains standing design elements, such as headers and footers, as well as nonprinting layout guides, such as grids and rulers.

masthead. An area of the newsletter that lists information about its operation, such as staff members, mailing address, website, copyright notice, and reprint policy. The masthead should appear in the same spot in every issue—the second or last page of a print or PDF publication, or at the end of an e-mail or web newsletter are recommended.

matte. A dull finish on paper.

monospace typeface. A typeface in which an equal amount of horizontal space is allotted to every *character.* See also *proportional typeface.*

nameplate. The area across the top or side of the first page of a newsletter or other periodical that includes the full name of the publication. The *tagline*, issue date, and *volume* and *issue numbers* are also often found within a nameplate.

navigation tools. Elements within a publication, such as table of contents, page numbers, *jump lines*, and *hyperlinks*, that help readers make their way through it.

news story. An article covering recent events and happenings, particularly ones that are notable or unusual.

nonsubscription newsletter. A newsletter that is distributed free or as a membership benefit to prospective or current customers, clients, supporters, members, donors, or employees. See also *subscription newsletter.*

nut graph. See *nut paragraph.*

nut paragraph. The summarizing paragraph of a *feature article* that immediately follows the *lead paragraph* and lets the reader know what's coming. It often contains details like dates, names, and locations. Also called a *nut graph.*

offset printing. A method of print reproduction involving indirect image transfer. After the page-layout file or camera-ready copy is photographed to create film, the film is used to make printing plates, which are placed around a press cylinder. As the cylinder spins, ink adheres to the image areas of the plate and is then transferred to a smooth rubber-covered cylinder, which, in turn, prints the image on paper.

opacity. The degree to which you can see through a sheet of paper.

orphan. A single word or short last line of a paragraph that is isolated at the top or bottom of a page or column.

Pantone Matching System (PMS). A set of standard, numbered ink colors used by printers and graphic designers to match *spot colors.*

paragraph formatting. The designing of paragraphs through line spacing, spacing before and after the paragraph, and text alignment choices. See also *character formatting.*

passive voice. A sentence construction in which the action is performed upon the subject. "The tree was hit by a car" is written in passive voice; "The car hit a tree" is written in *active voice.*

PDF. See *Portable Document Format.*

PDF newsletter. A newsletter produced in *Portable Document Format* that is usually posted on a web page. Publishers usually distribute an e-mail notice to subscribers of PDF newsletters, informing them when a new issue is posted.

Periodicals mail. A discounted class of mail for magazines, newspapers, and other regularly distributed publications that meet certain requirements of the US Postal Service.

per-issue cost. The amount of money required for the publication of each newsletter issue. Printing and postage expenses are examples of per-issue costs. See also *fixed cost* and *startup cost.*

pica. A unit of measure used by typographers that equals 0.167 inches. There are 6 picas in 1 inch. See also *point.*

plain type. See *Roman type.*

PMS. See *Pantone Matching System.*

point. A unit of measure used by typographers to specify the size of type or the amount of *leading.* There are 12 points in 1 *pica,* and approximately 72 points in 1 inch.

point-and-shoot camera. A camera that automatically adjusts settings, such as focus, exposure, and shutter speed.

pop-up ad. An online advertisement within a small window that displays (pops up) over a browser window.

Portable Document Format (PDF). An electronic file format created by Adobe Systems that captures text, fonts, graphics, and even the formatting of a document, so that it appears on any computer screen (Mac or PC) exactly as it does on the original composition software. Viewing a PDF file requires Adobe Reader, a free downloadable program from Adobe Systems.

postmortem. Term for an analysis or review of a publication after distribution.

press release. A news announcement that is distributed to media outlets.

primary audience. A publication's main (target) group of readers. See also *secondary audience.*

process color. A method of color reproduction in which four primary ink colors (cyan, magenta, yellow, and black) are mixed in varying proportions to create all other colors. Since process color requires four printing plates and four runs of paper through the press, it is more expensive than *spot color.* Also called *four-color printing.*

production editor. See *layout artist.*

production manager. See *layout artist.*

production schedule. The deadlines for the writing, editing, laying out, printing, and distribution of each newsletter issue.

professional newsletter. A type of newsletter whose purpose is to help professionals and business people keep up with developments in their fields and do their jobs better.

profile. A *feature story* that outlines a person's work, contributions, and personality.

proof. The typeset copy of a publication that is examined for any changes or corrections before the final printing.

proofread. To read over the content of a publication

for errors in spelling, punctuation, capitalization, and the like.

proofreaders' marks. A standard set of symbols used by proofreaders to note changes or corrections in a manuscript.

proportional typeface. A typeface in which a varying amount of horizontal space is allotted to each *character,* depending on its shape. See also *monospace typeface.*

publication schedule. The frequency and day/date on which a publication is produced and distributed.

publisher. The person at a publication who oversees the entire operation. At some publications, the publisher may also be the *editor.* Also, the business entity that edits, produces, markets, and otherwise makes a publication available.

pull quote. An eye-catching phrase or sentence extracted from the main text of an article, set in display type (often inside a box), and placed within or alongside the article itself. Pull quotes are designed to pique interest in the entire article. Also called a *display quote.*

ragged right. See *left justified.*

rate card. A card specifically designed to answer common questions of advertisers. It contains information such as the publication's circulation and reader demographics, as well as production requirements, deadlines, and prices for ads.

ream. A quantity of paper, usually 500 sheets.

registration. Correct positioning of printing relative to the edge of the page, and to other elements on the page, such as colors, letters, and/or *rules.*

regular type. See *Roman type.*

response list. A mailing list containing the names of people who have already responded to a *direct mail* solicitation. Response lists typically draw more customers than *compiled lists,* so they cost more to rent.

response rate. Percentage of people who respond to a *direct mail* campaign or other promotion.

reversed type. Type that appears as white (or the color of the underlying paper) and is surrounded by a block of black or colored ink.

rights. The entitlement to reproduce, adapt, distribute, perform, or display a contributor's work. When a *publisher* accepts material for publication, he purchases some or all of these rights, based on the agreement with the contributor.

Roman type. The most common style of type in which the *characters* have vertical stems, rather than the slanted stems of italic type. Also called *regular type* or *plain type.*

rule. A line used as a graphic element, often to separate or organize copy.

saddle stitch. A binding method in which folded sheets are stapled along the outside of the fold.

sans serif type. A typeface that lacks *serifs.*

second person. Writing style in which the writer addresses the reader directly though use of the pronoun "you." It is commonly used in how-to articles, which provide advice or information.

secondary audience. A group of people who have an interest in reading a publication, but are not part of its *primary audience.*

sentence caps. A style used for *display type* in which only the first letter of the first word (plus the first letter of any proper nouns) is capitalized. See also *all caps* and *initial caps.*

serif. The small lines that appear at the top or bottom of a *character's* main stroke.

shells. Preprinted pages produced in large quantities that contain a publication's standing color elements. When folded, each sheet forms the front and back pages of each issue. The black text and graphics are printed on the shells during the production of each issue.

sidebar. A short boxed article that accompanies a main article and provides supplementary information, such as helpful hints, a list of resources, or a summary of the article's main points. Sidebars are placed near the main article.

single-lens reflex camera. A camera that enables the photographer to see through the lens while looking in the viewfinder. This is done by means of a mirror behind the lens, and a prism above the mirror and in front of the viewfinder. Single-lens reflex cameras give the photographer the choice of manually selecting focus and exposure settings or having them set automatically.

skimming aids. The *headline, subheads, pull quote, captions,* and other eye-catching elements of an article that readers "skim" over. Typically set in larger type and a different font from that used in the body of the article, skimming aids pique reader interest. From a visual point of view, they make pages more organized, attractive, and accessible.

slant. A writer's particular approach or manner in presenting the information in an article or story. Also called an *angle.*

spam. Junk e-mail.

spot color. A method of color reproduction in which a second or third color (in addition to black) is used in areas or "spots" on the page, such as *subheads, rules,* or boxes. Spot colors are printed as solid areas, using premixed inks. Also called *two-color printing.*

spread. The two facing pages of a publication.

Standard Mail. A discounted class of mail service offered by the US Postal Service that requires preparation and sorting of the mailpieces by the customer. It is commonly used for mailings of at least 200 pieces that do not require expedited delivery.

standing head. See *kicker.*

startup cost. The expense incurred for new equipment, supplies, and/or services at the outset of a publication's operation. See also *fixed cost* and *per-issue cost.*

stock photography. Professionally shot pictures that are available for purchase or rent.

stock. The type of paper used for printing.

style. A set of conventions adopted by a publication pertaining to spelling, punctuation, capitalization, typography, word use, and other details. Also, a set of formatting instructions in page-layout software that the user specifies for text elements, such as *headlines, body text,* and *subheads.*

style guide. A commercially published or internally produced book that describes a set of conventions pertaining to spelling, punctuation, capitalization, typography, word use, and other details. *The Associated Press Stylebook and Briefing on Media Law* and *The Chicago Manual of Style* are style guide examples.

subhead. A short heading that appears between two paragraphs of an article.

subscription newsletter. A newsletter that is distributed upon request for a fee. See also *nonsubscription newsletter.*

syndicated newsletter. A newsletter (usually marketing) that is produced by a company that sells it to businesses or professionals, who, in turn, distribute it to their customers and clients. Also called a *franchised newsletter.*

tabloid. A newsletter or newspaper in which each page measures 11 x 17 inches.

tagline. A brief line of text, usually appearing in a newsletter's *nameplate,* that summarizes its audience and purpose.

teaser. See *kicker.*

template. A computer file that serves as a pattern for the layout of newsletter issues. Templates contain the *nameplate, masthead, folios,* and other standing items, as well as preformatted columns, styles, and colors.

text editor. A program for creating and modifying text files that allows very little or no formatting of the text.

text e-mail newsletter. A newsletter that is distributed via e-mail and contains plain *ASCII* text and no graphics.

third person. The most distant of all writing forms. In this type of writing, "he," "she," and "they" are the pronouns used. Third-person writing is generally used in objective articles such as *news stories* and *feature articles,* and is sometimes used in profile pieces as well. It is appropriate when the writer is trying to present important information or show an unbiased front.

tight registration. A design element that requires exact alignment of two or more colors on a page, such as a colored box with a black outline.

tone. The mood or tenor of a newsletter, conveyed through its writing style and physical design. Formal, informal, cost-conscious, and upscale tones are examples.

trademark. An officially registered name, phrase, or symbol that distinguishes the goods or services of one manufacturer or service provider from another's. Registering a newsletter name as a trademark gives the publisher certain advantages in the event of a legal dispute over its use.

two-color printing. See *spot color.*

type style. Characteristics of a *typeface,* such as bold, italics, *Roman,* or *condensed.*

typeface. The complete set of *characters* of a single design. Times New Roman, Helvetica, and Garamond are typeface examples. See also *font.*

typography. The arrangement and appearance of type.

UBIT. See *Unrelated Business Income Tax.*

Unrelated Business Income Tax (UBIT). A tax levied on income of nonprofit organizations that is earned from trades or businesses unrelated to their missions.

volume number. A number that represents how many years the publication has been in existence. It usually appears in a newsletter's *nameplate,* but may also appear in the *masthead.* See also *issue number.*

web newsletter. A newsletter that appears as a set of pages on a website. Publishers usually distribute an e-mail notice to subscribers of web newsletters, informing them when a new issue is posted.

white space. Areas of a page that contain no text or graphics. White space causes the eye to focus on the text and surrounding graphics and gives pages an uncluttered look. It also helps organize material—items with a little white space between them appear to go together, while those with more white space appear separate.

widow. A short last line of a paragraph that appears at the top of a page or column. Also refers to a single word or syllable on the last line of a paragraph.

word count. The number of words in an article, not including the *headline* or *byline.*

work for hire. A legal doctrine giving the company or employer ownership of any work that is produced or prepared by employees within the scope of their job—unless an agreement has been signed to the contrary.

zine. See *e-zine.*

$\mathcal{W}$ORKSHEETS

For your convenience, blank forms of the worksheets used in this book appear on the following pages. You can make photocopies of the forms and fill them in with the specific details of your publication, or use them as guides for creating forms of your own.

- Newsletter Planning Worksheet, 316–317
- Budget Worksheet, 318–319
- Article Tracking Log, 320
- Printing Quote Form, 321

A completed sample of the Newsletter Planning Worksheet is found on pages 26 and 27, the Budget Worksheet is on pages 56 and 57, the Article Tracking Log appears on page 82, and the Printing Quote Form is found on page 239.

1. What are the purposes of your newsletter?

___ Inform about _____

___ Motivate to:

    ___ volunteer   ___ donate   ___ join or renew membership

    ___ attend meetings   ___ participate in activities

___ Improve organization's image

___ Build community interaction and involvement

___ Persuade of a political, religious, or moral view

___ Thank donors, volunteers, and customers

___ Solicit media coverage

___ Coordinate procedures among offices

___ Reduce number of mailings

___ Other: _____

2. Write a purpose statement for your newsletter (25 to 40 words).

_____

_____

_____

_____

_____

3. Who is your primary audience?

Demographics:

Age _____

Sex   ___ M   ___ F

Race _____

Ethnic group_____

Religion _____

Geographic location _____

Income level_____

Disability status _____

Educational level:

___ Some high school   ___ High school graduate

___ Some college   ___ Bachelor's degree

___ Master's degree   ___ Doctoral degree

Familiarity with topic:

___ High   ___ Medium   ___ Low

Interest, motivation to read your newsletter:

___ High   ___ Medium   ___ Low

Familiarity with organization:

___ High   ___ Medium   ___ Low

4. Can you identify any secondary audiences for your newsletter?

_____

_____

_____

_____

_____

_____

_____

_____

_____

5. What is the appropriate tone(s) for your newsletter?

___ Conservative   ___ Stylish   ___ Cost conscious   ___ Upscale   ___ Casual   ___ Formal

6. What is the appropriate editorial posture for your newsletter?

___ Advocating   ___ Objective   ___ Predicting   ___ Personal

	Itemized Amount	Total Annual Amount
PROJECTED INCOME		
Subscription revenue		
Advertising (per issue)		
Advertising total for year		
TOTAL ANNUAL INCOME		
PROJECTED EXPENSES		
STARTUP COSTS		
Equipment:		
Services:		
Total Startup Cost		
Total Annual Startup Cost		

	Itemized Amount	Total Annual Amount
PER-ISSUE COSTS		
Total Per-Issue Cost		
Total Annual Per-Issue Cost		
FIXED COSTS		
Total Fixed Costs		
Total Annual Fixed Costs		
TOTAL ANNUAL EXPENSES (includes startup, per-issue, and fixed costs)		
PROJECTED PROFIT		
Total Annual Income		
minus Total Annual Expenses		
equals Total Annual Profit		

Article Tracking Log

Article	Writer & Contact Info	Word count	Assigned? Date	Received? Date	Edited? Date	Placed in layout?
			❏	❏	❏	❏
			❏	❏	❏	❏
			❏	❏	❏	❏
			❏	❏	❏	❏
			❏	❏	❏	❏
			❏	❏	❏	❏
			❏	❏	❏	❏
			❏	❏	❏	❏
			❏	❏	❏	❏

Printing Quote Form

PRINTER

Name: _____   Contact: _____

Phone: _____   E-mail: _____

CUSTOMER

Newsletter: _____   Editor: _____

Phone: _____   E-mail: _____

DETAILS

QUANTITY

Pages per issue: _____   Issues per year: _____   Copies per issue: _____

PAPER STOCK

Grade: _____   Weight: _____   Color: _____   Finish: _____   Brightness: _____

Brand: _____   Trim size: _____

INK COLOR

____ Black

____ Spot PMS # _____   PMS # _____

____ 4-color process (CMYK)

____ 4-color process + spot / PMS # _____

____ Shells / Quantity: _____

PHOTOS

____ Scan / Quantity: _____

PROOFS REQUIRED

____ Laser   ____ Color key   ____ Blueline   ____ Digital   ____ Matchprint   ____ Press proof   ____ Contact

BINDERY REQUIREMENTS

____ Fold: _____   ____ Collate   ____ Saddle stitch   ____ 3-hole drill

SHIPPING

____ Deliver to mail house _____
                                                (address)

____ Deliver to customer _____
                                                (address)

____ Customer to pick up

____ Other _____

PRICE QUOTE

Price per issue: $ _____   Turnaround time required: _____

Payment terms: _____

RESOURCES

Many fine books, periodicals, and websites offer valuable insights into the world of newsletter publishing. The entries listed here provide helpful guidelines on a variety of different subjects—writing effective articles; designing visually appealing page layouts; understanding copyright laws; developing budgetary, technical, and management skills; and much more—for producing high-quality newsletters and for familiarizing yourself with the ins and outs of the newsletter industry. In addition, you will find a number of groups and organizations that can offer helpful information and support. A variety of seminars, workshops, and training courses to further hone your skills as a newsletter publisher rounds out this list of resources.

BOOKS

The Associated Press Guide to News Writing, 3rd edition
Rene J. Cappon. Lawrenceville, NJ: Arco, 2000.
In this book, long-time Associated Press editor Rene "Jack" Cappon gives reporters and other writers advice on writing news and feature stories that are compelling and accurate. Eliminating subtle bias, avoiding the "anemia of abstractions," and writing precise leads are among the topics discussed. One of the strongest chapters—"Quotes: Your Words or Mine?"—illustrates the author's sense of humor that makes this book such a pleasurable read.

The Associated Press Stylebook and Briefing on Media Law

Norm Goldstein, editor. New York: Perseus Books, 2002.

Many newsletter editors use this book as their style guide. It provides useful facts and references as well as information on usage, grammar, and spelling. Separate sections discuss writing for the Internet and writing about sports and business. The briefing on media law covers issues of copyright and libel.

The Chicago Manual of Style: The Essential Guide for Writers, Editors, and Publishers, 15th edition

Chicago: University of Chicago Press, 2003.

This reference offers guidelines for writers, editors, publishers, copywriters, proofreaders, indexers, and everyone in between. Information is provided on all aspects of word usage and style, from how to properly number the pages of a book to how to use a hyphen. While this book focuses on book publishing, some newsletter editors use it as their style guide, particularly if they write for scholarly audiences. This edition includes sections on electronic publishing.

Community Sourcebook of ZIP Code Demographics, 19th edition

Vienna, VA: ESRI Press, 2005.

If you are doing audience research, you may want to consult this book, which provides, by state and ZIP code, data on the likelihood of consumer spending for financial services, home products, entertainment, and personal items.

The Copyright Permission and Libel Handbook: A Step-By-Step Guide for Writers, Editors, and Publishers

Lloyd J. Jassin and Steven C. Schechter. New York: John Wiley & Sons, 1998.

Written by publishing attorneys, this guide explains copyright and libel law in straightforward, jargon-free language. The summary checklists and examples help explain the complicated, often tedious laws.

The Elements of Style, 4th edition

William Strunk and E.B. White. New York: Allyn & Bacon, 2000.

Long considered a classic book on grammar and style issues, *The Elements of Style* covers elementary rules of usage and basic principles of composition, provides a look at commonly misused words and expressions, and presents tips on refining your writing style. This reference is a must for every writer.

Encyclopedia of Associations

Kimberly N. Hunt, editor. Farmington Hills, MI: Gale Group, updated annually.

This directory of international, national, regional, state, and local nonprofit organizations can help you find your newsletter's audience, as well as locate experts and information sources. Description, contact information, size, publications, sponsored meetings and conventions, and membership fees are among the items reported for each of 23,000 associations.

Encyclopedia of Business Information Sources

James Woy, editor. Farmington Hills, MI: Gale Group, updated annually.

In this book you can look for an entry that defines your newsletter's subject area—personal finance, or the plastics industry, for instance—and find a list of directories, abstracts, indexes, statistics sources, databases, and more, that you can use to research your audience. You might also find the listing for "newsletters" helpful in locating publishing resources.

Essentials of English Grammar, 2nd edition

L. Sue Baugh. Lincolnwood, IL: Passport Books, 1993.

This book serves not only as a handy reference to parts of speech and punctuation, but also gives advice on constructing sentences, writing concisely, dividing and hyphenating words, and using gender-inclusive language. The appendices include lists of frequently confused and misspelled words, as well as proper verb-preposition combinations.

Getting Permission: How to License & Clear Copyrighted Materials Online & Off, 2nd edition

Richard Stim. Berkeley, CA: Nolo Press, 2004.

Written by an intellectual property lawyer, this book guides writers through the gray areas of copyright law. The author explains the law, discusses ambiguities such as public domain, and provides information on tracking copyright holders and writing permission letters. The book comes in both print and digital (Adobe Reader) forms.

How to Do Leaflets, Newsletters & Newspapers

Nancy Brigham. Cincinnati, OH: Writer's Digest Books, 1991.

If you produce an issues-oriented advocacy newsletter, this is the book for you. The author draws on her public relations and editorial experience with labor unions and alternative newspapers to cover virtually every aspect of newsletter publishing. Some of the book's information on layout and production is dated, but the chapters on research, writing, editing, and photography are still pertinent.

Hudson's Subscription Newsletter Directory

Howard Penn Hudson, editor. Rhinebeck, NY: Newsletter Clearinghouse, updated annually.

This directory provides listings of all the subscription newsletters published in the United States. If you are thinking about starting your own newsletter, this directory will give you a good idea of the publications that are already out there.

Kirsch's Handbook of Publishing Law: For Authors, Publishers, Editors and Agents, 2nd edition

Jonathan Kirsch. Los Angeles: Acrobat Books, 2006.

Written by an attorney, this manual covers legal issues relevant to writers, publishers, editors, and agents. All discussions are written in easy-to-understand language, and are accompanied by helpful examples and sample forms.

Newsletter Sourcebook, 2nd edition

Mark Beach and Elaine Floyd. Cincinnati: Writer's Digest Books, 1998.

This richly illustrated book, filled with color illustrations of print and online newsletters, shows how to create successful newsletters through creative design of pages, type, nameplates, graphics, and other elements.

Newsletters in Print

Farmington Hills, MI: Gale Group, updated annually.

This directory lists 11,000 newsletters published in the United States and Canada that are readily available to the public. Contact information, description, publication frequency, advertising policy, size, price, and audience are among the data reported.

The Non-Designer's Design Book: Design and Typographic Principles for the Visual Novice, 2nd edition

Robin Williams. Berkeley, CA: Peachpit Press, 2003.

This classic book is aimed at those without a background in graphic design. Using simple, clear illustrations, the author demonstrates how to achieve each of four characteristics of good graphic design: proximity, alignment, repetition, and contrast. She then discusses the categories of type and helps readers understand which typefaces work well together. The book includes quizzes along the way to help readers check their understanding of the material.

The Non-Designer's Web Book, 3rd edition

Robin Williams and John Tollett. Berkeley, CA: Peachpit Press, 2005.

This book extends the principles set out for print publications in *The Non-Designer's Design Book* to the Internet. It is primarily devoted to web design topics like navigation, color, typography, and the use of graphics, but the authors also help new web designers get started by explaining the workings of everything from modems to browsers to plug-ins. Testing, fixing, uploading, and registering websites are also covered.

Oxbridge Directory of Newsletters

New York: Oxbridge Communications, updated annually.

This directory, available in print and on CD-ROM, lists over 20,000 newsletters, loose-leaf publications, bulletins, and fax letters. Oxbridge also offers subscriptions to Mediafinder, an online database of print media in the United States and Canada. Limited searching of Mediafinder is available free on the company's website.

Poor Richard's E-Mail Publishing

Chris Pirillo. Lakewood, CO: Top Floor Publishing, 1999.

Chris Pirillo, publisher of the Lockergnome electronic newsletters, provides a guide to creating newsletters, bulletins, discussion groups, and other e-mail communication tools. After starting with e-mail basics, he moves on to topics like communicating without spamming, managing subscriptions, working with both text and HTML e-mail newsletters, and finding list-hosting services. Rounding out the book are a number of articles of advice from e-mail publishers and an extensive list of resources.

Publishing Newsletters, 3rd edition

Howard Penn Hudson. Rhinebeck, NY: H & M Publishers, 1998.

This book is an essential guide for editors and owners of for-profit print newsletters. It contains comprehensive chapters on finding markets for newsletter publications, and on obtaining and keeping subscribers.

Quick Service Guide. Publication 95.

Washington, DC: US Postal Service, January 2001.

If you distribute your newsletter by mail, contact your local post office to receive a free copy of this publication. Based on the Domestic Mail Manual, it describes eligibility, rates, addressing standards, and preparation and sorting requirements for First Class, Standard, and Periodicals mail. It also includes a guide to the Postal Service's Internet resources. Also ask about the wealth of other information available at no charge, such as a glossary of postal terms, and templates and booklets for designing mailpieces.

Standard Periodical Directory

New York: Oxbridge Communications, updated annually.

Available in both print and CD-ROM versions, this directory includes information on a variety of periodical publishers in the United States and Canada. Its companion website *www.mediafinder.com* offers additional information and updates, and includes both a free and fee-based search feature.

Starting and Running a Successful Newsletter or Magazine, 4th edition

Cheryl Woodard. Berkeley, CA: Nolo Press, 2004.

Written by Cheryl Woodard, a consultant to newsletter and magazine publishers and founder of several computer magazines, this book is a valuable resource for newsletter managers and owners. It covers business-oriented topics such as researching an audience, developing a circulation strategy, starting ancillary products, managing employees, working with investors, and developing an Internet publishing strategy. Numerous examples from real-life start-up publications bring the information to life. Woodard's website *www.publishingbiz.com* offers additional resources.

Ulrich's Periodical Directory

New Providence, NJ: RR Bowker, updated annually.

Published in five volumes with an Internet update option, *Ulrich's* includes nearly 250,000 entries. Each edition contains contact information for publishers from 200 countries; information about online and CD-ROM serials; listings for 7,000 United States newspapers; and more. Divided into different media categories, Ulrich's information is comprehensive, but not always up to date. Therefore, be sure to check the contact information by other means when possible. Ulrich's website (*www.ulrichsweb.com*) offers a fee-based search and indexing service.

The Ultimate Guide to Newsletter Publishing

Patricia M. Wysocki. Arlington, VA:
Newsletter & Electronic Publishers Association,
1999.

This book, which is written by the executive director of the Newsletter & Electronic Publishers Association, emphasizes the business side of starting and running a successful newsletter. It offers valuable information on subjects ranging from evaluating the competition to gathering news to selling newsletter properties. It also includes profiles of a number of for-profit newsletter publishers.

Writer's Market

Kathryn S. Brogan, Editor. Cincinnati: Writer's
Digest Books, updated annually.

This book is a guide to publications that accept freelance submissions. While most of the listings are for book publishers, magazines, and trade journals, a chapter entitled "How Much Should I Charge?" provides estimates of the amount of time required for newsletter writing, editing, and layout, as well as the range of hourly rates commonly charged for these tasks.

PERIODICALS

Before & After: How to Design Cool Stuff

323 Lincoln Street
Roseville, CA 95678-2229
Phone: 916-784-3880 (voice mail)
Website: www.pagelab.com

Each issue of this four-color newsletter provides beautifully illustrated, easy-to-follow step-by-step instructions on "how to design cool stuff," including newsletters. In addition to subscribing, consider buying back issues of this magazine, so you can pick and choose those that contain articles on newsletter design.

Copy Editor

McMurry Campus Center
1010 East Missouri Avenue
Phoenix, AZ 85014
Phone: 888-626-8779
Website: www.copyeditor.com

Copy Editor offers "language news for the publishing profession," including articles on controversial usage questions, reviews of dictionaries and style guides, and a column that defines recently identified words by the *Oxford English Dictionary*. A must for copyeditors who want to keep current on language trends.

Corporate Writer & Editor

Ragan Communications
111 East Wacker Drive, Suite 500
Chicago, IL 60601
Phone: 800-493-4867
         312-960-4100
Website: www.ragan.com

This monthly newsletter covers writing, editing, layout, format, and design issues from the perspective of those who write and edit company newsletters. Interesting topics have included editing the boss's work, negotiating the approval process, and choosing between print and online distribution. Each issue showcases a real-life corporate publication and analyzes why it works.

Dynamic Graphics

Jupiter Images
600 North Forest Park Drive
Peoria, IL 61614
Phone: 888-698-8542
Website: www.dynamicgraphics.com

This bimonthly magazine covers all aspects of graphic design with emphasis on both inspiration and technique. Regular features on trends and media (print, web, packaging) share space with how-to instruction for popular software packages. Content is available in both print and online editions.

The Editorial Eye

EEI Communications
66 Canal Center Plaza, Suite 200
Alexandria, VA 22314
Phone: 703-683-0683
Website: www.eeicommunications.com/eye

As its title implies, this twelve-page monthly newsletter covers issues of language and usage. It also illuminates the broader workings of the publishing industry with articles on topics such as how to manage a telecommuter and who is financially responsible for changes that are found *after* a publication goes to print. It can also help you negotiate publishing-related questions about technology, such as how to catch errors in Internet addresses and use online graphics.

First Draft

Ragan Communications
111 East Wacker Drive, Suite 500
Chicago, IL 60601
Phone: 800-493-4867
        312-960-4100
Website: www.ragan.com

This monthly newsletter offers filler articles on health, consumer, business, technology, and safety topics. Paid subscribers are authorized to copy and paste the online articles into their own newsletters. *First Draft* also offers reprintable quotes, statistics, anecdotes, jokes, and calendars.

The Newsletter on Newsletters

20 West Chestnut Street
PO Box 348
Rhinebeck, NY 12572
Phone: 845-876-5222
Website: www.newsletterbiz.com

This newsletter is published twice a month for publishers of print and online newsletters. It offers news on the newsletter publishing industry, as well as tips and techniques for marketing newsletters, hiring staff, writing and designing, and managing finances. The newsletter also sponsors an annual Newsletter Awards Competition.

WEBSITES

101 Newsletter Answers

Website: www.101newsletteranswers.com

Former newsletter editor Mike Alexander offers a free e-mail newsletter focusing on newsletter content and usage for small or home-based businesses. He also offers free customizable theme newsletters on health, small business, and home and family. If you want to publish your own e-mail newsletter on one of these topics, you can insert your own articles into the ones on this site, and eliminate most of the work of writing and editing an original publication.

About.com

Website: www.about.com

This site helps you use the Internet more efficiently by having an expert sift through available web pages and recommend only those of high quality. Of the dozens of experts available on About.com, newsletter publishers will be most interested in those who cover publishing, graphic design, web design, desktop publishing, and photography. You can access the recommended pages by visiting *http://publishing.about.com; http://desk top pub.about.com; http://graphic design.about.com; http://web design.about.com;* and/or *http://photography.about.com.* Most of these sites also offer free e-mail newsletters.

Adobe Systems

Website: www.adobe.com

This is the site where you and your readers can download the free Adobe Reader software that is required for opening PDF documents. At another Adobe site, *www.createpdf.com*, you can subscribe to a service that lets you convert files to PDF right on the Internet. Free trial conversions are also available.

American List Counsel

Website: www.amlist.com

The website of the American List Counsel, a mailing list manager and broker, lets you browse hundreds of data card lists for an idea of your potential markets.

American Society of Media Photographers (ASMP)

Website: www.asmp.org

ASMP is a trade organization of photojournalists. At this website, you are able to search through its directory of members to locate a newsletter photographer in your area.

Bartleby.com

Website: www.bartleby.com

This site enables you to use online reference books. Type in a word and find a dictionary, encyclopedia, or links to both *Bartlett's Familiar Quotations* and *Simpson's Contemporary Quotations*. Plus, an extensive section with links to classic reference manuals answers your questions on usage.

BCL Technologies

Website: www.gobcl.com

BCL Technologies makes "plug-ins" (supplementary software) for Adobe Acrobat. Registering on its website allows you to convert your newsletter to a PDF file, without having to download or purchase any software.

Brownstone Publishers

Website: www.brownstone.com

Brownstone publishes plain-English newsletters for managers in health administration, education, real estate, and construction. If you are interested in browsing through some samples of professional newsletters, visit this site, where several are available as PDF files.

Chuck Green's Ideabook

Website: www.ideabook.com

You can browse this site for articles on graphic design and production by Chuck Green, the well-known author of *The Desktop Publisher's Idea Book*. Visit the site's Design Store, where you will find clip art, books on graphic design and production, and various templates for Adobe PageMaker publications, including newsletters.

ClipCopy Newsletter Content

Website: www.clipcopy.com

ClipCopy, sponsored by Mike Alexander of 101news letteranswers.com, offers articles, quotations, crosswords, and jokes that you can use as filler for your newsletter. Members can search the database and copy and paste articles into their newsletters.

Copyright Clearance Center Content Exchange

Website: www.copyright.com

The Copyright Clearance Center manages the reprint rights for over 1.75 million works. On this site, you can request permission to reprint the works they manage, and also set up a system for granting permission (and earning royalties) for publication of your newsletter's content by others.

Dictionary.com

Website: www.dictionary.com

If you have a quick spelling, definition, or grammar question, this site is likely to have the answer. Offering writing resources such as grammar guides, dictionaries in several languages, a language discussion forum, a language translator, and a quick search option for both dictionary and thesaurus questions, Dictionary.com is a one-stop shop for all your language needs.

Direct Marketing Association (DMA)

Website: www.the-dma.org

This trade association for direct marketing users and suppliers maintains a directory of members on its website. You can search it for list brokers and compilers, marketing consultants, and other direct marketing companies in your geographic area.

Edith Roman Online

Website: www.edithroman.com

Edith Roman Associates offers list brokerage, management, and consulting services. The company's website has a searchable database, which can help you locate available mailing lists of your newsletter's audience. It also has helpful articles about direct marketing, as well as online calculators to help you determine the cost-effectiveness of running a direct mail promotion for your newsletter.

Email Universe

Website: www.emailuniverse.com

Email newsletter publishers should visit this site to subscribe to its daily or weekly newsletter, and to peruse its archived articles on content, formatting, list management, promotion, and revenue generation.

FedStats

Website: www.fedstats.gov

For anyone working on a project that requires statistical backup, this site is the place to go. FedStats offers statistics from over a hundred United States agencies, searchable by topic or agency name.

Getty Images Creative

Website: http://creative.gettyimages.com

Visitors to this site can search and download images from a number of collections of stock photography and clip art. An advanced search feature lets you select images based on characteristics, such as black and white or color, horizontal or vertical, and royalty-free or rights-managed.

Google

Website: www.google.com

I find that this powerful search engine produces the most complete results because it searches PDF files that are posted on the Internet, as well as the usual HTML web pages. Use it to research your articles or to find examples of web, PDF, or e-mail newsletters.

How Stuff Works

Website: www.howstuffworks.com

This site explains in simple terms the workings of just about everything from laser beams to jet engines. Newsletter publishers may be interested in articles on such subjects as digital cameras, copyrights and patents, web pages, Internet advertising, computers, and offset printing.

Inetmedia

Website: www.markovits.com/journalism

The Journalistic Resources page of Inetmedia's website includes links to schools, organizations, and other sites of interest to journalists. Based in Sweden, this website provides a number of international resources that could be helpful in locating writers abroad.

Internal Revenue Service (IRS)

Website: www.irs.gov

If you need tax forms or publications, you can get them from this website. Newsletter publishers will also be interested in the information on tax regulations for independent contractors, on the Unrelated Business Income Tax (UBIT), and on the extent of political advocacy activities allowed for various categories of nonprofit organizations.

Internet News Bureau (INB)

Website: www.internetnewsbureau.com

Designed for businesses and journalists, INB offers morning e-mails of relevant press releases to anyone who signs up for the service. Much like PR Web, INB provides writers with story leads and informs them of experts in a given field.

Internet PR Guide

Website: www.internetprguide.com

Among the resources available on this site sponsored by INT Media Group are lists of links to clipping services, media guides, and wire services, as well as PR tips and archived articles from PR Insight.

Internet Public Library

Website: www.ipl.org

The Reference section of this site models itself after a traditional library, with links organized into subject categories, such as sciences and technology, arts and humanities, and business. In addition, the site offers links to online texts, magazines, and newspapers, as well as a guide to Internet search engines.

InterNIC

Website: www.internic.net

Affiliated with the nonprofit Internet Corporation for Assigned Names and Numbers, InterNIC maintains a list of accredited registrars of Internet domain names, as well as answers to frequently asked questions about the process of registering a domain name.

Juno Internet Services

Website: www.juno.com

If you publish an e-mail newsletter and you want to test it in more than one e-mail program, sign up for a free e-mail account at this site.

List-Resources.com

Website: http://list-resources.com

If you are starting any type of online newsletter and need help creating and maintaining lists, you'll want to visit this site. Here, you'll find directories of list-hosting services and list software. You can also subscribe to a number of free e-mail newsletters on online newsletter publishing.

Merriam-Webster OnLine

Website: www.m-w.com

Here you can look up word definitions or synonyms in an online version of the *Merriam-Webster Collegiate Dictionary* or *Collegiate Thesaurus*. For proofreaders' marks, go to www.m-w.com/mw/table/proofrea.htm.

NewEntrepreneur.com

Website: www.newentrepreneur.com

This is the website of Roger C. Parker, whose books on desktop publishing for laypeople helped spark the newsletter-publishing boom of the 1980s and 1990s. While the focus of his recent writings has moved away from graphic design, you can still find articles pertaining to newsletter publishing on this website, as well as information about his books. Titles of interest to newsletter publishers include *Desktop Publishing and Design for Dummies, Looking Good in Print,* and *The One-Minute Designer.*

Newsletter Strategy Session

Website: www.nwsltr.com

On this site, newsletter developer David M. Freedman offers a collection of resources for publishers of non-commercial newsletters. It includes articles on newsletter publishing, reviews of books about newsletter publishing, and links to online reference works and newsletter directories.

NewslettersOnline

Website: www.newslettersonline.com

This site helps newsletter publishers convert printed publications to HTML or PDF, post them online, and employ online subscriptions or pay-per-view access.

Newswise

Website: www.newswise.com

Newswise maintains a comprehensive database of news releases from institutions engaged in scientific, medical, liberal arts, and business research. You can search, browse, or download any article or abstract, and you can locate experts to serve as interview subjects.

Nolo

Website: www.nolo.com

In addition to selling law books for laypeople, this site contains a wealth of free legal information. Its Plain English Law Center offers articles on trademarks, copyrights, and starting a small business; a legal dictionary; and a small-business loan calculator.

PDFZone.com

Website: www.pdfzone.com

PDFZone offers tips, answers to frequently asked questions, lists of software, discussion groups, and an electronic newsletter for those who create PDF files.

Planet PDF

Website: www.planetpdf.com

This is a helpful site for those who create PDF files. It offers informative articles, a list of software, a forum for information exchange, product reviews, and more.

PR Web Press Release Newswire

Website: www.prweb.com

This site offers recent press releases organized by industry. The service is available in Spanish and English.

ProfNet Experts

Website: www2.profnet.com

A service of PR Newswire, ProfNet provides writers with access to expert sources. You can fill out an online form with information on the type of expert you are seeking, and the staff will connect you with qualified experts.

Proofread.com

Website: www.proofread.com

Writers as well as proofreaders can benefit from a visit to this handy site. Included are a list of proofreaders' marks, an interactive writing workbook, and definitions of foreign phrases.

PS to PDF converter

Website: www.ps2pdf.com

If you create PDF files only occasionally, you might want to use this site to convert page-layout files without purchasing conversion software. The page of frequently asked questions provides step-by-step instructions for the procedure.

PubList

Website: www.publist.com

This site offers a free, searchable online directory of over 150,000 print and online magazines, journals, newsletters, and other periodicals.

The Rainwater Press Publishing Primer

Website: www.rainwater.com/glossary.html

This glossary of electronic publishing, graphic arts, and printing terms includes over 1,000 entries.

Search Engine Guide

Website: www.searchengineguide.com

Divided into four main areas, this site includes a directory of Internet search engines, search engine news, search engine marketing, and search engine books and services. It offers free online newsletters on the best methods for getting your site listed on search engines.

Search Engine Watch

Website: www.searchenginewatch.com

This site offers a number of articles on how to make sure potential subscribers to your newsletter find your website when using a search engine. It also offers both free and paid e-mail newsletters on the topic.

Topica

Website: www.topica.com

Topica offers free list hosting for publishers of online newsletters as well as paid services for those with more sophisticated needs. From this site, you can also search for and subscribe to any of the hundreds of free e-mail newsletters they host.

US Census Bureau

Website: www.census.gov

If you need census data, this site, which offers dozens of avenues for accessing data from the US Census Bureau, is for you. The handy State and County Quick-Facts feature provides a fast way to find basic demographic and economic data about your area of interest.

US Department of Labor

Website: www.dol.gov

On its website, the Department of Labor maintains a Small Business Regulatory Compliance Assistance page that can answer your questions about labor laws and regulations. You can also search the site for information on regulations for independent contractors.

US Patent and Trademark Office

Website: www.uspto.gov

If you are interested in applying for a trademark of your newsletter's name, or if you want to check for existing trademarks for your proposed name, visit this site. Here you can search the agency's trademark records and read basic facts about applying for a trademark.

US Postal Service

Website: www.usps.gov

On this website of the US Postal Service, you can calculate postage on items you want to mail, find ZIP codes, and change your address. Of particular interest to newsletter publishers is the Business Mail 101 course, which guides you through the regulations for designing and sorting mailpieces, as well as the Direct Mail Guide in the Small Business Tools section.

Usability.gov

Website: http://usability.gov/guidelines

This site, sponsored by the Office of Communications of the National Cancer Institute, provides guidelines for creating easy-to-use web pages. It covers the full range of usability topics, from determining optimum page length to reducing download times.

UseIt.com

Website: www.useit.com

Visit this site to subscribe to Jakob Nielsen's free e-mail newsletter, *Alertbox,* which provides biweekly information on making websites easy to read and navigate. You'll also find information about books and conferences relating to website usability.

WebWire

Website: www.webwire.com

WebWire provides free press releases, a means by which you can post your research needs, and a free service that lets you customize a home page to display recent releases and news articles of interest to you. Use this site to keep up with current events and trends in your industry.

Webmonkey

Website: www.webmonkey.com

This site, sponsored by Lycos, offers a set of free online tutorials on authoring, design, multimedia, and cascading style sheets for beginning web-page developers. An "HTML Cheatsheet" places the codes for formatting, color, and special characters at your fingertips.

WebScout Lists

Website: www.webscoutlists.com

This is a central site where you can subscribe to (and unsubscribe from) e-mail newsletters and discussion groups in hundreds of subject areas. It offers yet another way to check out the competition for your electronic newsletter.

WriteContent Editorial Services

Website: www.writecontent.com

This site offers a number of valuable links to writing, editing, and publishing resources.

Writers Write

Website: www.writerswrite.com

If you are looking for writers, you can use this site to post a job listing, and to link to schools of journalism that can refer you to students or recent graduates. The site also maintains links to writers' newsletters, conferences, organizations, and more.

Yahoo

Website: www.yahoo.com

In addition to being a well-known site for Internet searches, Yahoo offers free e-mail accounts. If you publish an e-mail newsletter and you want to test it in more than one e-mail program, sign up for a Yahoo account to supplement your primary e-mail service. You can use a related site, YahooGroups (www.yahoogroups.com), as a free list host for your e-mail newsletter. And at Yahoo Alerts (http://alerts.yahoo.com), you can register to receive notices, via e-mail or a mobile device, of news pertaining to topics of interest. You can select the sources you want searched for your news alerts, including press release wires, newspapers, and online publications.

GROUPS AND ORGANIZATIONS

Editorial Freelancers Association (EFA)
71 West 23rd Street, Suite 1910
New York, NY 10010
Phone: 212-929-5400
Website: www.the-efa.org

Founded in 1970, the EFA is a national, not-for-profit, professional organization of self-employed writers, researchers, editors, desktop publishers, and other publishing industry professionals. The group sponsors seminars on topics of interest to publishing professionals. If you have a job opening for a freelancer, you can post it on their website.

International Association of Business Communicators (IABC)
One Hallidie Plaza, Suite 600
San Francisco, CA 94102
Phone: 800-776-4222
            415-544-4700
Website: www.iabc.com

IABC is a professional organization for people working in corporate, employee, or marketing communications; public relations; and other areas. It provides print and online publications, an online member directory, international conferences, seminars, and professional accreditation.

National Press Photographers Association (NPPA)
3200 Croasdaile Drive, Suite 306
Durham, NC 27705
Phone: 919-383-7246
Website: www.nppa.org

Photographers who specialize in photojournalism have the skills best suited to newsletter photography. Contact the NPPA, an association of photojournalists, to find a photographer in your area.

Newsletter & Electronic Publishers Association (NEPA)
1501 Wilson Boulevard, Suite 509
Arlington, VA 22209
Phone: 800-356-9302
Website: www.newsletters.org

Formerly known as the Newsletter Publisher's Association, NEPA is a well-known international nonprofit group whose focus is on serving newsletter and electronic publishers through education, training, and networking. Among its member benefits, which are geared to publishers of for-profit professional newsletters, include a subscription to the bimonthly *Hotline* newsletter, assistance with legal representation and counseling, discounted fees for attendance at conferences and seminars, and access to subscription areas of NEPA's website.

Public Relations Society of America (PRSA)
33 Irving Place
New York, NY 10003-2376
Phone: 212-460-1442
Website: www.prsa.org

PRSA provides professional development classes, publications, job search assistance, and mentoring for public relations professionals. Over 100 local chapters provide opportunities for networking with the local public relations community.

Society of American Business Editors and Writers (SABEW)
Missouri School of Journalism
134 Neff Annex
Columbia, MO 65211-1200
Phone: 573-882-7862
Website: www.sabew.org

SABEW is a professional society for business journalists throughout North America. Benefits of joining this organization include educational opportunities, awards, networking, and a subscription to *The Business Journalist* newsletter.

Society of National Association Publications (SNAP)

8405 Greensboro Drive, #800
McLean VA 22102
Phone: 703-506-3285
Website: www.snaponline.org

SNAP is a nonprofit organization designed to serve the needs of those who create association and society publications. Members receive *Association Publishing*, a bimonthly magazine that covers the ins and outs of the industry. The website offers a calendar of events, conference listings, and a career center to assist both members and nonmembers in finding employees or employers.

Society of Professional Journalists (SPJ)

3909 North Meridian Street
Indianapolis, IN 46208
Phone: 317-927-8000
Website: www.spj.org

Founded in 1909 as Sigma Delta Chi, the SPJ was created to promote the free practice of journalism as well as high ethical standards for journalists. The organization offers a wide array of programs to assist its members in professional development, as well as monetary awards and student fellowship. Members receive a subscription to *The Quill* magazine, access to an online directory of sources and resources, and online publications and discussion boards.

SRDS Media Solutions

1700 Higgins Road
Des Plaines, IL 60018-5605
Phone: 800-851-7737
Website: www.srds.com

Publications of SRDS include *Direct Marketing List Source* (for mailing list rental information), *Lifestyle Market Analyst* (of local, regional, and national audiences), and *International Media Guide* (a directory of consumer and professional magazines in the United States and abroad).

US Copyright Office

Library of Congress
101 Independence Avenue, SE
Washington, DC 20559-6000
Phone: 202-707-9100 (forms and publications)
           202-707-3000 (general information)
Website: www.copyright.gov

Although your work is copyrighted with or without official documentation, if you are still worried that a publishing company might steal your work, the Copyright Office can provide you with legal protection by officially copyrighting your manuscript. You can order the necessary forms over the phone or download them from the website.

US Small Business Administration (SBA)

409 Third Street, SW
Washington, DC 20416
Phone: 800-827-5722
Website: www.sba.gov

The SBA was founded in 1953 to provide financial, technical, and management assistance to small business owners, thus helping owners start, run, and expand their businesses. The SBA website offers a wealth of information on every aspect of starting and operating a small business, as well as data on local SBA offices.

SEMINARS, WORKSHOPS, AND TRAINING COURSES

EEI Communications

66 Canal Center Plaza, Suite 200
Alexandria, VA 22314
Phone: 703-683-0683
Website: www.eeicommunications.com

EEI offers both traditional and online courses on dozens of communications topics, including newsletter publishing, business writing, editing, and design.

nSight

1 Van de Graaff Drive, Suite 202
Burlington, MA 01803
Phone: 781-273-6300
Website: www.nsightworks.com

nSight offers a range of courses for both the print and online publishing industries. Included among the many course topics are newsletter publishing, marketing communications, grammar and word usage, publication design, and editing.

Ragan Communications

111 East Wacker Drive, Suite 500
Chicago, IL 60601
Phone: 800-493-4867
          312-960-4100
Website: www.ragan.com

Ragan Communications sponsors conferences and workshops throughout the United States on topics relating to corporate communications. They also offer telephone seminars for those who are unable to travel.

CREDITS

I would like to gratefully acknowledge the many writers and newsletter publishers who have allowed the following graphics, articles, and sample forms to appear in this book:

Housing Affairs Letter newsletter figure on page 10. Reprinted with permission of CD Publications.

Update newsletter figure on page 11. Reprinted with permission. Karen L. Krause, Editor. American Red Cross, Greater Nashua and Souhegan Valley Chapter, Nashua, NH.

E&P Weekly Briefing newsletter figure on page 12. © 2001 ASM Communications Inc. Used with permission.

Copy Editor newsletter figure on page 13. Vol.13, No. 2. Reprinted with permission of *Copy Editor.*

Résumé Writers' Resource newsletter figure on page 14. Copyright National Résumé Writers' Association, 2001. www.nrwa.com.

Health After 50 newsletter figure on page 15. Reprinted with permission of www.hopkinsafter50.com.

Intellectual Property Bulletin newsletter figure on page 17. Published with the permission of Edwards & Angell, LLP.

Heart Murmurs newsletter figure on page 34. Reprinted with permission. Patricia O'Brien and Julie-Anne Evangelista, Cardiovascular Program, Children's Hospital, Boston, MA.

The May Report newsletter figure on page 34. Reprinted with permission of Ronald May, *The May Report.*

Advocate newsletter figure on page 34. Courtesy of Monadnock Humane Society, West Swanzey, NH. Bert Troughton, editor.

Westlaw Edge newsletter figure on page 34. Source: Westlaw Edge for Associates. Published by the West Group. Reprinted with permission.

deal memo newsletter banner on page 41. Reprinted with permission of Informa Media Group.

Andrew Harper's Hideaway Report newsletter banner on page 41. Reprinted with permission of Harper Associates, Inc.

property manager's protector newsletter banner on page 41. Copyright, Brownstone Publishers, Inc., 149 Fifth Ave., New York, NY 10010-6810. Reprinted with permission. For a free sample issue or to subscribe, call 1-800-643-8095.

Population Council newsletter figure on page 47. Reprinted with the permission of The Population Council from *Population Briefs,* Vol.6, no.3 (September 2000), contents page of Web edition.

Inspired2Write newsletter figure on page 48. Reprinted with permission of Susan J. Letham.

The SitePoint Tribune newsletter figure on page 49. Reprinted with permission. *The SitePoint Tribune* is published bi-weekly by SitePoint Pty Ltd. Subscribe at SitePoint.com. Copyright 1999–2006.

ICES Newsletter figure on page 50. Reprinted with permission of *ICES Newsletter* (www.ices.dk).

Contributor Rights Agreement on page 94. Reprinted with permission from *How to Publish Your Articles* by Shirley Kawa-Jump (Square One Publishers: Garden City Park, NY).

Professional Apartment Management newsletter figure on page 97. Reprinted with permission from the monthly newsletter *Professional Apartment Management,* Dec. 2001. © by Brownstone Publishers Inc., 149 Fifth Ave., New York, NY 10010-6801. To subscribe, call 1-800-643-8095 or visit www.brownstone.com.

The Nor'easter newsletter figure on page 98. © 2000 by the Northern New England Chapter of the Society for Technical Communication. Reprinted with permission.

Professional Apartment Management newsletter figure on page 99. Reprinted with permission from the monthly newsletter *Professional Apartment Management,* Dec. 2001. © by Brownstone Publishers Inc., 149 Fifth Ave., New York, NY 10010-6801. To subscribe, call 1-800-643-8095 or visit www.brownstone.com.

The information on doing research and interviewing in Chapter 6 was adapted from *How to Publish Your Articles* by Shirley Kawa-Jump (Square One Publishers, Garden City Park, NY, 2002).

Sample News Story: "Anti-Terrorism Law Imposes New Rules on Charity Telemarketers" on page 143. Reprinted with permission of the *Chronicle of*

Philanthropy. http://philanthropy.com.

The Ragan Report newsletter figure on page 167. Reprinted from *The Ragan Report*, Lawrence Ragan Communications, Inc.

Campus Journal newsletter figure on page 191. Reprinted with permission of Lori Gula, editor, *Campus Journal.*

at Home newsletter figure on page 191. Courtesy of Public Service of New Hampshire.

Page grid figure on page 192. ©1997 Adobe Systems Incorporated. Used with express permission. All rights reserved. Adobe and PageMaker is/are either (a) registered trademark(s) of Adobe Systems Incorporated in the United States and/or other countries.

SuperPages@work newsletter figure on page 196. Reprinted with permission. Copyright © 2002 Gruner + Jahr USA, publisher of *Inc.* magazine.

Best practices newsletter figure on page 222. Courtesy of The Center for Information-Development Management.

Boston Broadside newsletter figure on page 223. *Boston Broadside, STC Boston Chapter Newsletter,* July/August 1999, pages 4 and 5. Reprinted with permission.

Page grid figure on page 231. ©1997 Adobe Systems Incorporated. Used with express permission. All rights reserved. Adobe and PageMaker is/are either (a) registered trademark(s) of Adobe Systems Incorporated in the United States and/or other countries.

American Bowling Congress newsletter figure on page 253. This image courtesy of www.bowl.com and the American Bowling Congress.

International Programs Newsletter figure on page 257. Reproduced with permission from the March of Dimes Birth Defects Foundation.

Catch of the Day newsletter figure on page 271. © Rafe Needleman, *Catch of the Day.* www.catchoday.com. Reprinted with permission.

Dot Org newsletter figure on page 275. Dot Org Media is a content publishing and syndication service that offers a free e-mail newsletter, Web content, and special reports on selected topics such as ASPs, online advocacy, fundraising, and Internet strategy. We present case studies, effective practices, techniques and tools to help nonprofits maximize their Internet presence. Dot Org Media is a coproduction of Marc Osten at Summit Collaborative and Michael Stein. Back issues and more information: www.dotorgmedia.org.

Driver/Education newsletter figure on page 290. Courtesy of *drivers.com.*

Dateline Houston newsletter figure on page 295. Courtesy of the Society for Technical Communication, Houston Chapter.

*I*NDEX

OTHER SQUAREONE WRITERS GUIDES

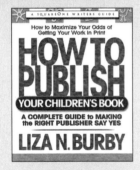

HOW TO PUBLISH YOUR CHILDREN'S BOOK

A Complete Guide to Making the Right Publisher Say Yes

Liza N. Burby

A successful children's writer explains the world of children's books and offers a proven system for approaching the right publishers.

$17.95 • 288 pages • 7.5 x 9-inch quality paperback • ISBN-7570-0036-3

HOW TO PUBLISH YOUR ARTICLES

A Complete Guide to Making the Right Publication Say Yes

Shirley Kawa-Jump

Here is complete information on getting articles into magazines, journals, newspapers, and newsletters. Tips are included for building a freelance career.

$17.95 • 352 pages • 7.5 x 9-inch quality paperback • ISBN-7570-0016-9

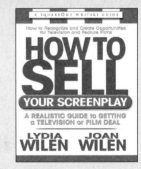

HOW TO SELL YOUR SCREENPLAY

A Realistic Guide to Getting a Television or Film Deal

Lydia Wilen & Joan Wilen

Veteran screenwriters tell you how to properly format your script, work with industry "players," prepare a perfect pitch, and make the best possible deal.

$17.95 • 320 pages • 7.5 x 9-inch quality paperback • ISBN-7570-0002-9

HOW TO PUBLISH YOUR POETRY

A Complete Guide to Finding the Right Publishers for Your Work

Helene Ciaravino

This guide to print poetry helps you focus on appropriate publications, write a persuasive submissions package, and submit it in the best way possible.

$15.95 • 192 pages • 7.5 x 9-inch quality paperback • ISBN-7570-0001-0

HOW TO PUBLISH YOUR NONFICTION BOOK

A Complete Guide to Making the Right Publisher Say Yes

Rudy Shur

Designed to maximize success, this book guides you in choosing the best publishers, crafting a winning proposal, and effectively submitting your package.

$16.95 • 252 pages • 7.5 x 9-inch quality paperback • ISBN-7570-0000-2

HOW TO PUBLISH YOUR NOVEL

A Complete Guide to Making the Right Publisher Say Yes

Ken Atchity, Julie Mooney, Andrea McKeown

To get your work of fiction into print, this book explains how to find a literary agent, develop an effective proposal package, and much more.

$18.95 • 320 pages • 7.5 x 9-inch quality paperback • ISBN-7570-0049-5